BK 745.4 B571
DESIGN THROUGH DISCOVERY /BEVLIN, MA
D1285903

WITHDRAWN

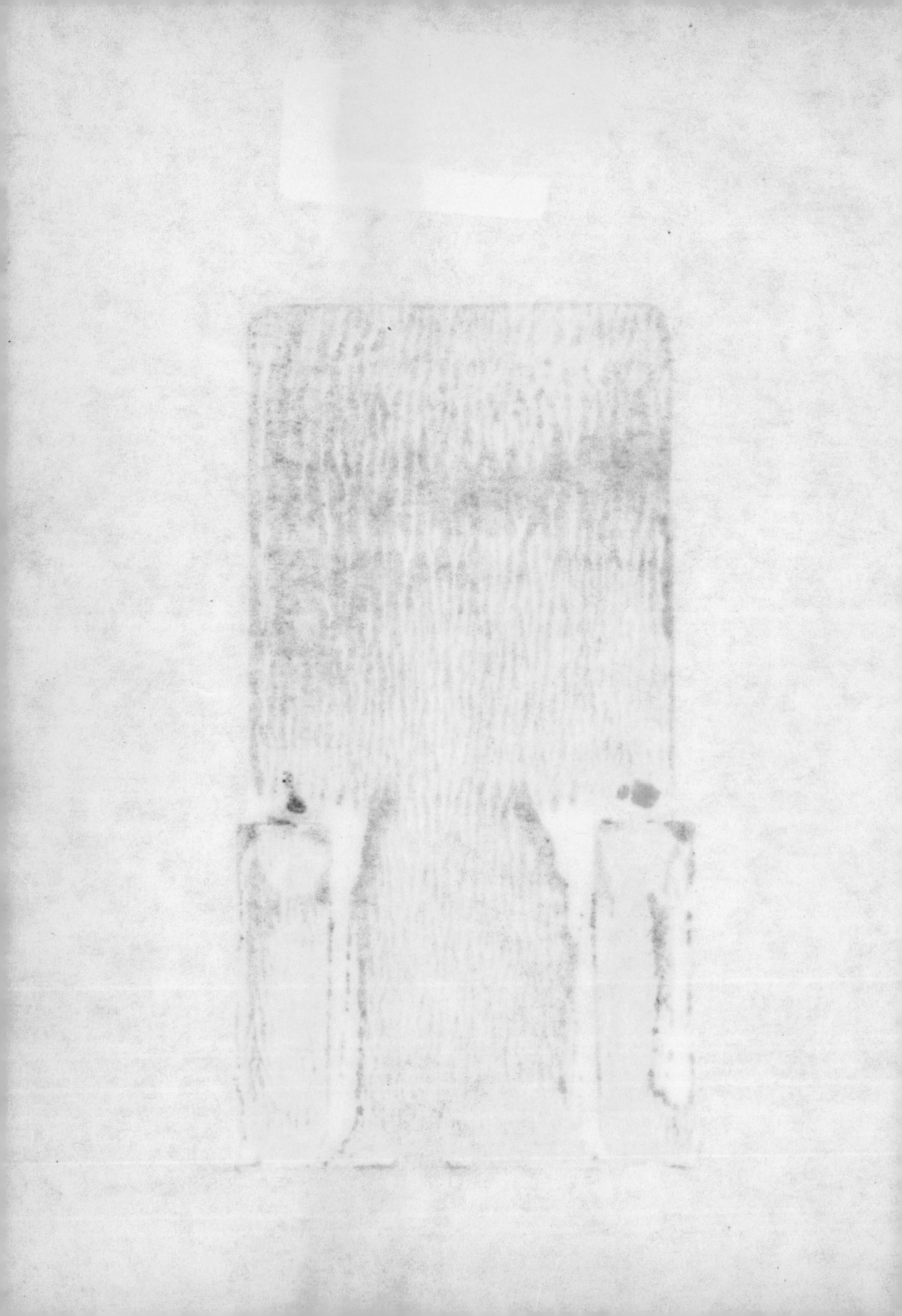

Design through Discovery

DESIGN
through Discovery

MARJORIE ELLIOTT BEVLIN

Otero Junior College

HOLT, RINEHART AND WINSTON

New York · Chicago · San Francisco · Toronto · London

Library of Congress Catalog Card Number 63-15112
20930-0113
Printed in the United States of America

Preface

THIS BOOK is intended as a threshold, an opening through which the beginning design student may pass into new and exhilarating worlds. It has been planned to provide a background of artistic philosophy which will supplement the studio projects assigned in class and lead the student into new depths of understanding of both his own work and the work of professional artists.

The purpose of *Design through Discovery* is to show the link between creative design processes and the fundamental creative methods inherent in nature and thus help the student realize that design is not a man-made discipline but a natural development clearly visible in the universe. It is hoped that through its pages he will learn to make discoveries of his own, leading him ever further in the pursuit of his own contribution, whether in a professional career, as an amateur artist, or simply as an individual better trained for appreciation.

The first chapters explore the general principles of design found in nature, identify these elements, and assess their significance. Later chapters deal with the application of these principles to specific fields of design. Pictorial material is used to illustrate explicit statements relating to these principles and their application. At the end of each chapter is a list of suggested projects for either classroom or outside assignment to assist the student in applying what he has read to his own creative efforts. A list of pertinent titles for further reading is also included at the end of most chapters.

The material has been organized so that the reader may survey design in its general scope, then apply over-all concept to particular areas of activity. The highlights of artistic achievement are touched upon in order that the student may view his own period in its historical perspective and thus understand more clearly both his creative heritage and the efforts of contemporary artists.

This book strives to speak to the student in practical terminology. Progress through its pages will give him an idea of the area wherein his own interests lie as well as a respect for what is being done and an awareness of what needs doing in many fields. It will acquaint him with the processes of both two-dimensional and three-dimensional design and make him conscious of space problems and the importance of form. It should awaken him to new horizons in the crafts and the possibilities of the artist's making a significant contribution to industry as well as to human environment. It is hoped, above all, that it will guide him into a deeper understanding of the relationship of art to nature and thus help to lead him toward his own evaluation of life, which is the foundation for all artistic expression.

M.E.B.

La Junta, Colorado
March 1963

Acknowledgments

EVERY BOOK is the result of an author's total experience, but there are always individuals and organizations without whose help any single work could never have emerged.

Special appreciation must be given to Professors Ray Faulkner of Stanford University and Mildred Fairchild of Teachers College, Columbia University, who read the manuscript and offered many practical suggestions; to artists, architects, and craftsmen who contributed photographs of their work; and to commercial firms which made available photographs and descriptive material.

The staff of the New York Public Library and personnel of many museums sought out photographs—particularly Miss Emma Papert of the Metropolitan Museum of Art and Willard Tangen and Joseph Messing of The Museum of Modern Art. Sam Richardson, director of research for the American Craftsmen's Council, was most liberal in lending photographs. Hal Halverstadt, *Craft Horizons'* editor, and his staff devoted considerable time to locating the work of outstanding craftsmen. Edward McLean contributed valuable suggestions to the section on hand bookbinding.

Nor would this book have been possible without the help and cooperation of many photographers, particularly Alison Franz, Professor Clarence Ward, Bruce Roberts, Harold Finke, and J. F. Burshears. Professor Sybil Moholy-Nagy, Beaumont Newhall, and others generously assisted in finding necessary photographs; G. Alan Turner, editor of *Design* and Paul H. Bonner, Jr., of Condé Nast, were especially helpful. Elwayne Carter contributed measurably, and Virginia Debolt Pike gave unswerving interest and hours of cheerful labor.

Many students contributed by helping me to grasp their need, and Neva Daniel provided continued inspiration. Ervin W. Bevlin, my husband, helped in countless indispensable ways.

Contents

Design through Discovery

CHAPTER 1

Design and Life

THE FEELING FOR DESIGN IS AS OLD AS MANKIND, but design itself is millions of years older. Ever since the first mineral, plant, or animal forms appeared in the universe, distinct patterns have been evolving naturally and logically in infinite variation.

The structure of a mineral deposit, the skeleton of a fish, the veining of a leaf are all designs based on the structural laws of nature. With the emergence of man into an intellectual being, these forms were used consciously to create attractive settings in which he could move and find expression. The palace, the cathedral, and the skyscraper finally developed from a strong feeling for design which found expression not only in esthetic values but in such well-ordered principles of engineering as stresses and strains, thrusts and counterthrusts. Yet the primeval cave with its areas for eating, sleeping, and keeping warm and the simple farm with its pattern of cultivated fields are just as surely examples of design, emerging logically and naturally from a need. All of these illustrate the basic characteristic of design: a design is, first of all, *a plan for order.*

From the beginning of time, order has been the cornerstone of creativity. The world began when order was created out of chaos. Not only in the Old Testament story but in ancient Greek mythology, the entire complicated genealogy of the gods is traced back to ancestors who sprang from chaos and then sorted the universe into categories by taking upon themselves such entities as earth and love and the darkness under the earth. The ancient Chinese believed in a nebulous state that existed before the earth came into being. In all of these versions the world as we know it began only when confusion or nothingness gave way to form and order—in other

Figure 1–1 (Opposite). The tapestry of human life as it appears from the air. Man's efforts and activities weave a design filled with interesting shapes, varying textures, lights, and darks. Photograph by L. Moholy-Nagy. Courtesy of Sibyl Moholy-Nagy.

words, to design. As Alexander Pope expressed it: "Order is heaven's first law."[1] Order, or design, can in fact be interpreted as the foundation of all living. The study of the way design permeates life is an unending adventure in discovery.

The great fallacy in approaching design is the idea that design is decoration superimposed upon a surface. The view from an airplane reveals one of the most spectacular of designs, the blocks of field and forest, of plowed ground and winter wheat, of towns and cities and cornfields all woven into a vital living tapestry that is the earth itself (Figure 1–1). This is not a superficial pattern laid upon the surface of the ground by climate and man's efforts. It is the character of the earth coming to its surface from deep within: the areas of fertility yielding patches of feathery green or burnished gold, the roots of towns and cities with their deep networks of pipes, gaslines, wells, and subways making a richly textured area of concrete, glass, and trees delineated by streets swarming with thousands of lives and their intermingled perplexities. So *any design should be an outgrowth of the material of which it is a part; it should spring from life and living, not be an external attempt at decoration.*

An example of true design is seen in the totem poles created by the Indians of the Pacific Northwest (Figure 1–2). Stylized characters of exciting variety and color are carved into the huge poles of the Northwest cedar, maintaining the shape and character of these trees so characteristic of the Indian's native habitat, yet adding tremendous drama and meaning in the depiction of the history of a clan. Nothing is stuck on for decoration, even the colors of the paint become a part of the meaning of the pole. The majestic tree remains but with it and in it stands the social and religious philosophy of a people, as well as the personal and familial legend of a proud individual. Yet, even to persons who understand nothing of the interpretation of the totem pole, the dramatic designs and colors have held enough attraction to be borrowed as motifs for paintings, for fabric designs, and for various commercial uses. In these settings, it is still the intangible flavor of the Northwest and the mystery of the tribal philosophy *combined* with the native color and design which provide the interest. *A true design has validity because it fulfills the possibilities of its material and its purpose, and its esthetic appeal stems from this validity.*

One of the most functional uses of design is in the creation of architecture. It is a significant fact that a well-designed building will have a floor plan which makes a good two-dimensional design on paper. The plan which shows variety in the use of space, an harmonious arrangement of sizes and shapes representing rooms, and a pleasing rhythm in the flow of traffic from area to area will, when built, be a structure that is satisfying and

[1] Alexander Pope, "An Essay on Man," *Pope's Poems* (New York: John W. Lovell Co.), [n.d.] p. 211.

Figure 1–2. The Northwest cedar, carved by the Coast Indians, depicts the history of a clan: coats of arms, exploits, deaths, even notices of debts are carved into a unified design expressive of these Indians and of the great forests in which they live. Totem Pole at Prospect Point, Vancouver, British Columbia. Courtesy of Canadian Government Travel Bureau.

functional in its three-dimensional form. The plan of the early Christian church was based upon the shape of a cross for symbolic reasons and this two-dimensional figure has survived through the ages as the basis of varying three-dimensional forms of architecture—all related by this vital symbolism, yet fulfilling the needs of their congregations in diverse ways.

We have weathered the conglomerate period of American architecture in which buildings were designed first for outward show (with all the periods of past glory getting a jumbled representation) and interior rooms fell wherever they might. Thanks to Frank Lloyd Wright, contemporary architecture follows instead the principle found in nature where shelters are constructed according to the needs of the occupants with the structure evolving outward into birds' nests or honeycombs or beaver dams. For integrity of design, buildings should be created for the life within them. The floor plan should be all-important and the exterior adapted in an attractive and functional way.

New Mexican architecture exemplified this principle long before the artists' colonies had sprung up in its midst, for it was not art but necessity that fathered the design of adobe churches and pueblos. The designing of a pueblo church (Figure 1–3) was simply a matter of laying out the size needed for the interior of the church with its sanctuary and vestibule and then enclosing this designed space. The method of enclosure was as expedient as the allotment of space within. The ground is hard but malleable; with the addition of straw it was formed into bricks baked in the hot New Mexico sun, held together with mortar made from the same adobe mud, and the whole wall plastered with the same mud to provide protection and a certain smoothness. Cedar poles were brought from the nearby Sangre

Figure 1–3. The pueblo churches of New Mexico seem to rise right out of the ground from which they are built. Church at Ranchos de Taos.

Figure 1–4. The architecture of this Alpine village is indigenous to its setting. Logs and boards of larch and roofs of stone slab come from nearby slopes. Shuttered windows and steeply pitched roofs adapt to cold winters with heavy snow. The forms of the buildings themselves seem to echo the peaks of the mountains and the solid bulwarks that separate one valley from another. Village of Zermatt, Switzerland. Courtesy of Trans World Airlines.

de Cristo mountains to form rafters or *vigas* to support the roof. The poles, being long, stuck out beyond the walls, creating fascinating shadow patterns that change throughout the day. The mild New Mexico winters preclude the need to shed great quantities of snow; therefore the roof is flat. Meanwhile, the thick walls with their little windows not only provided a haven from enemies in the early days but remain to keep a cool dim interior, practical as to weather and appropriate to the mystical rites of a church that is early Spanish with overtones of ancient Indian. Here is true design of the land and of the people. It is not so much erected structure as a flowering of the ground itself; from a distance any line of demarcation is scarcely discernible. And just as the color is of the earth, the texture is of the people, being the imprint of many hands, smoothing, patting, building flat-palmed, with piety and devotion.

The high mountain valleys of the Alps have produced an architectural design entirely different but just as honest (Figure 1–4). Built of heavy logs and boards from the larch-covered slopes below timberline, the Swiss hut and chalet proclaim readily their affinity to their dramatic surroundings. Powerful boulders from the mountain slopes form a solid foundation and serve decoratively for the fireplace so necessary for heat against chill evenings. The stone-slab roofs are steep to shed the heavy snowfall of an Alpine winter. Plaster chinking blocks the wind that would whistle through the cracks between the logs. And after the necessities have been provided in heavy doors and small-paned windows which are secure against high winds, shutters and interior frequently reflect the blossoms of the Alpine meadows in colorful designs taken directly from fields above the village. This is decorative design applied to enhance the basic structure, but reflecting its surroundings, relating it more closely to them.

Nature, of course, is the supreme master of inherent design. The smallest granite pebble has its patterns, the result of centuries of building up and washing away until the round smooth core of design remains, each one different from the others (Figure 1–5). The trunks of trees are rich in design, drawn in concentric circles through the seasons, then twisted into writhing lines and textures by winds and snows and lightning which man could not withstand but which the tree uses to improve its own intrepid character. The outer bark, too, has its individual design quality. The satiny gray-green of aspen trunks which turns to black-streaked silver in winter has little in common with the irregular roughness of fir or spruce but becomes more dramatic from the contrast. The winter white of the silver poplar stands out starkly and beautifully against the mottled elms among which it grows (Figure 1–6). Each has its own design, a beauty of color, texture, or line which has been part of the tree from its beginning, registering each scar from wind or the hand of man and molding it into its total being.

Underlying the individual characteristics, however, exist the eternal laws of growth and order. Each blade of grass unfolds in an orderly way characteristic of its kind. The leaves of every tree, while limitless in variation, appear in precise order from the trunks or boughs of the tree, each becoming first a bud, then a tiny shape emerging until it reaches maturity and takes its place in the design of the tree. It is true that the total effect of such growth is frequently disorder. One plant grows on top of another and the dead growth that nature has weeded out lies about to add confusion to the scene. Yet this is a matter of quantity rather than quality. The fact that fertile soil and propitious growing conditions create a tangled jungle does not alter the fact that each facet of that growth is accomplished according to basic and orderly procedures. From this discovery we deduce another of the qualities of creative design: *good design is related to the basic natural laws of growth and order.*

Figure 1–5. Stream-washed stones. Each has its own visual textures built up through centuries of mineral deposits washed smooth by the impact of rushing streams.

This order is found wherever we look. We may classify design into certain basic movements: the spiral, the circle, and similar symbols, but truly creative design is found not in standardized patterns but in individual variations. Not only is each variety of tree different in its characteristics, each tree is unique because its peculiar design is the outgrowth of its individual life. Trees in the same clump will be of varying shapes because of the way in which they crowd one another. The woodpecker will carve a hole in the trunk of one, the storm will rip a branch from another. Hail will pelt the surface of still another, while its neighbor may be sheltered from the direct beat of hailstones. A basic shape and salient characteristics may be attributed to an entire species, but each individual tree has its own design story to tell.

It is well-known that snowflakes, though following basic patterns, are

Figure 1–6. The designs of nature change from season to season. As leaves begin to fall, the branches of silver poplars trace their delicate patterns against the sky.

never exactly alike. Neither is any seashell exactly like any other seashell, nor any tongue of flame, nor any ocean wave, nor cloud alike. The artist who would create truly original designs must learn to see the individuality of his inspirations and to respect it. He must train his eye to look beneath the general shape of things to the variation that creates interest. *For the creative artist, individuality is the most important design characteristic of all.*

It has been said that nothing new is ever created in the world of matter. This truth carries over into the field of design. Every design is based on age-old forms whether they are found in nature or simple geometric lines and figures used in an abstract way. Yet a new approach is like a spring bubbling out of a hillside; the water is the same as the water that has been used and drunk for centuries, yet it is always new, always fresh, always satisfying because it comes forth in its own way, in its own place, and with its own individual degree of coldness and freshness. A talent for design, using elements and methods long grown old, can bring forth a freshness and originality in its own inimitable style.

Individual interpretations of design are not limited to the graphic artist. The orderly mind is a creative mind, a mind that sorts and arranges for creative use, whether it be figures, with the statistician, facts, with the historian, or theories, with the philosopher. The creative writer must have an orderly mind before he can build the design for a plot or a piece of poetry, and the musician must have an orderly vision of his themes and harmonies before he can set down creative music so it can be played by instruments.

The person who insists that he has no creative ability frequently builds his life on designs without being conscious of the fact. The handyman whose shop is a model of neatness with nails sorted into jars and every tool in place is a designer in spite of himself, for his work is based on order and the order itself is pleasing to him. The woman who hangs her washing on the line in a certain way, with all the socks together and all the white shirts in a group, is creating design without realizing it; no doubt she feels creative satisfaction and refreshment from her labors when she views the neatly hung rows. A clothing store usually has its stock hung according to the sizes and shapes of garments and their colors, with blues running into greens and then into grays and so on, because the merchant knows that if his stock makes an attractive design he is more apt to sell it. When we straighten the furniture in a room we create a more orderly appearance, a better design within which to live. We plan our gardens in a certain order, not only so plants will have sun and shade according to their needs, but so areas of pattern, color, and texture will be created; this is a part of landscape design.

Look around you and notice how many examples of design are created in your own day-to-day life. You will discover that most of living depends upon design of one sort or another for no one can live satisfactorily or creatively in confusion, either mental or physical. And the minute confusion gives way to order you have design: design for living, design for working, design for creating—for design is, above all, a plan for order.

STUDIO PROJECTS

1. For a fuller understanding of the importance of design in life, list five instances of design in everyday living not usually associated with artistic endeavor.

2. Find and display four examples of design in nature and show how each evolved as the result of an orderly growth process.

3. From magazines or museum catalogs clip five examples of man-made design, each one of which exhibits at least one of the five basic requirements stated in Chapter 1. Mount each example and explain your choice.

CHAPTER 2

Design and Nature

DESIGN IS IMPLICIT IN NATURE in even its simplest forms. While everyone is conscious of the beauty of a flower, a leaf or a seashell, the wonderful world of the microscope is frequently familiar only to the scientist. Yet, here is to be found some of the most fundamental truth about design and many of the most fascinating patterns and space relationships existing anywhere.

Chapter 1 highlighted the fact that design began when chaos was converted into order. Harlow Shapley states the approach of the scientist who senses a world beyond the realm of human knowledge when he says: "Chaos is but unperceived order; it is a word indicating the limitations of the human mind and the paucity of observational facts."[1]

Rhythm

One of the most vital facts uncovered by scientific study is the existence of basic rhythms throughout nature. Any good design is based on rhythm and unity; and the realization that not only the animal kingdom but the plant and mineral worlds ebb and flow in a constant yet flexible rhythmic pattern can do much to make the artist realize that these principles are not restrictions imposed upon the designer but basic truths blending all of existence into a related whole.

We take for granted the rhythm of the seasons; much of our economy is based upon the sowing and reaping of the harvest. This has always been

[1] Harlow Shapley, *Of Stars and Men* (Boston: Beacon Press, 1958, p. 63).

Figure 2–1. The alternating egg and dart of the upper molding is equivalent to a loud drumbeat alternating with a soft, while the bead and reel of the lower molding is a graphic representation of a loud and two soft beats. From a base on the Acropolis in Athens. Photograph by Alison Frantz.

so with even the most primitive peoples. The pattern of life has revolved around an eternally recurring cycle of spring festivals celebrating the sowing of seed, harvest celebrations in honor of the reaping and storing of crops, and winter festivities to relieve the long monotony of the barren months. Centuries before the Christian church translated such events into the holidays of Christmas and Easter, spring and winter festivals were annual occurrences with primitive tribes, with the Egyptians and Greeks, as well as with Oriental civilizations. Today, in our highly complicated lives we take such rhythms for granted, yet who has not looked out upon a bleak winter landscape and wondered if it can be possible that the world will billow forth in greenery and bright blossoms once again? Most of us have moments of consciousness of the miracle of growth and rhythm around us. How many artists, however, realize that even the simplest one-celled organism has a rhythmic pattern that relates it to the complex world outside? Usually this pattern is governed by periods of day and night. The reproduction of the organism takes place during daylight hours and can be predicted by the regularity of its rhythms.

In more complex structures the rhythms of day and night have varying manifestations. When a bean plant is raised in darkness it has no daily sleep movement in its leaves, but if exposed to a flash of light it will show a definite natural reaction. When it is returned to darkness the pattern remains; every day at the time of that single exposure to light the leaves will persist in elevating.[2] The fiddler crab starts to turn black at sunrise, wearing a protective cloak against the glaring sun and predators. At sunset it speedily blanches out again to a silvery gray. Even captured crabs when kept in a darkroom will continue this natural rhythm.[3]

With other organisms rhythms have a seasonal basis. At exactly the time of the third-quarter moons in October and November in the southwest Pacific, the Palolo worms break off their long posteriors which are filled with reproductive cells. The worms then swarm from their burrows and are washed ashore. The South Sea Islanders who relish these tasty worms set their feast days to coincide with this sudden arrival, so dependable is the cycle each year. The reef heron is closely attuned to the cycle of the tides in its activity. Each day it leaves its Australian homeland to prey upon a reef as far away as thirty miles, arriving at the time of low tides when more food is uncovered. Even though the tide goes out fifty minutes later each day, the heron still alights at precisely the moment of low tide.[4]

The relationship of moon and tides has long led to theories about the

[2] W. Pfeffer, *Abbandl. sachs Akad. Wiss. Leipzig,* Math-Phip. K-1 30:259, 1907.

[3] F. A. Brown, Jr.: *Living Clocks* at Northwestern Medical School, Chicago, Illinois; March 22, 1960; The Rhythmic Nature of Animals and Plants, *Tri-Quarterly,* Northwestern Univ., Fall 1958.

[4] F. Ratcliffe, *Flying Fox and Drifting Sand* (London, Anglo Books, 1952).

effects of the moon upon human events. The *Farmers' Almanac* tells of the advantages of planting according to the moon, and the study of astrology endeavors to determine the fate of individual human beings according to the positions of certain stars and constellations at a given time. Recent studies have indicated that these relationships may be more than superstition. A Florida eye-ear-nose-and-throat specialist became concerned when he noticed cycles of difficulty in patients having surgery. Frequently, excessive bleeding occurred in all his patients followed by periods when they all showed a "normal" reaction. When his nurse suggested that it was the "time of the moon," he dismissed the idea; however, the nurse began circling the dates of difficult cases on the calendar, and in a few months it became obvious that the hemorrhages invariably occurred between the moon's first and third quarters. The doctor continued to study reactions and found that 82 percent of all bleeding crises came at these times. Inducing a colleague to undertake a similar study, he discovered comparable results. While the doctor did not feel prepared to make a scientific statement as to his conclusions, he did write up his experiences in the Florida state medical journal. All of these studies indicate that much of folklore may have valid bases stemming from the close association of primitive peoples with nature and their observations of and dependence upon cycles that go unobserved in the highly complicated structure of modern life.

We tend to elevate art to a higher sphere, setting it above the biological aspects of human life and keeping it on a spiritual plane where it will remain unsullied and inspirational. This reaching for an ideal is an essential part of human nature and the mainspring of all religion and art, yet a truly ideal art removed from the needs of human existence is an impossibility. By nature art is an expression of human experience and all the concomitants, biological or emotional, that comprise it. The Greeks, whose art is often referred to as "idealized," based their interpretations on human form and frailty. Their statues were depictions of the human biological structure glorified to the highest degree, and their mythology is an intriguing tapestry of superhuman powers interwoven with human pettiness. Their gods could accomplish anything except the conquering of their own emotions. This frailty-in-common was the secret of their tremendous influence on the daily lives of their devotees, for it was believed that while maintaining their stronghold on Mount Olympus they still descended frequently to share the concerns of men and women. Thus the gods became a part of men's lives instead of merely constituting a remote ideal for homage at stated intervals. Processions and sacrifices were made but these mythological contacts with everyday life were the basis for the influences which outweighed the effects of the vengeful and impersonal gods of other civilizations. The contact with human life remains essential in religion, in political leadership, and in art.

Man's earliest designs show a significant reflection of his own basic rhythms. From his first heartbeat man is a creature of cycles, of systole and diastole, of the beat pattern of his pulse, of the regularity of breathing, of waking and sleeping, of eating and fulfillment, of activity and rest. His reproductive processes follow set patterns of fertility and sterility and his gestation period forms a precise design of development that can be clearly charted from month to month. It is only natural when he celebrates the cycles of the seasons or his struggles and victories that festivities should take a rhythmic form in keeping with his own being. Primitive man's first expressions were his beating on a simple drum of animal skins, of dancing to the beatings, and of chants in monotonous rhythms. Gradually the structure became more complex with enactments of events merging into drama and new instruments added to accompany the drums. Voices began to vary and harmonize. From these beginnings emerged Greek drama, medieval morality plays, Elizabethan instrumental music, and the varied dances of the American Indian. It is interesting that no matter what the period or the geographical location these manifestations follow similar rhythms, whether they are the beat of native dances or the more intricate patterns of suspense, climax, and denouement in drama.

Graphic expressions follow much the same patterns. Anyone who has seen an electrocardiogram or a tracing of human brain waves can see immediately the relationship of natural rhythms to graphic representation. We think of an electrocardiogram in terms of sharp peaks of systole and diastole, a definite design of heights and depths. The tracing of brain waves may be more varied, with calm thoughts indicated by smooth rolling lines and tumultuous thoughts tracing patterns of greater angle and wider variation. These are designs made by man unconsciously, yet through the years he has also tried consciously to interpret his emotional reactions to his environment with visual symbols.

The alternating bead and reel of the ancient Greek molding (Figure 2–1) can be likened to the beat of native drums with their repetition of loud and soft tones. The same can be said of the egg and dart with its repeated patterns. The alternating units of triglyph and metope are an excellent example of design emerging from natural forms, since the triglyph was originally the end of the wooden beam needed to support the roof of a Greek temple (Figure 2–2).

The stylization of a lotus blossom on the Lotiform Cup (Figure 2–3) is the graphic equivalent of the use of lotus in an ancient Egyptian poem:

> Death is before me to-day
> As the odour of lotus flowers,
> As when one sitteth on the shore of drunkenness.[5]

[5] A. Erman. *Literature of the Ancient Egyptians* (London: 1927), pp. 91–92.

Figure 2–2. Triglyph and metope create an alternating rhythm with variety contributed by the sculpture in the metope. This detail from the southeast corner of the Temple of Hepaistos in Athens is only a small part of the frieze which continues the rhythm around the top of the building. Photograph by Alison Frantz.

Figure 2–3. Egyptian Lotiform Cup. Faience, Nineteenth-Twentieth Dynasty. Courtesy of the Metropolitan Museum of Art, Carnarvon Collection. Gift of Edward S. Harkness, 1926.

Association of the lotus with death is as individual as the simplified modeling on the cup. Neither is a realistic *description* of a lotus blossom; each is an interpretation in rhythm, one in the cadence of a song and the other in the pattern of shapes upon the base of a decorative goblet. Again, the carved figures in a Greek frieze with their fluid folds create a feeling as rhythmic as the music to which the procession must have moved when in actuality it progressed to the temple to present an offering to the gods (Figure 2–4).

The major difference between music, drama, literature, and the visual arts is the matter of timing. The musician and the writer can manipulate an audience over a period of minutes or hours, attracting attention, building suspense, sweeping to a climax, and finally unfolding the denouement be-

Figure 2–4. Figures on a Greek frieze. Demeter, Triptolemos, and Persephone carved in Pentelic marble around 450–440 B.C. Roman copy of the original Greek relief. Courtesy of the Metropolitan Museum of Art, Rogers Fund, 1914.

fore spellbound eyes or ears. In painting, particularly, except in the case of very large murals, the complete composition is placed before the observer all at once and it is his own receptivity which determines how much he gleans from it. People who would not dream of darting in and out of a symphony concert will walk past a painting with only a cursory glance, yet lyric passages should be enjoyed within a painting just as much as within a symphony, and a little time and study will reveal that the dramatist's formula of suspense, climax, and denouement may be discovered just as readily in a fine visual work of art.

A Gothic cathedral illustrates this point (Figure 2–5). Approaching the portal (Figure 2–6), interest is awakened by the carved figures in their niches, and the eye is carried upward to the more elaborate carvings on the tympanum, or semi-circular area above the door. Suspense mounts as the gaze goes upward and a point of major interest is reached in the rose window. Further carvings of figures and finials lift the observer's eye to the base of the spires and to a primary climax at the apex of the nave where a figure leads the eye ever upward. The final climax is attained at the tip of the spires with their urgent upward surge pointing still higher until the eye and the mind reach a peak of ascendancy toward which the total design is directed. Since denouement in drama is concerned with the final untangling of the intricacies of plot, visual denouement may be considered to be the more searching scrutiny which the eye now gives to elements composing the cathedral; the realization that the figures are pertinent saints, that much of the carving is of symbolic forms, and, finally, appreciation of the glowing patterns in stained-glass windows. Although he may have seen many details that interest him in a temporal way, the receptive viewer will have experienced through looking at the cathedral an adventure following the same basic pattern he might feel in seeing a great religious drama or listening to a masterpiece of religious music. In each case he will have felt the rhythm of interest, suspense, and climax which governs his biological life, in eating, in reproduction, and on a smaller scale in many of the functions of his body which go largely unnoticed, and which he also experiences repeatedly in the tumult of his emotional existence.

We have discovered that there are two elements in rhythm: *repetition* and *climax*. A more common name for climax is *emphasis* since the climax of any experience is the point of greatest emphasis. It is interesting that these two elements are interactive. There is a certain amount of suspense involved in repetition: will the next beat be the same as the one before it? Will there even be a next beat? Surprises in rhythm are frequent in jazz and part of its interest. Again, the pattern of emphasis, of suspense and climax, gains rhythm through repetition. We are hungry, we are in a state of suspense until a meal is put before us. The promise of fulfillment is the

Figure 2–5. Cathedral of Notre Dame at Chartres, famous for its rose windows and for its contrasting towers showing a difference of 350 years in style. Photograph by Professor Clarence Ward.

Figure 2–6. The north portal of Chartres Cathedral is full of esthetic interest in its sculpture, stained glass, and architectural detail. Photograph by Professor Clarence Ward.

Figure 2–7. The variety of design in the wings and shapes of butterflies has led men to travel the world over in search of rare specimens. Courtesy of Bruce Carnes.

climax of the experience. The feeling of satisfaction becomes the denouement. The experience has its own rhythm of suspense and emphasis yet it is only when this experience is repeated three times a day week after week that it becomes a major rhythm in our lives, an ever recurring theme threaded through the pattern of existence.

The same is true of emotional experiences. The beginning actor finds his first performance almost devastating in the nervous suspense of appearing before an audience. He reaches his climax at some point during the performance when he feels that everything is going to be all right. The denouement follows as he concentrates wholly on the role, forgetting his suspense and working until exhaustion follows as a result of his performance and as a reaction to his suspense. This anxiety may be repeated in every performance for the rest of his life, as we are told it does in the greatest artists, but it is the repetition of the experience at regular intervals that gives rhythm to his total existence, and the rhythmic pattern of anxiety, climax, and exhaustion form the design for that larger rhythm.

Variety

Another characteristic of nature is variety. The existence of rhythm insures variety for it is the contrast of light with dark, of winter with summer, of height with depth and of a loud beat with a soft beat that makes for rhythmic pattern.

Variation in nature is infinite and fascinating. How much is the green tree enhanced by the tracery of black branches through its leaves! People make careers of the variations in flowers, in trees, in rocks or birds or butterflies (Figure 2–7). Men have lost their lives because of the lure of the changing faces of mountains, clear and challenging in the sunlit morning, lowering or smiling under passing clouds, and remote and menacing as the sun disappears and the uncertainties of darkness grow imminent. The farmer thrives on the varying patterns of his fields and his horizons; it is doubtful if his independent spirit could long be satisfied if every morning he viewed exactly the same sights and projects.

Figure 2–8. Careful selection and placement of plants and stones give this tiny Japanese garden infinite variety of textures and forms. Photograph by Ezra Stoller. Courtesy of *House Beautiful* Magazine.

Figure 2–9. The variety in a field of daisies includes not only the flower heads with their many differences but the spaces between the flowers, no two of which are the same in size and shape. The textures of the flower centers, petals, stems, and leaves offer still more examples of variety. Photograph by Herbert Matter.

The most obvious variation found in nature is in *size and shape.* The landscape architect makes use of this in his planning, for a plot filled with shrubs and trees of the same size and shape would not be a garden but a nursery. In an area so small that it could go unnoticed, the Japanese create an atmosphere of infinite beauty (Figure 2–8). Trees are pruned radically to present unusual shapes and to keep size in scale with surroundings. Foliage is combined for contrast, with fronds of ferns accenting azalea leaves and the whole interlaced with the tracery of branches. The supreme achievement of the Japanese artist is his willingness to obscure himself in the larger designs of nature. His surroundings are designed to look uncultivated and natural, and in this way they achieve the unity with nature that is the essence of good design.

Dramatic variations among different species of trees as well as individual differences which make for interest in design have been noted earlier. In Figure 2–9 we see how interesting a field of daisies becomes because of differences in size. Close scrutiny reveals a wide variation from the tiny flowers half hidden in the grass to the largest heads with prominent button centers. A closer look shows that the shapes also vary, for some petals bend forward while others curve back. Again, notice the arrangement of pattern in the field, no area of grass between the clumps of flowers is of the same size and shape as any other area.

A similar situation is found in a tide pool (Figure 2–10). Looking at the scattered shapes of foam and water it would be impossible to find two shapes exactly alike, yet if one had to design that many different shapes and sizes in a given area it would be extremely difficult. Once again, in the world of astronomy we find variety of size and spacing. While many stars at a distance may seem similar in size, the aspect of the heavens as a whole is one of infinite variety (Figure 2–11).

It is easy to see why nature is the best possible instructor for the creative designer. Anyone who learns to see as an artist can discover the principles of design all around him.

Turning to the world of the microscope, we find more evidence of the variety in nature. Figure 2–12 shows a section of cell structure taken from a glandular secretion in a guinea pig. Notice the varied character of the large cavities of the network and again of the dark round granules within them. The round areas are separated by different shapes and sizes and by the textured pattern of the endoplasmic reticulum which surrounds them. Figure 2–13 pictures another section from a guinea-pig pancreas with an entirely different pattern. Here again, it would be difficult to emulate nature in designing shapes and sizes in so much variation.

Figure 2–10. Tidepool. Notice the variation in size, texture, and spacing which gives the feeling of an ever-changing yet ever-related design. Photograph by Edward Weston. Courtesy of Brett Weston.

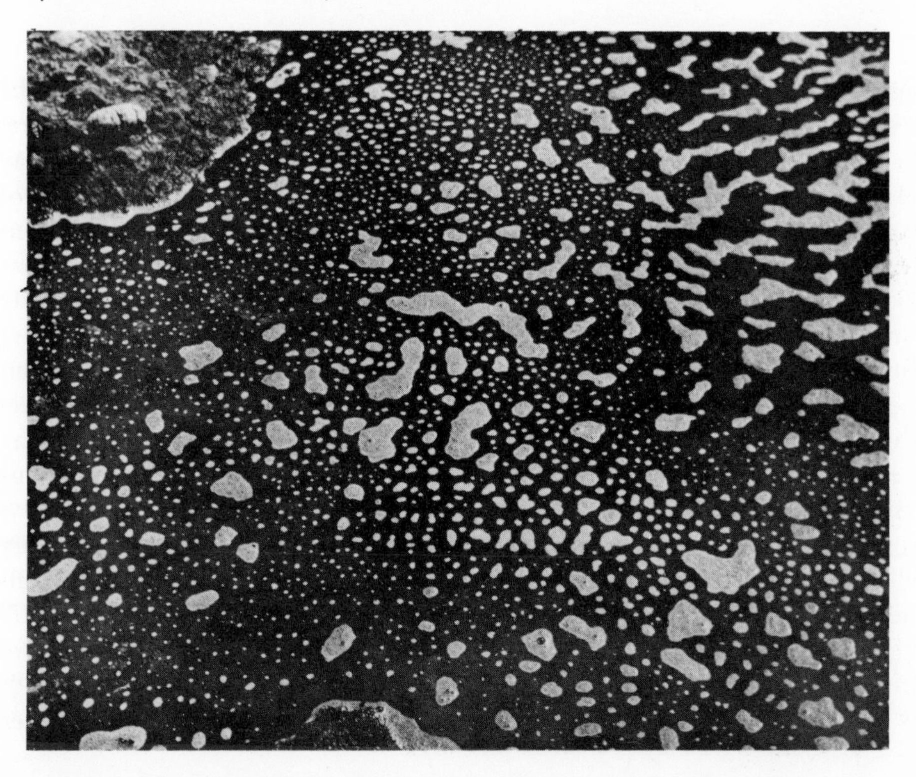

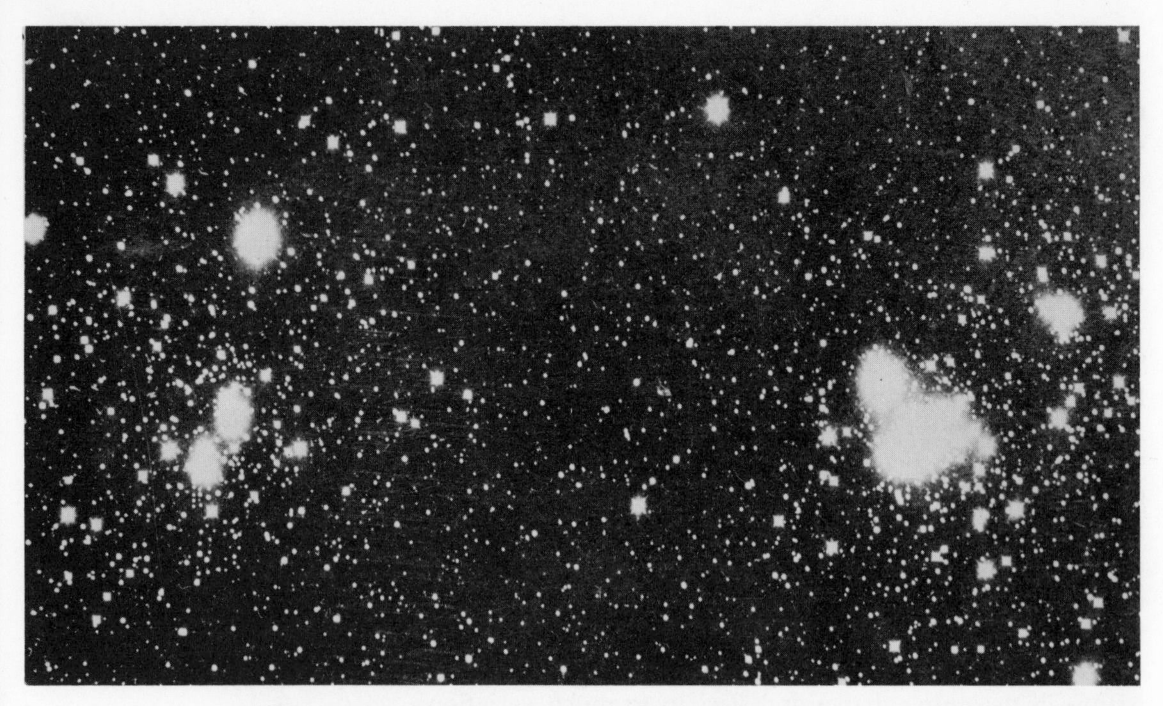

Figure 2–11. Even at a tremendous distance the stars and planets have infinite variety, not only of size but of brilliance. Although the photograph seems evenly covered, close observation shows how difficult it is to find any two areas that are similar in design. Photograph by Herbert Matter.

Perhaps the best way to appreciate variation in *color* is to paint a landscape. To the beginning painter the most beautiful spots seem the best material for a painting, for what is more logical than wanting to preserve something that inspires us with feelings of pleasure? The novice may select a peaceful meadow or a grove of trees yet after an hour or so of work frustration sets in. The green trees, the green fields, and the green bushes in the foreground suddenly become a mess of bright paint that has taken control of the canvas and turned a scene of beauty into a gaudy jungle. It is only after scrutinizing study that the artist discovers the infinite variety and subtlety of nature's greens, not only the differences between the green of leaves and the green of grass but of various areas within the leaves or grass, where a ray of sunlight hits or a cloud shadow makes the green darker and cooler. The scene can be painted but only with tremendous care in the mixing and use of the varying greens, and even then the finished work seldom has the interest and freshness of the original scene. The sky offers another pitfall as there is no surer sign of an amateur painter than the garishness of blue in the sky he paints. To produce a sky with the look of nature requires great subtlety and a willingness to see that what we think of as blue is often green or rose. The same holds true of stone with its various mineral deposits which give a wealth of earth colors under changing lights. While color in nature is all around us, there is much that is hidden from us—not by outward circumstances but by our own blindness and preconceptions.

Before an artist can work creatively he must learn to see. This is why the great Expressionist painter, Oskar Kokoschka, called his school in Salzburg the School of Vision. Here he gathered together art students from all over the world, and in four languages scolded, cheered, coaxed, and gestured in an effort to make students "learn to see." This ability to see is so vital to the young painter that the entire school was built upon this premise. It is no less vital to the designer.

The exploration of *texture* is one of the larger adventures in the artist's study of nature. Texture has two dimensions: *tactile* quality and *visual*

Figure 2–12. Secretion in an acinar cell of a guinea-pig pancreas, a study in texture and variety. Courtesy of Doctor George E. Palade and Doctor Keith R. Porter, the Upjohn Company, and *The Journal of Biophysical and Biochemical Cytology.*

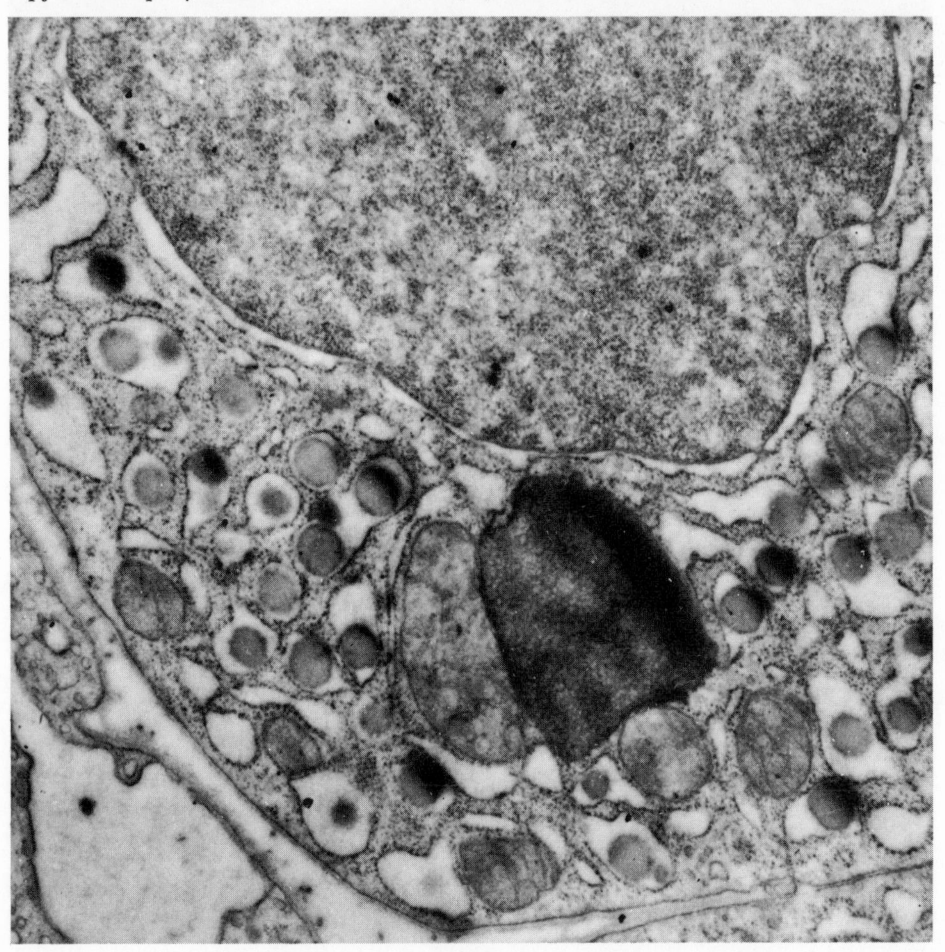

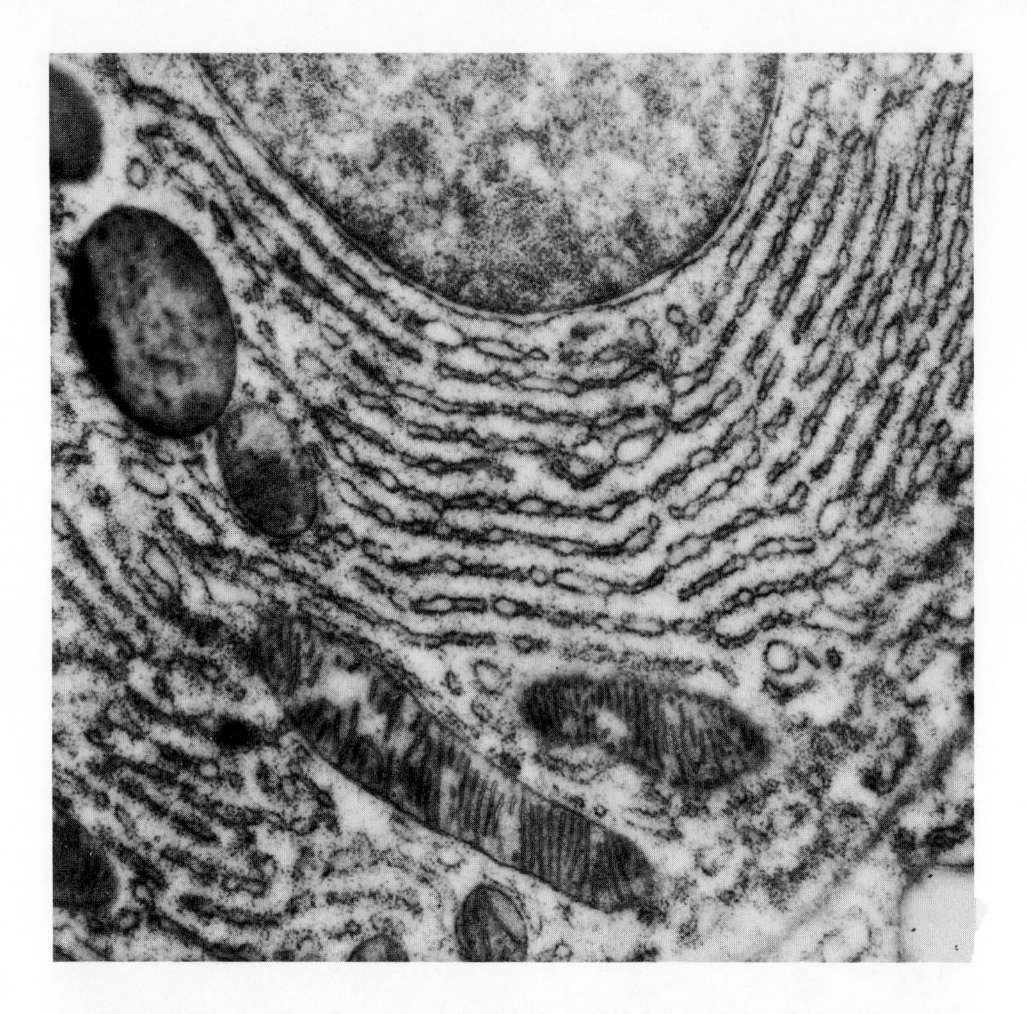

Figure 2–13. Section of a pancreatic exocrine cell of the guinea pig. An even more varied texture is found in the cross section. Notice how no two shapes or sizes are exactly alike. Courtesy of Doctors George E. Palade and Keith R. Porter, the Upjohn Company, and *The Journal of Biophysical and Biochemical Cytology.*

quality. The tactile quality can be felt and enjoyed with the fingers, like the ridges of an old log or the soft fur of a kitten. Visual texture can make one *feel* its presence without actually being discernible to the fingers. In Figure 1–5, for instance, one senses the roughness of the stones, a roughness of granite particles, sand, and ridges; yet if one could feel the stones, he would find that most of them felt very much alike because they have all been worn smooth by centuries of washing by mountain streams. In design the tactile quality often comes from the nature of material used, like the roughness of a stone jar or the nubbiness of a tweed fabric, and the design takes its own texture from the material itself.

Glance again at Figures 2–8 through 2–13 and explore their textural qualities. We spoke of the variation in size and shape of leaves in the Japanese garden. Large leaves make for rough textural patterns even though the leaves themselves may be smooth, while delicate fern fronds give a lace-like feeling. The field of daisies actually has three textural patterns. One comes from the nobby centers of flowers, another is created by the soft curving of petals silhouetted against the dark areas of grass and, finally, the textural quality of the grass itself makes a linear pattern with its stalks and blades, yet gives us an instinctive feeling of combined prickle and smoothness. The tidepool offers a contrast of smooth and rough textures of a strictly visual quality. One feels that he can reach out and touch the rough surface of the foam, yet if he did so his fingers would find only the smoothness of water. Great variation in texture can be found in the pancreatic tissues of the guinea pig, for here, as in the Japanese garden, the variety of size and shape contributes ultimately to the variation in texture. Look now at the textural design in Figure 2–14. All of the smaller textures of the earth's surface combine into one gigantic pattern when seen from afar, a master design in which rivers and forests, hills and valleys contribute their own distinctive textures.

Weathering is the great creator of texture in nature. Sometimes, as in

Figure 2–14. All of the textures of field and forest, river and stream combine into the larger textures of the earth's surface when we raise our eye level beyond the ground and are able to see it as a whole. Photograph by L. Moholy-Nagy. Courtesy of Sibyl Moholy-Nagy.

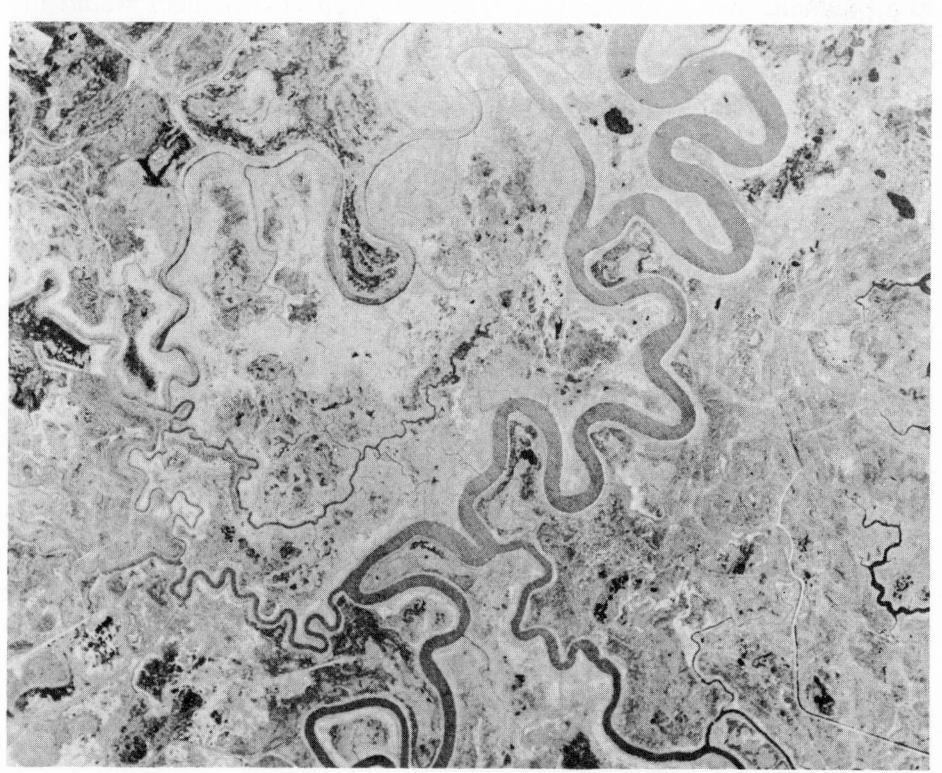

the case of stones or driftwood, the visual textures created by the elements will remain although the tactile textures disappear under the polishing action of water. Leaves of trees attacked by insects develop fascinating patterns as cells disintegrate, and even mineral deposits acquire texture as they weather, causing areas to flake off and roughen.

Look about you for further textures. The pattern on the skin of a pineapple, the shell of a turtle, the seeds of a dandelion or milkweed, a patch of cattails growing in a marshy roadside—these are but a sampling of the immensity of texture in nature.

Balance

If we study variety in nature perceptively, we make a further discovery. The presence of variety is not an end in itself; the variations in size and shape, in color and in texture are placed with purpose and design. The blue sky is not an isolated area; its color is repeated in the forget-me-not and gentian, in the pansy and delphinium as well as in the wings of the butterfly and the feathers of the bluebird. We find it difficult to imagine vast areas of red to correspond to the areas of blue and green around us. Because red is brilliant and exciting and because we have become adjusted to a predominance of cool restful colors, such an environment would undoubtedly have violent effects on us. Certainly, we would not appreciate large areas so much as we now enjoy the sudden flash of a red bird or the brief glory of red leaves in autumn. This presence of bright color as an accent in the stretches of green field, forest, and blue sky is nature's way of counteracting great cool areas by small bits of exciting color. This is *balance.*

If all our land were as high as the mountains we would have only a high plateau. It takes a valley to make a mountain, an ocean to make a continent. The rough bark of a tree is balanced by the smoothness of its leaves, and we note that smaller flowers frequently have the greatest fragrance while the showy blossoms of the tropics may have no noticeable scent. This, again, is balance. In the animal kingdom the little porcupine has quills, the skunk odor, and the insects a potent sting to compensate for lack of size and ferocity. This is nature's balance of power.

In human life balance is indispensable. For every intake of breath we have to exhale and our days of activity must be balanced by nights of rest. This we sometimes discover in college when we study until morning and then take an examination. When we destroy the natural balance of our lives we often run into complications. Disease is an upset of balance, either by germs or virus or by the action of environment on our chemical make-up. We hear frequently of people being mentally unbalanced. Recent research indicates that mental illness may be an upset in body chemistry, that balance may be restored by proper medication. This is one of the great hopes for the future.

Emotionally, we also find the pendulum swinging in an effort to achieve a state of balance. We do not experience serenity without knowing anxiety, and it is only after being involved in conflict that we appreciate the true meaning of peace.

Form

We have spoken of variety in size and shape. But nature takes us one step further, into three-dimensional qualities. We see the shapes of trees silhouetted against the horizon but when we approach them at close range they become *forms* that we can walk around and view from all sides. The contour of the land is a flattened shape at sunset when lighted from behind, but as we drive on it we find ourselves surrounded by hills and hollows—in other words—by forms. Even a blade of grass has form when we handle it or blow through it to make a sound. Nature embodies all her animal life in forms, from man to the so-called shapeless jellyfish. The round pebble that we hold in our hand and the mountain peak that requires days to climb are both natural forms. To understand the meaning of the word form, imagine for a minute that the world is a stage set with all the scenery made of flats, and the people and animals cut from cardboard. This would be a world of shapes and sizes, but the minute we round out the flats into real trees, rocks, and buildings, and the people into many-sided forms, we achieve depth and movement and the capacity to view objects from all angles. This is form, one of nature's most important tools.

Unity

Throughout the discussion of rhythm and variety, balance and form, one fact becomes increasingly clear. Nature in all its parts has a certain similarity. The life rhythms occur in weather, in seasons, and in man—and all are interrelated. The rotation of electrons around a nucleus is not unlike the ordered movement in which infinite galaxies orbit throughout the universe, extending more than two billion light years from us in all directions. Variety is characteristic of nature in all its manifestations, whether it is in the skin of a hippopotamus or in the microscopic tissues of a guinea pig. The textured pebble, which we think of as inanimate, is actually a manifestation of centuries of living, in which it has been water, vegetation, and stone, and then has become in part vegetation and water again as its roughness is washed away into the soil. This cycle of creation and disintegration illustrates the great basic fact of nature, the characteristic of over-all relationship that we identify as *unity.*

As physics and the other physical and biological sciences point more and more toward the oneness of the universe, we realize that this is what the philosophers have been trying to tell us for centuries. The seventeenth-century philosopher Spinoza maintained that all reality is one substance, one in cause and one in origin, and that God and this reality are one. By substance, however, he did not mean the material contents of nature such as hills and forests, but an active and vital process involved, among other things, in the creation of these contents. This is the eternal order as opposed to the temporal order of things that exist in time and finally die; it points to the very structure of existence, underlying all events and things and comprising the essence of the world itself.

Two hundred years later Schopenhauer pursued a similar train of thought in saying that only in time and space do we become separate beings, that space and time are the illusion hiding the unity of things. In his masterpiece, *The World as Will and Idea,* he states:

> To understand clearly that the individual is only the phenomenon, not the thing-in-itself, [to see in] the constant change of matter the fixed permanence of form—this is the essence of philosophy. . . . The true philosophy of history lies in perceiving that, in all the endless changes and motley complexity of events, it is only the self-same unchangeable being that is before us, which today pursues the same ends as it did yesterday and ever will. The historical philosopher has accordingly to recognize the identical character in all events . . . and in spite of all the variety of special circumstances, of costumes and manners and customs, has to see everywhere the same humanity. . . .

These are comparatively modern restatements of a basic belief relating to one of the world's oldest religions, Hinduism. The Vedas, sacred Hindu writings dating back four thousand years, are believed to be the teachings of Brahman, who represents the totality of all creation; and stress is laid upon the underlying unity of all life and the presence in the universe of one great spirit called Atman, in whom all existence is a part.

No one can find deeper meaning in such revelations than the creative artist. The painter, writer, composer, or designer must have a sense of timelessness and continuity as well as a feeling of his own destiny in reaching toward the ideal and striving to improve or interpret what he finds. George Santayana says in *The Sense of Beauty:* "He who lives in the ideal and leaves it expressed in society or in art enjoys a double immortality. The eternal has absorbed him while he lived, and when he is dead his influence brings others to the same absorption, making them, through that ideal identity which is best in him, reincarnations and perennial seats of all in him which he could rationally hope to rescue from destruction."

The objective of the creative artist, then, must be the ideal based in the truths of living, for any work to be truly creative must have a basic unity: unity within its parts and, even more vital, unity with the fundamental qualities that we continually rediscover in our search for design in nature.

STUDIO PROJECTS

1. List four examples of natural rhythms not mentioned in the text.
2. Using ink or paint make a design using the simple rhythm of a native drumbeat.
3. Listen to a musical composition and make a graphic representation in India ink, using your own symbols to represent phrases.
4. Cut five different shapes of varying sizes from colored paper. Mount all five in such a way that a unified design results.
5. Using a bright-colored paper and a dark-colored one cut out pieces and mount them to create a design showing balance.
6. List five ways of achieving unity in a design.

CHAPTER 3

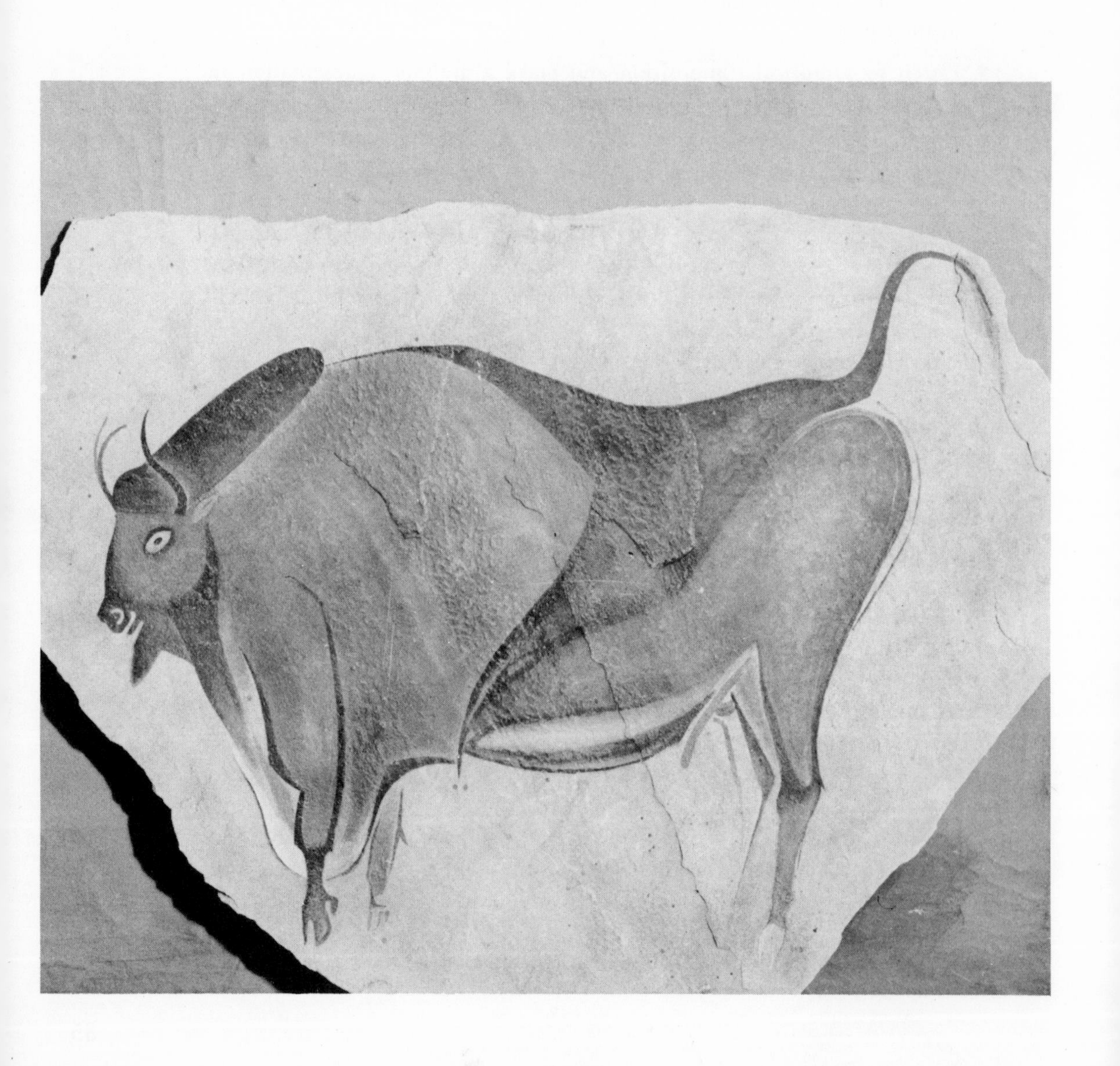

Basic Ingredients

In acknowledging the magnitude of design possibilities around us, we can assume that our environment is the result of definite methods on the part of nature. Such elements as color, texture, size, shape, and form are combined by means of rhythm, variety, and balance into a unified whole in which we live and find our inspiration for work. Attractive as his natural surroundings may be, however, man feels the need to reflect their beauty in a more immediate way; in other words, to enhance his man-made environment by design and ornamentation.

Our earliest relics show signs of man's creative need in simple designs carved upon the handles of tools and weapons. The famous cave drawings at Altamira and Lascaux have been interpreted in many ways: as superstitious talismen planned to insure success in the hunt, as records of animals already encountered, as personal victory over the animal needed for sustenance by capturing him in vegetable dye and charcoal on the walls of a cave. Regardless of the motivation, the esthetic quality of the drawings is undeniable. The flow of line, the richness of color, and the feeling for design that capture the essence of the animal continue to awaken admiration in artists of each succeeding generation (Figure 3–1).

As man's shelter became more than a cave his attempts to improve its design became increasingly ambitious. He discovered two ways of making his immediate environment attractive. First, he could use natural elements. He could plant trees and flowers, dam streams, make clearings in the wilderness. He could use natural materials to build his shelter, combining wood and stone in their original state, merely shaping them to form the beams and corners needed. Second, he could produce new shapes and materials with his own hands, creating designs based on natural forms but

Figure 3–1. Facsimile of "Standing Bison of Altamira" from early cave drawings in northern Spain. Courtesy of the Denver Art Museum.

indigenous to his own taste and creative ability. In this way, through the centuries, he has produced all the textiles, tapestries, ceramics, glass, metalwork, painting and sculpture with which he has enriched his surroundings.

The immediate problem for the creative artist is how to make his own contribution. We have seen how nature creates an environment, but how does the human artist begin? He does not have time for the gradual development of his designs through evolution. He needs means of creating something that will be effective immediately and that will retain its original effectiveness throughout the duration of its usefulness. Using nature as his guide, he still needs to discover ingredients he can use in his own way. Some of these have counterparts in nature; one, at least, does not.

Line

The first ally in creative design, as in drawing, is *line*. This is a man-made tool. What we think of as line becomes on closer observance a joining of two surfaces, a dark form against a lighter one, a round vein in a leaf through which the food and water flow, a spider web which has a cross-section under a microscope. The only pure lines are made by man with a pencil, pen, brush, or other instrument, yet his use of line is necessary and important. It is by use of line that we enclose space and create shape and thus have the beginning of design (Figure 3–2).

Figure 3–2. Fragments of line mean little but when continued and joined a shape results which can become form or the beginning of design.

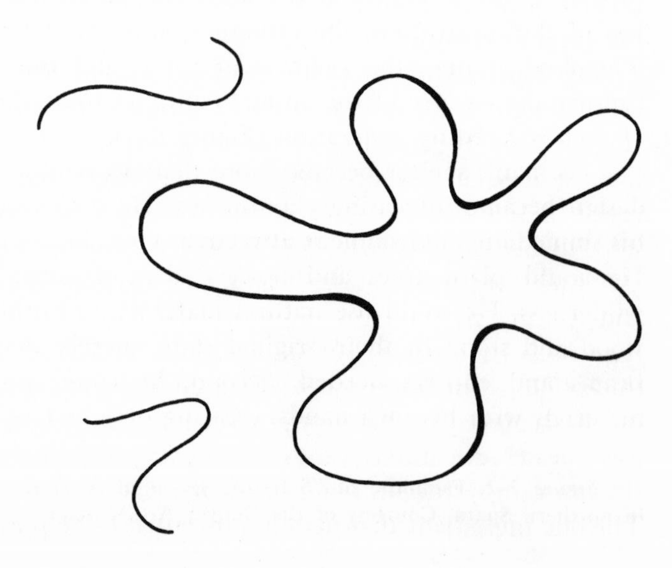

Figure 3–3. Deserted ranch buildings in the Rocky Mountains. Notice the diagonal lines of the decaying buildings as opposed to the strong verticals of the spruce trees in the background.

Lines assume expression and meaning through association with natural forms. We find horizontal lines restful as a still lake or a far horizon are restful. Trees and mountains reach up to pierce the sky, so we think of vertical lines as climbing, reaching, aspiring and use them in our buildings to create a feeling of awe and inspiration. Diagonal lines, on the other hand, make us think of lightning, of falling timber, of buildings in the process of decay (Figure 3–3). These associations cause us to interpret slanting lines as chaotic.

If deprived of all other elements except line we could still create a good design. Line can be used to simulate texture (Figure 3–4) or value (Figure 3–5). It cannot produce color, but it will give an effect of dark and light if used in certain ways. We have seen that size and shape are the result of line enclosing space, and form can be created by carrying line a step further, into a three-dimensional treatment (Figure 3–6).

Lines express motion, leading to rhythm. The motion may be slow and flowing like a river, or short and fast like the staccato beat of jazz (Figure 3–7). Variety can be achieved with line: long lines, short lines, thick lines, thin lines, wavy or jagged lines, smooth straight lines. Balance can be achieved by the grouping of lines in certain ways. Line also can be used to achieve unity. Lines flowing in the same direction or moving in rhythm can be the unifying force that makes a composition a good design. The one ingredient that man has invented to help him in simulating nature

Figure 3–4. Line can be used to create many kinds of texture.

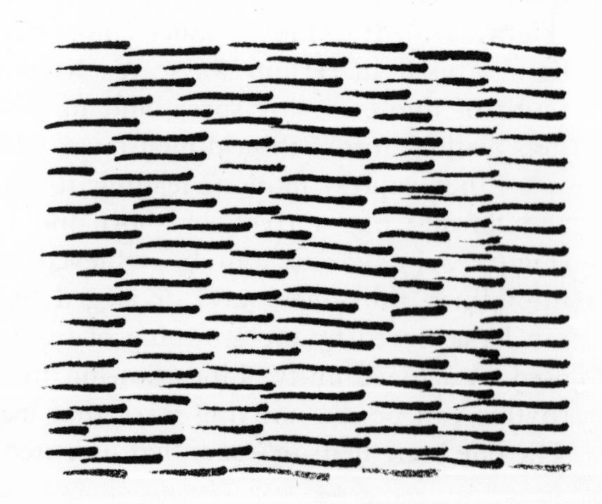

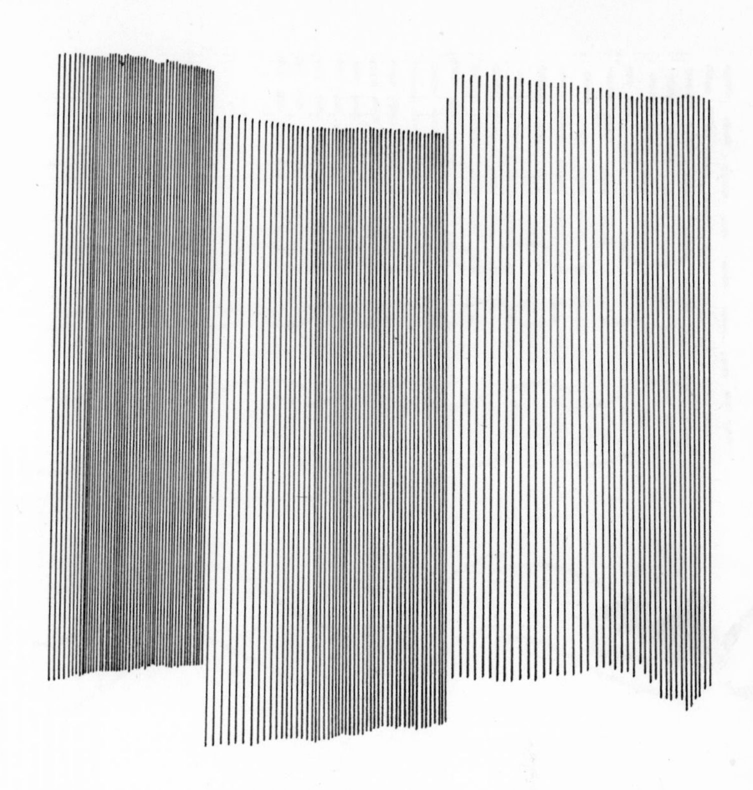

Figure 3–5. Varying values from light to dark can be created by the use of line alone, by width of the lines, and by the distances between them.

Figure 3–6. Simple line can be used to create form.

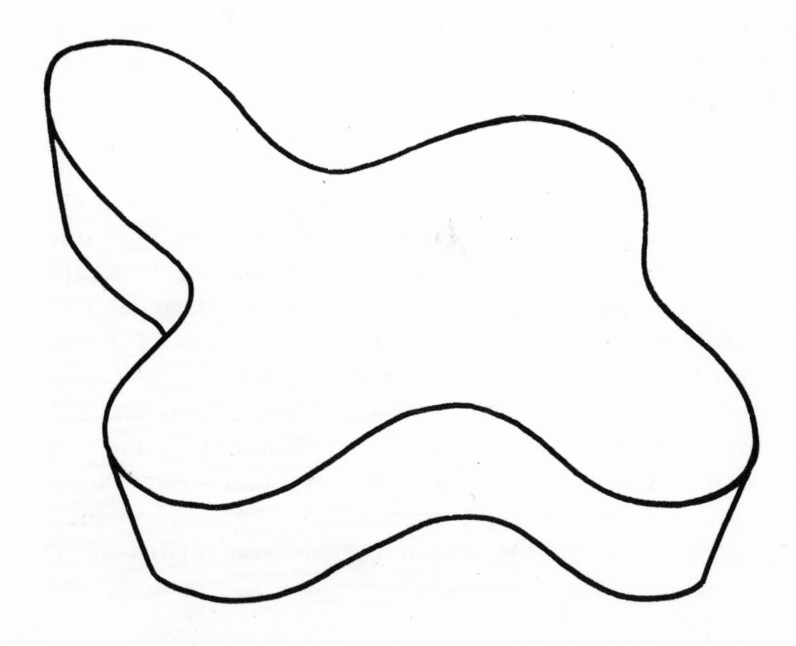

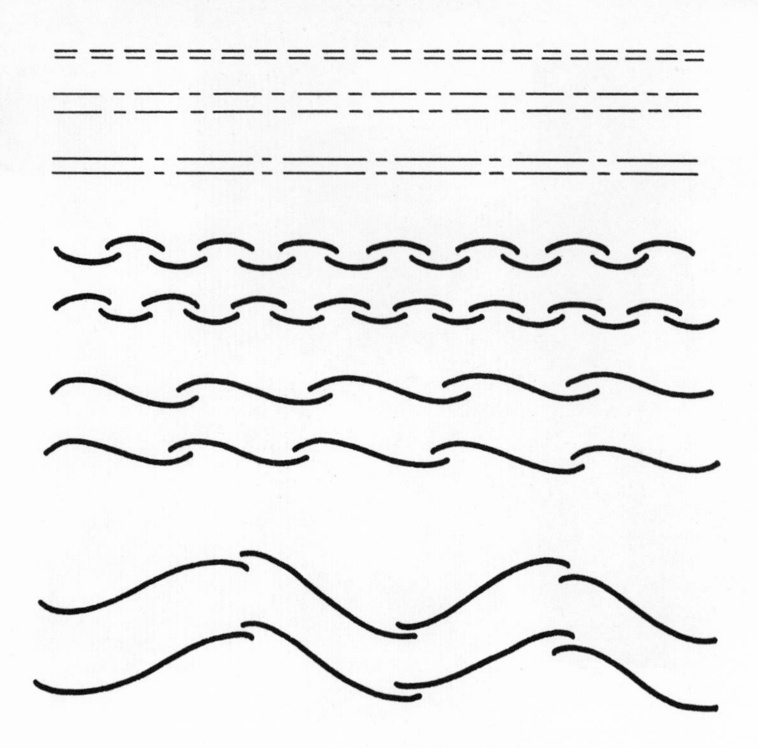

Figure 3–7. Line creates a variety of rhythms. Try "reading" the lines like a piece of music, making a sound in keeping with the size and shape of each line. You will find that rhythmic sounds result which translate back into the visual symbols.

can take on the guise of most of the elements found in natural design.

We have been speaking of line as a specific element, drawn with a man-made tool. However, there is another connotation in which line does have existence in nature. In describing any artistic work, the word "line" is used in a larger sense to express the general feeling of the work, with an implication of rhythm, unity, and balance. We speak of the lines of a building, the flowing lines of a dress, the interesting lines of a painting, just as we speak of the rolling horizon line or the rugged shore line or the curved line of the hills. This is our way of stating the all-over feeling of a work or a scene, of describing its essence. A building with horizontal lines connotes informality, designed to blend with the surrounding landscape, a structure with vertical lines furnishes dramatic accent. Diagonal lines designate still another type of architecture, the peaked roofs of Alpine chalets, Finnish churches, and many of the modern chapel buildings created to give a feeling of aspiration. It is the writhing, seething lines that give El Greco's paintings their strong emotional quality (Figure 3–8), the calm horizontal lines combined with soft atmospheric effects that create a mood of restfulness in a Constable landscape (Figure 3–9). This is line in its fullest sense, expanded to become the most important basic quality of any work of art.

Figure 3–8. The twisting curves of El Greco's "The Assumption of the Virgin" give it a feeling of emotion and movement. Oil. Courtesy of The Art Institute of Chicago. Gift of Nancy Atwood Sprague in memory of Albert Arnold Sprague.

Figure 3–9. The horizontal lines of this painting by John Constable give a feeling of serenity accentuated by the peaceful quality of the subject matter. "Wivenhoe Park, Essex," oil on canvas. National Gallery of Art, Washington, D.C. Widener Collection.

Texture

A second ingredient of design is *texture*. We have seen how much texture adds to the visual and tactile interest of our natural environment. When plastics first began to prove their versatility a vast smoothness came into interior design. The ultimate in modern interiors in the 1930's was the room with the "streamlined" look, with smooth bare walls and chromium and plastic furniture curved to fit the body. One of the recommendations for such rooms was that the concrete floors could be hosed down instead of swept or vacuumed, thus simplifying upkeep. However, as people lived in these models of efficiency they began to feel something missing. There was a sterility about such complete bareness and smoothness, a lack of warmth and comfort, even though the plastic chairs were scientifically designed to support the body better than the old ones with soft cushions. As we approached mid-century, houses began to acquire areas of rough-hewn fieldstone and inside walls of used brick, preferred to new brick because it was rougher and more interesting in color. The smoothness of floors now came from flagstone or brick or wood parquetry. Planters were built indoors so the texture of leaves could relieve the wide expanse of walls still preferred to the cluttered walls of the early part of the century. Even the scientifically designed furniture cast off its smooth bright chromium for the tones and textures of wood and textiles. Carpeting began to be more important than simplicity of upkeep and pile frequently became long and looped. Interesting weave was emphasized in draperies and table linens, in upholstery, and even in grasscloth wall and floor coverings. Warmth and color were felt in interiors, qualities stemming principally from texture. This was not new. Through the centuries texture has been important in all civilizations, from the thick-piled Persian rugs to the grass tatami on the floors of Japanese homes. It is as though some atavistic need relates us to the rough bark and thick moss of the forest, making us feel most at ease among the natural textures in which early life developed (Figure 3–10). Having carried to excess Victorian interiors with horsehair upholstery and wall decorations woven from human hair, it was necessary for the pendulum to swing to the other extreme of severe functionalism before arriving at a middle ground of balance.

It is not in the visual arts alone that texture is essential to human satisfaction. We find texture in music as a result of sustained tones or staccato notes, of flowing rhythms or sharp beats, of harmonic arrangements or martial treatment. We find it in literature in characterization, figures of speech, conversation, description, as well as in the use of words and their placement. Dance has texture depending upon the fluidity or violence of movement.

Figure 3–10. Old wood and sand, two products of the relentless weathering processes of nature.

In the hands of the graphic designer, as in nature, texture has two faces. The *tactile* quality comes from the choice of interesting materials: rough stone, nubby fibers, wood in which the soft grain has been worn away leaving interesting ridges. Frequently this is an inherent quality in a work of art, one that comes from the initial selection of materials rather than from anything the designer does to them. What he does *with* them, of course, will determine what the implicit quality does to the finished design, but the existence of this quality comes from his original choice. The tactile quality can also come from treatment of a given material, as in the carving of wood or the incising of design on plaster or pottery. Metal can be given a tactile quality by hammering or treatment with acid. Even when such materials are not actually felt by the fingers, the tactile quality is an important part of the enjoyment, giving a sensory satisfaction related to actual touch but going beyond it.

Visual quality is more obvious and is more apt to be an active contribution of the designer. A textured glaze is achieved on a piece of pottery by use of a formula in which flecks of one substance hang in suspension. Visual texture is given to a fabric by design printed upon it in repetition. An Impressionistic painting is built entirely of texture. This may be tactile texture if the paint is put on *impasto,* in thick layers, or it may be more visual in quality (Figure 3–11). The Impressionists were primarily interested in light and color, and in order to achieve the maximum effects they used small dots of paint placed side by side to give a shimmering quality. Instead of mixing their pigments on the palette, they relied upon the eye of the observer to mix the paint into the desired colors and forms. Consequently, their painting is a study in texture, and since the forms are built up from the texture, the texture is an organic part of the painting; in fact, it IS the painting—as any texture should be, in design as well as in painting.

Figure 3–11. Most impressionistic paintings are rich in texture, both visual and tactile. An excellent example is provided in the lush strokes of Claude Monet in "Le Bassin des Nympheas." Courtesy of the Denver Art Museum.

In creating a design we find that there are three kinds of sources for either visual or tactile texture. First, as we have seen, there are infinite textures in *nature*. Second, there are *man-made* textures, created by carving, stippling, cross-hatching, scratching into the surface of a pot, combining rough fibers in weaving and many other processes. Third, there are *machine-made* textures brought about by pressing, stamping, machine engraving, raised printing, and so on. Visual texture exists in the type on a page and tactile texture is obvious in the holes of a cheese grater. All three sources are authentic and each kind has its place. The designer must know where each type of texture will be most effective.

Color

We have stated that it is possible to have a good design without using *color*. Considerable time is spent in arranging space and type on title pages of books and magazines; such pages have no color yet they are good composition. We have seen effective all-over prints in black and white on fabric. The use of color in design is not necessary but it plays an important role in our psychological reaction. A design that is interesting in black and white becomes an exciting thing when done in warm bright colors. The same design becomes soothing and restful when done in soft tones. We react differently in different color settings; this is why the psychology of color has become so important in interior design. Soft colors are used in doctors' and dentists' offices to calm our nerves and warm stimulating tones are painted on the walls of restaurants where it is hoped we will enjoy our food and eat heartily.

Color is the most flexible of all materials used in design. Not only can it change the entire character of a design, it is never absolute but varies continually through its juxtaposition with other colors. Color does not exist without light. A closet full of bright-colored clothes is without color when the door is closed and the light turned off. Consequently, variations in light cause color to modify constantly, assuming endless variations.

Because of the importance of color in everyday living, man-made restrictions have grown up around its use making people afraid of combining colors without definite rules to follow. A careful study of color in nature can free anyone from such arbitrary limitations and open up a new and exciting world. For instance, some people will state that certain colors "clash." This is a word that, at least in its derogatory sense, should be eliminated from the vocabulary of any person interested in design. A clash of color in a positive sense can have shock value which will be effective in architectural design or in dress, but the idea of colors clashing in the sense that they cannot be used together is an unnecessary and limiting consideration. The case of blue and green is an example. Many people have the idea

Figure 3–12. A dramatic quality pervades this painting by Theodoros Stamos by virtue of the exaggerated size of a few vital elements. "Greek Orison," oil on canvas. Collection of the Whitney Museum of American Art, New York.

that blue and green cannot be used together, although it is difficult to find any basis for this opinion. On the contrary, consider the green of the ocean against a blue summer sky, the blue of the harebell against the green of a meadow, the innumerable other blue flowers that we admire in our gardens, surrounded as they are by green leaves. Pink and orange are another combination questioned by the average person, yet who has objected to the splash of pinks and oranges in a field of poppies? It is true that we can appreciate colors in nature that we could not live with at close range under artificial light. Most people would rebel at a room with one pink and one orange wall and with good reason, but the reason is not that the colors do not harmonize. The reason is that both are exciting colors and living with large areas of them could be disturbing. A cushion of each color against a brown sofa might be just the touch that would lift a room from monotony to a level of interest. This is an example of following nature, for the flowers in their bright colors are actually only dots of color on a landscape.

Size

Still another element that we must consider in creating a design is size. Scale is another term, implying the relationship of various sizes within a given design. As with a clash of color, exaggerated size may be used for emphasis or dramatic impact (Figure 3–12), but on the whole the various parts of a design will be in scale with one another, be basically related in size. When small units are used they usually are repeated to create texture, as in the painting by Georges Braque (Figure 3–13). One area of texture would be lost if used individually but repeated in balance, textural areas create a rhythm which gives a strong feeling of unity. Size is always determined by the original area in which the designer starts to work. The size of a house should be prescribed by the size of the lot combined with the restrictions of how much lawn and garden the client wants around it. The size of elements in a fabric design will be affected by how the fabric is to be used and how much of it will be seen at one time. Larger elements will be used in a design for draperies than will be used in material for a small girl's dress. Sizes in a mural will be much amplified over the sizes of the same elements in an easel painting. The designer may be more conscious of color and rhythm and the general feeling of his work, but none of these can come into being until he has solved the problems of size.

Shape

In our last basic ingredient to be considered we come back to line, for whenever we use line to enclose an area we create *shape*. Shape can also

Figure 3–13. Variety of texture repeated throughout the composition relates the different sizes and shapes in this oil on canvas by Georges Braque, "Oval Still Life" (*Le violon*). Collection, The Museum of Modern Art, New York. Gift of the Advisory Committee.

Figure 3–14. Geometric shapes comprise this painting by Piet Mondrian. No two shapes are just alike in either size or proportion. "Composition in White, Black and Red," oil on canvas. Collection of The Museum of Modern Art, New York. Gift of the Advisory Committee.

be created by masses which exist as areas of color or of dark and light. Wherever a mass exists two shapes are created, the shape of the mass and the shape of the area around it. Whenever two masses or shapes overlap a new shape is created. In a painting the center of interest may have importance because of subject matter which has a psychological appeal, but in a design the center of interest depends primarily upon shape. What we do with a shape in the way of color or texture can add interest, but basically the shape must have significance in itself before it can assume importance as the basis for a design.

Shapes can be *geometric,* as in a painting by Mondrian (Figure 3–14). At first glance one would say that all of the shapes in this painting are similar, yet actually, although all are rectangles, no two are really alike in size or shape. Making a composition of such closely allied shapes takes more skill than combining varying shapes because the differences are so subtle. If any two areas were identical the composition would immediately lose its interest.

Shapes can also be *nonobjective.* Nonobjective shapes rarely resemble the object used as model. A simple way to understand this is to draw a geometric figure and then pretend that you are giving it a push. A triangle, a circle, or a rectangle can thus in effect become an abstraction (Figure 3–15). The nonobjective painter uses shapes to represent his own *subjective* thoughts and emotions.

Shapes can also be *natural.* Certain leaves are more interesting to us than others. The rooster and giraffe have long been popular for designs because of their unusual forms. Natural shapes need an imaginative touch to avoid triteness; their obvious interest is frequently overworked. Snowflakes, palm trees, cactus, and waterlilies need not be ruled out as points of departure. It simply takes the original touch of a gifted designer to re-establish them on a higher plane in design.

Mass

We cannot discuss shape without becoming involved in its three-dimensional counterpart, *mass.* When a shape takes on a third dimension it becomes a mass, something that can be lifted or turned over. It is not necessary to have mass in a painting or design. Mondrian's painting does not have mass in the usual sense. It has shape, composition, and color, and it has its own kind of form, but it has no mass in the connotation of third dimension. We say that a work of art "takes a certain form" but not in the sense of mass that goes into space with a feeling of volume and weight. Mass is not essential to all works of art. In a mural or fabric design, in fact, the feeling of mass can be distracting, giving the viewer the feeling that there are holes in the wall or the drapery. Some wallpapers are designed as *trompe-l'oeil,* "fool the eye," as in life-sized murals of Southern gardens or Venetian canals. In living with an all-over design, we are usually more comfortable with a flat pattern of interesting shapes. In a realistic painting, on the other hand, mass is important. We want to feel that the buildings have weight and that we could walk around and see what is behind them if we wished. We usually want our portraits to look as though we are sitting in a room, surrounded by air and space, not flattened against a wall. Even in nonobjective paintings we speak of the interesting masses and the feeling of solidity in certain parts.

These, then, are the ingredients that the designer has at his disposal. As in making any one cake we do not use all the materials in the cupboard, so it is not necessary that we always use all the elements of design. The artist must be able to understand the possibilities of line, texture, color, size, shape, and mass and to decide which will be important in each of his creations. These are his tools and he can choose them to suit his goals. It is important to have the knowledge to choose wisely.

Figure 3–15. A triangle, circle, and rectangle when given a push form nonobjective shapes.

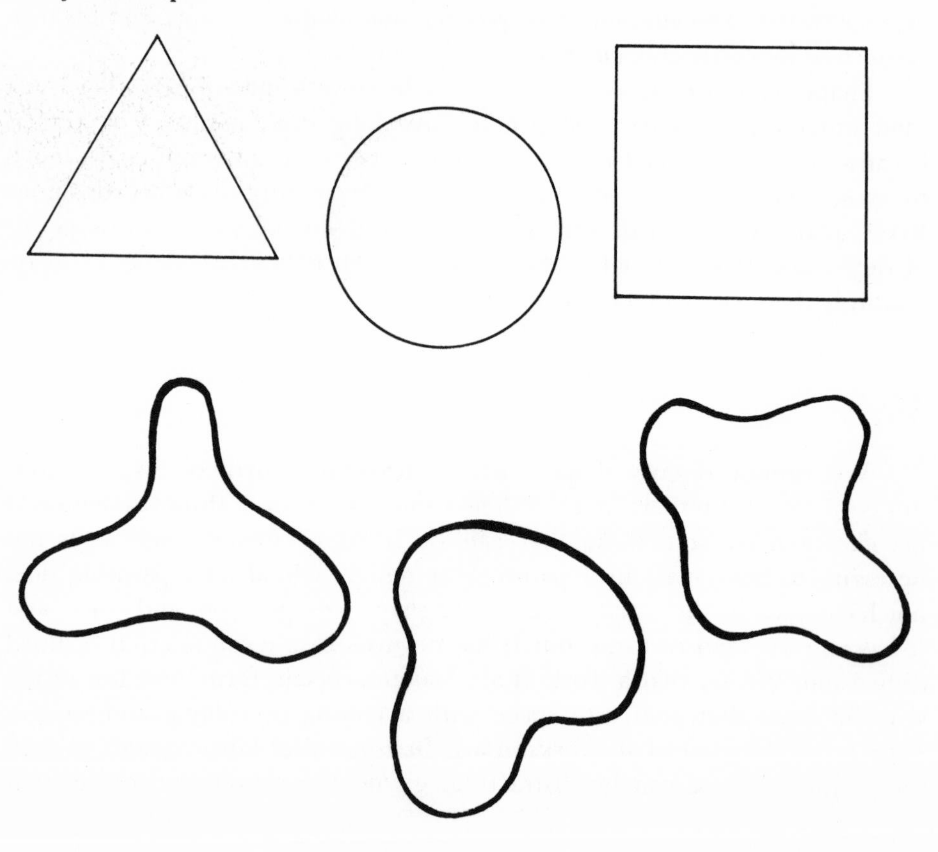

FOR FURTHER EXPLORATION

Design: A Creative Approach by Sybil Emerson (Scranton, Pa.: International Textbook Company, 1953). An excellent introduction to the elements of design, generously illustrated.

Design for You by Ethel Jane Beitler and Bill C. Lockhart (New York: John Wiley & Sons, Inc., 1961). An informative treatment of the elements and principles of design, handled informally and with extensive illustrations.

STUDIO PROJECTS

1. With brush and ink draw lines expressing as many different emotions as possible.
2. Mount examples of visual and tactile texture combined to form a "collage," or glued on design, making certain that you have variety of shape, size, and color as well.
3. Cut from paper three pieces of any shape in three different colors that you feel should not be used together. Now by cutting the pieces to different sizes and shapes see if you cannot make an arrangement which is harmonious. Mount on a black background.

CHAPTER 4

The Magic Touch

WE HAVE NOW ESTABLISHED SIX BASIC INGREDIENTS or elements for creating a design: line, texture, color, size, and shape or mass. This by no means places them in the category of rules for creating. Rules we leave to science; in art it is necessary to remain flexible with only an outline of possibilities to guide conception. There have been artists who reduced their work to three basic considerations: line, form, and value and considered anything further as confusing and extraneous. There are art teachers, on the other hand, who list as many as thirteen basic elements of design, breaking mass into space and shape, and color into hue, value, and intensity. There is no conflict here, just a shift of emphasis. Some people prefer to catalog information as minutely as possible, others like to think and work simply and in large areas of understanding.

Our six elements have been observed through an analysis of nature and they will be useful hereafter as the basis for further progress. If properly understood, they encompass everything that is found in a creative work of art.

Variety of Design

When we realize that the entire world of design, in architecture, painting, sculpture, clothing, industrial and commercial design, and all their many ramifications is based on these six ingredients, we marvel at the variety that is achieved. Even within the limits of one material the variations seem virtually limitless. Walk into the yard-goods section of a large department store and look at the bolts of printed cotton. Many of the

Figure 4–1. The simple rhythm of a drumbeat interpreted visually. To dramatize the relationship, read "Boom" for each dot.

patterns will be similar in motif but handled in different ways. Consider the table that holds only plaids. One can think of a plaid as a formula in which space is broken up by lines going at right angles, yet even here the necessity of design is evident if we study the variations that can be achieved by moving the lines a fraction of an inch one way or the other and by breaking up the space into bands of varying widths. Designing a plaid is akin to studying a Mondrian painting (Figure 3–14) where through geometric shapes a two-dimensional area is transformed into a composition. We find bold plaids, delicate plaids, thin lines and broad stripes, and some "shadow plaids" that are subtle variations on a simple check.

Secret of Creative Design

If all of these creations can be achieved through the use of six or fewer simple elements, we can come to only one conclusion: the determining factor in a design is not so much in the elements used as in the magic touch of the creative designer who uses them. In this touch lies the secret of exciting design.

One of the most important differences between art and science lies in the role of the artist. Although the scientist must have feelings and emotions about his experiments, he works primarily in rules and formulae in such a way that the same experiment can be performed in the same way by any number of people. The artist, however, is such a potent part of his work that even his apprentices will not execute the work in exactly the same way that he would. We have many instances of paintings done in the workshops of the Old Masters in which experts can distinguish the work of the helpers from the touch of the master himself, even when the master has given instructions as to how the work was to be handled. There is inspiration to be derived from working in a studio with other artists, in seeing the varying approaches, and the diversity of viewpoint regarding one particular model. Set up a still life and tell a class to paint it; no two paintings will be similar in their finished presentation. Even a simple object like an orange will appear in diverse sizes and colors, depending upon the viewpoint of the observer. The selection of composition and emphasis of various elements can actually be a key to the personality of the painter. This realization obligates the artist to develop his taste and knowledge to the fullest, for not only does he reflect the social and spiritual climate of his age but he shows forth what he is himself in the intangible quality of his art. Here the artist parts company with the craftsman. His skills express what he is, a person who not only has mastered a technique but uses technique, not as an end in itself but to say something to the world.

Figure 4–2. This rhythm would be expressed audibly as "BOOM boom BOOM boom" in the top row, and "BOOM boom boom BOOM boom boom" in the row below.

Nature Points the Way

Knowing that the ultimate result in a work of art depends upon the philosophy, personality, mental and spiritual qualities of the artist, we can still look for some general principles to guide him. In nature we have discovered the six elements of a good design, so it is only logical to look to nature for the principles by which these elements may be put together.

Rhythm

We know that in nature the underlying principle is rhythm. How do we inject rhythm into our work? The answer, of course, is that we do not. Rhythm must be, as in nature, *underlying*. It must be in the work from the beginning; it cannot be added after the rest is done. Some artists create to the sound of music in the hope that the rhythmic sounds will be transmuted to the forms in their work. Others study the dance hoping that they can translate these forms into line and color. Some have a natural sense of rhythm which comes out in visual work just as natural grace is apparent in certain dancers. Others have to cultivate this sense in the same way that they cultivate an eye for color, a feeling for proportion, and a sensitivity to good design, by studying the best work and analyzing it to see why it is superior.

There are, however, some specific procedures for achieving rhythm. We learn in studying nature that rhythm has two important components: *repetition* and *emphasis*. Simple visual rhythm can be created just as African natives achieve a simple rhythmic sound, by *repetition* of one motif at regular intervals. Translate the drumbeat into a form of any size or shape and repeat it at regular intervals and you will have a kind of rhythm (Figure 4–1). This is related to the human heartbeat under a condition of

relaxed regular breathing. However, we are aware that when anything of interest occurs this regular breathing varies, so if we wish to give interest to our visual rhythms we vary the motif or vary the intervals, or both. When a strong element is added to accent the original, we immediately find greater interest. When a strong element is balanced with two lesser ones, we find that the attraction increases even more (Figure 4–2). Kay Sekimachi has woven an unusual textile in which she uses the same motif but varies it in value, thus providing a difference in texture as well (Figure 4–3).

Figure 4–3. A simple rhythm is repeated throughout this textile, "Square Variations," by Kay Sekimachi, yet it is handled in an imaginative way that keeps it lively and full of surprises. Courtesy of the artist and of *Craft Horizons.* Photograph by Ernest Lowe.

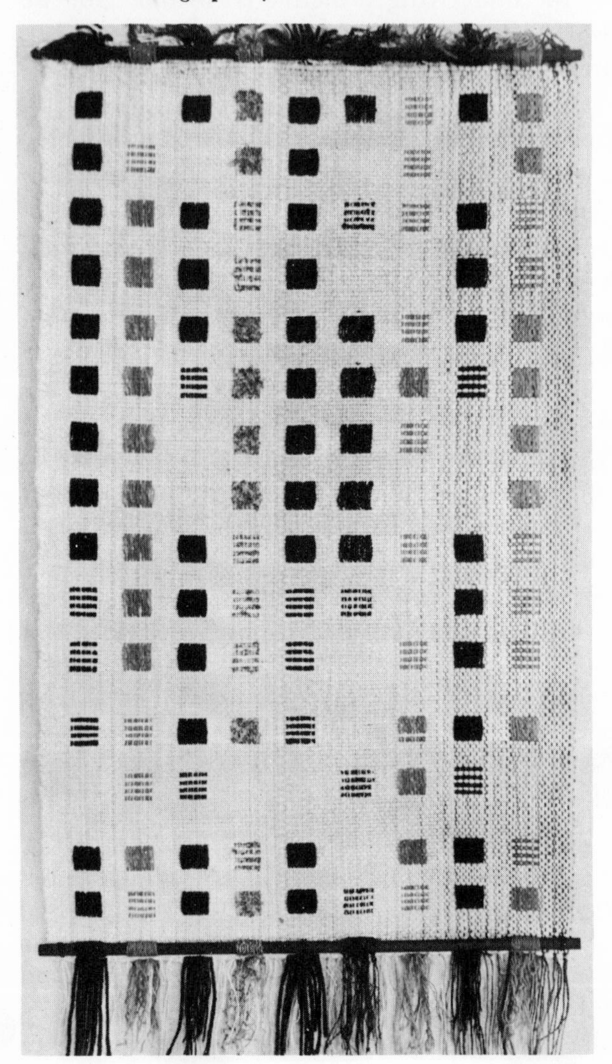

Figure 4–4. (*Opposite page.*) Two all-over designs created from repetition of a single shape. At left a square is used in solid and open spaces; new forms are evolved by placement of the solid square as emphasis. At right circles overlap to form two new shapes that are repeated to form an all-over pattern in which the original circles claim emphasis. Courtesy of Morris Kurtzon, Inc.

Notice the way in which she has omitted the motif from some areas, giving a surprise to the rhythm much as one finds in modern music.

As soon as a second size or shape is added to our pattern we express *emphasis* because the larger of the two motifs indicates a stronger beat or a more emphatic element in the rhythm. One can design in the same way as a dance is developed, by starting with a simple rhythm and then playing *repetition* and *emphasis* together until a degree of complexity is reached which best expresses the intent. Figure 4–4 shows two designs, each created from one simple geometric form repeated to invent other forms. In (a) two new forms are created each time the circles overlap, giving a vertical and horizontal pattern and a diagonal one as well. In (b) a simple square is used with the juxtaposition of the solid form on the open areas creating new forms.

We have been speaking of the simple rhythms formed by *repetition* and *emphasis,* but to most people the word rhythm means a flowing quality such as the rhythm of breakers rolling in on a beach or the swirling of draperies about a dancing figure. While this sort of rhythm depends upon *repetition* and *emphasis* just as much as the simpler rhythms, the flowing quality is derived from the use of more fluid motifs and a less rigid placement of them as in the room divider in Figure 4–5. Moholy-Nagy in his book *Vision in Motion* states that every drawing can be understood as a motion study since it is a path of motion recorded by graphic means.[1] Interpreting a design as the path left by the motion of the artist's hand, we realize that the artist's feeling of rhythm as he works will be the determining factor in the rhythm of his design.

In Figure 4–6 we can compare two designs three centuries apart in conception, both of which illustrate a free use of motifs. The tapestry from seventeenth-century Portugal achieves its rhythmic pattern from the interweaving of flowing lines representing the stems and tendrils of a flower, probably a thistle. The flower form itself is used in two variations, one simpler than the other and turned at right angles to lessen the regularity of the *repetition*. While the placement follows a set pattern, the flowing quality of the leaves, stems, and flower heads is so emphatic that the over-all feeling is one of movement akin to a satisfying emotional experience rather than to the simpler rhythm of the heartbeat in a relaxed, and perhaps bored, state of mind. The more complicated a design becomes the more it resembles the rhythms of the body in its higher emotional states. This does not mean that the more involved designs are necessarily the best. We would not choose to live in a continual state of high excitement; indeed it would be biologically impossible to do so. Similarly, we need simplicity in certain of our surroundings if we are to be able to function effectively in them. The exciting accent can "make" a room and stimulating patterns can be fascinating in public buildings or areas where great activity is carried on. In an atmosphere of relaxation, however, the simple pattern has its own essential place.

The Portuguese design is contrasted with a contemporary fabric design by Janet Erikson entitled "After Pollack." Using the paintings of Jackson Pollack for inspiration, Mrs. Erickson has created an individual interpretation of flowing rhythm which demonstrates two characteristics of twentieth-century design. First, in contrast to the Portuguese thistles, the motifs in Mrs. Erickson's design cannot be identified. One feels that they are figures and the longer they are contemplated the more one imagines about the activities that they represent. However, there is no complete statement. Not knowing definitely what any motif depicts, we are free to interpret it differently every time we look at it. Secondly, analysis of the different units discloses that while all are similar no two are exactly alike. Thus, while giving the effect of *repetition*, the fabric actually is done in a nonrepeating

[1] L. Moholy-Nagy, *Vision in Motion* (Chicago: Paul Theobald & Company, 1956), p. 36.

Figure 4–5. A flowing rhythm dominates this acrylic screen handwoven and dyed by Ted Hallman.

design. These characteristics give the design an emotional fluidity as well as graphic flexibility, for the viewer is not bound by any limits of interpretation. He can impart his own feelings to the design and he can sense the security of *repetition* without being encompassed by it, much as the composer or the dancer repeats phrases but with variations and elaborations, making the composition ever more interesting.

Figure 4–6a. Block-printed Portuguese textile showing use of natural forms in design. Printed in dark red on a tan ground of loosely woven linen, this seventeenth-century fabric has a feeling of flowing rhythm produced by intertwining stem forms and periodic but not mechanical repetition of flower heads. Courtesy of The Newark Museum, Newark, New Jersey.

Variety

This brings us to the second principle learned from nature—*variety*. We have mentioned the variety of texture and value in Miss Sekimachi's fabric in Figure 4–3. Variety here is the essence of the design since the motif is a simple geometric figure repeated over and over. A master touch of variety such as this can be more effective than wide diversity which tends to become complicated.

Variety in size and shape are infinitely useful in the hands of the designer. In Figure 4–7 we see a comparison of designs created from bottles. In the first one all of the bottles are of the same shape and while that form is interesting the effect of the whole is like that produced by a frieze in which the same unit is repeated in the simple rhythm of a staccato beat. The second design uses the original bottle shape combined with another form in a different size. While unity is maintained through the basic similarity of the shapes, interest is gained through the differences. No longer do we have a staccato beat but a flowing rhythm from the combined

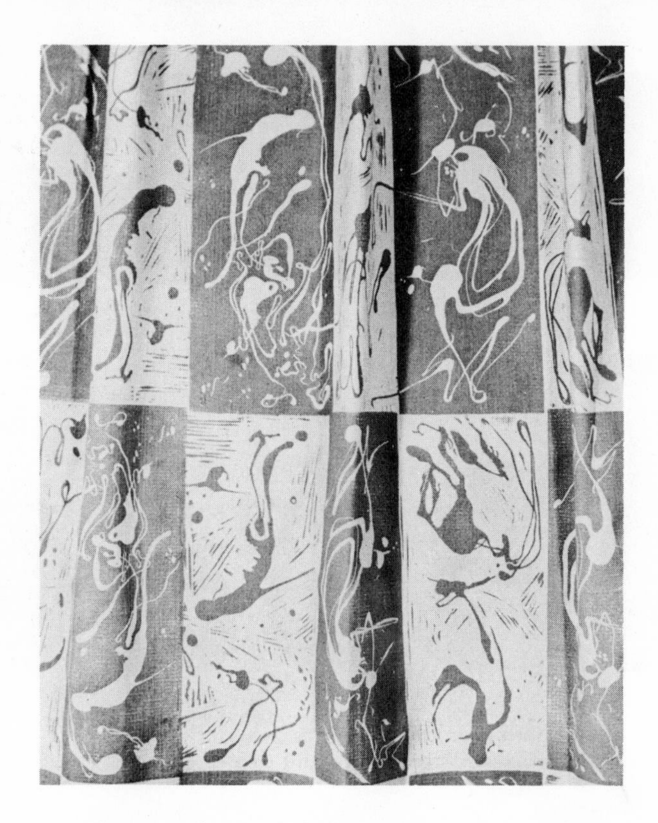

Figure 4–6b. Hand-blocked print by Janet Erickson entitled "After Pollack." The fluid forms of a painting by Jackson Pollack are suggested in this contemporary design which leads the imagination freely through positive and negative blocks. Courtesy of the artist and of Watson-Guptill Publications, Inc.

lines of the varying shapes. Similar results can be created through the use of leaf forms or the shapes of birds or geometric figures. The choice of motif is important but not nearly so important as what the designer does with it, and one of the simple methods of creating a beautiful design is the tasteful arrangement of various sizes and shapes. This is the basic principle used in flower arrangements and in the combining of objects of art in beautifully appointed homes. The creative process is always a matter of taste. The artist who has developed his taste to a point of refinement will see immediately that one combination of shapes or sizes is more pleasing than another and his designs will profit accordingly.

Look closely at the plastic screen designed by Ted Hallman in Figure 4–8. Here the entire design is dependent upon variations in size, shape, and texture of a single basic shape. It is elongated in some places and almost geometrical in others yet the fundamental similarity is there. Notice how no two shapes or sizes are exactly alike, then glance back at Figure 2–12 and you will find that there is a marked similarity between the plastic screen and the tissues of the guinea pig. Here is a design based on

Figure 4–7. Two rhythms, one a staccato beat and the other rising and falling as a result of variation in size and shape.

nature, showing the same variety combined with unity.

The possibilities of color for achieving variety are almost limitless. With one paint manufacturer now advertising 1322 different colors of paint available for home decorating the problem becomes not so much one of finding the right color as of knowing it when one sees it. Paradoxically, the reaction of most customers to such infinite choice is one of confusion rather than delight. Knowing that you want a blue room instead of a rose one is comparatively simple but faced with page after page of variations of blue and blue-green and blue-violet, the responsibility for decision becomes overwhelming. Of course, the artist has always had all these colors to work with and possibly even more. They are his for the mixing and the endless subtleties and variations are at his fingertips so long as he has the knowledge to blend them. What he needs to decide first in any specific work is just what he wants to accomplish with color.

There are many adjectives used to describe color in painting. Sometimes works which have little else to recommend them are lauded for their "vibrant color." Other paintings are described as exceptional for their subtle colors. Textiles and ceramics are frequently done in "earth tones," meaning the browns, ochers and soft reds found in natural rocks and soil. These are particularly appropriate to arts in which affinity to the earth remains apparent, such as pottery made from natural clay and weaving done with earth-grown fibers. The rugs and blankets of the early Indians are examples of this sort of color. In this case no choice was made since there were no dyes to be had except those found in the earth. The same is true of the pottery made in early periods. Browns and reds on neutral grounds cannot help being appropriate since they are intrinsic qualities of the earth from which the bowls and jars are made. Stylized patterns representing symbols of Indian life are worked out using the simple rhythms of their dances enhanced with careful variations in tone expressing a quality of natural design. Later, in the zerapes of Mexico and the rugs from Chimayo in New Mexico man-made dyes were employed, making brilliant designs of the same basic symbols. These rugs have quite a different feeling, yet one that is still characteristic of the civilization that produced them. Instead of the simple attachment to the earth, we view another side of Indian life—the flair for elaborate ceremonials, vivid costumes, bright feathers, and sparkling beadwork (Figure 4–9). Here we find the most brilliant of blues and greens, purples, reds and yellows, in variations shading one into the other in such a way that there is no conflict but a blending of brilliance entirely characteristic of the ceremonial life of the people.

Appropriate uses for such variety in color are limited. In our own environment the trend swings from a fashion for bright color to the deliberate understatement achieved by decorating entire rooms in neutrals. At one point the most elegant interiors were the ones with beige walls and off-white carpets and natural raw-silk upholstery. This trend was followed

Figure 4–8. Acrylic plastic and synthetic fibers combine to create an organic design reminiscent of cell structure in nature. Screen designed and executed by Ted Hallman. Courtesy of the artist and of *Craft Horizons.*

Figure 4–9. The Aztecs of Mexico express centuries of symbolism and a native sense of design, not only in their age-old dances but in the elaborately beaded costumes in which they perform them. Photograph by Harold Finke.

by a taste for rich colors in which the glamor of exotic places was felt, as with Persian blues combined with deep greens.

Variety in color is not only interesting but important to human life. Nature varies the color range of our surroundings with change in seasons, and people who live in regions of constant temperature, however comfortable, frequently cite the lack of change as the principal drawback. In our man-made interiors we make use of our power to achieve change whenever we feel the need. This, of course, is a boon to industry. Every season has its new colors in clothes, home furnishings, and cars and the outdating of one for another is what keeps industry flourishing.

The role of the artist is to be so familiar with the possibilities of color that he can select exactly the right tone or variation to express his intentions in his creative work. He may be designing a car or a pot for violets; whatever his goal he must know what colors do to people and to each other. He should know from research what colors the public will accept in the new car models, and he must know what glaze will bring out the color of violets without overpowering them. The uses of color are as unlimited as man's activities and emotional needs, and the only way the artist can choose effectively is to have a thorough knowledge of color through study and experiment with it. The subject will be gone into more thoroughly in Chapter 5.

Nature uses variety in texture as one of her most effective means of expression, and here again the artist can learn a great deal. Before he begins his work he must decide whether he is going to use tactile or visual texture. If the texture is to be tactile, he will have to choose his materials with this in mind. In weaving he will select fibers that are nubby or rough and combine them in patterns that create a looped or bumpy effect. Many beautiful textiles have been created in a single color and a single weave, depending for their entire interest on variety of texture. Figure 4–10, on the other hand, shows a tapestry woven by Mildred Fischer in which the fibers are used for their textural quality and blended by imaginative weav-

Figure 4–10. "Panel," a tapestry by Mildred Fischer in tones of gray, white, yellow, and black. The yarns are used not only for their color but for their textural value. Photograph by Jack Foster. Courtesy of the artist.

ing into a textile of considerable charm. This is contrasted with the visual textures in Figure 4–11 in which Alexander Girard has created a fabric design through graphic means. The patterns of "April" are printed on fabric rather than being woven into it. The eye experiences a feeling of great variety but the fingers feel only the smoothness of the cloth just as in the case of stream-washed stones. As designs the fabrics are both effective; the type of texture is simply a matter of choice according to its use.

Textures are used similarly in pottery. A band of tactile texture will become the area of greater emphasis on a bowl that otherwise is smooth. Such textures may be created by skillful use of an instrument, by sand in the glaze, by salt glazes, by incising or by other means. The bottle by Richard M. Lincoln in Figure 4–12 shows use of two textured areas, one tactile and one visual. The white lines over the body of the piece actually can be felt, both visually and by the fingers. There is a smattering of visual texture to emphasize them and an even stronger visual texture in the dark bands forming vertical panels between. A subtle reflection of these bands carries up the neck, providing an attractive contrast to the rougher section below.

The artist need know no limits in creating texture. He can put stones or glass or sticks in concrete, he can weave pods and grasses into fabrics, he can carve holes in plaster and eat grooves in wood with acid. The opportunities for texture are as great as his imagination and his needs. Here, as in all other aspects of his art, he must never cease to experiment to find his most effective means of expression.

Figure 4–11. In "April" by Alexander H. Girard, texture is printed on the fabric rather than woven into it. Courtesy of Herman Miller Textiles.

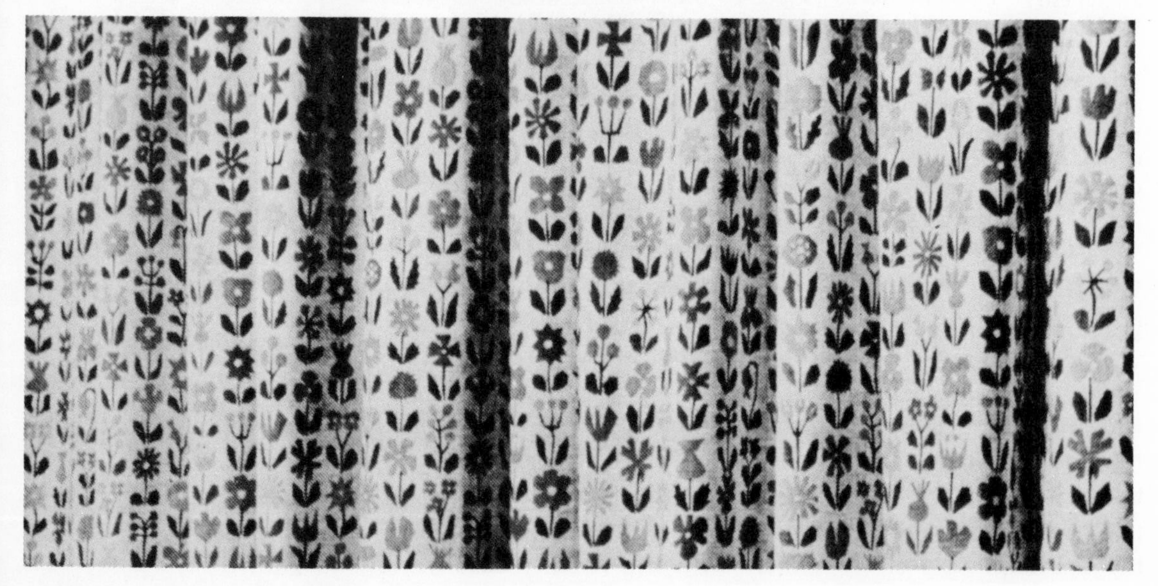

Figure 4–12. Visual and tactile textures combine to create a vibrant surface on a 20-inch pottery bottle. Designed and executed by Richard M. Lincoln. Photograph by Bob Abey. Courtesy of Carlin Galleries, Fort Worth, Texas.

Balance

There are many ways of accomplishing a state of *balance*. In chemistry we balance an equation so the same number of the same kind of atoms is on each side. In art we do not follow a formula and the balance is not always so obvious. We are familiar with the rigid symmetrical balance represented by the clock in the center of the mantelpiece with a candlestick on each side. This is balance by formula and a person who designs in this way can be certain that his compositions will be balanced. However, he may find that they are not particularly interesting. Moving the clock to one end of the mantelpiece with the two candlesticks together with a pot of ivy at the other end may make the effect less usual. It will also give the mantelpiece a closer affinity with the balance that we find in nature.

Figure 4–13. Balance of light and shadow, line and space give a striking texture to the exterior of the Ministry of Education and Health in Rio de Janeiro. Architects: Costa, Niemeyer, Reidy, Leão, Moreira and Vasconcelos. Photograph by G. E. Kidder Smith.

Seldom do we find perfect symmetry in our natural surroundings, either in an individual or in the arrangement of materials. We are aware that people are never the same on both sides of their faces or their bodies. Most people find their right foot larger than their left. We see evergreen trees that look perfectly symmetrical but closer inspection reveals that their branches do not grow out of the trunk symmetrically even though the over-all effect of the foliage gives this impression. Leaves, though regular in shape, are not symmetrical in their veining; stones, though perfectly round, will have differences in pattern on opposite sides. In photographs of landscapes we find a large tree in the foreground balanced by a body of water in the middle ground or a mountain at the back. This is not entirely the work of the photographer. Nature achieves balance in a flexible manner.

In working for balance in design, the artist should work for the fluid treatment found in rhythm, where principles are used as guides but not as formulae. He can follow nature in balancing a large area of dark or subtle color with a small spot of bright color or by balancing a heavy form with a smaller more interesting one. He should think of balance as a control over variety in which variety is kept from becoming too complicated by the simple measure of keeping the various colors, shapes, sizes, and textures in balance with each other.

The textile in Figure 4-6b shows balance of value in the alternating dark and light of background areas and the corresponding treatment of the figures on them. The over-all effect would not be nearly so interesting if the ground were not broken into areas of dark and light. Again, in the bottle in Figure 4–12 the balance of texture is effective. The larger rougher area is balanced by the fine visual texture near the neck. The shape of the neck area is more varied than the body of the piece, so the finer texture is placed there to balance the larger area of roughness. Moreover, the heavier texture gives a feeling of solidity by being located toward the base where we feel it is holding the bottle firmly on the table. This sort of balance not only gives us esthetic pleasure but makes us more comfortable from a mechanical point of view.

Figure 4–13 is an example of beauty in architecture achieved principally from balance. We see many skyscrapers with long lines of windows reaching upward, some of them esthetic in effect, some purely functional. The particular attractiveness of the Ministry of Education and Health lies in the balance of vertical line by horizontal louvers, making a striking pattern rather than a series of long lines. The fact that the louvers are designed in groups of four with alternate open spaces and are placed in recess giving shadow patterns, accounts for one of the most important features of the building, one that constitutes the essence of design.

Unity

Unity, the last principle that we found in nature, is the warp and woof that ties any design together as a whole. In a mosaic unity is achieved in one way by the grout that is used between the varicolored tesserae, weaving its way among all the various colors and shapes and tying them into a relationship with each other. Some contemporary painters leave patches of canvas without paint as a means of keeping the painting unified throughout. Unity can be created by using the same color or variations of it throughout a design, much as the musical composer uses variations of the same theme throughout a symphony. The novelist unifies his book by a basic premise that he develops through plot and characters, carrying it in and out so that it seems to disappear in places only to come forth more strongly later on.

The most important means of arriving at unity in any work is *to create with a definite objective in mind.* If the artist maintains a singleness of purpose throughout his work and attains a successful completion of that purpose, his work will have a basic unity. The painter who sets out to express an experience will find that he has to have unity before he can feel that he has succeeded. The writer who determines to put across a certain message and devotes an entire work to that end will have unity. The same is true of the sculptor or the musician or the choreographer. Devotion to his work as a means of accomplishing a certain objective will make the artist himself the strongest possible unifying influence.

Limiting what he uses in his work is another help in achieving unity. This applies to the actual materials as well as to the colors, textures, sizes, shapes, and lines. It is more effective to choose a few elements that will best express feeling and to use them over and over in different variations than to clutter the work with too much diversity. Some of the most striking compositions are monochromatic, that is, they use variations of one color only and bring out that color in all its ramifications. One or two colors threaded through a painting or design are more beautiful than a patchwork of many colors that fight for emphasis. The designer must learn to compose, by playing colors and forms, lines, sizes and shapes over and over again, varying them, emphasizing them, diminishing where necessary, choosing a motif and then bringing it out to its fullest, leaving other ideas for another design, just as the writer polishes his work, cutting words, phrases, and even sections to eliminate extraneous matter and keep to the basic unity of his writing.

It has been said that unity is the master design principle. This is true in the sense that any work, regardless of its other virtues, must have unity to be art. It is not a quality that can be imposed upon a work nor arrived at by a number of conscious steps. It is the intrinsic value of any creation, value that comes from rhythm flowing through it, variety lending interest, balance holding it in control, and above all the artist striving wholeheartedly to achieve the fulfillment of his own conception.

FOR FURTHER EXPLORATION

Elements of Design by Donald M. Anderson (New York: Holt, Rinehart and Winston, Inc., 1961). An excellent and extensive treatment of the elements of design as found in nature, in history, and in man's present-day creations.

The Visual Arts by Wallace S. Baldinger (New York: Holt, Rinehart and Winston, Inc., 1960). A thorough exploration into the major visual arts today with emphasis on artistic merit.

STUDIO PROJECTS

1. For a study in variety:
   a. On a sheet of paper 18 by 22 inches or larger, paint or block print an all-over design using a single shape repeated at intervals. Use only one color.
   b. Design a second sheet similar to the first but combine the original shape with a similar shape in either a larger or smaller size. Use only one color.
   c. Using the two sizes in (b) design a third sheet in two colors. Compare the three designs for variety and interest.

2. For a study in rhythm:
   a. On a large sheet of paper create an all-over design in which two elements are repeated at intervals as in the beat of music.
   b. On a similar sheet create an all-over design which shows emphasis as well as repetition by working up to a climax at specific intervals.

CHAPTER 5

The Glow of Color

COLOR IS THE MUSIC OF THE GRAPHIC ARTS. Great art can be created without color but its presence brings a mood and a depth of experience that cannot be achieved in any other way. Furthermore, it has as many variations as a symphony orchestra and as great an ability to manipulate our emotions. It, therefore, becomes one of the most powerful materials of the designer.

Color is both a science and an art, and the designer must have some knowledge of both approaches. The physicist can tell him much about the basic structure of color; the chemist formulates rules for mixing and using color; the psychologist can provide information about the reactions of human emotions to certain colors; but the artist must understand pigments and the effects of light, and he uses the chemist's information in mixing his paints or his dyes and glazes. From that point he goes further into the field than any of them, coordinating their information and developing his own variations in an effort to see the field as a whole in relation to his own work.

Color in Nature

In nature color is a matter of life and death. One of the treats of roaming through high wild country is to see a lichen-covered rock suddenly ruffle its feathers and move away, becoming a ptarmigan. This same bird turns white in winter along with the snowshoe rabbit and the ermine, thus making it possible to become a drift of snow if danger threatens. This is a characteristic found throughout the animal kingdom. In the White Sands of Alamogordo in New Mexico all of the common forms of insect

Figure 5–1. Protective coloring for lizards and other wild life in the White Sands of Alamogordo, New Mexico, consists of turning white. Photograph by J. F. Burshears.

and reptile life take on the whiteness of the sands (Figure 5–1). Not only the lizards but the grasshoppers and horned toads become albinos, protecting themselves from detection against the whiteness of their background.

With nature attaching so much importance to color it is logical to expect that it has an overwhelming influence on human environment. And none of the materials of the designer is more deserving of mastery.

The Essence of Color

The perception of color is a *neurophysiological process* not fully understood; however, we do know that color is actually light broken down into electromagnetic vibrations. The wavelengths of these vibrations vary, causing us to see different colors. The longest, which is 32 millionths of an inch in length, is seen as red, while the shortest wavelength of 16 millionths of an inch registers on our vision as violet.

The waves are seen by passing a beam of sunlight through a prism, breaking the light into hues corresponding to those seen in the rainbow and usually listed as violet, blue, indigo, green, yellow, orange, and red (Figure 5–2). Although the artist may think of his pigments as man-made materials, color itself cannot actually be manufactured. Instead, it is caused to occur by the manufacture of materials which absorb or reflect certain rays of light. When a substance is exposed to light, it will absorb all the rays but those creating a certain color, and the rays not absorbed will constitute the color that we attribute to the substance. When the manufacturer makes green paint he actually puts together the materials that will absorb rays of violet, blue, indigo, yellow, orange, and red. The green rays are not absorbed and we perceive them, saying the paint is green. Thus the process may seem to be in reverse, putting into the paint the rays of all the colors that will not show, with the one that is left out giving the paint its identity.

When all of the colors of the rainbow or prism are whirled together rapidly, as on a wheel, the effect is one of white light; therefore the sum of all colors is white. Similarly, when any color is put in a dark room the result is blackness. Since we know that the absence of light means absence of color we conclude that the absence of color is black. For this reason some experts believe that darkening colors with black paint, which actually is the absence of color, can deaden the original color, destroying its vitality. One of the most important things a designer needs to know about color is the process of mixing it to achieve the effects desired. To do this he must know some facts, terms, and at least a little theory.

We mentioned that vibrations with the longest wavelengths are seen as red while those with the shortest are seen as violet, putting these two colors at the opposite ends of the scale where wavelengths are concerned. Around 1666, Sir Isaac Newton in studying color realized that violet and red have a relationship, since together they form purple—a deeper variation of violet. Following this reasoning he made a circular chart in which he placed the seven colors of the rainbow side by side, bringing the violet at one end to a place beside the red at the other, thus unifying the scale into a continuous whole. This was the first color wheel. Other wheels have been worked out by color experts and the colors varied according to the theories of physics, human vision, or pigments; however, these do not actually represent a difference in theory. The physicist considers the basic colors to be red, green, and blue-violet because he is working with pure light, while the dyemaker and manufacturer of house paint thinks of them as magenta, yellow, and turquoise because these are the basic colors from which he mixes pigments. Because of the nature of the materials in which he works, the artist accepts *red, yellow, and blue* as the *primary* colors, since he finds that he cannot mix these colors from anything else but must have them as a starting point for all his painting. If his palette had to be limited to three tubes of paint, these three colors would give him the greatest possibilities for variety.

When he mixes these basic, or primary, colors together in approximately equal parts, the artist begins to create new colors. From yellow and blue he makes green, from blue and red he gets violet, and from red and yellow he creates orange. Thus he has three more colors, which we call *secondary* colors.

Going one step farther, he can mix combinations of the primary and secondary colors and create a third group whose origins are obvious: yellow-orange, orange-red, red-violet, blue-violet, blue-green, and yellow-green. When these three groups are placed in such an order that they seem to flow one from the other and the whole is bent into a wheel, we have the basic color wheel from which the artist can mix his color (Figure 5-3).

Figure 5–2. A ray of white light projected through a prism results in a rainbow of color.

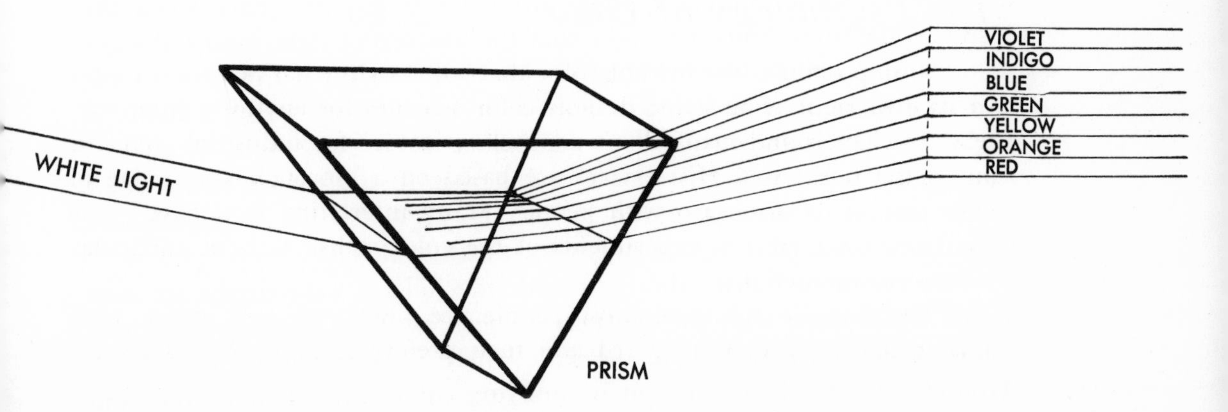

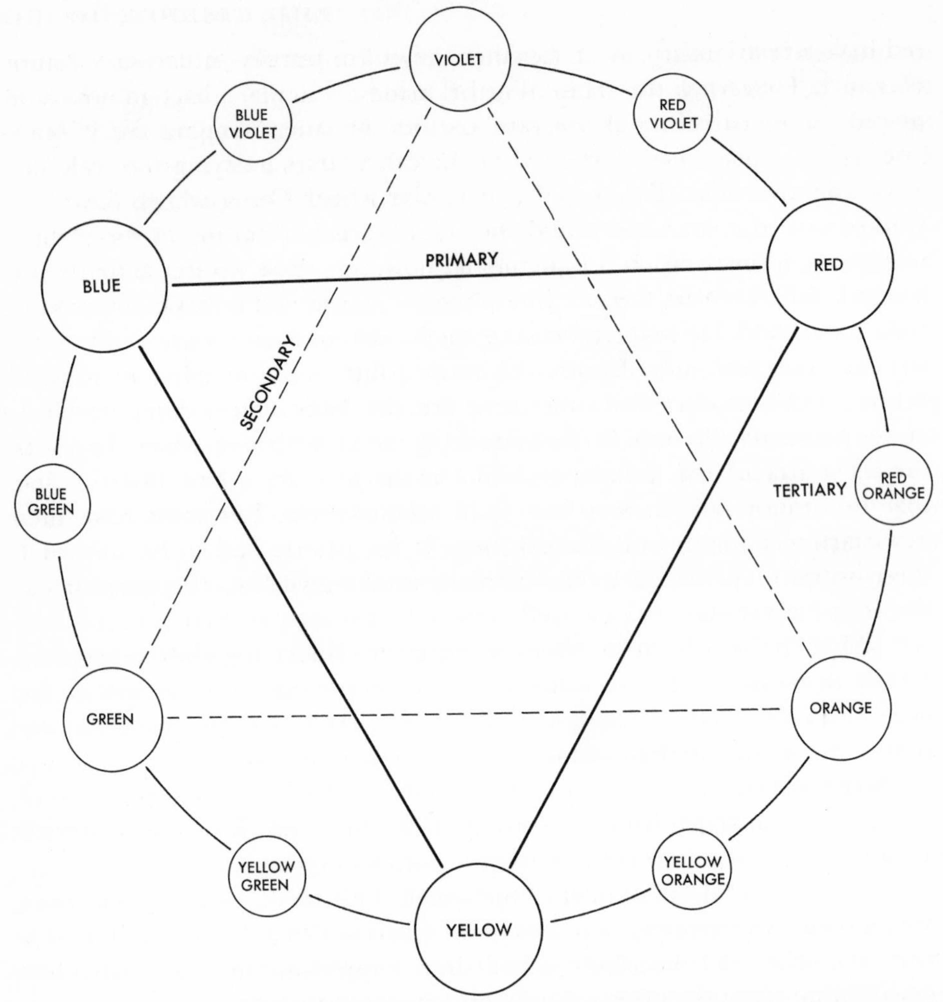

Figure 5–3. The color wheel generally used for pigments evolves in three steps. It starts with the primary colors which cannot be mixed, shown here connected by solid lines. From these are created the secondary colors, joined by broken lines. All other colors evolve from these six basic colors.

The Psychology of Color

So important is the field of color that color styling has become a career in its own right. The stylist designs color schemes for anything from subways to chapels and maintains a counseling service for industrial concerns and small businesses. His services are based on a thorough knowledge of color and its relationship with people. Many interesting facts have come into focus through the experiments of the color stylist, facts of particular interest to the designer.

The favorite colors of most people are blue, red, and green, with women generally preferring red and men preferring blue. Red is known to quicken the pulse, so it becomes useful in many situations. Knute Rockne, a former Notre Dame football coach, had the dressing rooms for his own team painted red and the visitors' dressing rooms painted blue, keeping the home team keyed up at half-time while the visitors relaxed. In Denver the stair area of the airport was painted tomato red to attract customers to the new observation deck. The move was so successful that business flourished on the deck but left the first floor coffee shop almost deserted. So acute was the situation that an expert was flown in to make a study and finally, at his suggestion, tomato red was put at the coffee shop entrance and highlighted with the proper lighting. Immediately interest picked up and the deck and coffee shop both maintained a thriving business. Of course, any color so effective has to be used with discretion. Walls of certain shades of red or orange will encourage a persistent thirst which might be propitious in a bar but could have adverse effects in a restaurant unless tempered with other colors.

Generally speaking, warm colors stimulate while cool colors relax. The terms *warm* and *cool* are well chosen. Green actually makes people feel cold and there have been instances of office workers having chills when they worked in rooms with blue walls. Although the temperature remained the same, the chills abated when the walls were repainted in yellow or the chairs were slipcovered in orange.

Some workers complained of the weight of dark-blue boxes they were lifting, even suffering from backstrain in a few cases. The simple device of painting the boxes yellow alleviated the complaints.

Yellow is a cheerful color, making people feel sociable and alert mentally and emotionally. In classrooms for retarded children, yellow is a good wall color. It is not recommended for a nursery, however, as it is not conducive to nap-taking.

Warm colors make objects look closer than cool colors do. A red chair seems closer than a blue chair placed at the same distance from the observer. We find in nature that as we look into the distance colors become grayed and cooler, even when they are actually bright and warm at close range. Knowing this, the designer will use bright warm colors to cut down the size of a room or to lower high ceilings and cool soft colors to make a small room look larger.

Color can be important even in traffic problems. Study has shown that most automobile drivers feel a greater urgency to pass a red, maroon, cream, or yellow car than a black, blue, or green one.

The effect of color on insects is another enlightening study. Although cats, dogs, and other mammals are color blind, mosquitoes react emphatically, avoiding orange but liking red, black, and blue. Beekeepers wear white to avoid being stung, finding that if they wear dark colors they are besieged. The knowledge that flies dislike blue has had great importance for the meat-packing industry, in which many plants now have blue windows.[1]

The Dimensions of Color

Color has been discussed in only one of its dimensions—*hue*. Hue is the name by which we distinguish one color from another. It is the basis for the other dimensions much as shape is the basis for form. Once we have established a color by hue, speaking of it as red or yellow or violet, we can go on to explore its other two dimensions.

Intensity is sometimes called saturation. Imagine that you are making a certain color of paint. You start with a binder, for oil paints, oil and a siccative to make the paint dry. Suppose you decide to make blue paint. You stir the pigment into the binder, using powdered cobalt or a manufactured chemical such as those used in ultramarine or cerulean blue. Gradually the color becomes more intense. If you want a soft color you will not add much pigment; however, you may decide to go on until the paint becomes almost dazzling. In either case, you are deciding upon the intensity of the color you want. Intensity is the degree to which the binder is saturated with the pigment. Transferred to paper or cloth or wax or any other substance, intensity becomes the degree of vividness in a color. Another term for it is *chroma*.

The third dimension of color is *value*. Value is the lightness or darkness of a color. Every hue has a gamut of values, from the middle value, which is equivalent to a medium gray, in both directions, through the tints, which are all the variations lighter than middle value, and down through the *shades*, which are darker than middle value. Technically, of course, it is incorrect to speak of a "shade of pink" since pink is really a light value of red and therefore is a tint.

The subject of value can best be understood through a study of the gray scale (Figure 5–4). Here the student can see all the gradations from white to black and will be able to relate them to gradations of a given hue. According to psychologists, the average person can distinguish nine steps from white to black with middle gray being the fifth value in the scale. Theoretically then, he should be able to differentiate the same number of values in any hue. A useful experiment for the student is the making of a value scale for each of several hues to determine how many gradations he can distinguish. He should then combine the variations in different ways to study their effects upon one another.

In addition to tints and shades, we have a third category of values—hues mixed with gray. These are soft and neutral and are known as *tones*. The tones are extremely useful in the blending of colors since tones

[1] Thomas J. Fleming, "Color Takes Courage," *The American Weekly* (January 24, 1960).

Figure 5–4. The gray scale showing variations in value from white to black.

frequently will go together where pure colors would not, (related as they are by the common addition of gray).

Color Schemes

A color "scheme" is a group of colors which are used together with pleasing results. There are many formulae for color schemes based on the color wheel, and people frequently derive a feeling of security from the knowledge that the living room is done in a complementary color scheme or the bedroom is analogous. These words should be in the designer's vocabulary but there are several reasons why he should not use them as rules for decorating. First, there actually are no hues which cannot be combined if the proper tints, tones, or values are used. Secondly, the fact that several colors appear at stated spots on the color wheel does not guarantee that they will combine better than other colors unless care is taken to select the most appropriate tints, tones, and values. Third, there is no reason why the designer should translate his taste into specific axioms. He is trained to a high degree of discernment and sensitivity. When he limits himself to formulae, his native talent and training are carrying him no further than the layman who has read a book on color.

In mixing colors, however, it is imperative that the artist be familiar with two basic terms. Any two colors directly across from each other on the color wheel are *complementary* (Figure 5–5). The important fact is that complementary colors, if mixed together in equal proportions, will make gray. This is a theoretical statement, of course. Some types of paint will tend more toward brown or black than gray, but the vital point for the artist is that any color may be grayed or softened by adding its complement. If you want to soften red, use a touch of green. If your orange is too bright, use a little blue. If you need gray, mix parts of violet and yellow or any other two complements until you get the kind of gray you need. It is quite possible to get an acceptable gray by mixing black and white but it will not have the life of the complementary grays.

Notice that in every set of complements there is a warm color and a cool color. The warm colors are the yellows, oranges, and reds which we associate with the sun and fire; the cool colors are the blues, greens, and violets of water and the deep woods. Your gray will be warm or cool depending upon whether you use more of the warm complement or the cool one. This knowledge expands the possibilities of gray alone from one rather dead tone to a whole family of vibrant grays. It can do the same thing for the hues on the wheel. A color made from a hue darkened with black loses the vitality of the original hue, and when several such colors are used throughout a painting the painting itself acquires a lifeless appearance. When complements are used to soften hues the lively quality of both the original hue and its complement are retained and the result is a subtle color, not a dull one.

The practice of simply adding white to get tints and black to get shades obviously detracts considerably from the effectiveness of color, since it dilutes the color more and more as it grows lighter or darker. The hue itself should always be retained to the greatest extent possible. An effective

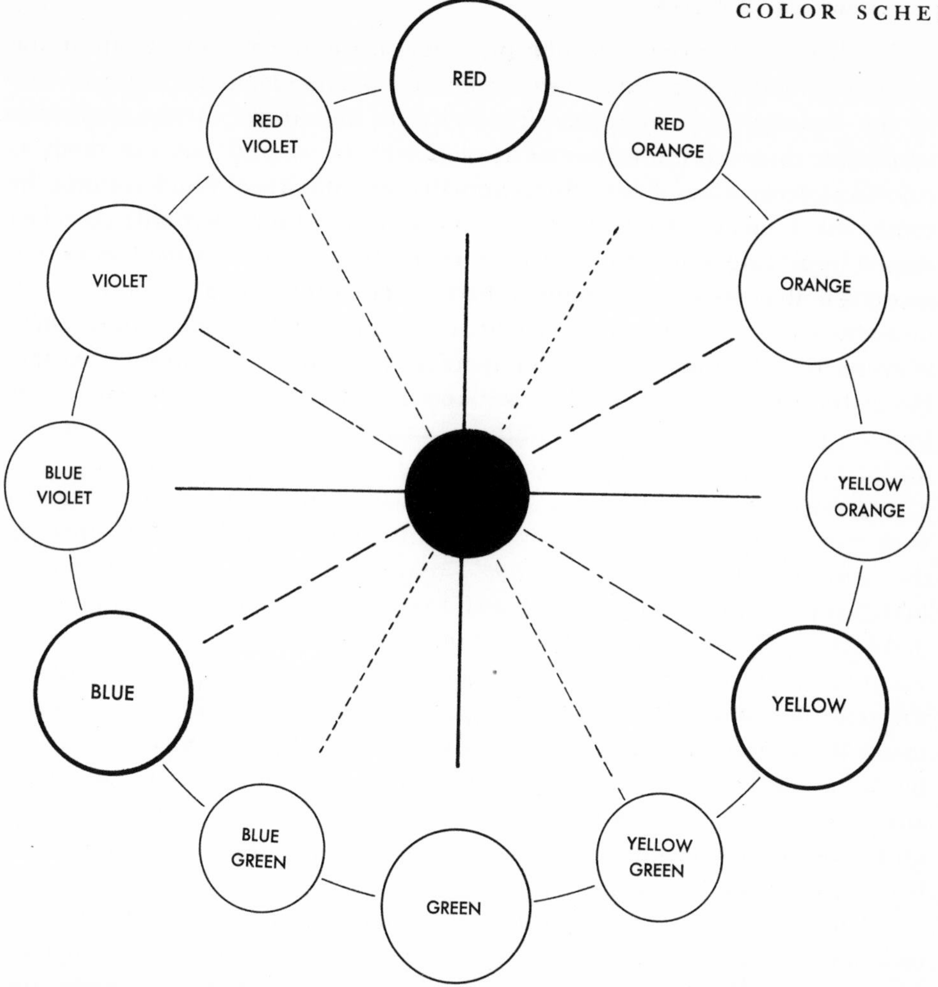

Figure 5–5. Complementary colors are those opposite one another on the color wheel. Here each pair of complements is shown connected by a different type of line. Red and green, for instance, are joined by a heavy solid line, yellow-orange and blue-violet connect with a medium solid line, and the other pairs have broken lines of various kinds.

way to insure this is to mix a tint, a tone, and a shade of the same hue and use these three as the bases for mixing variations. The tint may have a little white in it and the shade might have a touch of black and the tone will be achieved by use of the complement. Beyond this the changes will be made by intermixing the three, thus retaining as much of the quality of the color as possible. This method accounts for the luminosity of the work of the Old Masters, and the richness of the color that seems to increase with age.

Another interesting fact about complementary colors is that while mixed together they produce gray, placed side by side they tend to intensify each other. If your red is too bright mix a little green with it, but if you want it brighter place green beside it. This phenomenon is of great value to the designer since it makes it possible to accentuate anything that he may want to make the center of attraction.

In mixing colors it is well to know that equal parts of the three primary colors make brown. Here again the character of the brown will be determined by adding more of one of the colors. More red gives a reddish brown, more yellow a tan and more blue a darker chocolate brown.

Analogous colors are colors that are adjacent on the color wheel (Figure 5–6). It is important to be familiar with analogous colors since they have a relationship with each other and are always acceptable when used

Figure 5–6. Analogous colors are those adjoining one another on the color wheel. Various types of lines here show some of the analogous ranges possible.

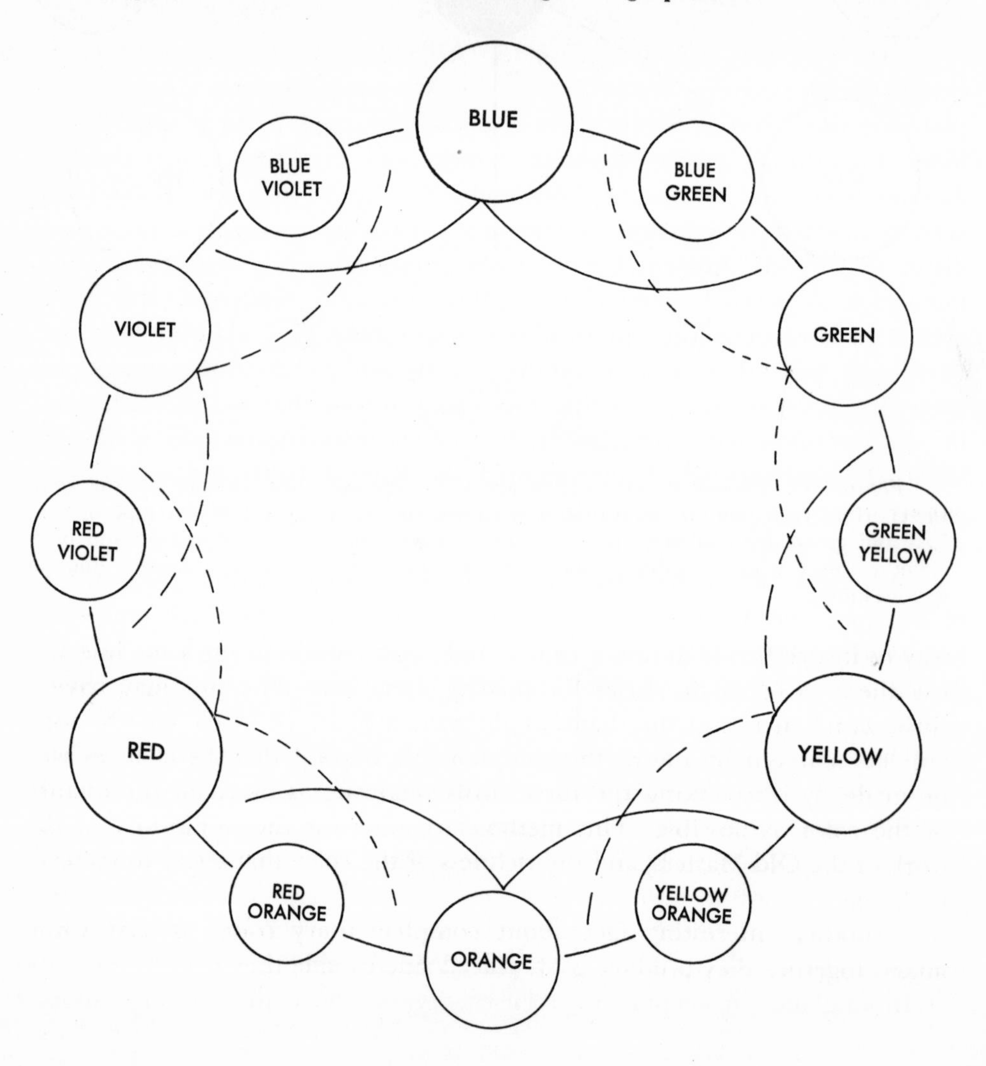

together in the right proportions. An analogous color scheme is one step more complicated than a *monochromatic* one, in which variations of one color are used. Nature uses analogous colors in the blending of flower petals, where a pink rose darkens to red-violet in the center, or a yellow tulip becomes yellow-orange inside. The blue of a lake turns blue-green at the edges and the green of the trees blends with the turquoise of the sky overhead. Analogous color schemes are pleasing because they have an inherent unity, being composed of colors that are basically related.

Still another way of relating colors is through *triads.* A triad is composed of any three colors equidistant on the color wheel (Figure 5–7). The primary colors form one triad; the secondary colors compose another.

Color and History

Each year the fashion stylists decree what colors will be featured in clothes for the coming season and the clothing manfacturers cooperate by planning their output within these bounds. The same trend is apparent in home furnishings, where upholstery colors and carpeting follow definite dictates from year to year. Although choice of color has not always been actively abetted by industry, we find that periods in history have their own distinctive trends. Ancient Egypt, Athens, and Rome all favored brilliant hues such as peacock blue, lemon yellow, carmine, tangerine, and vivid greens to ornament their homes and wardrobes. The sculpture on the Parthenon and other ancient buildings is known to have been painted in these bright colors and the white togas and chitons that we see on figures in our museums were actually of the richest hues trimmed in gold and silver. The mosaics which ornamented the Roman baths and villas were equally sparkling in color, lending a brilliance in keeping with the aspirations of the people of that era.

We think of the Renaissance as another colorful period, particularly in Florence and Venice where the arts reached one of the high points of history. Here the colors were richer and more subdued, such as bronze-greens, yellow-oranges, purple-blues and olive. Similar colors were used during the Baroque period which followed, until it reached France where it became the Rococo style of Versailles and Louis XVI. Here the emphasis was on the feminine and delicate, with life becoming a pageant of pastoral frivolity, powdered wigs, and elegant balls. Furniture was delicate with many soft curves, decorated with shell forms and garlands. Wood was painted in gold or white and pastels and the walls and upholstery echoed dainty colors. Soft blues, pinks, violets, and grays were the predominant background colors with much gold and white for accent.

In England, in keeping with the reserve of the British people, colors

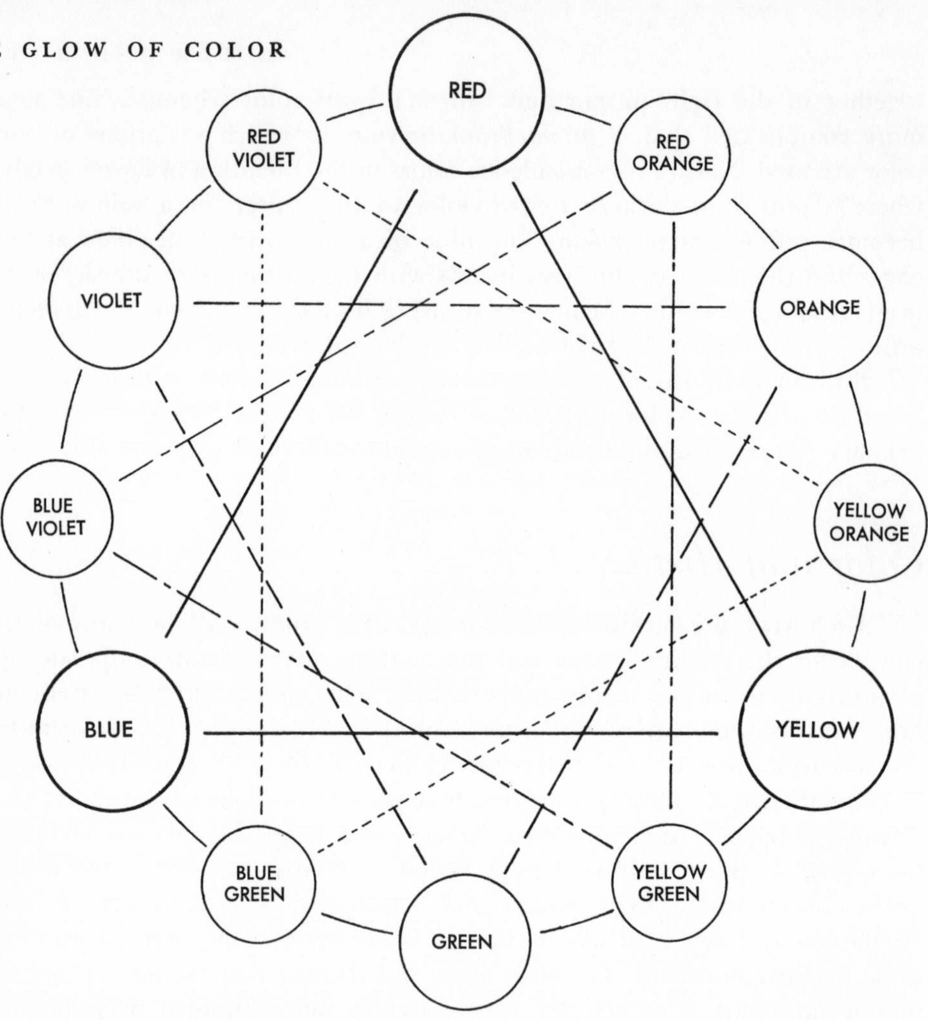

Figure 5–7. Triads consist of three colors equally distant on the color wheel. Various triads can be traced by following the different types of lines designating each. Red, blue, and yellow—the primary colors—form one triad connected by solid lines. Red-violet, blue-green, and yellow-orange, connected by dotted lines, form another triad.

have tended to be somewhat conservative. During the period of the great cabinetmakers—Adams, Chippendale, Hepplewhite and Sheraton—the individual pieces of furniture were greatly treasured. Inlay and carving were intricate and the grain and finish of the wood were of utmost importance. To keep from detracting from such masterpieces the colors of other furnishings were held to soft tones: misty greens, beige, dove gray, carnation pink, and hazy blue. The flagrant example of an exception to conservatism in British taste came during the Victorian era when interiors returned to the reds, greens, and purples of the periods of antiquity, culminating in a style, in both England and America, whose passing can scarcely be regretted.

In striving to recreate a specific period either in a stage set or in a period home, the designer can successfully set the mood in the beginning if he has a sound knowledge of historic use of color.

Even the names of colors have their history. While the connection may seem somewhat obscure, the term magenta for a form of red-purple derives from the battle of Magenta, Italy, in which the French and Sardinians were victorious over the Austrians at the time this particular dye was discovered. A soft reddish-gold color formerly known as Isabella obtained its name from the Queen of Spain. The story goes that during the siege of Granada she vowed not to change her linen until Spain had won. Assuming that the linen started out as white we can visualize the color somewhat from the fact that the siege lasted twelve months.[2] Prussian blue got its name from its discovery in 1704 by a Berlin colormaker named Diesbach, Berlin being one of the principal cities of Prussia at that time.

Color and the Designer

It is evident that color flows throughout the history of civilization in never-ending cycles. We have rising and falling fashions in literature, music, painting and philosophy, and we have color fashions in dress, in homes and in automobiles. Through the cycles the simple hues of blue, green, yellow, and red keep coming back like something basic to man's nature that cannot be destroyed. Recently children from forty-eight nations submitted over 4000 paintings in a competition for illustrations for a fairy-tale book. In the work submitted from all over the world these four colors over and over summed up the world as the children knew it.

Man uses color to clothe and interpret his greatest thoughts and moments, and the subsequent symbolism attributes to certain hues specific qualities that remain constant within a given civilization. In the Western world the Christian church has been a powerful influence in color symbolism. The use of color to depict the seasons of the church year has endowed individual colors with the attributes associated with those seasons. White is connected with purity because it is used for all the greater church festivals and especially for those pertaining to the Virgin Mary. Blue is the color attributed to her robe and it accordingly has a connotation of serenity, tranquility, and spirituality. Yellow has no specific symbolism in the church, perhaps for the reason that popular association attributes to it such traits as treachery and cowardice, as in calling a person "yellow." Wassily Kandinsky, the Expressionist painter, had a particular horror for yellow, calling it the color of madmen, yet we see it in much of the work of his contemporaries who find it suitable for expressing light, sunshine, and cheer.

2 Faber Birren, "Color Comes First," *House and Garden*, September 1957, p. 65.

Quite different associations have been carried into the field of sound by means of synesthesia, or color hearing. The proponents of this theory give each color a counterpart among musical instruments. The family of trumpets is red, the French horn is yellow, the flute sounds blue, and the oboe green. We have evidence that many well-known composers interpreted sound as color in their individual ways. Beethoven considered B minor a black key, Schubert described E minor as "a maiden robed in white with a rose-red bow on her heart" and C major as sunlight. Liszt is said to have used certain phrases in his conducting such as "That is too black," "More pink here, if you please," and "I want it all azure."[3]

All of these associations have more than passing interest for the designer. It is important for him to know how colors have affected people in the past although it is not necessary for him to be bound by traditional symbolism. The contemporary designer should use color as he uses all of the other elements of design, to express himself in his own way. Color is a personal thing, with widely varying meanings for different individuals. Blue, for instance, can mean coldness, aristocracy, purity, or a baby boy. Each period and each artist has the world of color at his command, to interpret in his own way and, if desirable, to establish an entirely new set of associations.

The designer is responsible for the fact that America now has more than ten million color telephones and takes for granted color in everything from paper towels to garbage cans. He is behind the emergence of colored houses along America's streets where formerly 65 percent of the houses were painted white with most of the other 35 percent subdued hues such as brown or gray. He has become an important force in American life through his realization that color is essentially tied up with nature and with living. Just as color does not exist without the ray of light, it does not have entity without the reactions and emotions of man. Color means nothing until it is seen and a reaction felt.

There are many excellent books on color which the aspiring designer would do well to study. Even more he should take every opportunity for his own explorations into the effects of light and of color upon color. A warm pink in one location becomes a vivid orange in another. This could be catastrophic to a working designer. He must be able to predict these changes by understanding the reasons for them.

We think in color, we respond to color, we are manipulated by color. It is the business of the designer to understand as much as possible about the entire exciting field, for through this knowledge color becomes a magic wand with which he can not only fill the needs of humanity but can become a veritable sorcerer molding people's reactions to their environment and in that way contributing to their mental, physical, and emotional well-being.

[3] *Ibid.* p. 178.

FOR FURTHER EXPLORATION

Creative Color by Faber Birren (New York: Reinhold Publishing Corp., 1961). A dynamic approach to the study of color by one of the foremost color experts of today.

The Art of Color by Johannes Itten (New York: Reinhold Publishing Corp., 1961). A comprehensive and up-to-date study of the principles of color theory as set forth by the famed Bauhaus teacher and painter.

Color, Form and Space by Faber Birren (New York: Reinhold Publishing Corp., 1961). A book devoted entirely to the use of color in three-dimensional forms. Well re-enforced with illustrations and suggested experiments.

STUDIO PROJECTS

1. Using black and white tempera, make a value scale of nine steps grading from white to black.
2. Make similar scales using the primary and secondary colors arranged in the same gradation from light to dark.
3. Make a collage of colored paper in various tints. Make a similar design in dark values. Make a third in bright tones. Compare the three.
4. Select a tone, such as gray-violet, and mix it in as many different ways as possible, using various complements, trying to get all of the results as nearly alike as possible. Mount chips of each and label as to procedure for mixing.
5. Using tempera colors or cut paper, make a simple design on white paper or Bristol board, then make the same design on black paper or cardboard. Compare the effects for brilliance and luminosity.

CHAPTER 6

Evolution of a Design

ALTHOUGH PRACTICALLY EVERYTHING surrounding us is designed in one way or another, to most people the word *design* means a *graphic* design, a design created by lines and strokes to express a certain feeling. The uses for graphic designs are many: we find them on book jackets and billboards, on plates and silverware, on fabrics, and enhancing architecture in carved panels or mosaic walls. In short, graphic design is the basis for all the facets of creative work and it would be well to understand its creation before delving into other aspects.

There are three ways of approaching the creation of a design. We may base our work on *natural forms,* depicting them much as we see them in nature. We may use *geometric forms.* Or we may create a *non-objective design.*

Natural Forms

We see an example of a design based on natural forms in Figure 6–1. It is entitled "Mexico." The calla lilies and butterflies, the clouds and mountains are all readily recognizable, yet they are not lifted from nature as they would be if they were illustrating a book on either botany or butterflies. Instead they have passed through the creative mind of the designer, and what he presents to us is his own interpretation of the feeling of Mexico, the features that impressed him that he wants to express. He has handled them in a flowing rhythmic way that is subtle and beautiful and that depicts his own special feeling about the subject. This is the talent of the designer, the faculty that raises him above his surroundings

Figure 6–1. The essence of a country is captured in this enamel-on-steel plaque in which many diverse elements are composed into a unified and immensely decorative design. "Mexico" by Edward Winter. Courtesy of The Cleveland Museum of Art. Gift of the Cleveland Art Association.

and gives him a touch of immortality. He takes pleasing objects and im parts to them a new kind of beauty because of his own sensitivity to them. His magic touch transforms them from the work of nature into a work of art.

A more whimsical treatment of a natural form is shown in Figure 6–2. Here the flounder is used as the basis for a cloisonné enamel pendant. In cloisonné the enamelled pieces are inset like mosaic, often with partitions of wire outlining them. The idea of wearing a fish around one's neck becomes surprisingly attractive when so original and decorative as this. Notice the way the designer has combined bands of color with circles and half circles to give texture and variety of shape.

Geometric Forms

The use of geometric forms can be seen in the stained-glass design in Figure 6–3 and the decorative paper in Figure 6–4. The interplay of textures among the varied rectangles and triangles makes the glass panel fascinating. The smaller forms of the texture are echoed in the larger areas and the heavy outlines of the leading contribute to a strong sense of unity. The paper design, on the other hand, is composed entirely of circles. The interest here comes from the blending of vivid colors and the

Figure 6–2. The imaginative approach to design is obvious in this cloisonné pendant by John Paul Miller entitled "Flounder and Fossil." From the Files of the American Craftsmen's Council Research Service.

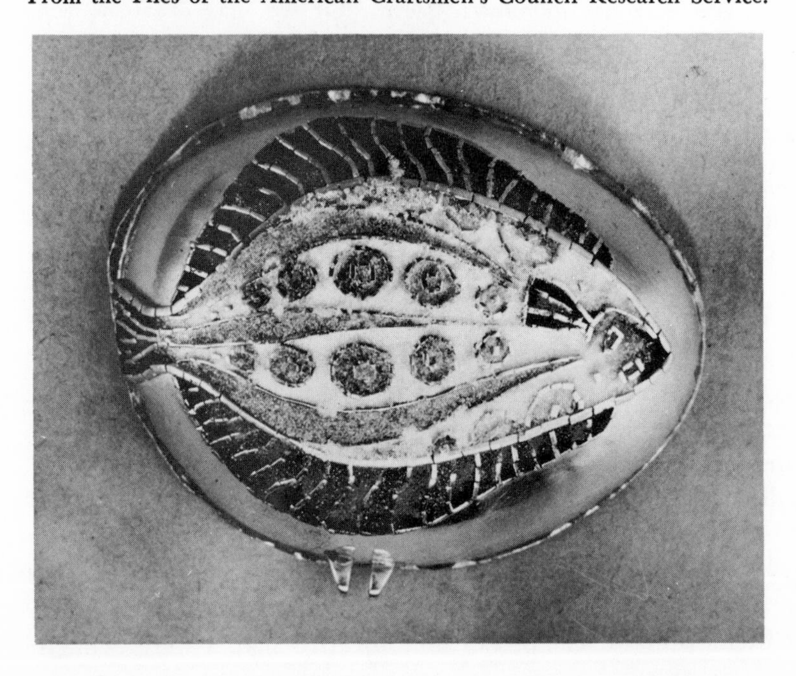

Figure 6–3. Geometric forms are the basis for this panel of fused and painted glass designed and executed by Joseph Meert. Courtesy of the artist and *Craft Horizons*.

subtle irregularity of the forms. The placing of circles within circles makes for depth and unity. In each of these designs the motif is simple. The designer has used it to an end that is creative and esthetically pleasing.

Nonobjective Designs

The ability to create a nonobjective design is one of the surest indications of creative ability, yet it is frequently one of the most difficult faculties to set in motion. In Chapter 3 nonobjective shapes were defined

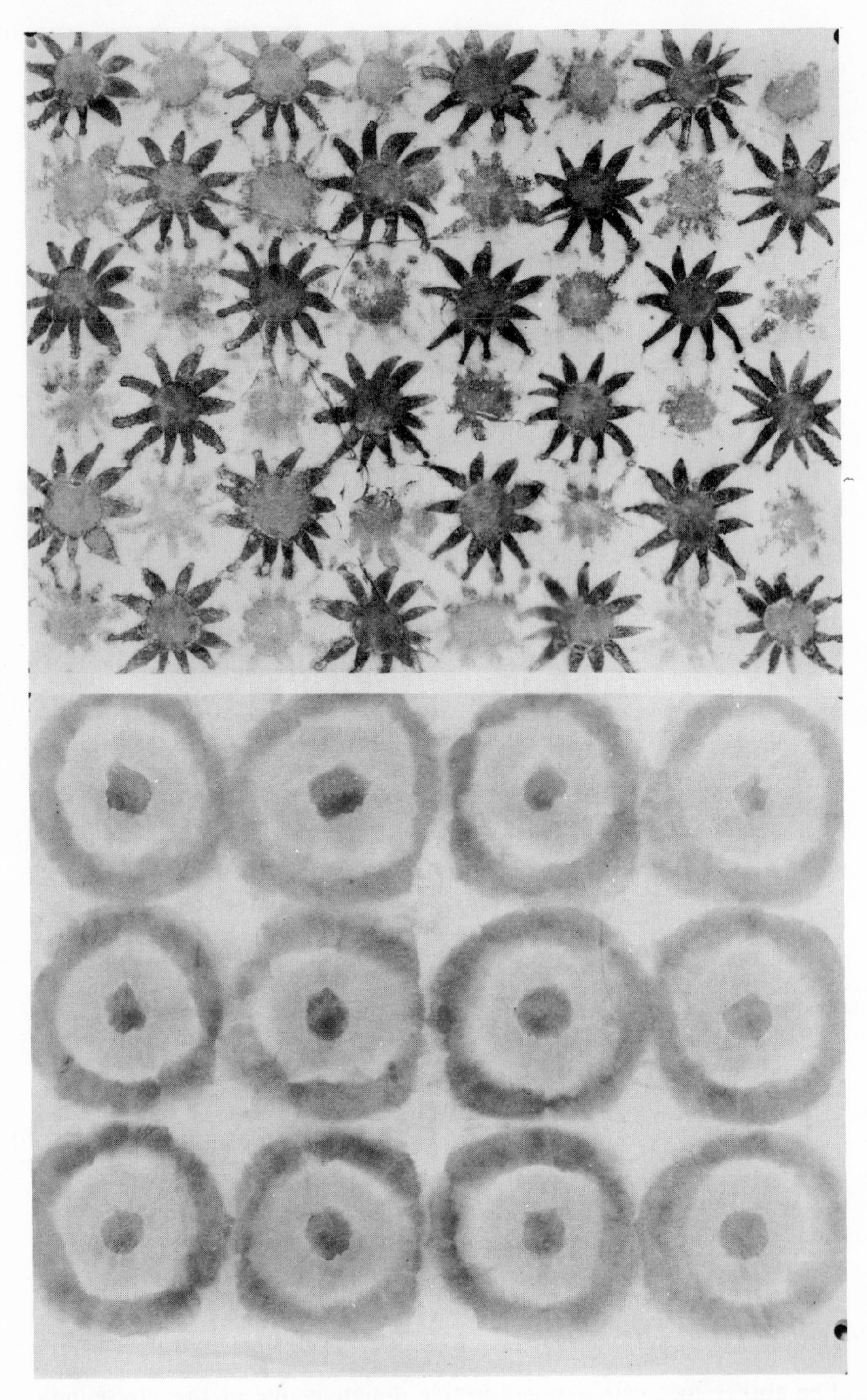

Figure 6–4. The simple circle is the foundation of these over-all designs. "Tie Die," papers by Barbara White. In a variety of colors. Courtesy of Karl Mann Associates and *Craft Horizons*.

as shapes which do not resemble anything recognizable, or abstractions. This is the mathematical use of the term *abstract* for in mathematics an abstract number is one without reference to a thing or things. In this connotation designs can be made in several ways. We can take a piece of string and drop it on a piece of paper and get an abstract design. We can cut paper into shapes that do not resemble objects and move them around until we arrive at an interesting combination of forms. We can crush fabric or paper and let it fall of its own accord and create a design from the forms that result (Figure 6–5). In each case the forms and shapes will be only the starting point. Possibly they will present their own rhythms, but we will have to build a design with balance and unity by combining these rhythms with texture and value and variety until we have an effective design.

Figure 6–5. The folds of satin fall in abstract forms. Although geometric shapes are suggested, the softness of the material carries them further into true abstraction. Photograph by Herbert Matter.

Abstractions

There is another use of *abstract* which has importance for the designer. As a noun, the word means something that concentrates the essential qualities of a larger thing; for instance, in literature an abstract is a summary or short form giving the essential structure of a book. This is what we attempt to do when we "abstract" an object to make a design. We try to pinpoint its essential feeling or flavor and translate it into simple forms which may or may not resemble the original object. The term *stylization* is often used when the object is identifiable but has been simplified to give it a design quality.

Now let us suppose that you are going to abstract an object to make a design. The most difficult step in any design is finding a point of departure. It should be emphasized that anything can be used as material. It is not the object but what the designer does with it that determines its esthetic success. Any of nature's infinite sources will serve: leaves, shells, vegetables, trees, birds, fish. Man-made objects can be handled just as effectively, objects such as keys, lamp-posts, kitchen utensils, or buildings. The designer should, however, choose something that holds a personal interest, an object that has meaning for him. It is only through feeling excitement about his work that the artist gains inspiration and is able to create something with meaning.

Once the subject has been chosen, the next step is to look at it in an entirely new way. You are going to catch the essence of this object, to express things about it that heretofore you have not suspected. To do this you will submit it to a scrutinizing anaylsis in which you take it apart and explore all its possibilities and those of its components.

Suppose you decide to make a design from a wire coat hanger. There are two basic forms here, the triangle of the base and the curved shape formed by the hook. However, closer inspection will reveal an interesting spiral where the two ends of the wire are twisted together. Furthermore there is the cross-section of the wire itself which gives you a circular shape with which to work. Here you have four basic units which can be amplified into larger forms, diminished into smaller ones, superimposed and interpenetrated. This is ample material for an interesting design, but if the coat hanger is hanging against a wall or an easel, you may want to make use of the background to lend texture. Figure 6–6 is a design developed from such a beginning.

When you have decided in a general way what you want to include in your design, a good way to start is to make a drawing of the object as it actually is, just to get the form on paper so you can analyze it more effec-

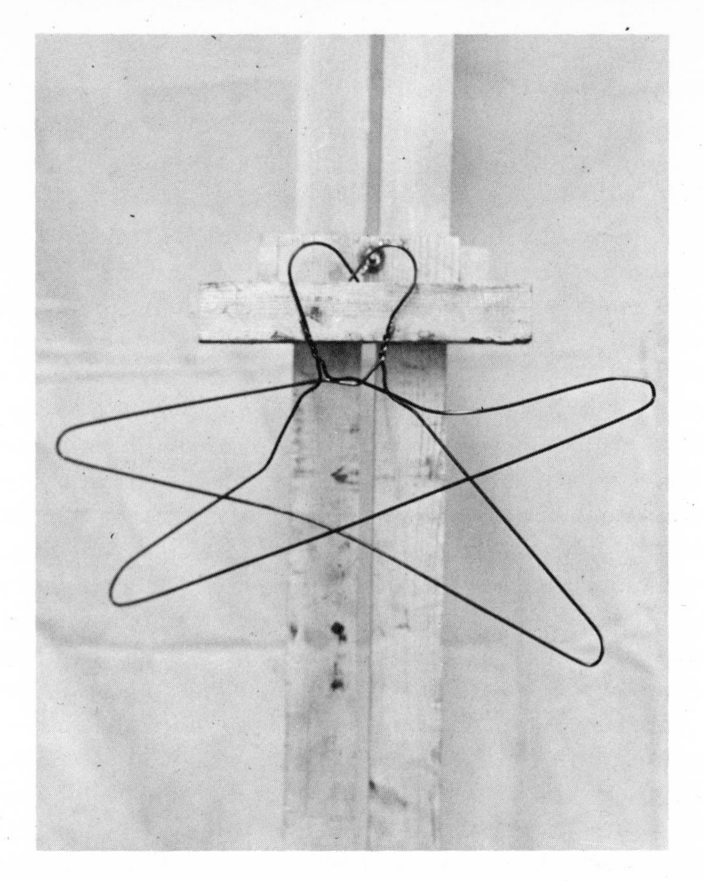

Figure 6–6. Student design evolved from two coat hangers suspended from an easel. Above, photograph of the original subject; below, development of the design, first in values of gray, black, and white; then, in the larger area, in three colors.

tively. When you have done this, make sketches of all the different shapes and forms into which you can break the object. What you actually are doing is tossing all of these units into the crucible of your own creative force and letting them evolve into a new and original entity. No one else will produce exactly the same result.

The next step is to start composing. This is the time to remember the facts learned from nature. First, decide what kind of basic rhythm your design will have. Will it have a flowing rhythm like a river or a rhythm like a heartbeat? The first lines should make this decision clear. Your lines thus become not only the edges of shapes and forms but the handwriting expressing the character of the design and its intrinsic nature.

In establishing the rhythm you will find that your shapes and forms emerge rapidly. There will be shapes drawn by lines and shapes formed by the space outside the lines. These should be made as interesting as possible. If you have two shapes of the same size, the design will be improved if you change one of them. In general, like shapes should be of different sizes and similar sizes should be in various shapes. This will probably be the most important step in making the design since the shapes form the framework for all the other elements.

As you think about variety of shape, you should think as well about variety of texture. In a graphic design the texture will usually be visual and must be supplied by a cross-hatching of lines or a stippling with dots or other such means. You will probably want the same or similar texture repeated in more than one area as a means of balance. Do not make two similar areas textured in the same way. If you apply cross-hatching to a large area, echo it in a smaller section of interesting shape in a different part of the composition. You may find that instead of balancing similar textures against one another you prefer to complement the interesting texture with an area of bright or unusual color. It is more creative to work for *balance of interest* than to adhere to a formula of texture for texture and shape for shape. Any of the elements of design can be balanced by any of the others, provided the elements used are of similar interest.

As you solve the problem of texture you will want to bring color into the composition. Sometimes we conceive an idea in color from the first; in that case the principal problem becomes one of distributing the colors for the subdominant or less emphatic shapes and making all of the areas blend in support of the center of interest. When color is dominant it will enter the design before texture and the texture will lend it interest.

If you have not decided in advance on the colors you will use, review your basic design idea before you make the decision. If you want a feeling of gaiety, as in a travel poster for Spain, you will use warm colors in their various dimensions. If you are designing a jacket for a book about the English countryside, you will use subdued colors with an effort to retain

Figure 6–7. The syrup bottle was the inspiration for the all-over fabric or paper design.

a feeling of freshness. Posters advertising cosmetics will be more subtle in color than billboards proclaiming the merits of a gasoline, with its implications of speed and energy. If you are designing for the printing of fabrics and wallpapers, of course, you have an advantage because your design will probably be printed in several sets of colors. Try it in variations with the idea of selling them to the manufacturer.

Now you have considered shape and size, texture and color, rhythm, balance, and variety. There remains the question of unity. If you had a clear feeling about your design in the beginning and were conscientious in solving the problems involved in the other principles of design, there is a good chance that your finished design will have unity. In Figure 6–7 we can detect the development of a design from a syrup bottle. In this case the basic shape of the bottle is retained and developed into an all-over design. A variety of values is employed, and varied shapes are abstracted from the design on the bottle to add interest. The larger circle has been echoed by several smaller ones to provide a balance which is carried through the distribution of dark areas. Finally, we feel a sense of unity through the rhythms of curved lines, through the repetition of values, and through the several manifestations of balance.

Although unity is a basic quality flowing through the design as it evolves, we sometimes have the feeling that an otherwise finished design just does not "hang together." When this happens, a careful analysis will reveal the reason and can teach the student more than a chance success he does not fully understand. First, analyze for balance. Is each area of special interest balanced by interest somewhere else? Are the sizes in scale; that is, are they related rather than miscellaneous? Are the shapes similar enough to look as though they belong together? Sometimes we have more success in composing entirely of angular forms, or entirely of round or curved shapes. If we combine the two, we will want *transition* by gently guiding the eye from one to the other through the variations on the original shapes. This is true of color as well. Transition from a warm color to a cool one can be accomplished by gradual change if the contrast seems too abrupt. On the other hand, you may want sudden changes to lend vitality and an element of surprise. Are you using too many colors? Are your hues too much like their primary state? Variations of a few colors will give greater unity than a gay mixture of all your favorites. Such an analysis will do much for your present design but even more for those that you will make in the future.

Creating designs in this fashion can give the student the firm foundation he needs for any type of design he wishes to pursue. Commercial design, in both advertising and packaging, is based on abstractions in varying degrees. Architectural designs such as murals, mosaics, wall panels, and decorative windows are all based on this same procedure. Fabrics and wall-

Figure 6–8. The design qualities here suggest a modern painting or the forms of plants. Photograph of the broken windshield of a wrecked and burned automobile.

Figure 6–9. Ordinary grasses form interesting abstract patterns when seen through an artist's eye. Photograph by Bruce Roberts.

paper, dress materials and rugs, metal sculpture and paintings can all be designed in much the way the simple abstract graphic design is created.

Designing in abstraction can do a great deal to open the eyes of the student to forms and shapes, colors and textures in the world around him. He will become acquainted with a whole new field of inspiration, that of the natural abstraction. This does not mean abstractions in nature alone, but abstractions that occur in all kinds of materials and situations where no thought of design was considered. Study the design qualities of the broken window in Figure 6–8. Here are balance and unity as well as variety in size, shape, texture, and value.

A concrete sidewalk cracks and makes a design. Paint peels off a wall, a mud puddle dries up, a rope falls to the grass: all form their own designs. Next time you walk by a building with glass bricks look at the design made by the opaqueness of the glass. Look for patterns on old walls where the bricks are broken or the plaster is cracking. Notice the color and interesting shapes of oil floating on puddles and the patterns formed in flagstones by mineral deposits and by wear. Notice the way a clump of grass divides space into shapes (Figures 6–9). Even the worn wooden steps of old buildings have design possibilities. The importance lies not so much in using *things* for inspiration as in learning to see the patterns and designs in your surroundings. When you have opened your eyes and your mind to the fascination of the world around you, there will never be any problem in finding inspiration for your work.

FOR FURTHER EXPLORATION

Forms and Patterns in Nature by Wolf Strache (New York: Pantheon Books, Inc., 1956). A book of beautiful photographs, many taken through a microscope, showing the fascinating forms and rhythms to be found in natural materials.

Teaching Portfolio Number Two—Pattern and Texture (New York: Museum of Modern Art, n.d.). A series of excellent photographs showing the possibilities of design in all kinds of natural surroundings.

STUDIO PROJECTS

1. Use the simplest or most prosaic object you can think of as a basis for an abstract design. Abstract the object in neutrals first (gray, black, and white), then translate the design into colors of corresponding values.
2. Find a design in nature which you can use as the basis for an interesting abstraction. Work out your interpretation in tempera.
3. To translate sounds into visual forms and colors, design to music, painting in tempera while you listen to a record. Compose the results into a well-integrated design.

CHAPTER 7

Structural Design

As knowledge of design is applied to specific projects, we find that the work falls into one of two categories. If designing *an object,* we are concerned with both categories since they are inseparable except from the standpoint of technique. First, we must be involved in *structural design* then with the development of surface, which can be termed *decorative design.* The interrelationship of the two is basic. While decorative design is sometimes used like counterpoint in music, structural design usually determines the decorative design in all its aspects: the shape and size, the techniques used, and the nature of the design applied, which must be related intrinsically to the materials and the structure of the object.

Meaning of Structural Design

Paul Weiss, head of the laboratory for developmental biology of the Rockefeller Institute for Medical Research, states that if there is one lesson to be learned from the study of organic nature it that there is order in the gross, or large forms, with freedom and diversity in the small.[1] The tree has an orderly growth and definite form but its bark is varied and its leaves show great diversity, especially under a microscope. The mountain builds through the centuries layer upon layer of glacial deposits, fossilized vegetation, and alluvium, growing with the rhythms of fire and ice into an

[1] Paul Weiss, "Organic Form: Scientific and Aesthetic Aspects," *The Visual Arts Today* (Middletown, Conn.: Wesleyan University Press, 1960), p. 184.

Figure 7–1. Enamel-on-steel panel, "Christ and the Apostles," designed by Thelma Frazier Winter and executed by Thelma and Edward Winter for Bethany Evangelical Lutheran Church in Ashtabula, Ohio. The structural design is emphasized by clearly discernible horizontals, verticals, and diagonals. Notice the pattern of light and dark areas. Colors are deep red, black, purple, deep yellow, blue green, gray, and 22- carat gold.

orderly structure. Yet on closer inspection its surface is a treasure house of variety, in textures of stone, alpine vegetation, and tundra.

In the same way man should build his edifices from the inside out, designing first for the function and letting the structure itself dictate what form the surface detail shall take. The activity within should determine the outer expression just as the configuration of the mountain shapes the glaciers and snowbanks. The architect should not design a building and then call in the muralist or mosaicist or sculptor to decorate it. The architect and the artist should work together from the inception of the design, in mutual respect, sharing the original vision and combining their talents for the creation of a beautiful building. This is the sort of relationship that can result in the highest form of art.

Structural design embodies the most fundamental aspects of any object: its purpose, its function, its very being. If the structural design is not successful, no beauty of decorative design will save it any more than a novel without structure can be rescued by brilliant characterization, or a symphony given form by harmony alone. Frank Lloyd Wright commented that the doctor can bury his mistakes, but the architect can only plant vines over his. Obviously, the most beautiful vines cannot hide from the occupants the fact that a building does not fulfill its function.

We speak of nature's amazing structural designs, particularly in the animal world. The mountain goat has sharp ridges around his soft foot pads enabling him to climb rapidly on ice, snow, and bare rock. The penguin, living on barren arctic wastelands carries her eggs with her in a special pouch until they have hatched and the young are old enough to face the outside world. The bat, seeking its food at night, has been found to guide itself with a special sonor system, uttering ultrasonic cries and then following the echoes to avoid running into other objects. The shells of snails have fascinated biologists and mathematicians alike for over 250 years because of the orderly growth pattern which follows the logarithmic spiral and can be reduced to the same mathematical formula as the golden mean of the Greeks. Even the most learned doctors profess to comprehend little of the miracle of machinery comprising the human body. In spite of its myriad susceptabilities, it appears to be a marvel of adaptability and recovery potential. We know that these structural wonders are the result of over a million years of adaptation, in which organisms gradually changed to meet the demands of their environment. Unfortunately, the designer can neither wait for evolution nor usually for knowledge based on trial of his designs. A designed object must be right from the time it is put to use, whether it is a building or a piece of power machinery or an iron. In machinery and appliances, of course, later models profit by the errors of the previous ones, but each successive model must be right for its own time or the manufacturer will be flooded with complaints and the designer will have failed. It is imperative that the professional designer know his field before he begins. His only protection against error is knowledge of what is needed, what the object is expected to do, what has already been done in the field, and how he can improve upon previous models. Beyond this, he must know the structural limitations of the sort of thing he intends to design.

In painting and two-dimensional design, structural design is frequently referred to as *composition*. Although they are actually decorative designs in one sense, such works to be successful must have a structural basis which is carefully planned and coordinated. One effective method of working out such construction is known as *dynamic symmetry*. In this use, symmetry is a two-dimensional composition in which the various lines, angles, and curves compose sections of a maplike arrangement which determines and defines the character of the design or picture. Frequently the design is based on related rectangles and triangles which have a mathematical alliance with the composition as a whole. Developed from this basis, the resulting work

Figure 7–2. Mrs. Winter's use of dynamic symmetry is obvious in this diagram showing the geometric forms which are the basis for the design. Related rectangles and triangles supply unity. The composition is further strengthened by the use of diagonals relating the three separate sections of the panel.

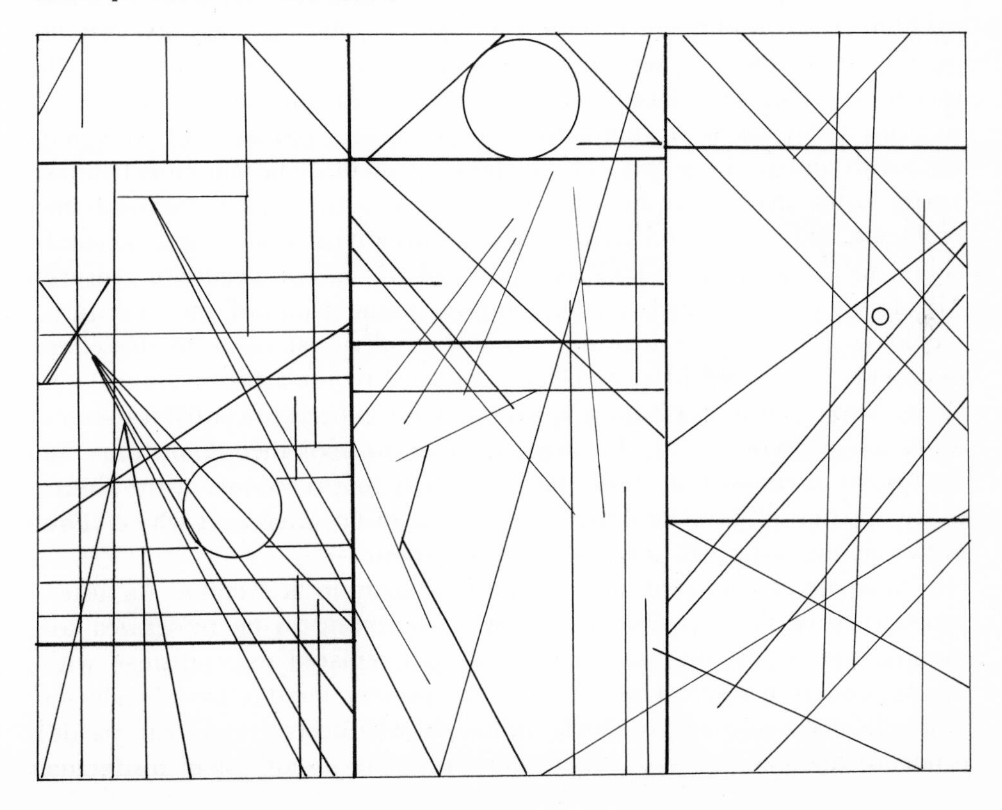

is comparable to an organism in its unity, for each part is related to every other part and all parts are elements in the total entity. Thelma Winter's enamel panel in Figure 7–1 shows clearly the workings of dynamic symmetry. The four figures accentuate the vertical lines but are delineated in part by the horizontals and diagonals which build the composition. Intersections of basic lines strengthen the unity and give a feeling of interrelationship of the various masses of light and dark (Figure 7–2). Exhaustive studies have shown dynamic symmetry to be the basis of much three-dimensional design as well, notably in Greek temples and Greek vases where extreme and mean ratio rectangles are found repeatedly, indicating that much successful design actually has a firm basis in mathematics.

Art and Science

We recognize differences between art and science, and they are many; but, as technology becomes more dominant in human life, it becomes increasingly clear that both art and science must play major roles in the design of environment. The artist must acquaint himself with the workings and developments of science. Both the artist and scientist must grasp the wholeness of existence instead of succumbing to the traditional pigeonholing of one field in opposition to the other. Since the Industrial Revolution human environment has burgeoned with developments in such rapidity that no one has been able to keep any kind of control, with the result that the present-day designer is faced by a vast ugliness and confusion. A trip across America today often is dominated not by scenic wonders but by gaudy billboards and junk-car lots. The increase in mental and emotional illness attests to the inadequate housing, the noise, the dirt, the shattering traffic problems, and a thousand irritations and annoyances that plague the individual in his struggle to lead some kind of life in the twentieth century. All of this can be overcome, but only by sound study of the biological, physiological, and psychological needs of the individual and a massive effort to provide for them. Little can be accomplished by the artist or the scientist alone. Never before has it been so necessary for experts to contribute to the wholeness of existence and to work together to pool their knowledge for the benefit of civilization. It has been said that genius consists of the ability to see apparently unrelated elements as parts of an integrated whole. This sort of genius is the great need of our generation.

Nowhere is the need more important than in the crafts. An interdependence of the machine and artist is beginning to be recognized for the first time since the Industrial Revolution replaced the craftsman with the power-driven loom, glass blower, and pottery mold. After decades of mediocre machine-made products, industrial engineers are realizing a dependence upon the artist-designer who can create prototypes of distinctive pottery, glassware, and fabrics which can be reproduced in quantity by the machine. The artist who understands the engineering of a glass factory or textile mill can be one of the outstanding influences in raising the taste of his generation.

Integrity of Materials

Integrity of materials is the first requisite of structural design. Not only must the designer know what materials are available, he must be aware of their limitations. If he is designing buildings he must know which materials are strong in *compression,* when pressed under weight, and which have more strength in *tension,* when stretched. If he is working with clay, he must know which clays are more plastic and how much weight they will support before he can design a specific shape or form. If he is creating textiles, he must understand fibers. A warp that will respond favorably to water combined with a weft that will mat or shrink can mean an unsatisfactory textile from the standpoint of daily use.

Generally speaking, materials fall into one of seven categories: wood, metal, ceramics, glass, stone, fibers, and plastics. Each group has its own inimitable characteristics and the designer has an obligation to make the most of them. Wood should not be used where great tensile strength is needed and stone cannot be used to supply the resiliency of wood.

It has taken drastic action, spearheaded by the architect Louis Sullivan in this country and the Bauhaus School of Design in Germany, to jar designers into using steel for its own qualities instead of simply as a framework to be camouflaged by other materials. The first skyscrapers were conglomerations of Renaissance stone ornaments and Greek columns stuck on *after* the steel construction was completed. Of course, this is not a fault of the nineteenth century alone. Even the Greeks were guilty of imitating the ends of wooden beams when they began to build their temples in stone, giving us the triglyph in the Doric frieze. If this was a fault, however, how much worse was it still to be using triglyphs on the tops of fourteen-story buildings nineteen centuries later! While Sullivan himself used stone and concrete in his designs and even decorated his skyscrapers rather lavishly, his work showed clearly the essential structure of the building and ornamentation was planned as part of the structure instead of being stuck on afterward. It was designed for its own period rather than consisting of Greek moldings and Gothic gargoyles, and his finished work did not look like a medieval castle or a Gothic cathedral raised high above the ground. Much controversy flared around these early innovations, but they led in a straight line to the simple functional beauty of many of our present-day tall buildings (Figure 7–3).

Figure 7–3. The simple beauty of a modern skyscraper is designed for equal effectiveness by day

Whichever type of material the designer chooses for his work he must explore all possibilities to get the maximum effect. If he is to work in wood, he should know the characteristics of the various types of wood, which are hard, which are soft, which will carve well, which splinter easily, which provide the most beautiful grain. In using metal for small objects or sculpture, the artist must know which will corrode easily, which can be molded or hammered and the comparative weight to expect in the finished product. Above all, he must be willing to accept the limitations of his materials. There is nothing but esthetic failure to be gained by imitating one material with another. Bricks painted to look like plaster have no more

or night. Seagram Building, New York. Architects: Mies van der Rohe and Philip Johnson.

justification than an iron bench textured to look like wood or a wooden candlestick painted to look like metal. Regardless of how well the deceit is accomplished, the article retains a basic lack of integrity that has no place in good design.

One of the most challenging areas for the designer is the field of plastics. This is a relatively new medium, having been anticipated only by celluloid which was the one form of plastic widely used before the nineteen-twenties. In the last decades hardly a month has passed without some new development in this field. At present plastics are divided into several groups on the basis of their chemical characteristics. Two of the groups most useful to the designer are the acrylic and the melamine plastics. *Acrylic* plastics are unusually clear and lend themselves to high polishing. They feel warm and pleasant and they withstand weathering and hard usage. They can be used for handles on brushes, decorative objects such as bowls, and electrical insulation. *Melamine* plastics are among the hardest of the plastics, they resist water and most other liquids and have excellent heat resistance. They are often used in laminates (thin layers glued together) and they come in a wide range of colors and textures. They are used in table and desk tops and for other working surfaces.[2] There are other plastics used for toys, for cushioning in mattresses and upholstered furniture, and for airplane parts. The term *plastic* comes from the fact that no other material is so easily shaped. It can be rolled into thin sheets, molded, or shaped through the use of dies.

The adjustment to such versatile new materials has brought problems to the designer. For years he simply made the same old shapes in new materials without correlating the two. Plastic handles on utensils and irons were exactly the same shape as those that had been turned on woodturning lathes and retained all the same limitations. When designers discovered that they could eliminate the ridges and turnings, they created handles that lent themselves to a firmer grip (Figure 7–4). Much plastic design was called "streamlined." This was design built to speed through the air with a minimum of resistance, with all corners smoothed out and any projections shaped to hug the body. However applicable these lines may be to rockets and automobiles they are not particularly necessary to vacuum cleaners and electric beaters; however, a certain simplicity of design resulted.

The designer has great need for a completely fresh outlook when he is dealing with a new material. He must experiment until he knows what it will do and then adapt his design with no backward glance. On the other hand he must not become so enthusiastic about the new substance that he discounts the past entirely. Nothing can replace the warmth and comfort to be derived from wood or the solidity and texture of stone and brick. Plastic imitations of these materials are so much wasted effort for while they reduce the cost they also cheapen the effect. There is nothing wrong with facing a building with plastic blocks but why must they look like brick or ceramic tile?

There are many instances where plastics have proven their limitations. Plastic measuring cups in their bright colors almost replaced aluminum and pyrex cups for a while. Then housewives found that when they measured hot liquids the cups disintegrated into a molten state. Plastic frames for glasses have a way of snapping in two across the nose and plastic couplings break when subjected to force. Through science such problems are being

[2] Ray Faulkner, Edwin Ziegfeld, and Gerald Hill, *Art Today* (New York: Holt, Rinehart and Winston, Inc., 1956), p. 186.

solved as new attributes are added to plastics, but the designer must not let himself be caught between. Although experimentation is necessary, he must know his materials thoroughly before he can be certain that his design will be effective.

Mass production of plastics has had much to do with the increased interest in crafts made by man's own hands. Ease of acquisition has always diminished the value of consumer goods. Most people have an innate longing for the beautiful and a deep desire to surround themselves with objects that indicate a refined taste. The machine cannot profitably be set up for production of isolated items, and objects sold in quantity defeat the purpose of the serious collector. For this reason handmade pottery and textiles, carvings, mosaics, sculpture, and painting have begun to enjoy a demand previously unknown in our era. Even Indian pottery, which has long been with us, is accorded a new appreciation.

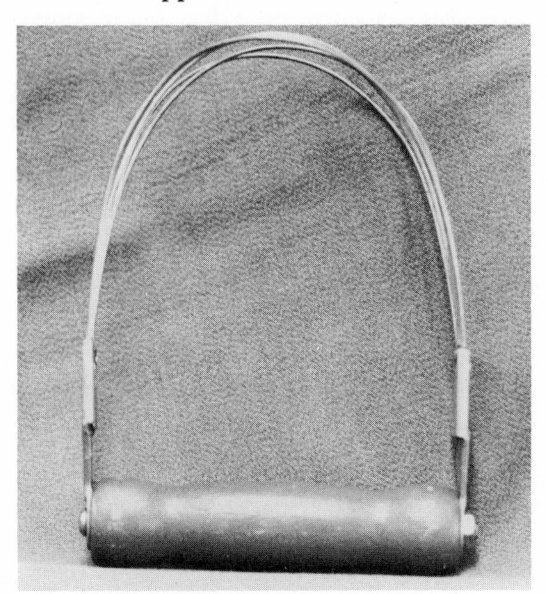

Figure 7–4. These two kitchen utensils, both of which require a firm grasp, demonstrate the difference between a wooden handle, turned on a lathe in a conventional way, and a plastic handle which has been molded to fit the fingers.

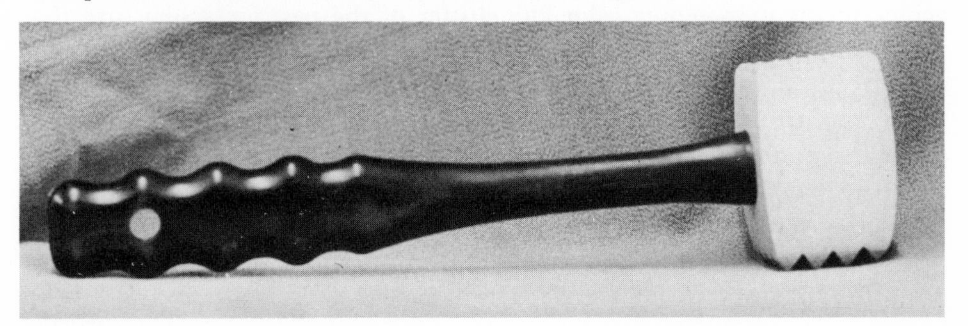

Integrity of Form

Simultaneously with consideration for materials, the designer must devote himself to *integrity* of form. Form will determine the materials and materials will modify the form so it cannot be said that either consideration takes precedence.

Integrity of form has been summed up for years by the expression "form follows function." Because of the dramatic evolution of the skyscraper, this concept has been associated with the Bauhaus and with Louis Sullivan although it has always existed in nature. Birds' nests, beehives, and beaver dams are all forms evolving strictly from function and with a minimum expenditure of effort or material. However, nature does not always reveal her methods readily. Raul France, who has made extensive biotechnical studies, states that if we could use the same structural principles in a skyscraper that appear in the stalk of a plant we could erect a building 700 stories high with the same material as is used in our present buildings.[3] Biology has much of value for the engineer if he can adapt what he sees for human purposes.

Integrity of Function

If we are to improve environment, we must go one step beyond form following function and make certain that function follows man's physiological, sociological, and emotional needs. Rooms without windows, however air-conditioned, can bring out latent feelings of claustrophobia, yet thousands of offices are designed in this way to utilize space. On the other hand, houses made of glass may look open and free, but they spell continual frustration for the housewife who must keep every room ready for constant inspection by anyone approaching the front door. Both of these forms fulfill their function, but they could easily contribute to the nervousness of their inhabitants. The simplicity of the modern skyscraper is one of man's great achievements in sweeping aside the clutter of the past for a structure that proudly states its function as an office building in an era in which efficiency and directness are valued, yet this same simplicity may have a certain sterility when applied to domestic dwellings. The very fact that man works in austere surroundings may accentuate his need for more warmth at home. It is true that the interior of the modern skyscraper is becoming more suited to man's needs. Murals appear in the hallways and thick carpets adorn offices in which tropical plants soften the firm lines of walls paneled in beautifully grained woods.

[3] Moholy-Nagy, *op. cit.*, p. 45.

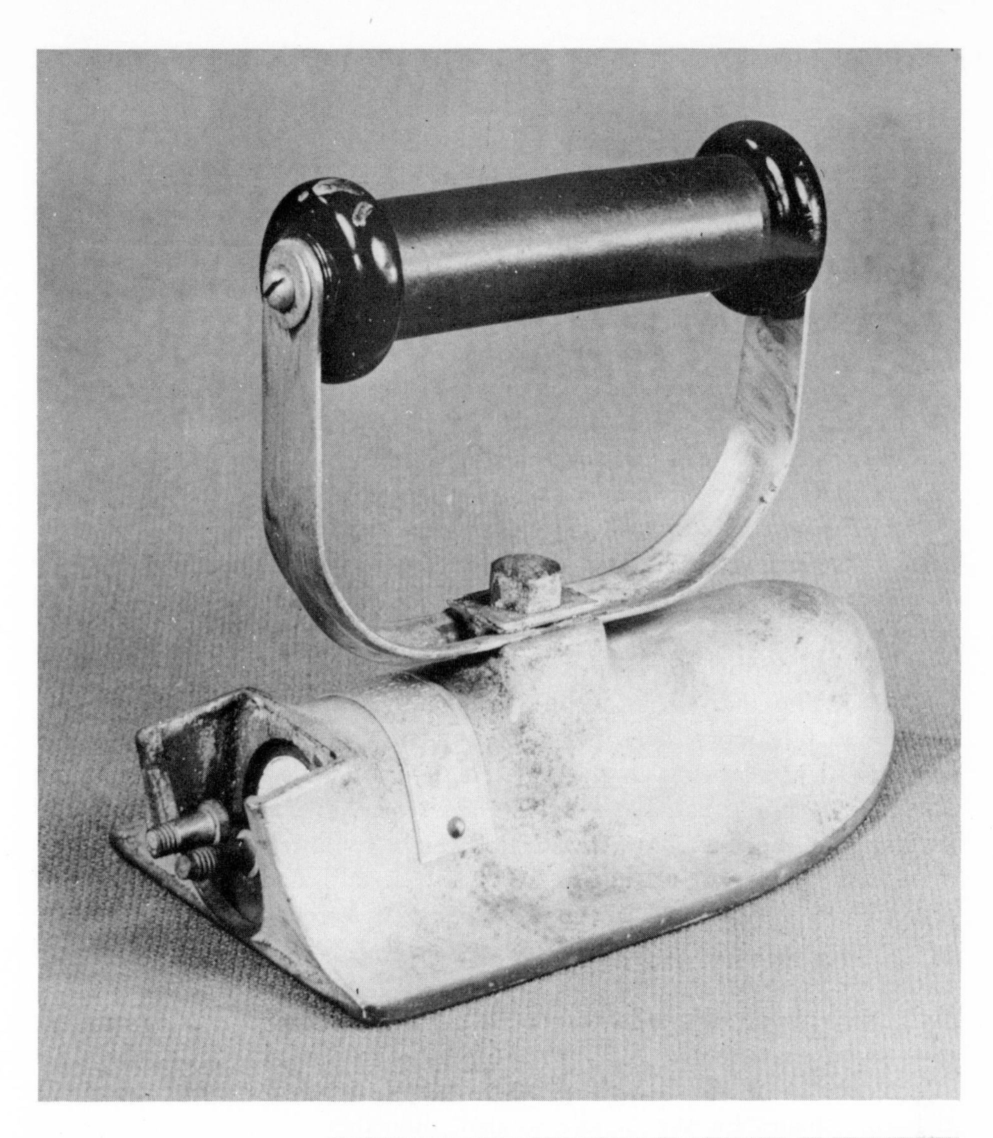

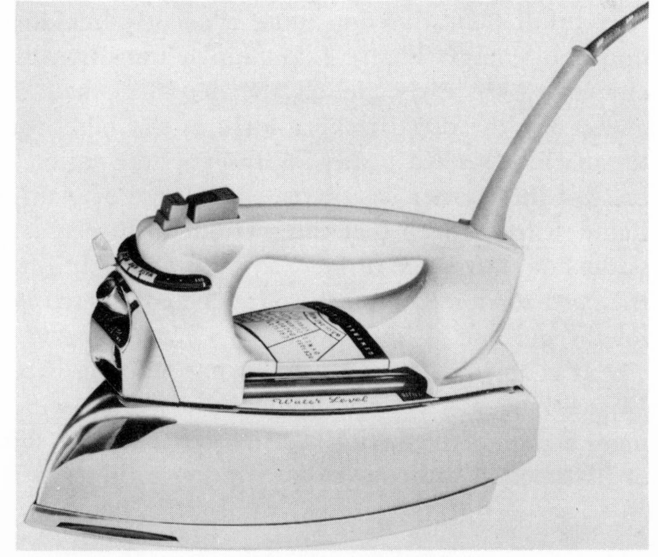

Figure 7–5. Two electric irons, fifty-two years apart in design. Above is a model used in 1910; at right is the 1962 model. Courtesy of General Electric Company.

However, for every executive ensconced in such an office there are hundreds of employees working side by side in large open rooms whose principal concessions to modern design are adequate lighting, air-conditioning, and the latest-model office machines. These same people are the ones whose economic status forces them to go home to simple boxlike houses side by side on treeless tracts where two or three basic designs are alternated so that every third family lives in the same house with the same yard, and a different color of roof or shutters becomes their sole claim to individuality. A child reared in surroundings so similar to those of his associates cannot be expected to exhibit strong traits of imagination, individuality, or willingness to break away from the "average," whether in an idea or a way of life. Standardization may have its advantages economically but we have reached the point where money can no longer be allowed to push human beings into molds that warp the best innate qualities of mankind. The designer of the future must find a way to provide for the tremendous increase in population without stifling the needs of man for self-expression, privacy, and a contact with natural surroundings.

While the idea of form following function and function following man's needs is more sweeping in the field of architectural design, the principle is just as vital in the smallest designed object. As in the use of materials, technology has opened up new ideas in function. The use of flatirons was associated with the idea of weight combined with heat and for years after the advent of the electric iron a certain amount of weight and pressure was exerted in the task of ironing. In recent years, however, we have discovered that with the proper temperature and dampness in the clothes to be ironed weight and pressure are not necessary. Consequently, the new irons are only a fraction of the weight of the older ones and the job of ironing consumes less energy. With lightness came the possibility of shaping for more skillful manipulation combined with the intelligent use of plastic shapes for the handle so that altogether the newer models not only fulfill their function more efficiently but do so with far less human output of energy (Figure 7–5). Similar transitions have occurred in vacuum cleaners. With early models the housewife had the feeling that she was extricating the dirt by sheer force as she bore down on the carpet while the machine sucked lustily. With experimentation in shapes and forms the body of the cleaner has increased the ease of manipulation while a greater lightness has proven that the suction works just as well when the machine skims slowly over the surface. Every innovation in the direction of lessening the need for force or pressure can be considered an improvement in form for the purpose of function.

It is obvious that form following function is basic to industrial design. No working mechanism should be disguised with the idea of making it more acceptable esthetically. Any enhancement should follow the dictates of its function rather than attempting to obscure it.

Figure 7–6. This stoneware demitasse set has honesty of form and material and great practical beauty. Designed by Karen Karnes. Photograph by Oswald Werner. Courtesy of the Everson Museum of Art, Syracuse, New York, and of *Craft Horizons.*

Figure 7–6 shows a stoneware demi-tasse set designed by Karen Karnes for a specific purpose. There is solidity here and integrity both of form and material. The stoneware will be heavy enough to protect the hands against the heat of the coffee while giving interesting color and texture. The pot is shaped for interest yet the cups have an honesty in their simple forms and their handles echo the shape of the handle on the pot, giving unity.

However, we must accept the fact that the sole function of some objects is that of affording pleasure to the eye. We have long brought functional objects from far places to decorate our homes with no thought of putting them to their intended uses. We have elephant bells that will never adorn an elephant and Russian samovars and Chinese teapots that will never make tea. While these objects have an exotic quality because of their origins we can hardly deny our own artists the right to create works to fulfill a similar function, that of visual pleasure. We must not let our penchant for efficiency overwhelm the needs of the spirit by insisting that everything prove itself by contributing to our material welfare. Even in the face of our notoriety as materialists, Americans still pay more for a fine painting or a piece of sculpture than for a high-powered automobile or airplane.

In contrast, Figure 7–7 shows four pieces made purely for visual interest. Although flowers or liquids could be put in these pots it is highly unlikely that they ever will be; actually the addition of flowers would destroy their simplicity. Singly or as a group they are purely objects expressing the qualities of the clay from which they are made, created to be seen and enjoyed.

Integrity of Ornamentation

There is one more aspect of structural design which must be considered. We have discussed integrity of materials, integrity of form and of function, and we must go one step further and consider *integrity of ornamentation.* Like many other problems of design this question has undergone radical changes in recent years. Moholy-Nagy states: "Texture is, at least for our time, the legitimate successor of ornament."[4] However, before we can dismiss the problem so easily it is necessary to review the field and study the developments that have led to our present-day approach. This will be done in Chapter 8.

FOR FURTHER EXPLORATION

Vision in Motion by Lazló Moholy-Nagy (Chicago: Paul Theobald and Company, 1956). A broad treatment of the interrelation of art and life, based on the work of the Institute of Design in Chicago, which brought the teachings of the Bauhaus to this country. Written by the most eloquent spokesman for the Bauhaus principle.

Art and Industry by Herbert Read (London: Faber & Faber, Ltd., 1947). The consideration of materials and their role in producing useful, though beautiful, objects.

[4] *Ibid.*, p. 44.

An American Architecture, Frank Lloyd Wright edited by Edgar Kaufmann (New York: Horizon Press, 1955). The writings of the master architect describing his work and his philosophy of organic design.

Dynamic Symmetry in Composition by Jay Hambidge (New York: Brentano's, 1923). An analysis of paintings showing the use of dynamic symmetry in their structure.

STUDIO PROJECTS

1. To explore the validity of structural design today, make a collection of clippings of objects in common use which you feel show integrity of form or of material.
2. Using India ink, design a useful tool, utensil, or small appliance combining integrity of form and beauty of line.
3. Using India ink or tempera, design an object in plastic which you feel could not be made as successfully in any other material.

Figure 7–7. These four pieces are designed purely for their decorative quality with interest in texture and form. Large pot by Don Wallace and three earthenware vases by Chizuko Shimano. Courtesy of the Canadian Guild of Potters and *Craft Horizons.*

CHAPTER 8

Decorative Design

Decorative design is frequently thought of as ornament yet in its true sense it goes deeper than mere ornamentation. We think of ornament as something not essential to the form of an object, something that is stuck on after the object is otherwise completed. Decorative design should be part of the object from the beginning, something which could not be removed without destroying the unity of the object. In its true sense decorative design simply brings out the structural design by enhancing it and playing up its most interesting features. It is never an independent entity.

Historical Symbolism

The first decorative designs were symbols carved into the handles of tools and weapons, either to insure success in their use or to record success as it occurred. Some historians believe that the carvings had much the same purpose as the notching of a gun handle to record the number of killings accomplished. From these beginnings we find symbols applied to pottery and to masks. Figure 8–1 shows two primitive African masks in which the spiral design is a direct interpretation of the simple tribal rhythms of drumbeat and native dance.

As we have progressed through the centuries the element of symbolism has remained strong in decorative design. The Greek vase (Figure 8–2), designed primarily for ceremonial use, incorporated paintings as part of the structure, shaped to the body of the vase, and frequently depicting in symbolic form the uses to which the vase would be put. Here symbolism took human form, depicting the lives of the people from battles and athletic

Figure 8–1. Masks of the African Kifwebe Society use the hypnotic spiral, originated as a symbol of this cult, which expresses the same rhythms as the tribal dances.

Figure 8–2. Attic vase of the fifth century, B.C. Red-figured design showing the departure of a warrior. Courtesy of the Metropolitan Museum of Art, Fletcher Fund, 1925.

contests to artistic endeavors such as carving or painting a statue. Each vase is an epic poem singing the song of a people. The esthetic quality lies in the homogeneity of structure and painting. Several techniques were employed, starting with archaic animal forms on a yellow ground, through a black-figured style on red clay adopted by the Athenians in the sixth century and, a hundred years later, reversing the process to produce red-figured funerary vases, or *lekythoi,* with a white ground. In all the styles the figures are combined in a stately rhythm which may be compared to the classic Greek chant.

The Early Christian Church in its conscientious sidestepping of anything resembling idolatry flowered into one of the most practical manifestations of symbolism through its mosaics (Figure 8–3). Although statues and paintings were not allowed in Byzantine churches during the iconoclastic controversy of the eighth century, the telling of Bible stories through mosaics was considered an important part of the teaching of the church. Entire walls were covered with stones or glass or ceramic tiles which, while decorating the surface, far transcended the usual conception of purely decorative art. Vaulted ceilings, arched niches, and wide wall panels were planned specifically for the combined decorative, structural, and instructional function of mosaics.

This Christian symbolism continued as a dominant force in the decorative design of Western art for six more centuries, just as the symbols of

Figure 8–3. Mosaic from the Byzantine period (sixth century) showing Empress Theodora and members of her court. Copy of original mosaic in the Church of San Vitale, Ravenna. Courtesy of the Metropolitan Museum of Art, Fletcher Fund, 1925.

Buddhism and Mohammedanism had dominated much of the art of the East. Painting, sculpture, mosaics, textiles and ceramics all attested to the strong part Christian faith played in the lives of the people. The Renaissance, with its interest in man as an individual and its dedication to the Classic era, saw the use of Greek and Roman mythology added to Christian symbols in decoration but these retained a symbolic meaning, even though it was a somewhat different interpretation than the original symbolism of fourteen centuries before. Instead of the ideal of human form and the expression of deity, the Renaissance Classicism was an expression of the importance of man as an individual and his reaching for renewed youth as a result of increased learning. It was symbolism for a time in which the literature and philosophy of the East were fused with the culture of the West through the fall of Constantinople and the subsequent exodus of Eastern scholars to centers of Western learning.

With the Reformation the uses of Christian symbolism were stifled in northern countries and the original vigor has never been restored. The gestures were continued and still continue but the embodiment of Christianity as a driving force of humanity has not found the strength in artistic expression that it achieved before and during the Renaissance. The Baroque period saw much elaborate decoration, not always structural, and the Rococo period refined this tendency into the delicate and fragile design that we associate with French furnishings. Wall decorations consisted of murals painted in soft colors depicting dimpled princesses or shepherdesses swinging or cavorting with dainty youths in powdered wigs and frilled shirtfronts (Figure 8–4). Cupids, sheep, garlands, and shells symbolized the frothy existence that led directly to the French Revolution. Similar decorative elements were extant on porcelain, silver, tapestries, and embroideries as well as in carved wall panels and furniture.

The use of animal elements was characteristic of the furniture of the eighteenth century, possibly because of the popularity of hunting as a pastime. The dainty hoofed leg of Rococo furniture grew into the heavy claw-and-ball foot of the English cabinetmakers. Interest in decoration for its own sake grew gradually until the Victorian era when humanity all but stifled under the excrescences of heavy furniture, heavy tapestries and draperies, heavy carpets full of Oriental design, and dark paintings, all housed in buildings heavily ornamented with classic moldings, Renaissance medallions, and Baroque arches which were admittedly stuck on for the simple purpose of making an "imposing" dwelling. Commercial buildings suffered from the same ailment. Architects of this era did not question the necessity of basing their designs on books of patterns drawn up by students of Classic and Renaissance art. The best architect was the one who could most faithfully represent these symbols of bygone eras while still fulfilling the purpose of his building.

Figure 8–4. "The Interrupted Sleep" by Francois Boucher (1703–1770). Courtesy of the Metropolitan Museum of Art, the Jules S. Bache Collection, 1949.

The Bauhaus Influence

A furious battle raged over the whole question of ornamentation at the turn of the last century. The Bauhaus School of Design founded by Walter Gropius in Breslau, Germany, in 1919 was hailed as the liberator of esthetic thought because it stood squarely for stern unadulterated design and carried out this teaching in its own buildings (Figure 8–5). Gathering students from all over the world, it taught the importance of the machine and sought to bridge the gap between artist and industry by seeking a common ground upon which fine art, handcrafts, and industrial art could flourish by interaction without conflict. Although the school fell to Hitler's armies, its influence continues to spread throughout the world of art and architecture as a harried world seeks to adjust itself to the confusion of facts and knowledge that leave little time for philosophy or symbolism. Modern man is so overburdened intellectually in his efforts to keep up with the progress of science and technology so vital to his existence that he either becomes submerged in the effort or sunk in hopeless apathy. Neither state is conducive to the development of meaningful symbols.

Return to Pattern

Man, nevertheless, needs more than utility in his buildings. Five years after the founding of the Bauhaus, Frank Lloyd Wright started a new trend by casting concrete building blocks into decorative forms for use in the construction of houses. Interesting singly, the blocks when put together with metal rods and poured concrete carried the decorative design throughout the building, inside and out, in a fluid rhythmic pattern that was not only full of variety but served to unify the structural design. Here the design *was* the structure, being cast into the very walls.

Mosaics followed, both indoors and out. Murals were encouraged by the federal government in the depression years when artists were commissioned to paint the walls of public buildings. Here a symbolism of sorts emerged in stylized depictions of the history of a region, or its geographical assets, or the activities for which the building was intended. Artists who disapproved of the sleek sterility of modern buildings were happy to create designs in a variety of media to add beauty and interest to contemporary architecture.

Walls are not the only surfaces lending themselves to pattern. In Mexico vast areas of pavement are inlaid with colorful tile mosaic. In this

Figure 8–5. The Bauhaus School in Dessau, Germany, was a powerful influence for functional and uncluttered design in architecture. Architect: Walter Gropius. Courtesy of the architect and the Museum of Modern Art, New York.

Figure 8–6. A creative kinship bridging twenty-six centuries is manifest in these two stoneware jars, yet each shows the subtle influence of its own time. Left, Etruscan vase of the sixth century B.C. Courtesy

country designed paving blocks add texture to garden areas or patios. Pebbles, crushed gravel, washed stones imbedded in concrete, or concrete laid in patterns outlined by strips of redwood are all accepted ways of achieving pattern.

What of the decorative design of small objects? The use of texture to supplant symbolic forms does not necessarily typify the twentieth century. The two jars in Figure 8–6 show a similarity in shape and texture that is particularly noteworthy when we realize that they were conceived twenty-six centuries apart in time. There are differences, of course, and it is not hard to guess which was made in pre-Roman times and which is an expression of an age of streamlining and fast movement, yet we feel the same basic principles in both, the combining of smoothness and texture, the sturdy shape, and interest in the handles as an accent. While such discoveries make us feel the eternal fellowship of creative artists, they can also have a disquieting effect on the young designer aspiring to make his own contribution. With the same basic principles effective through the ages can there really be new visual forms? Are there actually new emotions or sensations to express? What can the twentieth-century designer do to make his distinctive contribution?

of the Museo Etrusco Gregoriano, The Vatican. Right, contemporary stoneware jar in brown, black, and beige by Harrison McIntosh. Courtesy of the artist and *Craft Horizons.*

Contribution of the Artist Today

First, *he can make the most of the materials that are indigenous to his own period.* Plastic can be made in many forms and textures and will be made in many more when designers find the way. Decorative lighting fixtures are being designed that could never have been made without plastics and their propensity for being spun into thin sheets and molded into all kinds of forms. New alloys of metal are also opening doors from the standpoint of both durability and design.

Second, *the designer can concentrate on a sincere expression of his own reactions to his world, not leaning on the past nor imitating symbols that have no meaning for him.* In Figure 8–7 we see plates made by contemporary craftsmen in three different countries. Each constitutes a design within an eight-inch circle. The Swiss (top) has a bright-blue background on which wildflowers are strewn in fresh simplicity. At a glance one senses the blue skies above mountain meadows, with perhaps a reflection in an Alpine lake below. The Mexican (bottom) is also blue with the decoration applied in a creamy glaze. Here the forms are simple curved designs, bearing a feeling of flower and fern in the center but done in a stylized manner as on Indian pottery. The feeling is one of symbolism rather than a gay expression of environment. The center plate is of Finnish origin. The basic glaze is a cool gray with the design in soft blue-green. The pervading feeling makes one sense the tall forests and deep fjords and the restraint of a people used to long cold winters. These are authentic designs because they are honest expressions of the people from whom they sprang. Achievement of this authenticity is the highest goal to which the designer can aspire.

Last, *the student of design can realize that the fact of something having been said before does not diminish its importance for his own era.* Just as words of kindness are welcome in any age, so is a beautiful object always acceptable. If he is true to his own interpretation and speaks in his own idiom, his work will have its own distinctive quality no matter how many centuries of artists have done the same sort of thing. Even simple geometric forms can be adapted to new uses as can be seen in the room divider in Figure 8–8. Although the design is basically a combination of circles and squares, the use of aluminum makes a lightweight and practical screen with a modern feeling.

A fresh and individual interpretation of decorative design is apparent in the stoneware casserole by James McKinnell, Figure 8–9. The forms on the cover suggest plants or fish, yet we are not overly concerned with *what* is represented. The visual texture is carried throughout with smooth flecked areas repeated on the lower section and again around the handle; the solid tone of handle and edge lend effective accents. These decorative forms and textures are a part of the structure and each viewer can apply his own associations and experiences in interpreting them.

Perhaps this quality is the symbolism of an era in which man has come to realize how much lies beyond his knowledge. Even the natural forms that he sees every day have aspects which he does not fathom and which can mean dramatic new developments affecting his very life. The relationship of simple mold to the triumph over disease and the overwhelming consequences of splitting the atom are only two indications that there is much beyond what we see. Man's symbols can no longer be final statements because his reactions to his environment are neither clear-cut nor his knowledge conclusive. Each month brings new discoveries affecting human life and the artist depicts the ever uncertain status of his world by decorative design that is flexible, sometimes unfinished by previous standards. The viewer is given a suggestion to carry through his own interpretation according to his feelings at the time, much as the listener delves for the melody among the counterharmonies of modern music. There are those who insist that the artist of today is vague, lost, and has found no symbolism. Perhaps these very qualities of vagueness and ambiguity are the symbols of an age in which science, philosophy, and art have been unable to provide a conclusive statement.

Figure 8–7. Contemporary craftsmen express their own lands in their plate designs. (*Top*.) The example from Switzerland is reminiscent of Alpine meadows. (*Center*.) This Finnish plate is restrained in expression as are northern people after years of living with long winters, deep fjords, and forests. (*Right*.) This plate from Mexico shows the influence of Indian design. All three are in variations of blue and blue-green.

Figure 8–8. Simple geometric designs form an anodized aluminum screen which makes an effective room divider. Courtesy of Morris Kurtzon, Inc.

Figure 8–9. A free treatment of form and texture gives this stoneware casserole an exciting contemporary feeling. Designed and executed by James F. McKinnell. Courtesy of the artist and of the American Craftsmen's Council.

FOR FURTHER EXPLORATION

Bauhaus by Herbert Bayer (Newton Centre, Mass.: Charles T. Branford Co., 1952). Well-illustrated and informative discussion of the influence of the Bauhaus on twentieth-century art.

Bauhaus by Herbert Bayer, Walter Gropius and Ise Gropius (New York: Museum of Modern Art, 1938). A description of the Bauhaus approach in relation to use of materials.

STUDIO PROJECTS

1. To clarify the difference between decorative design and superficial decoration make a collection of clippings on each type. Label one group "design" and the other "decoration." Be prepared to discuss the reasons for your selections.

2. Design a plate, cup, and saucer, representing a set of dinnerware. Coordinate your decorative design with the structural design.

3. Design a decorative concrete block to be used as a repeat unit in a panel of decorative design on the facade of an industrial building. Show the panel with the blocks repeated as well as a large-scale detail of the block itself.

CHAPTER 9

Design for Living

ARCHITECTURAL DESIGN CONFRONTS US SQUARELY WITH SPACE, and in this era of pioneering beyond the limits of the earth, the word has many associations.

The Meaning of Space

Space as a limitless expanse stretching into infinity is an awesome thought that defies imagination, leading man into deep and unsolvable meditations. Yet it is this same space that circulates freely about him, making it possible for him to move and breathe and develop physically and spiritually. Some people who find themselves closed in with too little space suffer claustrophobia while others, when confronted with vast reaches of desert or water, become victims of an opposite fear which the psychologists label agraphobia. Both are real ailments with physical manifestations, brought on by one aspect or another of man's relationship to space.

The understanding of this space and effective use of it has a great deal to do with successful design. It is the positive and negative space that makes a piece of sculpture: the positive the space that forms the mass and the negative the space left around it and through it. It is the space left within a piece of pottery that determines its capacity and the nature of its use. We realize the importance of space in architecture if we think of space as being unlimited until the architect circumscribes it by erecting walls to contain it and allot it to certain uses. It is the amount and quality of the designed space that determines the success of a building. It is only *after* the space is determined that the material, surface color, or texture of the walls are considered. If we wanted to carry this point far enough we could even say that space is the *structural design* and the walls themselves are the decorative design enhancing it.

The consideration of space brings us to another characteristic of architecture, sometimes called the "fourth dimension." In music or literature we make use of time as part of our experience, letting it carry us to a climax and into the denouement. The viewer of a painting or of sculpture should spend enough time to feel an authentic reaction to the work. In architecture the use of time is imperative. To know architecture one must take time to walk through it, allowing his spirit to flow through the space, over and around the divisions or walls, out through the doors and windows. Anyone who has learned to "feel" a building in all its possibilities can sense almost endless dimensions in its relationship to the human spirit.

From the standpoint of space buildings can be divided into two types: closed and open. Referring to nature once more, we find in mollusks a protective shell that is carried with the animal wherever it goes. These are often remarkable in their structural development as in the snail and the starfish. The fundamental concern here is for protection and, while the animal within necessarily moves rather slowly, the protection afforded keeps his safety assured under most conditions. Progressing from the involuntary shelter that the animal carries with him to such voluntary protection as birds' nests, beaver dams, and honeycombs, we find the same principle, that of a simple outer covering serving primarily for protection. The structure is built *around* the bird or animal. As early man outgrew his cave and began to build freestanding shelters he followed this principle. The pueblo of adobe bricks is of this type as is the tepee of animal skins or the log cabin of the frontier. Any building consisting of outer walls carrying the full weight of the building with a roof thrown across beams or arches can be considered as an enclosed or protective shelter.

The vertebrate animals, on the other hand, have an inner structure, upon which the body is built not so much for protection as for support. The skeletal structure gives greater freedom, not only because the animal has no excess weight to carry but because of the greater versatility of his movements, his ability to reach out, to grasp, to run rapidly if necessary. His lack of built-in shelter is compensated for by his greater ability to attack or to escape. The open construction of buildings follows this principle. Stresses and strains are directed toward a basic inner structure rather than toward the outer walls, giving greater flexibility to design and allowing the walls to open out and flow into the out-of-doors.

The Parthenon is one of the outstanding examples of open structure (Figure 9–1). The cella, or inner sanctum where the statue of the goddess Athena was housed, is combined with a small treasury in an inner structure that forms the functional core of the building. No one but the priests was allowed to enter this area, yet provision was necessary for crowds in processions coming to pay homage on special days. The temple, therefore, has a *peripteral* plan, in which columns support the roof enclosing the cella on

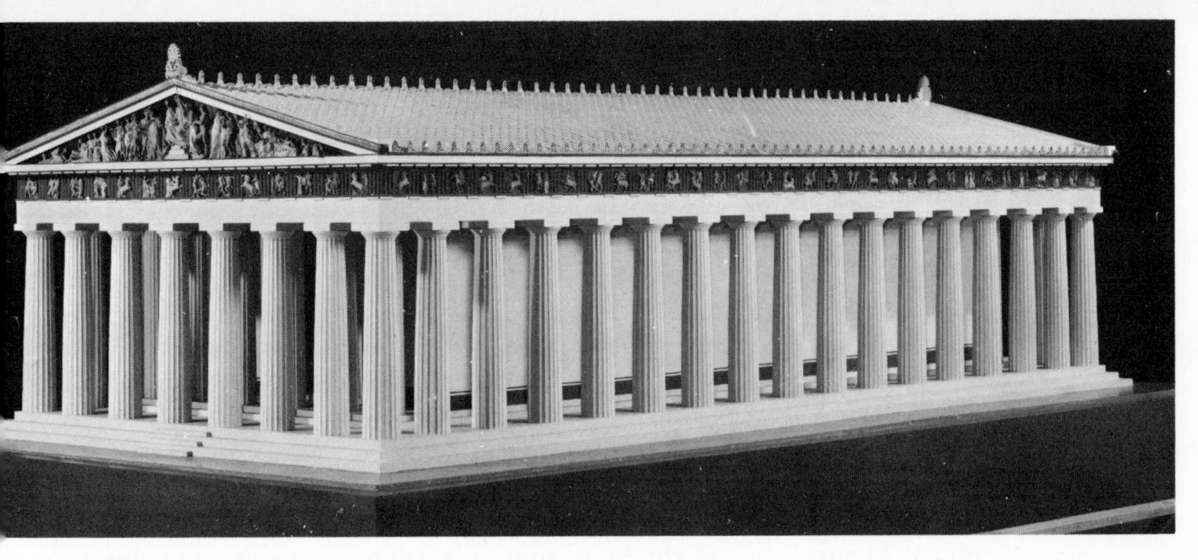

Figure 9–1. The Parthenon as it stands today, high on the Acropolis overlooking Athens (*page* 134), and (*above*) a model of it at its prime in the Fifth Century B.C. Photograph *today* by Alison Frantz, *model* courtesy The Metropolitan Museum of Art, Purchase 1890, Levi Hale Willard Bequest.

all four sides (Figure 9–2). The columns are an integral part of the structure yet the spaces between them give an openness which allows room for crowds to gather and overflow into the surrounding landscape. Standing proudly on the Acropolis, the sacred hill above the city, it appears as a series of columns drenched in sunlight and moving shadow, embracing space and shaping it. Each column bows out slightly in the center to give the illusion of greater strength and fluidity while the fluting diminishes in size as it reaches upward. This is particularly remarkable in view of the fact that the columns are actually a series of drums held together in the center by a bronze or wooden pivot about which they were ground to insure a perfect fit. Even the horizontal lines of the building are slightly curved. Every detail contributes to the feeling of grace, an interaction of solidity and space, of construction and environment.

Figure 9–2. The floor plan of the Parthenon shows a peripteral temple, so called because the colonnade completely surrounds the cella, which in this case has had a treasury added to it.

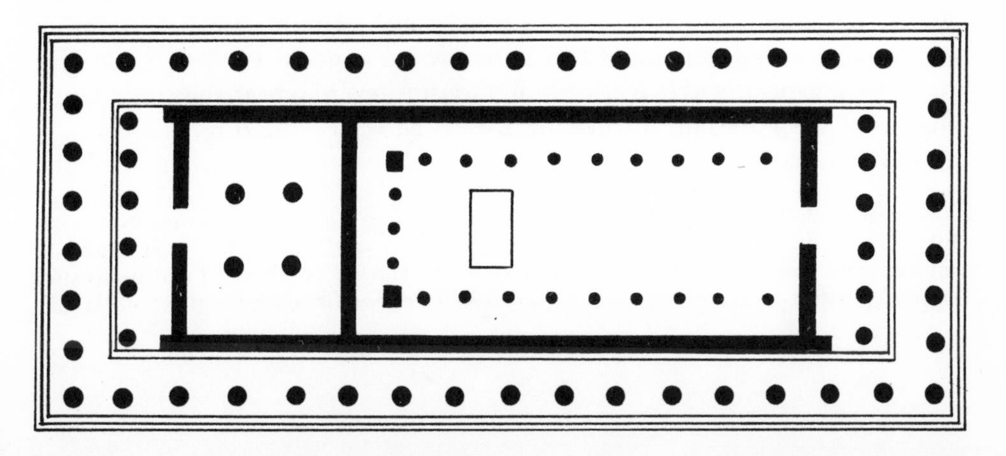

Less obvious manifestations of openness are to be found in Gothic cathedrals. Here a more organic building is found, a growing expression of a community over a period of several hundred years, rising higher, being added onto, developing in spite of time and innumerable changes into an integrated whole.

The success of the Gothic cathedral lies in the discovery of ribbed vaulting to solve the problems involved in use of the arch. Christian churches had used the arch from early times, but there were serious drawbacks because of the necessity for thick supporting walls. With the discovery of ribbed vaulting, the pointed arch, and flying buttresses, it was possible to secure the strength of the walls in such a way as to open up wide areas for windows, creating a jewel-like glow—one of the attractions of great cathedrals (Figure 9–3). At the same time, these three elements contribute to the sense of soaring into space and to a feeling of delicacy and refinement in keeping with the veneration of the Virgin Mary in the medieval church. The combination of height and light made it possible to attain a feeling of openness indoors and out, with the outside flowing in through the windows and the inner spirit of the building emanating from chapels, cloisters, niches, and flying buttresses (Figure 9–4).

Structural Classifications of Architecture

From the standpoint of structure, historic architecture can be classified in one of four general ways (Figure 9–5). The simplest form is the *post-and-lintel* system of the Parthenon, in which two posts are erected and the intervening space bridged by a beam, or lintel, thrown across it. The second type is the *arch* of the Romans, which was developed to a high degree in Gothic cathedrals. Today we see increased use of a third type, the *cantilever*. This consists of a beam or other structural member projecting from a wall where it is securely enough imbedded or otherwise fastened at one end to hold up while extended over considerable space, and even to carry weight in addition to its own. One of the outstanding examples of the cantilever system in our time is the home that Frank Lloyd Wright designed for Edgar Kaufmann at Bear Run, Pennsylvania (Figure 9–6). A series of overlapping cantilevers gives the structure an organic feeling, much like that of geological layers. Notice how the cantilevers repeat the stone layers that form the waterfall, integrating the home with its setting.

Figure 9–3. The interior of Amiens Cathedral as seen from the floor presents a dizzying study in quadrapartite vaulting, showing how the ribs of each four-part vault are supported by diagonally opposite piers or columns, making possible the soaring quality associated with Gothic cathedrals. Photograph by Professor Clarence Ward.

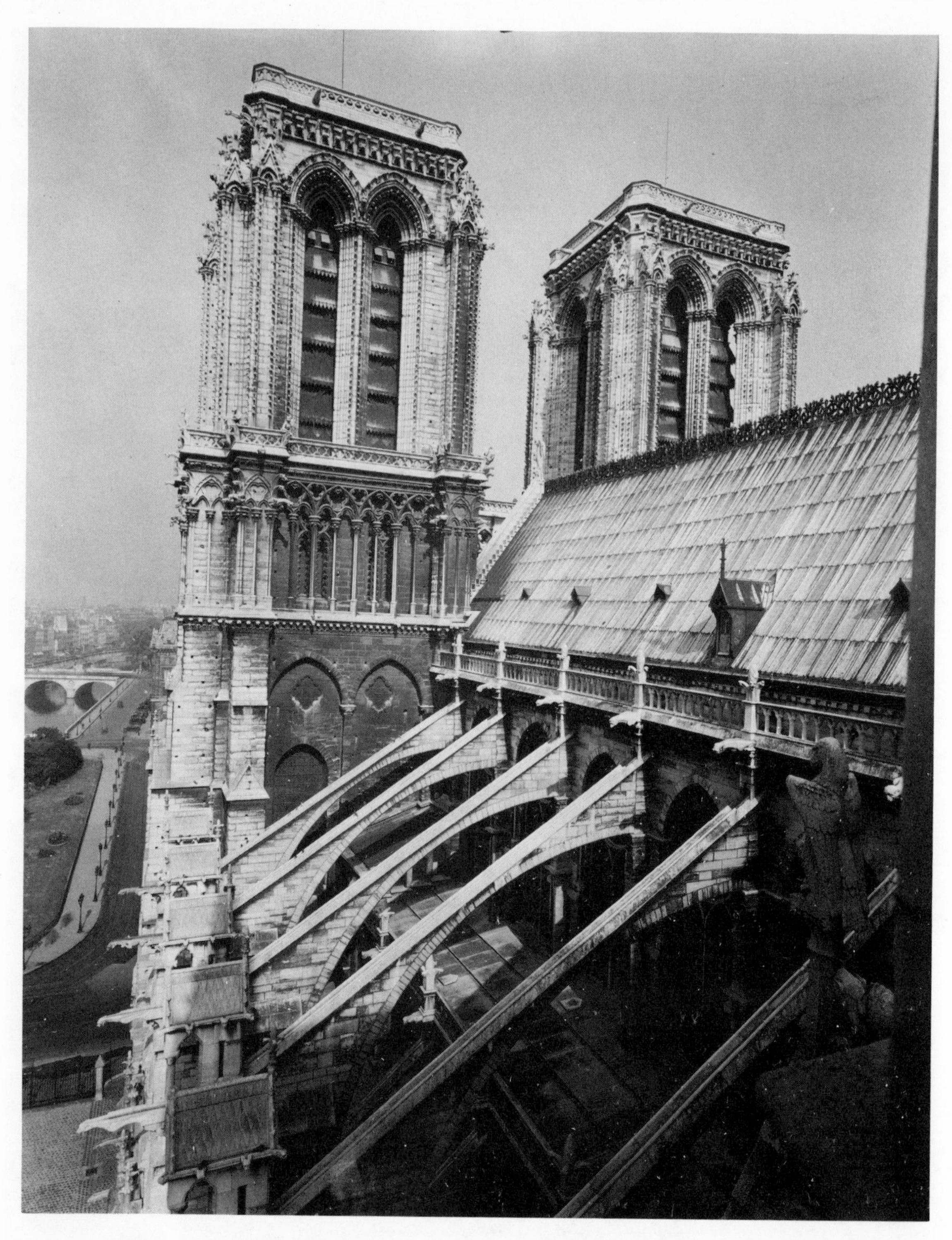

Figure 9–4. The flying buttresses of the Cathedral of Notre Dame in Paris contribute immensely to the feeling of lightness and grace. Notice the open work in stone railings, arches, and the detail of the ridgepole. Photograph by Professor Clarence Ward.

The cantilever system has come into increased use with the development of reinforced concrete, or ferro-concrete, as it is sometimes called. With immense strength under tension, steel beams can span greater distances in the post-and-lintel system than can either stone or wood. When this tensile strength is combined with the strength of concrete under compression a new and versatile material evolves. Beams embedded in walls of reinforced concrete and riveted or welded into place can support tremendous weights when extended into space.

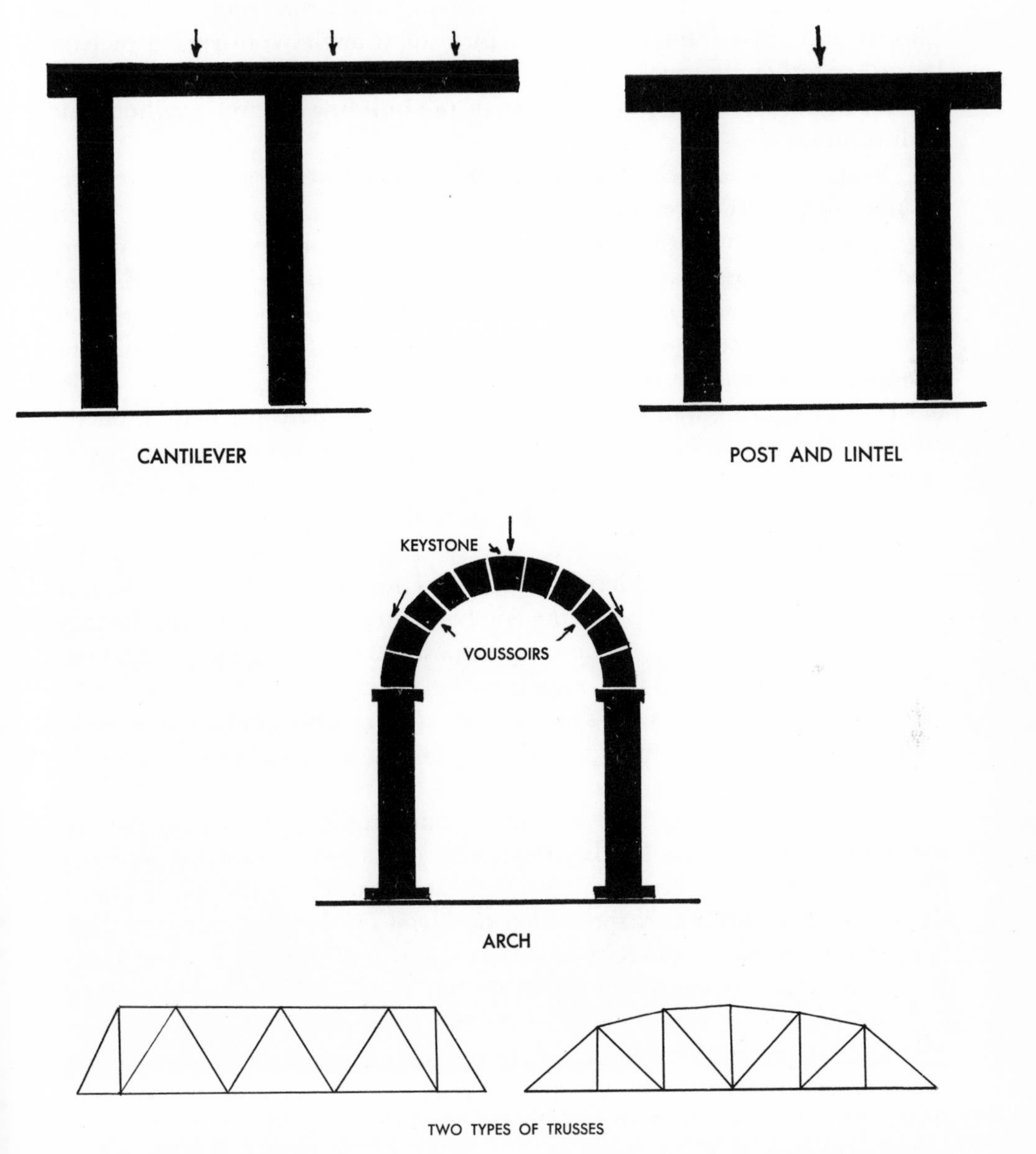

Figure 9–5. Most historic structures fall into one of four basic types of architecture.

Ferro-concrete has also contributed to the imaginative quality of contemporary architecture by its capacity to be poured into molds. This makes possible organic shell-like forms which can be used for such a building as the graceful hockey rink designed for Yale University by Eero Saarinen. The apparently billowing roof is supported by cables stretched from a huge concrete arch that forms the backbone of the building (Figure 9–7; see page 144).

The fourth system, *trusses,* is utilized where it is necessary to span longer spaces than can be bridged by post-and-lintel construction. The truss consists of a rigid framework in the form of triangles constructed of bars, beams, or other material (Figure 9–5). Truss construction has been used extensively for steel bridges as well as in the building of large pavilions and auditoriums.

While these four categories encompass most historic architecture, they do not adequately cover the subject of contemporary construction. There are a great many variations used by architects today, many of which do not readily accept classification. Two general types, however, are *bearing-wall construction* and *skeleton-frame construction.* In bearing-wall construction the wall actually supports the roof and the floors; in fact, from a structural standpoint the walls *are* the building. A building of concrete or cinder blocks is of bearing-wall construction. Skeleton-Frame construction, on the other hand, consists of a basic framework upon which the wall surface or "skin" is later hung. Skyscrapers with their "steel cage" construction are of this type; frame houses also fit into the classification with various modifications.

One of the most challenging problems for mid-century architectural designers has been the chapel at the Air Force Academy at Colorado Springs. Here is a building in which the very purpose necessitates a blending of two influences that at first glance appear to be widely opposed. Its association with the Air Force makes it a symbol of the future while its function relates it to the age-old traditions of Christianity and ancient Judaism. It must be nonsectarian yet it must have meaning for many faiths. It must relate to the functional classroom and dormitory buildings already completed, yet somehow retain an individuality expressive of its own distinctive function. The final selection of design offers a dramatic solution to the specific needs attendant upon this highly specialized problem. Of skeleton-frame construction, it combines two modern materials, glass and aluminum, in a design as functional as the classroom buildings but with forms strikingly in keeping with the soaring quality both of the Air Force and of the human spirit. The tetrahedrons of aluminum, while remotely related to accepted ecclesiastical forms, have a sense of being prophetic of unexplored worlds lying ahead. There can be no doubt of the function of this building or of the age which produced it (Figure 9–8).

Figure 9–6. Organic construction based on the cantilever system extends the Kaufman house as a continuation of the geological layers of rock on which it is built. House and setting become one entity, with no line of demarcation between. The Edgar Kaufman house, "Falling Water" at Bear Run, Pennsylvania. Architect: Frank Lloyd Wright, 1939. Photograph courtesy of Museum of Modern Art.

Man and Architecture

As important as civic and ecclesiastical architecture may be, nothing is more expressive of a civilization than its homes. Here the individual spirit of man is nurtured and here he most truly manifests himself. Dr. Carl Jung, the eminent psychologist, has said that the individual life is the only *real* life.[1] Any group is the sum of the individuals who compose it and a civilization is creative only to the extent that the individual man resists the pressures of the mob. The interaction of a man with his environment is a phenomenon whose limits have never been conclusively established. We do know that man placed in congenial and inspiring surroundings is a different person than the same man when battling irritation and frustration. The inspired home is not a matter of matching period furniture or blending certain colors, but an intangible creation of an atmosphere in which the inhabitants can reach the stature of their fullest possibilities, socially, professionally, spiritually and, of course, physically.

The creation of an architectural design is a tremendous responsibility, yet it is one of the most rewarding fields for the designer. Human development is dependent upon its surroundings and the surroundings become a

[1] C. G. Jung, *The Undiscovered Self* (New York: The New American Library of World Literature, Inc., 1960), p. 22.

Figure 9–7. The organic form and gently flowing quality of the David S. Ingalls Hockey Rink at Yale University characterize it as one of the imaginative buildings of our time. The huge concrete arch forms the spine of the building, from which the roof is supported by cables, much like vertebrate structure in nature. New Haven, Connecticut. Architect: Eero Saarinen.

Figure 9–8. New forms express an age-old spirit in the chapel at the Air Force Academy in Colorado Springs. Seventeen tetrahedrons (figures with four triangular surfaces) rise to a height of 150 feet to make it the commanding structure of the Academy. Three separate chapels on two levels serve the needs of Catholic, Protestant, and Jewish cadets. Architects: Skidmore, Owings and Merrill.

matter of buildings: of schools and churches, of libraries and museums, of office buildings and hotels, and especially of homes. The town becomes the sum of its buildings and the distant cityscape is a silhouette of its dominant structures. The intellectual climate of a community can be judged almost immediately by whether its factories or its museums hold the more important locations, whether it has beautiful parks or extensive slum areas. The architectural designer has the opportunity to put his mark upon an entire area, to make a contribution that can change the lives of vast numbers of people. As Eero Saarinen, one of the outstanding twentieth-century architects, expressed it: "Architecture should fulfill man's need for shelter but it should also fulfill his belief in the nobility of his existence on earth."

In planning any building the architectural designer is bound by at least four considerations: function, site, climate and environment. We know that *function* is the fundamental factor in any design. In designing a house, however, function can become a complicated matter. Shelter from weather and protection from insects and intruders are, of course, the basic functions of any house, from the primitive cave to the most elaborate mansion. Beyond these elemental considerations, however, the function of a house becomes an intensely personal thing. One person wants to use his home as a center for entertaining while another who works with people all day may desire a quiet retreat. The artist will want a home that can serve as his studio, where he can work uninterrupted at any hour of the day or night. A doctor or mortician may need his attached to his office, and will expect to have his patients or clients coming to consult him at all hours. It requires a diagnostician as well as an artist to design a home.

The Public Health Association recommends minimum sizes to fulfill physical needs for space within a home. One person requires only 400 square feet with two needing 750 and three 1000. A family of four should have at least 1150 square feet and a family of five 1400.[2] In addition to the requirements for physical space, every design needs attention to natural rhythms. The rhythm of the seasons dictates placement and landscaping. The daily rhythms of waking and sleeping must be considered in arrangements for light and air. The rhythm of family growth and development must enter into the over-all design. Through all of the stages of family development provision must be made for the rhythms of activity and rest, sickness and vitality, entertainment and contemplation, with care for man's physiological and psychological cycles provided in both material conveniences and spiritual satisfactions.

In an ideal situation the *site* will be determined by the function of the building, although this is not always possible. Frequently the client possesses a piece of land before he decides to build upon it, in which case the architect must adapt the building to its site. Such situations are a challenge and frequently result in unique designs. A group of young architects in southern California is meeting the crowded conditions by specializing in homes located on sites with a slope of fifty degrees or more. Not only does this utilize land formerly considered unusable, it creates highly individual houses.

Once the site has been established, *orientation* should be given primary consideration. Orientation may be described as *an interactive adaptation*

[2] American Public Health Association, Committee on the Hygiene of Housing, *Planning the Home for Occupancy* (Chicago: Public Administration Service, 1950), p. 36.

between house and land for the attainment of more healthful, comfortable, and attractive living. It means placing a picture window where it will command a view of scenery or a garden, instead of merely looking into the picture window of the house across the street. It means not putting large expanses of unshaded glass where they will catch the hottest sun on summer afternoons. It means locating bedrooms where they will have seclusion instead of facing on a busy thoroughfare. This stage necessitates the most important planning done by the designer.

Figure 9–9. Imaginative orientation to site means emphasizing existing characteristics that might be removed with less creative planning. Here a big boulder accents the entrance to a house in a mountainous area, setting the mood for its surroundings as well as serving to separate the carport, left, and the house. Concrete walks border a large grass terrace behind the boulder. Kenneth Norton house in Boulder, Colorado. Architect: James M. Hunter. Photographer: Warren Reynolds.

The more man can identify himself with natural surroundings the more at ease he will be in his leisure hours. Consequently, orientation involves making the best use of any existing natural attractions. A clump of trees, interesting boulders, a stream, a pond, or a view are all features that should determine the placement of the house and its external appearance. The use of an existing boulder to accent the entrance of a home built near the mountains is shown in Figure 9–9. While establishing the spirit of the setting the boulder serves as well to separate the house from the carport.

Both function and site orientation will be influenced to large degree by the third consideration of *climate*. The out-of-doors should be integrated into the total design in varying extent according to the kind of weather expected throughout the year. Naturally, the warmer climates are better suited to truly open architecture, although the feeling of openness can be achieved in regions of rain and snow by expanses of glass, if provision is made for adaptation by closing louvers or screens when the weather is bleak and by opening the glass to the full warmth of the sun when it is available.

Hot regions require special measures for controlling the climate by orientation. There are several ways in which this can be done. First, the sun should be kept off windows and walls to the greatest possible degree. Shading from the outside, trees, vines, or overhangs are all helpful. Second, light-colored materials should be used to reflect the sun rather than absorb it. A roof as close to white as possible is the best reflector of solar heat, and light walls are further protection. Third, air should be kept moving. Fans can be used to bring in outside air where advisable, and to circulate the air already inside. Controlled openings in walls and ceiling can admit cool evening air, forcing the day's accumulation of hot air to give way. Of course, in cases of extreme heat air-cooling systems are used with air circulation accomplished through ducts. Fourth, the use of water is helpful. Throughout the world, the fountain has been a fixture of the garden and town square, where the sound of splashing water serves to soothe and refresh all who listen, and when the water evaporates, actual coolness results.

Perhaps the ultimate accomplishment in adapting a building to its climate has been worked out in an experiment by architects who have built circular buildings which rotate gradually on an axis by the force of the sun's rays, thus providing solar heating within the building throughout the day. The heliodon is another development by architects to determine the angle of the sun's rays at any given time. Studies based on this and similar instruments can predetermine exactly what steps need to be taken for ultimate control of the various factors involved in climate.

While the term *environment* could be extended to include site and climate, we think of it more specifically as the immediate neighborhood in which a building is located. Once anyone has a definite idea of what he

Figure 9–10. Taliesin, showing master bedroom. Native stone and wood relate the structure to the rolling wooded Wisconsin hills of which it seems to become an integral part. Architect and owner: Frank Lloyd Wright. From *An American Architecture,* published by Horizon Press, Inc., New York 10, N.Y.

wants in a home, he must choose a site in a suitable environment; otherwise he may find himself limited by existing prejudices or even by zoning laws. For the most part, zoning laws are for the protection of the home owner, making it impossible for commercial or industrial buildings to plague a residential neighborhood. Some areas, however, are zoned according to the price range of homes to be built, some have restrictions on the style of building. In a hilltop area it is natural to expect zoning against two-story houses that would hide the view, while other sections may specify two-story homes.

Even without laws to set definite requirements, it is desirable to adapt a home to its social environment as well as to its physical surroundings. Generally speaking, nothing is gained by either side when a pretentious home is built in a modest neighborhood. The modest homes shrink in size and attractiveness and the larger one looks out of place and is in no way enhanced by its setting. Conversely, a small home built in the vicinity of imposing homes loses itself and detracts from the neighborhood rather than gains prestige from it. In either case, the concomitant psychological reactions of the inhabitants are obvious. Harmonious living is no closer than harmony of environment.

Two Classic Examples of Organic Architecture

The relationship of a house to its physical environment is the basis for the organic concept of domestic architecture. Classics in the tradition are the two homes Frank Lloyd Wright built for himself: Taliesin in Spring Green, Wisconsin (Figure 9–10), and Taliesin West in Scottsdale, Arizona.

Figure 9–11. Taliesin West, designed by Frank Lloyd Wright as his own home in Arizona, seems an outcropping of the desert more than a structure placed upon it. Photograph by J. F. Burshears.

Figure 9–12. The alliance of house and sun is dramatically displayed in this view of the interior of Taliesin West. Heavy stone piers give a feeling of cool protection yet let the sun pour in to cast ever-changing lights and shadows. Taliesin West at Scottsdale, Arizona. Architect and owner: Frank Lloyd Wright. Photograph by Hedrich-Blessing. From *An American Architecture,* published by Horizon Press, Inc., New York 10, N.Y.

The contrast of the two settings is striking, yet the same concept is applied to each house. Native materials were used to create a sense of naturalness, and the lines of the design complement the neighboring country to make an organic structure in harmony with its surroundings.

Wright spoke of the rolling green hills of Wisconsin in an intimate way, describing how they cradled Taliesin lovingly, and of the human scale of the landscape with its slow winding stream and pastoral beauty:

> . . . The buildings became a brow for the hill itself. . . . Then stone, stratified, went into the lower house walls and up from the ground itself into the broad chimneys. This native stone prepared the way for the lighter plastered construction of the upper wooden walls. Taliesin was to be an abstract combination of stone and wood as they naturally met in the aspect of the hills around about. And the lines of the hills were the lines of the roofs, the slopes of the hills their slopes, the plastered surfaces of the light wooden walls, set back into shade beneath broad eaves, were like the flat

> stretches of sand in the river below and the same in color, for that is where the material that covered them came from.[3]

Built in 1925, Taliesin still embodies many features of the finest houses being designed today.

Taliesin West (Figure 9–11), built thirteen years after Taliesin, has a more rugged setting with greater challenge. Any building designed for desert country must establish in the beginning its relationship to the sun. The first impulse is to construct a protective shelter where man can withdraw against the dazzling brightness and relentless heat. In this approach man builds in defiance of nature; he braces himself against it as a force to be resisted. In Taliesin West, however, nature is welcomed as an ally. Surfaces are broken into patterns to catch the sun, transforming it into endlessly changing lights and shadows and rendering it harmless. Here again, natural materials are used, stone from the desert outcroppings, wood from the nearby mountains, and the contour of the desert is continued in the lines of the house. Interior comfort is assured by deep overhangs and thick cool walls, yet the feeling of openness persists, creating a rhythmic interplay of light and space with coolness and protection (Figure 9–12). Light balances shadow, wood balances stone, and variety and unity are achieved by the imaginative use of materials relating to the setting.

As in most of Wright's architecture the emphasis is not on physical comfort. We know that his homes are eminently comfortable, but it is not the comfort of physical requirements alone. The importance of his designs lies in the creation of an atmosphere that nurtures both body and spirit. The soul of man is at ease with the materials of nature. It is free to soar out the windows into the trees or over the desert with the clouds and birds. There is no sense of retreat or resistance but a feeling of growth and development where a man can contemplate life's deepest meanings and reach out to find his own level.

This organic relationship of architecture to setting has been achieved in other widely differing sections of the country. Figure 9–13 shows a home built on a promontory overlooking Puget Sound and the Olympic Mountains west of Seattle. Here the problem is one of catching a breath-taking view without succumbing to the glare of sun and water, of dealing with wind and rain from the southwest without blocking out the feeling of kinship with the out-of-doors. Glass areas face the view but with deep overhangs, while vertical cedar walls protect the southwest side from the onslaught of the elements. Materials are native woods and no attempt is made to effect a modern formula by use of stone where the design does not require it. The simplicity of the walls and plantings shows an interest in Japanses forms quite in keeping with this area where Japanese fishing floats wash upon the beaches and Japanese ships dock regularly in the ports.

[3] Edgar Kaufmann, *An American Architecture, Frank Lloyd Wright* (New York: Horizon Press, 1955), p. 190.

Figure 9–13. Overlooking Puget Sound and the jagged peaks of the Olympic Peninsula, echoing its environment with cedar siding and accents of stone, this home reflects integration of architecture with surroundings. Even the plantings suggest the fact that the Orient is easily accessible, as well as the mountains with their slopes of pine and rhododendron. The David Stimson house. Architect: Paul Thiry. Photographer: Charles R. Pearson.

Importance of the Floor Plan

Obviously, no home is better than its floor plan. The arrangement of space for convenience and efficiency is as important as any other consideration. The home is, after all, a base of operations where cooking, washing dishes, laundry, and food storage must all be provided for, as well as the care of lawn and garden and the making of repairs. Such operations will be routine or time-consuming depending upon the placement of equipment and its proximity to related activities.

In general, a home may be divided into five specific areas: living; cooking; laundry and work areas such as sewing, indoor gardening or carpentry; sleeping, dressing and bathing; and storing. The relative importance of each area will depend upon the habits and tastes of the inhabitants.

A plan must "work" from the esthetic standpoint as well as from the aspects of utility. The placement of baths in full view of the living areas may save steps but certainly does not produce a gracious atmosphere. A bedroom may be quiet, but if it overlooks garbage cans it fails to achieve its fullest function as a place for pleasant relaxation. So many of the unattractive aspects of contemporary life are the result of situations that could have been eliminated or vastly improved with intelligent analysis and careful planning.

A study of Paul Thiry's floor plan for the Stimson house (Figure 9–14) shows an abstract design as well as a working drawing. Look at the division of space without thinking of rooms, and imagine the various areas filled in with color and texture. The design could stand by itself with no relationship to utility. This is true of any good floor plan. Emphasis is placed on the large area forming the living room and the surrounding terrace which lends an accent. Balance is achieved by the extension forming the kitchen, breezeway, and garage which counteracts the heavier more intricate area containing the bedrooms. The predominant feeling is one of variety with larger areas progressing in transition to smaller ones. Rhythm and unity are created by openings in the walls, providing a feeling of circulating, flowing space.

Now look at the plan from the standpoint of utility. The living room is at the back of the house and can be entered from the front only through the entry hall. This protects it from unwanted callers, from the driveway and outside activity, lends a touch of suspense to anyone entering the house from the front and centers its interest on the view to the back with its sweeping lawns stretching to the sound and the mountains. It is not necessary to cross the living room to get to any other room although the adjoining den can be entered from it as well as from the hallway leading to the bedroom. The den forms a buffer between the living area and the isolated bedroom wing where privacy and quiet are assured. At the opposite side of the living room, the dining room, kitchen, laundry, and garage extend one beyond the other, in that order. The dining room is easily served from the kitchen, and the laundry, while separated from the kitchen by a covered breezeway, can be supervised while work is being done in the kitchen. There is easy access to the service yard and the location of the recreation room downstairs keeps all of the areas of possible noise in one end of the house. All of the rooms take advantage of the view, except for two smaller bedrooms ostensibly designed to serve as children's rooms. Taken strictly as a floor plan, the design is as successful as it was when viewed as an abstraction, and one feels that the opportunity to move and live in the house in all its dimensions would be an infinitely satisfying experience.

Figure 9–14. Floor plan of the Stimson house. Architect, Paul Thiry.

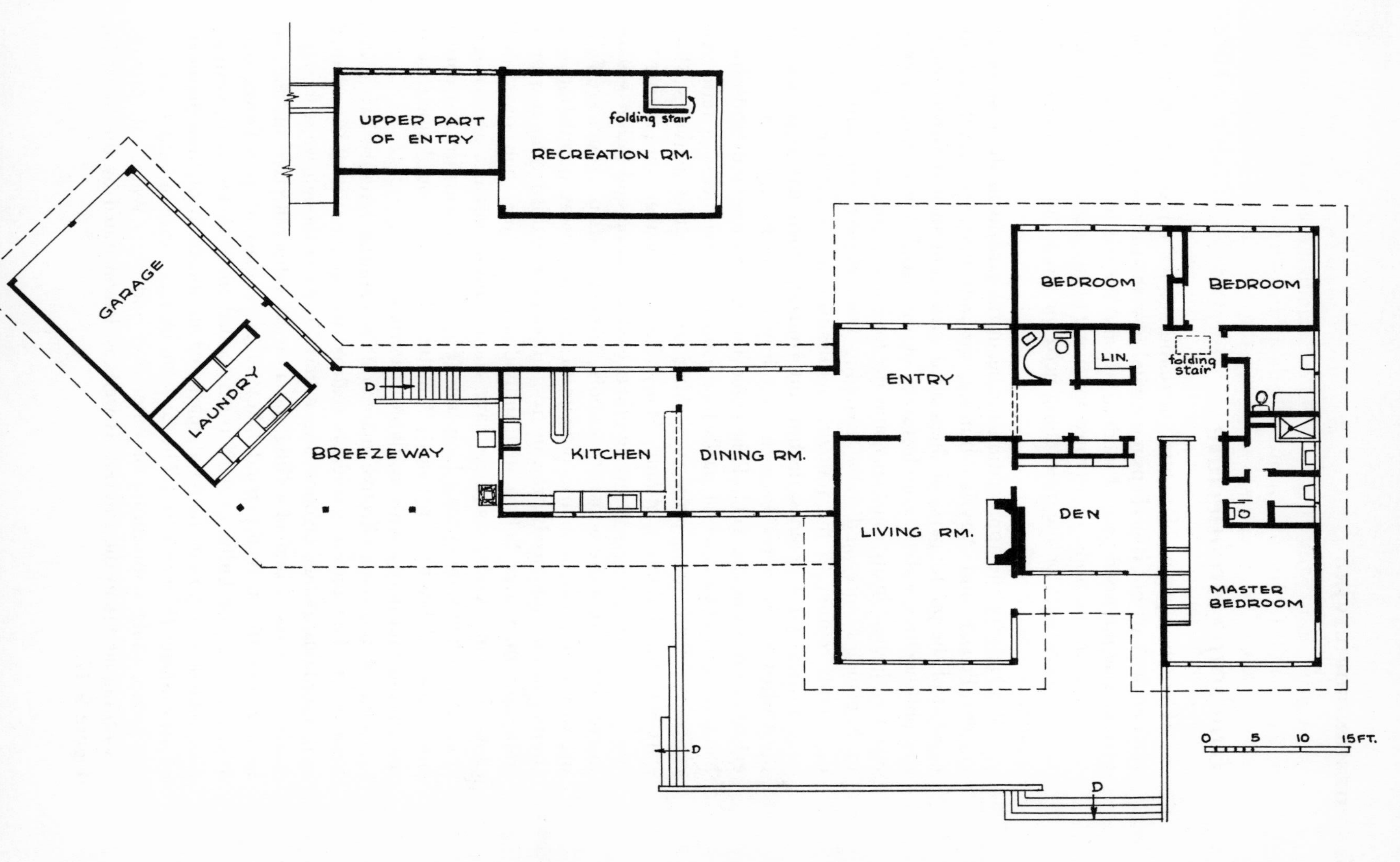
UPPER PART OF ENTRY
folding stair
RECREATION RM.
GARAGE
LAUNDRY
D
BREEZEWAY
KITCHEN
DINING RM.
ENTRY
LIN.
folding stair
BEDROOM
BEDROOM
LIVING RM.
DEN
MASTER BEDROOM
0 5 10 15FT.
D
D

Landscape Architecture

The development of natural surroundings for relaxation and beauty is an ancient art but is perhaps more vital now than it has been at any past period. The increased pace of modern life and the rise in population which keeps man in the midst of a crowd for many of his waking hours are only two of the reasons for the quickening need for serene surroundings during leisure.

We know of the appreciation for beautiful gardens in the past, of the ancient Persian and Assyrian hunting grounds that first developed the concept of the public park, of the shaded gardens of ancient Greece where the philosophers walked and lectured, of the arcaded patios of Moorish Spain with their many fountains, and the long history of gardens and villas in England, France, and Italy, changing from clipped formality in the eighteenth century to the romantic naturalism of the nineteenth. These were gardens on a grand scale but unfortunately their day is passing. In the United States, today, even the public parks are having a struggle for existence. Washington, D.C., long noted for its planning and landscaping, has lost nearly 600 acres of parks to so-called improvements, a term generally used for housing projects, parking areas, and other activities which start with the bulldozing of land. Many cities have garages on parking lots where city parks used to be, while others have lost parks and public squares to everything from fire houses to schools. Aroused citizens' groups are fighting to retain parks in many communities but the rising population continues and the civic needs press in from all sides. For this reason it is more important than ever before that individuals landscape their own small plots of ground. Older countries have known the importance and satisfaction of such landscaping for a long time (Figure 9–15). Turning any corner into a place of beauty is primarily a matter of imagination, knowledge of design and familiarity with available materials.

One of the most effective materials for creating serenity has always been water. The ancient gardeners realized its therapeutic value and used it in fountains, ponds, lagoons, and waterfalls. Even though we work on a smaller scale the sound of falling water or its calm reflective surface can be available to us. A lily pond takes no more space than a flower bed. Waterfalls can be built up with rocks hauled in from the mountains or constructed of a porous material marketed in the form of huge boulders of little weight (Figure 9–16). The flow can be taken care of with a circulating pump, using a minimum of water over and over. Water can provide a soothing accent to the interior as well, as demonstrated by the fountain, Figure 9–17.

Figure 9–15. The people of southern countries have long appreciated the value of secluded spots of beauty for refreshment of the spirit. Patio of the College of Roses at Morella, Mexico. Photograph by J. F. Burshears.

Figure 9–16. A pond and waterfall such as this can be built in a small area, providing beauty of sight and sound. Photograph by Maynard Parker. Courtesy of *House Beautiful.*

When soil will not grow lush vegetation, a spot of beauty is possible through the use of stones and gravel. Notice in Figure 9–18 the variety found in texture, the balance of a few simple plants with the forms of rocks, and the unity achieved by careful placement of forms in repetition. The succulent plants in the right foreground repeat the green forms of the cactus in the background and the total effect is one of restfulness and beauty.

There are many ways of achieving privacy even on a city lot. Hills can be constructed of earth to hide the view of traffic or of neighbors' yards. Plantings and fences or walls can achieve a sense of complete isolation even though the sidewalk may be only a few feet away. By balance in planting, variety in foliage, and a careful leading of the eye toward dominant areas of wooded solitude, the effect of remoteness can be created in the midst of the busiest city. The clamor of traffic becomes muffled by the foliage, and the sounds of falling water push the less desirable noises into the background, creating an atmosphere where even the busiest life can find an occasional moment of refreshment.

Figure 9–17. An atrium fountain plays cheerfully against a background of chased copper mounted on old wood. Designed and executed by Irv Burkee. From the collection of E. F. Armstrong in Aspen, Colorado. Photograph by Bonnie Burkee.

Figure 9–18. A touch of beauty is possible with only a suggestion of growing things so long as attention is given to shapes, textures, and unity of design. Entrance plaza of The First National Bank of Fort Worth, Texas.

FOR FURTHER EXPLORATION

The Natural House by Frank Lloyd Wright (New York: Horizon Press, Inc., 1954). Wright's beliefs and teachings presented informally and with illustrations.

Masters of Modern Architecture by John Peter (New York: George Braziller, Inc., 1958). A photographic survey of some of the outstanding architectural works of our time by thirty-eight leading architects.

Architecture as Space: How to Look at Architecture by Bruno Zevi translated by Milton Gendel (New Horizon Press, Inc., 1957). An excellent discourse on architecture as distinct from the other arts, dealing with the architecture of the past, the present, and emphasizing the fourth dimension of time.

Space, Time and Architecture: The Growth of a New Tradition by Siegfried Giedion (Cambridge, Mass.: Harvard University Press, 1949). An important work incorporating study of the architecture of the past with an analysis of twentieth-century styles.

STUDIO PROJECTS

1. To get a fuller understanding of the relationship between two-dimensional and three-dimensional design draw in pencil on a large sheet of heavy white paper your own design for a house of any size, using the scale ½ inch = 1 inch. Give careful consideration to the use of space, the esthetic aspects of the manner of entry and location of rooms. When you are satisfied with the practical operation of the plan, think of it as an abstract design, filling in the various rooms with colors and textures in tempera or oil paint, keeping in mind the principles of emphasis, balance, repetition, and unity. If the abstract design seems lacking in some way make the necessary adjustments and analyze how the changes would affect the working floor plan.

2. To develop further the concept of space, make a model based on the floor plan above using illustration board or other heavy cardboard or plywood. As the rooms develop, concentrate on the flow of space from area to area, thinking of the entire structure as a manipulation of space to practical and esthetic purposes. Mount the model on a large board and continue the flow of space into landscaping, letting the exterior and interior space combine into a single entity.

CHAPTER 10

Design for Environment

If the neighborhood is the environment for the home, the interior of the home becomes the intimate environment of all who live there. Everything that the architect strives to accomplish in creating a setting for the individual comes to a climax in a well-designed interior. Architecture and interior design are not only closely related, in actuality they are the same thing. Together they comprise the creative effort whose primary objective is the composition of beautiful space.

The Organic Approach to Interior Design

The organic concept of the interior involves creating an environment which will express the total personality of the people who live within it. Although the elements and principles of design are used extensively in any well-designed home, there is one basic principle which becomes the keynote. *Any successful home expresses its occupants.* Interior decoration is concerned with expression through furnishings, but interior design involves not only the furnishings but the structure, the environment, the experiences, and personalities of the people within.

Four Kinds of Integration

Integration of Structure with Interior Design

Perhaps the most obvious keynote of organic architecture is the honest treatment of structural elements as part of the interior design of the home.

Figure 10–1. The feeling of warmth in this living room results from extensive use of wood, and the exposed ceiling joists are an important factor. The large windows are another structural feature that contributes to the decorative design. The Fisher residence in Hollywood. Architect: John Lautner. Photograph by Julius Shulman.

In Figure 10–1, for instance, the redwood ceiling joists not only contribute to the appearance of the interior but they serve to carry the eye outward where the redwood is continued in an overhang sheltering the patio. The use of wood is repeated in the wall paneling and the bookshelves, and the forthright regard for structure is continued in the fireplace in which concrete blocks make no attempt at disguise. The structure of this house is not something to be sheathed or veneered but plays an important part in the furnishings, contributing warmth and attractiveness.

Integration of Interior with Landscape

Another aspect of organic design lies in the integration of indoor and outdoor living areas. This is important today for two reasons. First, with the population increasing and available space decreasing it is essential that we make the best possible use of any space at our disposal. This means not only utilizing indoor areas but extending our living into the surrounding landscape. Second, the enjoyment of a home can be multiplied many times by expanding the activities of living into a natural outdoor environment. Breakfast on a terrace, barbecue on a patio, badminton or croquet on the lawn, and even a relaxing view from a window all add to the pleasures of living and contribute to a family's well-being. In Figure 10–2 we see the correlation possible in a modest home with a small plot of land. The chief factor in the indoor-outdoor relationship here is the use of glass for walls separating interior and patio. With the dividing wall thus invisible, every foot of outdoor space is developed for the specific purpose of extending the living area within. Textures of rug and planting harmonize, with accents of planting brought within. Forms of garden beds and coffee table follow the same organic or *biomorphic* lines, and the wood of floors and walls continues outward to form decking and garden screens dividing the property from adjoining yards. No great amount of space is involved here, either indoors or out, but nothing is wasted. Man is related to nature instead of being closed within his shelter, and his experience is extended to the enjoyment of earth and sky and the changing seasons.

The integration of indoors and out can be carried into a further dimension by creative use of lighting. We have become familiar in recent years with many variations of lighting effects, ranging far from the traditional over-all lighting from a central chandelier. Indirect lighting from behind window valances bathes the interior in a soft glow, heightening the effect of the furnishings and causing intriguing changes in the colors of walls and fabrics. Suffused lighting from recessed fixtures in the ceiling dramatizes furniture groupings. The effects of light can be carried outward by lights places under the soffits outside the windows, by spotlighting in the

Figure 10–2. Harmonious integration of indoor and outdoor areas is achieved by indoor use of redwood in paneling and beams and outdoor use in deck and garden screens. The large window relates living room and patio while the organic form of the coffee table echoes the shapes of planted beds and rug texture carries through to the plantings. Architect: Ward Thomas. Photographer: Phil Palmer. Courtesy of California Redwood Association.

garden, or by detail lighting placed strategically among the shrubbery. With movement of breeze the shadows change continually and when there is a pond or waterfall the combination of light, shadow, and reflection become a fascinating play which opens the mind to new horizons of contemplation and relaxation.

Integration of Periods and Interests

The Importance of Taste. Taste is a quality that permeates all of our activities, from the records we collect to the things we say, but nowhere is it more apparent than in our home furnishings. These are the materials with which we build our personal environment, the base of operations to which we return for reinforcement and sustenance. Taste is an acquired trait, built and refined through years of observing, studying, and analyzing the beautiful things of the world. There are four specific ways in which it can be developed:

1. By seeking constantly for beauty; by exposure whenever possible to beautiful surroundings, and by studying museums, books, and magazines.
2. By delving into other cultures to widen experience and appreciation.
3. By gaining an understanding of history and philosophy so that artistic expressions will have meaning and depth.
4. By constant awareness of and sensitivity to our own environment with a continuing desire to improve it.

When an individual embodies his taste in the design of a home, it usually involves many influences. Mementos from travels, antiques, or family heirlooms, and treasured gifts all have their associations. When studying the homes of people who have lived full and interesting lives, we rarely find these homes limited to one style or period; they are more apt to be a rich mixture of varying influences, blended together by the force of each owner's personality. This is the integration of time and interest that makes possible the complete expression of an individual.

Such an expression is found in the bedroom in Figure 10–3. Against a background of modern furniture, Aztec and Incan pottery and other objects make a colorful display. Instead of disintegrating into clutter the consolidation of the collection creates unity and the dark tones of the walls form a rich and unobtrusive background which brings out the best in the pieces themselves. There is a span of nine centuries between the objects of art and the furniture in this room yet the texture of the carpet, the simple lines, and the coordination of colors blend the various elements into a unified design.

Integration of Sensory Responses

The organic approach to interior design creates a pervading atmosphere which involves all of man's senses. The *eyes* respond to the colors, shapes, forms, and textures as well as to the principles of balance, emphasis, rhythm and unity. The *ears* are affected by the acoustics which may cause sounds to echo or be muted. The furnishings can control the way ordinary sounds are transmitted just as the placement of components affects the reception of stereophonic sound. The *smells* of building materials, fabrics, rugs, and the woods of furniture have a potent effect on reactions to our environment. These elusive scents are heightened or overpowered by the odors of living, from cooking, from wood burning in the fireplace, or from cigarette or pipe smoke hanging in the air. The textures of walls and furnishings become *tactile* as well as visual experiences to people living with them: the feel of the fabric on a chair, the roughness of the stone of the fireplace, the smooth finish of the wood paneling or of a table. Even the *taste* is affected by the general atmosphere created. Foods taste better in a congenial relaxed environment, where the sights, sounds, and smells contribute to the anticipation and enjoyment of eating. Beyond all of these there is a sense of well-being that comes from living in surroundings where the spirit moves freely in attractive space involving rooms and surrounding landscape.

Figure 10–3. This man's bedroom greatly increases its versatility and interest by housing a collection of Aztec and Incan objects, yet there is no feeling of clutter or restlessness. From *House & Garden*. Copyright © 1957, 1960 by The Condé Nast Publications, Inc.

A Sense of Timelessness

When a home is integrated in these four ways it achieves a sense of timelessness that makes it impervious to change. This does not mean that it is static. Any successful room adapts to the expanding tastes of its occupants, and occasional changes in color or a piece of furniture are refreshing. Nevertheless, a skilled handling of the elements and principles of design can place a home beyond the limiting boundaries of changing fashion.

Such a home is seen in Figure 10–4. Although designed by Frank Lloyd Wright in 1940, no detail marks it as having been designed in any particular decade. We note that much of the furniture is built-in, becoming a part of the architecture. Wright used this practice to express his belief in the unity of buildings and furnishings. To carry the integration further, he designed a line of tableware, linens, and accessories specifically coordinated with the homes he designed.

Because Wright did believe so strongly in the unity of buildings and furnishings, he sometimes refused to design a house unless he could specify the furnishings to go in it, feeling that this was the only way he could be certain of achieving the flexible timeless quality which characterizes his homes.

In this house we have a strong impression of balance. The textures of used brick and carpeting balance the smooth polished surfaces of the built-in shelves and tables. The horizontal lines of ceiling, bricks, and furniture give a sense of serenity broken only by the occasional vertical of doors, windows, and fireplace wall. Rhythm is achieved by the *repetition* of the brick and natural wood textures and by the *emphasis* on the fireplace as the center of interest. Variety comes from the three basic textures combined with plants and objects of art. There is nothing superfluous or meaningless. The unity that permeates the room emanates from the use of natural materials throughout as well as from the repetition of specific textures. This is a room where one could read, listen to music, talk with friends or doze by the fire, a place to remember with pleasure during times of stress. It is a room that is not dependent upon fashionable colors or current trends, that will remain in good taste through innumerable generations of changing fashions.

Figure 10–4. An interior, contemporary in feeling but expressing a timeless quality—not a period but a way of life. A wide variety of treasures could be at home in this room without destroying its basic unity. The Lewis House. Architect: Frank Lloyd Wright. Photograph by Hedrich Blessing. From *An American Architecture,* published by Horizon Press, Inc., New York.

Figure 10–5. New uses of traditional materials result in refreshing designs particularly suited to the informality of contemporary life. Here the grain and luster of oiled walnut and oiled teak are combined with satin chromium legs to create a coffee table of classic lines but distinctly modern feeling. Photograph courtesy of Herman Miller, Inc., Zeeland, Michigan.

Contemporary Furniture Design

Much of our contemporary furniture is designed with this sort of timelessness in mind. One of the most important trends is found in furniture such as the coffee table in Figure 10–5. Although this is of Danish modern influence, it shows restraint and adaptability which enable it to fit into interiors touched by other styles as well. In fact, the combination of traditional woods with satin-finish chromium seems to bridge the chasm between period and modern furnishings in a style that holds to the best in both. The teak and walnut are oiled to bring out the grain and to supply a *patina,* or finish, that we associate with old and well-loved pieces. The chromium is softened to the luster of old pewter, yet the lines are smooth and the lack of ornamentation gives it the simplicity typical of the best modern pieces.

This versatility is evident in chair design as well. Where the so-called modern furniture of the nineteen-twenties stressed streamlining and shiny surfaces, furniture today uses woods and textiles which contribute textural interest. The chair in Figure 10–6 has an organic form that relaxes and supports the body, yet there is nothing clinical in its design. Here again, oiled teak is used for warmth with an interesting textile forming an accent in upholstery.

Actually, the simplicity admired today is not far removed from the influences of the past. A careful study of Figure 10–7 will show much of the same honesty of design and beauty of proportion that is stressed by contemporary artists. These characteristics have a sound basis in history, not only in Colonial American furnishings but farther back through the periods of the great cabinetmakers to the early Greek and Egyptian tables and couches. This is the reason for strong emphasis on historical knowledge in the training of any interior designer.

Figure 10–6. Upholstered side chair of teak reflects the contemporary feeling of simplicity and exploits materials. Designed by Danish architects Hridt and Mølgaard. Courtesy of John Stuart, Inc.

Functional Planning

Regardless of how attractive the furnishings may be, the design for a home is not successful unless it fulfills the various functions for which it is intended. As in architecture, each individual family must be analyzed as to its tastes and needs in order to establish these functional needs in the designer's mind. Whether the home is a one-room apartment or a mansion there are six phases to be considered.

1. *Deciding upon the spirit of the home.* This will depend largely upon whether the home is to be a center for entertaining or a retreat from a busy world. The decision will affect the choice of colors, textures and furniture as well as the way in which they are used. A room for entertaining may have warmer, livelier colors and more pattern than a retreat, which would require a feeling of restfulness. The textures may be coarser for hard wear or smoother as represented by more formal furnishings. The furniture should adapt to varied use and be placed to accommodate more people. Each room should have its individual spirit as well. Bedrooms may be study rooms, sitting rooms, or strictly for sleeping. Baths may be dainty, virile, or whimsical depending upon their location and the tastes of their occupants. Examples of both types are seen in Figure 10–8. The kitchen, especially, has propensities for wide variation, whether planned as a family room or as a laboratory.

2. *Pinpointing the needs and wishes of the occupants.* In order to express the occupant, a home must be designed to function according to his needs, tastes, and aspirations. It is important to consider not only such matters as the size of closets and the number of baths but the individual dreams which make a home distinctive and a true answer to all the owner's desires. This may mean a view from a dining-room window, a sunken bathtub, a patio off the children's rooms, or a big window over the kitchen sink. It could indicate a special kind of workshop in which to pursue a favorite hobby. It might well be a matter of a special color of carpet. All of these things should be listed and given careful consideration.

3. *Organizing allotted space according to these needs.* Choices are the expression of the individual, forming the warp from which an individual life is woven. Where a home is already built the space is distributed, but it is not necessarily specified as to how it will be used. The floor plans in Figure 10–9 give an idea of how flexible one basic plan can be, for in this case the same space is adapted to the needs of three different families. Family (a) has three small children who use the smaller rooms as bedrooms. The room between kitchen and living room becomes a family room with dining area at one end, and other activities including television available

Figure 10–7. The dignity and simplicity of contemporary furnishings is apparent as well in this eighteenth-century interior from Colonial Williamsburg. The hoop-backed Windsor chairs with their turned backs and saddle seats, the high chest and gateleg table, and the paneled door are all examples of a heritage that can teach us much about proportion. Courtesy of Colonial Williamsburg.

where the mother can keep an eye on the family from the kitchen. In Family (b) there is one child of school age. The family room becomes a dining room and the farthest bedroom converts to a study for the father. With this retreat available, it is possible to move the television into the living room which becomes a center for family activity. Family (c) consists of two parents of grown children. The family room–dining room now becomes a workshop where the husband can work near the kitchen without creating disorder in the rest of the house. The study becomes a guest room for the children coming home, and the small bedroom is a sewing room for the wife. A dining area is built into the kitchen. These are just three possible arrangements. If a family has special needs such as a studio, a dark room, or an office for a dentist or doctor, these could also be fitted into this basic plan. The dining room could be blocked off from the living room and used as a utility room. It could be closed off from the kitchen and used as a library. With the exception of the kitchen and bathroom with their permanent fixtures, the adaptability of given space need be limited only by imagination and the family's needs.

4. *Selecting colors, fabrics, and furnishings on the basis of use, appropriateness, and beauty.* This can be one of the most satisfying and most trying of the phases of interior design, for the choices involved determine to a large extent the entire feeling of the interior. The use of light colors can make a room seem larger while darker colors will lower the ceiling or make a large room small. Knubby textures reflect the feeling of bricks or fieldstone and printed fabrics can serve as accents for wide expanses of smooth walls. The scale of pattern in fabrics can do much to regulate the size of the room and its sense of activity or restfulness. Perhaps a panel of interesting wallpaper or a room divider in an unusual design are needed for accent. Should the carpet be solid or textured? This will depend upon the amount of design in the other furnishings. Would wallpaper or wood paneling be preferable? This choice may well affect the lightness of the room. These are a few of the many decisions which must be made on the basis of personal taste. Professional designers come to the job armed with large swatches of carpet or paint and drapery lengths of fabric, for no imigination is equal to the task of visualizing the effects of fabrics, colors, and textures upon one another. Even the bathroom can be varied by choice of material. Figure 10–10 displays the difference between plain floor and patterned walls and plain walls with patterned tile floor. Both are attractive but each expresses an individual preference.

5. *Choosing furniture to fulfill the expressed needs and wishes of the owner.* The function of each room should be the determining factor in the selection of furniture. A playroom requires sturdy pieces with hardy upholstery whereas bedrooms tend toward refinements. The relative importance of comfort and beauty have relegated more than one ample leather chair to the study while more graceful pieces are ensconced in the living room. The furniture cannot be chosen independently of the other furnishings but must be in harmony with the colors and textures which will surround it.

Figure 10–8. Two treatments of bathrooms showing the effects of different choices in pattern. (a) The use of wallpaper and draperies accents a plain design in the floor. Courtesy of the Kohler Company.

Figure 10–8. (b) The tile pattern in the floor provides the only accent for plain tiled surfaces and frosted windows. Courtesy of the Mosaic Tile Company. Photographer: Hans van Nes.

6. *Arranging furniture for comfort, attractiveness, and ease of circulation.* Once again, the function of the room contributes heavily to the decisions as to placement of furniture. Where much entertaining will take place, small groupings for conversation are important. There may also be centers for reading or listening to music or watching television. In each case, position of chairs in relation to lamps and tables is a first consideration. Essential, too, is the allowing of space for circulation. Every room should have a lane through which people can walk easily without the feeling of having to go *around* the furniture. Over-all circulation includes the ease of entry into the house proper and into the service entrance through which deliveries and repairs can be handled without crossing functioning areas.

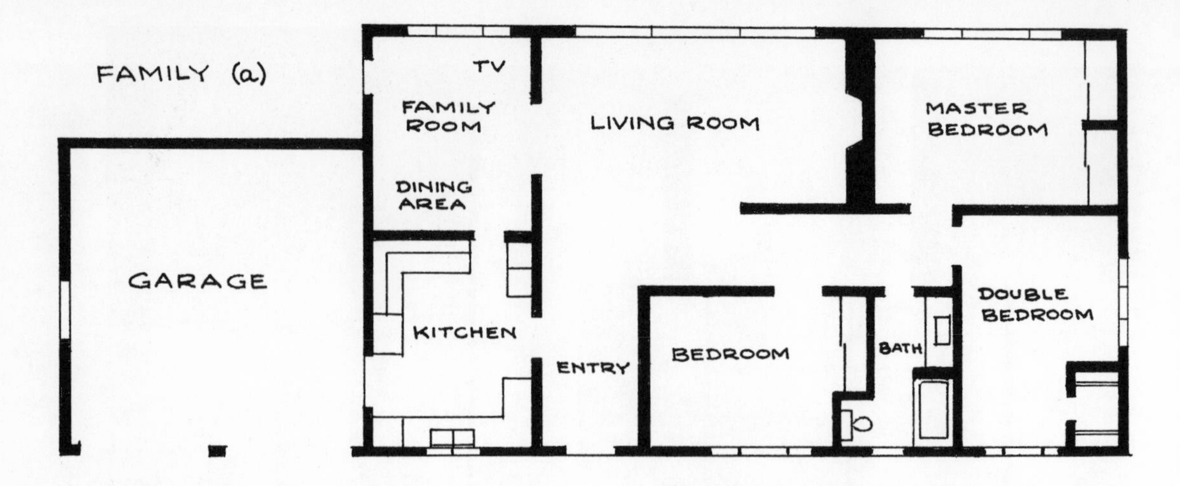

Figure 10–9. A basic plan adapted to three different families. Family (a) has three small children.

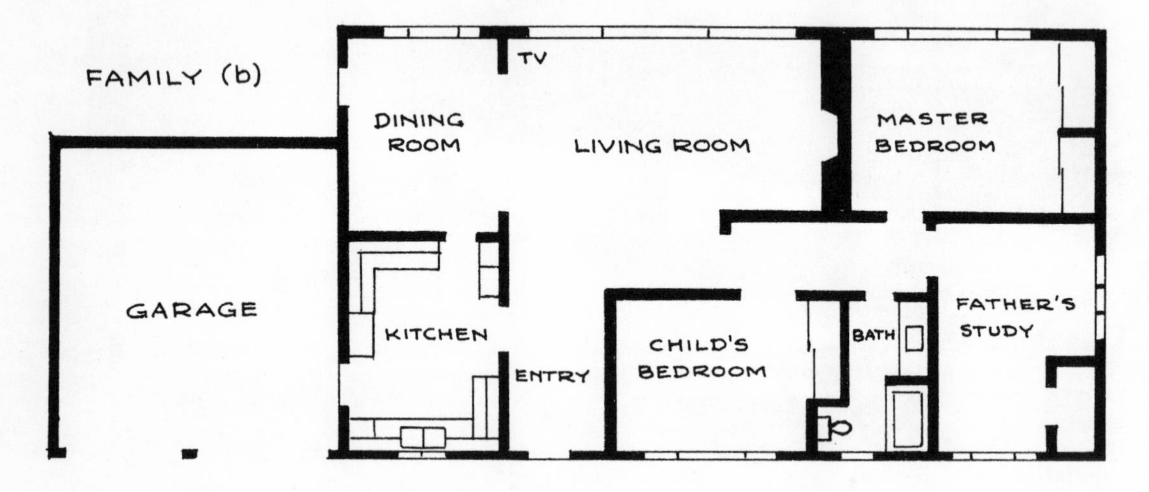

Family (b) has one school-age child, and family (c) has children who have grown up and moved away.

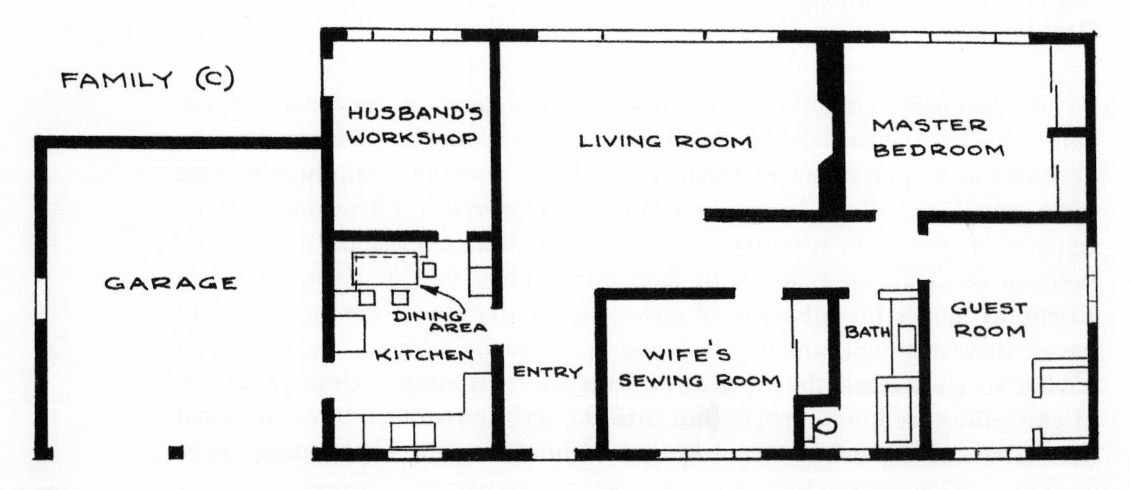

Figure 10–10. Two kitchens, equally attractive and equally efficient but expressing widely divergent points of view. Kitchen (a) is essentially a laboratory with nothing out of place and no extraneous decoration. From *House & Garden.* Copyright © 1957, 1960 by the Condé Nast Publications Inc.

Three Specific Problems

The Efficient Kitchen. To some people the kitchen is "the heart of the home" and should be warm, cheerful and cosy, while others think of it as a workshop where everything should first be neat, sanitary, and efficient. Examples of each type are shown in Figure 10–10a and b. With increasing numbers of homemakers working outside the home, the kitchen has become the object of considerable research directed toward conservation of time and energy. Functional planning involves many specific problems. It has been discovered that the most convenient arrangement is based on either an L-shaped or a U-shaped plan as shown in Figure 10–11. This makes possible the easy accessibility of the three basic work centers, the stove, the refrigerator, and the sink. Ample work surfaces and cupboard space supplement constantly improving appliances, cutting steps and motions until the time spent at cooking and clean-up has been diminished immeasurably.

Plans for Leisure-Time Activities. The increase of leisure time for working people as well as the lengthening of active later years has led to a trend toward more hobbies which, in turn, has emphasized the need for various kinds of work centers within the home. These may vary from woodworking shops to greenhouses, pottery workshops, or sewing rooms. The primary consideration in any case must be ample floor and wall space not only for working in comfort but for storing equipment. Location should be off the line of traffic to minimize the effects of clutter and to facilitate the actual work and transfer of equipment and materials in and out. This may well be one of the most important areas in the home of the future.

Effective Storage Space. Perhaps the greatest aid to the smooth functioning of a home is adequate storage space. This is not always so much a matter of a great deal of space as it is of efficient planning. Cupboard space should not be a haphazard matter. The most effective storage is space planned specifically for certain objects. Music and records require quite different areas from picnic baskets or film projectors and there should be no need to try to interchange them.

Many activities connected with daily living can be chores or pleasures depending upon the facilities provided. Such an instance could be cited in connection with Figure 10–12. Here all of the equipment for wrapping packages is assembled in one spot for quick and convenient use. When not in use the area is hidden behind attractive plastic-covered panels which also conceal compartments for blankets, pillows, and linens. Although such a wall requires a depth of at least eighteen inches, the sacrifice of room space is well compensated for by the benefits in organization and efficiency.

Importance of Interior Design

The interior of a home is a complex design problem involving many decisions. Each room has its problems of color and texture, of balance and emphasis. Yet there is no creative problem more worthy of the effort and concentration involved. A beautiful interior affects everyone who comes in contact with it, adding something to his satisfaction and pleasure and his consciousness of the dignity to be found in living. The use of genuine materials instills a sense of integrity and respect for honesty. Cheerful colors and an inspiring view give courage to face the problems that lie beyond. Appreciation of other cultures broadens understanding and endows an interested and open outlook. More important, a depth of spirit develops where the things of the spirit are nourished and considered important. The interior of a home not only *reflects* the individuals who live there; more than any other influence it molds and shapes them, determining their relationships with the world beyond their walls.

Figure 10–10. Kitchen (b) has a warmth that makes it inviting not only for homemaking chores but for lingering and visiting as well. Photograph courtesy of St. Charles Custom Kitchens, St. Charles, Illinois.

Figure 10–11. The most efficient kitchens are usually a variation of the U or L shape with all main appliances within reach by means of a few steps.

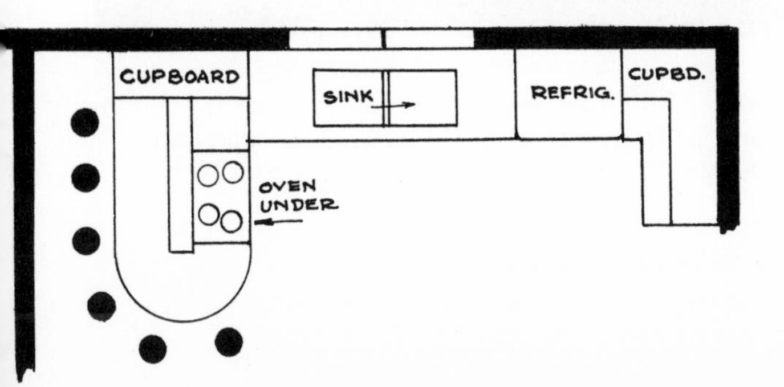

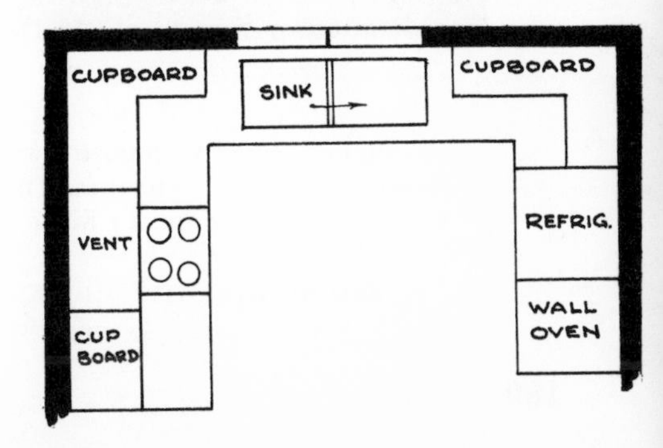

Figure 10–12. A center for wrapping packages with plenty of materials at hand transforms a chore into a pleasure. The desk can be concealed behind the sliding panels when not in use. Photograph by Maynard Parker. Courtesy of *House Beautiful.*

FOR FURTHER EXPLORATION

The Art of Interior Design by Victoria Kloss Ball (New York: The Macmillan Company, 1960). An excellent text on all aspects of interior design.

Inside Today's Home by Ray Faulkner (New York: Holt, Rinehart and Winston, Inc., 1954). A discussion of the elements necessary to the design of an attractive home. An excellent text.

New Horizons in Color by Faber Birren (New York: Reinhold Publishing Corp., 1961). A complete handbook written especially for architects, interior designers and others who work directly with color.

The Practical Book of Period Furniture by Harold Donaldson Eberlein and Abbot McClure. (Philadelphia: J. B. Lippincott Co., 1914). A guidebook to period styles for the decorator or student.

STUDIO PROJECTS

1. From a magazine, clip a photograph of a single art object or piece of furniture that might be used as the keynote for a living room. Establish the correct period of the piece and then, referring to the text on color in history on page 85 and to any other reference at your disposal, determine how you would design the room around the object. Be careful to give the room a timeless and livable quality, not adhering to period too strictly, *suggesting* the original setting rather than attempting to reproduce it. Using two-point perspective, sketch the room in watercolor.

2. Using two-point perspective, sketch in watercolor a workroom for a specific hobby or interest. Under the sketch draw a floor plan using the scale $\frac{1}{2}$ inch equals 1 foot. Include all storage space.

3. To bring into focus your own ideas on interior design, keep a portfolio of clippings of rooms or details that you would like to have in a home for yourself. Make a floor plan and list each room with color scheme, chips of color, swatches of fabrics, and a notation about the pervading spirit of the room.

CHAPTER 11

Design in Pottery and Glass

THE FASCINATION OF CLAY IS OLDER THAN RECORDED HISTORY. The same instinct that makes children fashion mud pies must have moved primitive man to dig in the mud of the river banks, patting, rolling, molding, and shaping until he found he had created a vessel that could hold something. The thought that his actions would evolve into a process for fashioning some of the most beautiful objects in the world probably never occurred to him.

Development of Pottery

The discovery of clay led to fascinating explorations from the beginning. The earliest pots were patted and *pinched* into shape and left to dry in the sun. Later the clay was rolled into *coils* or ropes the diameter of a man's finger and laid coil on coil to form a wall, after which it was smoothed with a piece of shell or gourd. This method is used by the American Indian today and is the preferred method of many contemporary potters. Still another method discovered was the rolling or patting of clay into *slabs* from which pieces were cut and built into boxlike structures.

As pots grew more ambitious in size a piece of mat or woven basket was used for support to make it possible to hold the work up and survey the results from all angles as the potter progressed. Eventually, someone placed a pot on a smooth stone and found that it could be turned *while* working, making for uniform smoothness and symmetrical form. Thus emerged the *potter's wheel.* Wheels were arrived at independently by many

Figure 11–1. The potter and his creation become inseparable for those magic moments when every movement brings a corresponding modification in his work. Photograph by Bruce Roberts.

cultures and have ranged in variation from those turned by donkeys to the Renaissance version driven by a cord strung over a pulley. Today, with numerous kinds of electric wheels available, many potters still prefer the ancient method of propelling the wheel by moving the foot. Body and wheel work together relating physical and creative energy in one concerted operation during which hands and clay become almost indistinguishable until the final separation of creation and creator (Figure 11–1).

It is interesting to imagine what accident or trick of fate caused the first pot to fall into the fire and come out *bisque.* The increased durability of such ware and the fact that it would not melt when wet apparently were considered real improvements, for *firing* in an open fire became an accepted development.

There remained the matter of making vessels waterproof so that they could be used for holding liquids. Early man painted his fired ware with plant resins and animal fats, forming a protective coating. He decorated them with incised designs or outlines in clay of a contrasting color. We are not sure when the process of *glazing* was discovered but it, like firing, was undoubtedly an accident. We do know that it opened up one of the most fascinating fields of artistic endeavor, elevating pottery-making since the time of the Egyptians to the level of a true art (Figure 11–2).

The Nature of Clay

Clay is the very substance of the earth's crust, the result of weathering and change, a process that has taken place over the centuries through the action of ice and snow, wind and water, air and decomposition. It is fre-

Figure 11–2. Egyptian hippopotamus. Faience, Twelfth Dynasty. Courtesy of the Metropolitan Museum of Art, Gift of Edward S. Harkness, 1917.

Figure 11–3. Three bowls, varied in form but similarly honest in both structural and decorative design. Richard M. Lincoln, potter. Photograph by Bob Abey. Courtesy of Carlin Galleries, Forth Worth, Texas.

quently an accumulation of vegetable matter which has petrified and become feldspar, later to be converted into a bank of clay somewhere in a hillside. This variety, known as *residual* clay, has stayed in the same spot since its formation. Or it can be the product of many movements, of wind and storm and rushing streams which have carried it from its starting point and finally in a calmer moment deposited it in the bed of a lake or along the bank of a river. Such clay is worn fine by its adventures and it may pick up many fascinating colors. It is known as *sedimentary* clay. It may be red from iron, green or blue from copper content, white or gray or yellow depending upon its own individual history. It can be mixed together with other clays and left to age in damp crocks for weeks at a time, for clay, like wine and cheese, improves with aging.

Clay can be fired at a wide range of temperatures in a variety of kilns. The results of firing depend upon the origin and innate qualities of the clay itself. *Earthenware,* which fires at the lowest temperature of all the clays, has a heavy porous quality. It includes the "baked earth" known as *terra cotta,* which is used for sculpture and roof tile. *Stoneware,* which fires at a higher temperature, is a favorite of contemporary potters for its solidity and for its affinity for textured glazes. *China* is made from a combination of clays and is widely used in commercial pottery. *Porcelain* fires highest of all and is a specially prepared clay body which becomes extremely hard and vitreous as a result of firing. It contains *kao-lin,* Chinese for "high hill," the fine white clay originally loved by the Chinese. Each type of clay has its own unique personality challenging the potter to discover the most effective methods of expressing its creative qualities.

Structural Design

As in other design fields, structural design in pottery is concerned primarily with honesty of form. This does not imply limitation but rather an exploration of possibilities within the scope of an object's function. A bowl may be deep or shallow, large or small, curved out or in, as in Figure 11–3. It may be free form or geometric. It is only when it begins to look like something that it is not that we wonder whether there is justification in its structure. Ceramic bowls are not pineapples, cantaloupe or green leaves and the only reason for such resemblance is novelty. This, of course, has little to do with serious design. Honesty does not mean trite or unimaginative form, however. The jar in Figure 11–4 is as forthright as an Indian water jug yet it has a flair that makes it highly original. The combination of interesting structure and unusual textural treatment sets it apart as a piece of distinctive design.

Honesty of form also means honesty of function. Lids must fit, spouts must pour; cups, bowls, or pitchers must be balanced for sitting and for active use. Casseroles must be oven proof and teapots should have an escape vent for steam. Neither beauty of line nor subtlety of glaze is sufficient to compensate for a piece that does not serve its primary purpose.

Decorative Design

In pottery, decorative design is, to a large degree, part of the process of glazing. A glaze is actually a layer, or layers, of molten material fired on the clay, making the glaze part of the original clay but imparting color, texture, and design. Glazing is a fascinating example of chemistry which has had widely differing manifestations in cultures throughout the world. A glaze may be transparent, translucent, or opaque. It may be high-fire or low-fire. It may be mixed from a lead or an alkaline base. Some glazes are glossy, some matt, and some have interesting textures and speckles. The crackle, crystalline, and luster glazes all have distinctive characteristics. Glaze may be applied by brushing, dipping, or spraying, or it can be put

Figure 11–4. Pottery vase 19 inches high with simple forthright form and an imaginative use of texture. Richard M. Lincoln, potter. Photograph by Bob Abey. Courtesy of Carlin Galleries, Fort Worth, Texas.

on with stencils to form patterns. With so many possibilities it is not surprising that the centuries have provided a sparkling variety of outstanding glazes.

Historic Examples

The Chinese are known as the world's greatest potters and several of their glazes are especially noteworthy. The rich *Ming blue* which we associate with much of their porcelain resulted from the use of cobalt which the potters of the Ming period found would endure the high temperature needed to melt their glazes. Cobalt is still an effective colorant but it is difficult to procure since the advent of the cobalt bomb.

Celadon is another glaze that we associate with Chinese porcelain. It consists of a porcelain or semi-porcelain body of gray-white with a thick translucent glaze varying from gray and blue-green to sea green and grass green. It is produced by firing black oxide of iron under reduction, in which extraneous material is burned in the kiln to *reduce* the amount of oxygen, thus producing unusual effects on the chemicals in the glazes. The *sang de boeuf,* or ox blood, widely used by Chinese potters is also a product of reduction, using red oxide of copper. The Chinese used other glazes combined with elaborate designs (Figure 11–5). *Cloisonné* is a combination glaze and mosaic technique that is seen in much Chinese work. Small areas of glaze are separated by gouging, applying clay-coil ridges or by carving grooves which are filled with contrasting glaze. The usual method of separation is by thin strips of brass which give a rich linear unity to the all-over design.

Majolica is a ware made by many potters today, yet it has elements of European history and geography in its background. It is earthenware coated with a glaze containing tin oxide which gives an opaque white background on which is painted a design in metallic oxides. The name is derived from a process used in the fifteenth century for wares exported to various countries in Majorcan trading ships. It was mistakenly supposed to have been made in Majorca, when actually it was a product of the early Renaissance in Italy. Designs have varied in different periods, from fruit and arabesques to complicated pictorial subjects (Figure 11–6).

Faience is a more involved type of majolica originating in Faenza and Florence in the late sixteenth century and later blossoming in France where

Figure 11–5. Chinese porcelain vase of the K'ang Hsi Period (1662–1722). Seeded green ground. Courtesy of the Metropolitan Museum of Art. Gift of Robert E. Tod, 1937.

Figure 11–6. Majolica Plate. Italian (sixteenth century). Courtesy of the Metropolitan Museum of Art. Gift of V. Everit Macy, 1927, in memory of his wife, Edith Carpenter Macy.

it was called Faience ware instead of the Italian *porzellana di Faenza.* Spain and Portugal have their Faience ware, and much of the early Egyptian pottery is actually of this same type. The term Faience applies to any earthenware of coarse texture covered with an opaque glaze and fired, then decorated and fired again.

There have been many well-known potteries in western Europe, each renowned for a particular type of ware. The Delft ware of Holland, Meissen of Germany, Wedgwood of England and Sèvres of France are all known for their individual treatments of blue-and-white glazes. English Royal Doulton and Staffordshire are other familiar names in fine pottery, both known for figurines as well as for dinnerware.

Decorative Design Today

The contemporary potter not only finds glazes an exciting field for experimentation and discovery but he makes use of several other methods of creating decorative design. While the clay is in the plastic state, he can use his fingers or a fork or comb to impress a ridged design in the clay as it turns on the wheel. He can make designs from dies of various materials and press them into the side of the pottery while it is standing still. When the clay has dried to the leather-hard stage, he can *incise* designs by using a sharp tool or a fine wire loop. He can *inlay* by cutting out pieces of clay and filling the spaces with clay of a contrasting color. *Slip trailing* is another device by which contrasting clay is poured through a glass tube or syringe in a design on the surface. *Sgraffito* may be used, coating the piece with glaze and then scratching through it in a design that shows the natural color of the basic clay underneath. *Sprigging* consists of applying designs made of cut-out clay, or rolls of clay, onto the surface.

Expression of the Material

The potter working at his wheel is not merely forcing clay into shape through exercise of will and fingers, but he is creating a symbol of the very essence of the earth and its eternally changing history. For a few moments he becomes an extension of the clay, experiencing its plasticity, feeling its willingness to go in certain directions, sensing how far and how long it will be worked without collapsing. He cannot arrive at his conclusions through facts or logic; no amount of discussion will tell him as much as

his intuition when he feels the clay. This is skill but with a deeper connotation. It is hands and mind and heart concentrated on extracting from the clay its most poetic possibilities (Figure 11–7).

Figure 11–7. To the spectator the development of a bowl from a ball of clay seems a creative miracle. *Opposite page:* (*Top*) The clay is centered on the wheel and "opened up" in the center. (*Bottom*) The potter begins to draw up the sides. Both photographs courtesy of the American Craftsmen's Council. (*Above*) Potter Richard M. Lincoln creates texture on his bowl by using his fingernails. (*Below*) The final touches consist of smoothing the edges. Both photographs by Bob Abey. Courtesy of the Carlin Galleries, Fort Worth, Texas.

The creation of a piece of pottery is a complete and totally related process from beginning to end. The type of clay is determined by the function of the piece, the form is decided by the qualities of the clay, and the decorative design must be integrated with the form. Thus the design is never something stuck on as an afterthought but rather a continuation of form and clay. There are many ways this can be done. The Dutch pitcher in Figure 11–8 is a fluid form with a smooth glaze. The decorative design is painted with overglaze in a soft blue with variations of gray and violet on a subtle background of blue-white. A fine mist of the same blue is sprayed at the base and around the lip and handle. The use of the bird form as a decorative motif is not arbitrary. The bird and form of the pitcher are integrated and treated with the same flowing quality. The graceful posing of the body, the uptilt of the beak, and the sweep of the decorative tail feathers serve to emphasize the form of the pitcher in such a way that it would seem incomplete without them.

Figure 11–8. The forms of the bird and of the pitcher are completely integrated. Handpainted in soft blues, grays and violets on a gray-white background, the bird seems almost to direct the flowing shape of the pitcher rather than having been added to it. Royal Holland ware. Photograph by Virginia Pike.

Figure 11–9. Unusual textures and subtle decorative forms complement the sturdy honesty of contemporary stoneware by Richard M. Lincoln. Photograph by Bob Abey. Courtesy of Carlin Galleries, Fort Worth, Texas.

In contrast, many contemporary American potters rely more on texture and sgraffito than on meticulous painting in overglaze. They scratch through glazes or they use broad strokes that express an affinity with the clay or a suggestion of a natural form. The two pieces in Figure 11–9 display the best traits of such pottery. Interesting yet honest in shape, each achieves distinction through both structural and decorative design. The elements used for surface design do not depict specific motifs, yet there is a feeling of natural forms which arouses the viewer's imagination and allows him to develop his own conception.

Figure 11–10. Two examples of what can be accomplished with the cooperation of artist and industry. The china (*above*) was created by designer Hermann Gretsch for contemporary interiors, emphasizing simplicity and purity of line. The designs (*right*), originated by Heinz Loeffelhardt, retain contemporary lines yet show an affinity with sixteenth-century pewter. Courtesy of H. E. Lauffer Company, Inc.

The Potter and Industry

While we tend to associate creative pottery with the studio, the potter is becoming aware that industry is not so far removed as he once suspected. The machine is fast and efficient but it has one great lack: it cannot produce beautiful objects by itself. The need for artist-craftsmen who can design objects to be produced in quantity is creating a partnership between art and industry that might once have been thought highly unlikely. Where once the artist rebelled at mass production he now realizes that it offers him an opportunity to replace machine-made mediocrity with a high level of design. He realizes, too, that the machine has one great advantage over the craftsman: it does not tire and its output does not vary in quality once the standards are set. In the field of pottery this mutual need of craftsman and industry is producing increasingly beautiful results. The china in Figure 11–10 (a), for instance, was created from designs by Hermann Gretsch, one of the leaders of the Bauhaus, and was manufactured in a factory in the hills of northeastern Bavaria. The designs in (b) were originated by another German designer, Heinz Loeffelhardt. Both have won gold medals for these particular designs as being among the best designed products of twentieth-century Europe. These men are only two of many artist-designers who realize the vast and inviting market which awaits the artist who allies his talents with the technological processes of his time.

Figure 11–11. Today most objects of blown glass are formed in molds. The hot gob of glass is formed, then placed in an open mold. When the mold is closed, the gob is blown out against the walls of the mold, thus determining the shape and dimensions of the piece. Courtesy of Corning Glass Works.

Glass

The characteristics of glass have endeared it to people in many ways. Its transparency, fluidity, and sparkle are a challenge to the designer to exploit the material to an extent hardly possible in other media. The affinity of light with glass results in a unique and fascinating beauty, and the expression "clear as crystal" indicates a purity not associated with any other material.

Although thousands of formulae are possible, glass is basically fused silica with other ingredients added. Most of the known chemicals have been used as constituents, making possible a wide range of colors and characteristics. Crystal, for instance, has a high lead content which contributes luster and clarity.

Hand blowing is an ancient art; however, for the past few hundred years most glass blowing has been done in molds (Figure 11–11). A hot glob of glass is formed and placed in an open mold, which is closed around it. The glass is then blown out against its walls, thus determining the final size and shape of the blown piece. In commercial production a machine carries out the motions of a glassblower, although in finer ware the process is sometimes finished by the glassblower himself (Figure 11–13). Glassware, like pottery, can also be *cast* from molds to reproduce the work of the designer.

Figure 11–12. Crystal bowl and candlesticks have their sole ornamentation in a laid-on design in clear crystal. Courtesy of Steuben Glass.

Figure 11–13. Crystal stemware is made by a machine which carries out the motions of a glassblower, gathering the glass by suction. By this method similar pieces can be turned out in quantity, yet maintain the quality of hand-blown pieces. Courtesy of Corning Glass Works.

Decorative Design in Glass

Although the inherent beauty of glass makes ornamentation unnecessary, the temptation to combine this quality with decorative design has led artists and craftsmen to create many distinctive effects.

Laid-on designs are associated with Venetian glass on which separate shapes of contrasting colors are applied for added interest. The modern application is usually simple and without color, as in the bases of the bowl and candlesticks in Figure 11–13.

Cut glass enjoyed tremendous popularity around the turn of the century when a collection of heavy glass with its sharp designs of flowers and starlike forms was an accoutrement of every sideboard. When flaw-free glass was developed, taste inclined to smooth surfaces leaving cut glass a collector's item.

Etching on glass usually results in a frosted texture. The parts of the glass to be left plain are coated with wax and the piece submerged in hydrofluoric acid which eats away the surface of the exposed parts. This process is used principally on less expensive glassware.

Enameling and gilding have not been widely used in recent years, but it is possible to see in museums treasured pieces of historic glass handled in this manner.

Engraving is probably the most adaptable of the decorative processes for glass, principally because it enhances the surface without detracting from its inherent qualities of brilliance and clarity. Because of the hardness and smoothness of glass, it is possible to obtain lines of great delicacy or vigorous boldness. Since the process is painstaking, however, it is limited to the finest crystal. The tools consist of copper wheels of many sizes and shapes turned rapidly by motors while the glass is pressed against them. Figure 11–14 shows a prism designed for Steuben Glass by George Thompson displaying this technique at its finest. Engraved to suggest a cathedral spire, the design gives the illusion of being suspended in three dimensions within the glass itself. This piece was presented to President de Gaulle by former President Eisenhower on a visit to France.

Like the contemporary potter, many present-day designers in glass express their ideas through structure and inherent qualities rather than by using decorative design. The fluidity and molten quality that is unique in glass as a medium is utilized to the fullest in the pieces in Figure 11–15.

Figure 11–14. "Cathedral," crystal prism engraved to suggest a cathedral spire. Because of the illusion presented by the crystal, the engraving appears to be suspended in three dimensions within the glass itself. Steuben Glass designed by George Thompson.

Color combines with light to give a fascinating surface that seems to go clear through the form itself, constantly changing. These pieces express the contemporary belief in the importance of material by using the qualities of the material both for structural and for decorative design.

Figure 11–15. The fluidity of glass is beautifully apparent in these three pieces by contemporary designers. (a) Made by N. V. Koninklijke Nederlandsche Glasfabriek Leerdam, designed by Andries D. Copier. (b) Made by Seguso Vetri d'Arte, Venice, designed by Flavio Poli. (c) Made by Skrufs Glasbruk, Sweden, designed by Bengt Edenfalk. Courtesy of the Corning Museum of Glass, Corning, New York.

Stained Glass

The art of stained glass has long been associated with church architecture, yet not since the Middle Ages has it received the personal attention that it is inspiring today. Following the example of a few European craftsmen who preserved the old techniques, the contemporary artist is experimenting with stained glass as an art in itself and adapting it to his original expressions.

Figure 11–16 exemplifies the approach of the artist today to the integration of stained glass and church design. With a literate congregation it is no longer necessary to use paintings and windows as a medium of instruction as they were used in the early days of the Christian church. Instead an attempt is made to establish an atmosphere of worship and contemplation in which soft lights filter in, and the mind is allowed to follow its own direction as thoughts weave through the colors and forms of the panel without intrusion by realistic shapes.

Liturgical art is not the only field in which stained glass is being used. Contemporary design in glass makes panels which form effective room dividers as well as accents set in outside walls. Turn back to Joseph Meert's design in Figure 6–3 for an example of textural interest achieved in a panel of stained glass. Some artists are engaging in experiments in fusing their own glass, working for new colors or variations, thus coming even closer to the approach of the medieval glassmakers who executed designs with their own hands.

Mosaics

Hand in hand with the renewal of interest in stained glass has come the revival of mosaic as an art form. The increasing enthusiasm for the integration of decorative design with architecture finds mosaic holding a place no other art can fill. The color, sparkle, and texture afforded by a panel or wall of mosaic cannot be achieved by either painting or sculpture. Furthermore, mosaic is durable and easily cared for, often outlasting the structure itself. Many of the examples of early mosaics found have been uncovered from the debris of crumbled walls.

Figure 11–16. The contemporary treatment of stained glass is particularly effective in this window by designer Robert Sowers. Holy Trinity Methodist Church in Danvers, Massachusetts. Photograph by Gerda Peterich. Courtesy of architect John A. Carter.

Figure 11–17. The history of Mexico in mosaics forms the walls of the library at the University of Mexico in Mexico City. Mosaics by Juan O'Gorman. Photograph by J. F. Burshears.

There are two methods of creating mosaics, the *direct* and the *indirect*. In the direct method the pieces of glass or ceramic (*tesserae*) are inlaid directly on a wall of wet mortar. The artist works with the realization that irregularities of surface will add to the interest of the total surface, catching the light, casting tiny shadows and making a tapestry of pattern which emphasizes the subtleties of the design itself. In the indirect method, the work is done from a full-scale drawing or cartoon which is drawn in reverse of the desired effect. The tesserae are placed on the paper with a special paste and the large areas are completed before the bed of mortar is applied to the wall. When the mortar is ready the paper-backed mosaic is placed face down against it and pressed gently, smoothing the mosaic into the mortar. When the mortar has cured, the paper is peeled off, revealing the mosaic as it was originally designed. Any *grout* that is used is added at this stage, by working it into the crevices between the tesserae and then wiping off the surplus with a damp cloth after it has set.

The truest mosaic quality is being achieved by individuals who are reviving the technique as a method of expression rather than as a means of covering a wall. Some designers glaze their own tile or make their own glass tesserae. Others combine mosaic with wood carving. The fact that the color is in the structure and, in the case of glass, goes clear through it, gives mosaics an advantage that few other media enjoy. Some artists have given this quality full play by creating transparent mosaics of stained glass, designed to be suspended with the light shining through from both sides.

The first integration of mosaics and architecture in the twentieth century was seen in Juan O'Gorman's monumental designs for the University of Mexico City as shown in Figure 11–17. A total of 4000 slabs, each a meter square, comprises a full acre of exterior walls in which the history of Mexico is depicted in millions of colored stones gathered from many parts of the republic. Since no separation is visible between slabs, the panorama unfolds uninterrupted as it progresses around the building. In this case the mosaics are not ornamentation but become in reality the building itself.

In contrast, Figure 11–18 shows a mosaic designed for a thirty-story office building in downtown Manhattan. In a space approximately 86 by 12½ feet, artists Lee Krasner and Ronald Stein designed a panel retaining the quality of handmade mosaic, something heretofore considered impossible on such a large scale. They achieved this effect by procuring glass plates from Italy which they smashed into tesserae, letting the spirit of the glass determine the shapes, and by personally overseeing the laying of the pieces to create a study in light and spacing which brought out the best in the mosaic technique, As a result, a rather drab downtown business district now has a colorful accent and the building itself has acquired a face that will withstand weather and smog and retain its vivacity and interest as long as the building stands.

Quite a different use is seen in the "Tree of Life" mosaic which forms the backdrop for the sanctuary of the San Marino Congregational Church.

Figure 11–18. Mural by Lee Krasner and Ronald Stein at 2 Broadway, New York. In spite of the great size of the mosaic, the hand set quality was achieved by a sensitive use of varying sizes of tesserae and by diligent supervision of the setting by the artists themselves. Uris Buildings Corporation.

Figure 11–19. The Tree of Life mural makes use of one of the most ancient symbols of life, of wisdom, and of eternity. Four colors of stone are used: pink, silver-gray, white, and deep brown, with fossil marks clearly defined in the silver-gray area. Top lighting creates changing lights and shadows that guide the worshipper into his own interpretation of the mural and of the service taking place below. Designed by Thomas R. Van Sant for the San Marino Congregational Church, San Marino, California.

This is an example of ancient technique and modern design which exemplifies the best work of contemporary artists. Like the larger mural it has the hand-set look, catching the subdued light and shadow of its setting just as the early Christian mosaics were designed to do fourteen centuries ago. Yet the design is a fresh interpretation of an old theme, simple, direct, and without elaboration. The various textures of stone are particularly effective in providing contrast without overemphasis. As with the stained-glass window in Figure 11–16 the viewer is left with his own thoughts and the design guides him in his meditations without intruding. Meanwhile it becomes a part of the building itself which is, after all, the highest function of decorative design.

FOR FURTHER EXPLORATION

The Complete Book of Pottery Making by John B. Kenny (Philadelphia: Greenberg Publishers, 1949). The most comprehensive guidebook in the field today.

Ceramic Reference Manual by Glenn C. Nelson (Minneapolis: Burgess Publishing Company, 1957). A technical handbook with emphasis on the chemistry of glazes.

The Story of Glass by Freda Diamond (New York: Harcourt, Brace & World, Inc., 1953). Informative discourse on the history of glass.

Glass Craft: Designing, Forming and Decorating by Kay Kinney (Philadelphia: Chilton Company, 1962). Detailed text giving basic information on all kinds of glass techniques.

Course in Making Mosaics by Joseph L. Young (New York: Reinhold Publishing Corp., 1957). A well-illustrated discussion of techniques and methods.

STUDIO PROJECTS

1. To develop your awareness of materials, design two bowls, vases, or bottles—one in clay and one in glass. Draw the designs using the scale ½ inch = 1 inch and render in water color, showing any decorative design. Explain why each is more appropriate to its own material.
2. Using the scale ½ inch = 1 inch, design a stained-glass window or panel suitable to a church or synagogue. Assume that it will be located in a focal position where it will command the eyes of the congregation. Use some symbolism, but handle it in a contemporary manner. Render in water color with India ink.
3. To acquaint yourself with the mosaic technique, design a mosaic panel in actual size using small pieces of colored paper cut in the same size and shape. Now redesign the same mosaic using pieces of colored paper in different sizes and shapes.
4. Execute the mosaic in glass or tile tesserae, taking care to create lights and shadows in the setting, but give an all-over effect of skillful handling rather than deliberate crudeness.

CHAPTER 12

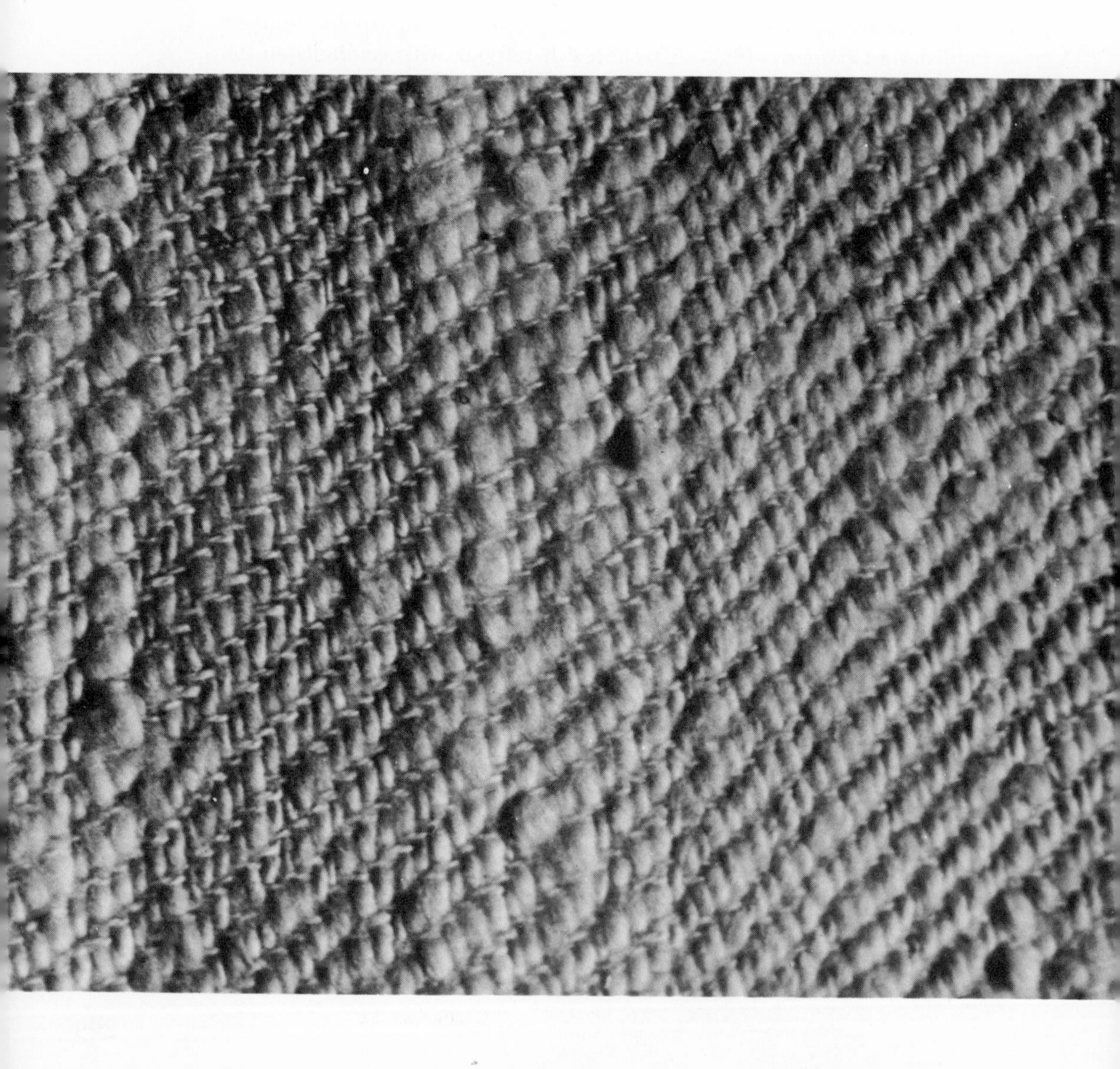

Design in Fabrics

Nowhere is the handcrafted look more effective than in the field of fabrics. Whether it is a handblocked fabric or a piece of distinctive weaving, the idea of a fabric made by an artist's hands has wide appeal.

Weaving as an Art

After centuries of weaving from necessity, hand weaving practically disappeared when machine looms came into use in the nineteenth century. Textiles were limited to those that could be woven of natural fibers, and novel weaves were introduced only by occasional changes in fashion. The revival of hand weaving arose from the same causes that prompted the renewal of pottery-making. Quantity production from mechanized industry had flooded the market with monotony, and a discriminating public was beginning to look for something with an individual flavor. People seeking the unusual turned to the handcraft cultures of backward communities or to the collection of materials from the past. When designers revitalized the hand loom they found an appreciative market.

The horizons of the contemporary weaver stretch to realms never envisioned by the craftsmen of the past. Not only do power looms and a world of new fibers offer unlimited challenge but the possible uses of textiles in contemporary living tantalize the imagination. Interiors featuring rough brick, stone, and wood paneling require fabrics with weight and variety in which the artist–craftsman can explore all the facets of textural interest and creative treatment. Open architecture invites room dividers in which fabrics can be one of the most appropriate materials, modifying the

Figure 12–1. Haitian cotton. The irregular, pleasing texture comes from wild cotton that has been handspun and then handwoven. Courtesy of Jack Lenor Larsen, Inc.

acoustics as well as supplying a visual accent. Ecclesiastical needs suggest symbolic hangings, woven reredos and altar cloths, all ancient accouterments which are experiencing a revival in modern terms. As a result, the weaver is enjoying a new status. In addition to being a craftsman, he has become an artist who is expected not only to produce but to *design* unusual textiles. He has developed the viewpoint of the artist, experimenting, finding new fibers, trying unexpected color combinations. Artists, on the other hand, have turned to weaving as a medium for their designs. Textile-making is no longer a process but an art.

The difficulty of supplying the market with hand weaving has led to an unprecedented collaboration between artist and industry. Textile engineers have established machinery of such versatility that almost any effect can be achieved quickly and skillfully, including designs that the artist works out in advance on a hand loom. As a result, some of the large textile manufacturers are employing top creative talents to develop new fabrics and designs and a high level of quality and originality is being achieved by quantity production.

The Importance of Fibers

Any fabric is the expression of the fibers which compose it. The world of fibers reaches into the far corners of the earth and is enriched continually through science and the designer's imagination. Luster, softness, delicacy, opacity, sheerness, absorbency, elasticity—all are characteristics of fibers which are ingrained in fabric and which determine the appearance, character and durability of the finished material. Such a textile as the one in Figure 12–1, for instance, displays the individual qualities of wild Haitian cotton woven by hand into a distinctive fabric, interesting in weight and texture.

For centuries the heavier fibers used for warmth have come from the fur or hair of animals: the wool of the sheep; angora, mohair, and cashmere from various species of goats; alpaca from a variety of llama, and combinations of woolen fibers with fur from rabbits and other animals. The lighter fibers originate with plants; for example, cotton from the bolls of the cotton plant and flax which, for at least seven thousand years, has been cultivated for linen. Hemp from Asia and jute from East India are used to make a fiber much like linen but coarser, from which door mats and rug backing are woven. A combination of plant and animal produces the luxury fiber of silk, which the silkworm creates from mulberry leaves or from oak leaves when a rougher texture is desired. Whenever a fiber is used it must be carded, spun, or twisted into yarns before it can be transformed into fabric. This is a process which has taken place for centuries.

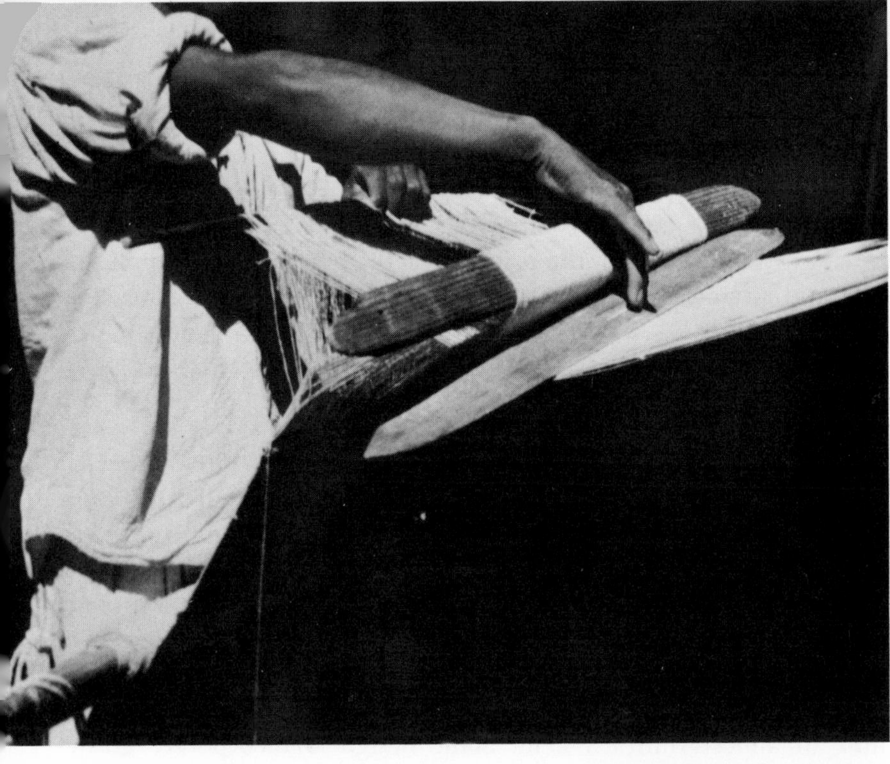

Figure 12–2. The rhythmic motion of the weaver's arms is obvious in this picture of a native weaver at work on a simple loom. Courtesy of American Craftsmen's Council.

Designers today make use not only of natural fibers but of synthetics, or man-made fibers, which have opened new doors in fabric design. Fibers are made from chemicals, from glass, wood, feathers, and even from steel. Recently an upholstery fabric was woven of mohair and stainless-steel filaments which could be molded to the furniture. Another textile is woven entirely of aluminum, making it flexible, flameproof, and durable. Plastic mesh, yarns of Saran, Dacron, Lurex and Orlon are often combined with natural fibers creating fabrics with the best qualities of both natural fibers and synthetics.

Methods of Making Fabrics

The term *fabric* applies to any cloth that is manufactured. The process can be a matter of *felting* which consists of rolling and pounding fibers together under heat and pressure to form a compact and even sheet. It can be *lacing,* which is done with a single thread fastened onto itself as in knitting, knotting, crocheting, tatting, looping, or hooking. It can be *sheeting,* which consists of rolling various plastics into sheets. Or it can be *intertwining,* which involves two sets of threads interlocked one with the other. The most usual form of intertwining is weaving. The term *textile* specifies fabrics that are woven.

The *structural design* of any fabric includes weaving and hooking and any other processes that establish pattern as the result of fabric structure. *Decorative design* refers to all of the printing methods as well as to appliqué, embroidery, and any other methods applied after the fabric is constructed.

Weaving

Weaving is a process by which two or more series of flexible materials are interlaced at right angles, the longitudinal series being called the *warp* and the transverse series the *weft*. With the advent of spinning, the possibilities of unusual effects in weaving were much increased. Whereas in the earliest weaving the variations depended upon use of color, spinning made possible the addition of many other characteristics which could be given to the combed or carded fibers when they were spun or twisted into yarns. The inventive attitude of the fabric designer today has expanded these possibilities into an almost limitless field. Some designers incorporate grasses and seed pods into their fabrics, using the distinctive shapes as integral elements of the structural design. The subtle earthy colors of broom corn, cattails, thistles, goldenrod, and various barks add accent to warps of linen and wool, making exciting textiles with a harmonious natural quality. Glycerin prevents brittleness and a coating of plastic preserves the forms indefinitely.

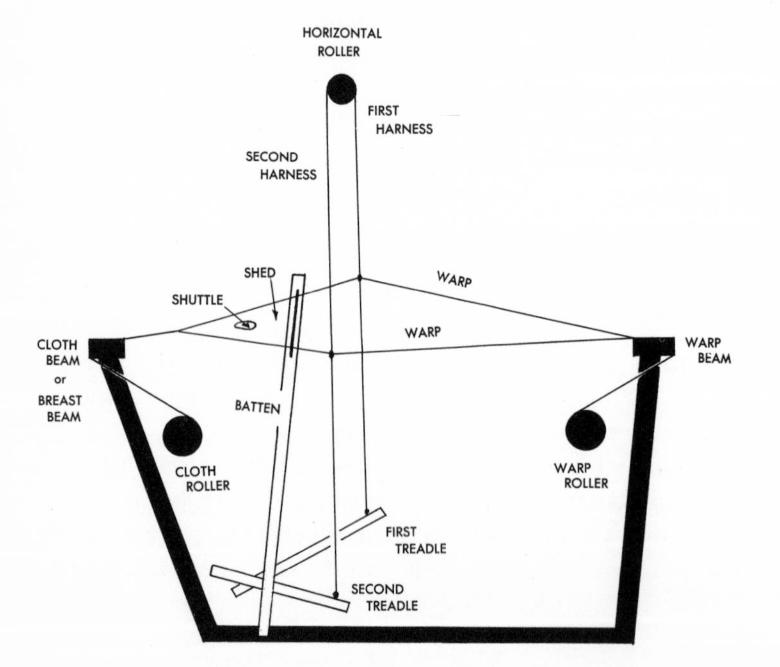

Figure 12–3. A cross-section of a hand loom shows the basic parts and the principal steps in operation. The shuttle carries the weft back and forth through the shed with the weaver reversing the warp threads by moving the treadles between each passing of the shuttle.

There is a certain philosophical connotation in the use of seed pods in weaving. In the Upanishads, which are part of the Hindu Vedic literature, the story is told of a sophisticated young man whose father feels that he needs some basic learning in addition to his intellectual theorizing. He tells the son, Svetaketu, to get a fruit from the banyan tree and break it open and then to break open one of the seeds and tell him what he sees. The son answers, "Why, nothing at all."

"Ah, my son," answers the father, "but this great tree cannot possibly come from nothing. That subtle essence which you do not perceive there, of that very essence this great banyan tree exists. Believe it, my son. That is the power, that is the spirit unseen which pervades everything. It is the Self. It is at the root of all existence and that also art thou." Thus the weaver who blends seed pods and grasses into his work may well feel that he is imparting to it not only interesting textures but a quality of universality.

In spite of new technological developments, the basic requirement of the textile designer remains a knowledge of the loom. This is the organ upon which the weaver plays, pouring forth his harmonies of color and texture. His entire body moves in a simple rhythm, culminating in the design that flows from the loom as textiles. Even in a simple form of loom such as the one shown in Figure 12–2, the weaver's harmonious movements are obvious.

The simplest loom is a rectangular framework of wood with the warp threads stretched parallel to each other across the length of the frame and secured at opposite ends. Weaving is accomplished by passing a needle carrying the filling thread, or weft, back and forth across the loom, placing it alternately over and under the individual threads of the warp. Obviously, this sort of loom is very slow in operation as well as being unsuitable for large pieces of fabric. To facilitate operation, the hand loom was developed. This machine, with only minor variations, was invented independently by every civilization which practiced the art of weaving. It is still the accepted method for creating handmade fabrics and for developing new designs for adaptation by machine weaving.

The hand loom is mounted on a sturdy frame of wood or metal to give support to the activities of the moving parts (Figure 12–3). The principal difference between the hand loom and the simple loom is that on the hand loom the warp threads are run alternately under and over a pair of flat wooden rods and the two sets of warp threads are controlled separately by treadles. Thus the weaver can raise one set of warp threads by pressing the treadle with his feet, forming a triangular space known as a *shed* between the two sets of alternate threads. He then throws the *shuttle* containing the weft thread through this space and raises the alternate set of warp threads, automatically interlacing warp and weft. As a repeated process, the motions become easy and rhythmic with the rows of fabric developing rapidly into a length of textile.

The threading of the loom plays an important part in fabric design (Figure 12–4). For special effects varied arrangements are possible. Flowers and other irregular patterns require the Jacquard mechanism which may have 1200 or more hooks and needles and is guided by a series of cards which are perforated to correspond with the pattern being worked. Power looms work at speeds up to thirty-two miles per hour and the rhythms become a rapid and continual process.

Figure 12–4. Two steps in the threading of the loom. In (a) the warp threads are separated and held apart by wires. Photograph by Dennis Martin. In (b) weaver Irene Mitchell works the yarns through the heddles, vertical wires with eyes which hold the yarns in position for raising and lowering. Photograph by Paul Parker. Both photographs courtesy of the American Craftsmen's Council.

Structural Design in Textiles

Structural design depends upon two factors: the fiber used, and the way in which it is woven. With all of the synthetic fibers now in use weaving is still a matter of natural rhythms, of warp and weft, of systole and diastole. As the weave becomes more complicated we can sense the accelerated rhythms of an emotional state—greater interest, suspense, climax. Furthermore, we find that the most attractive weaves still have natural fibers

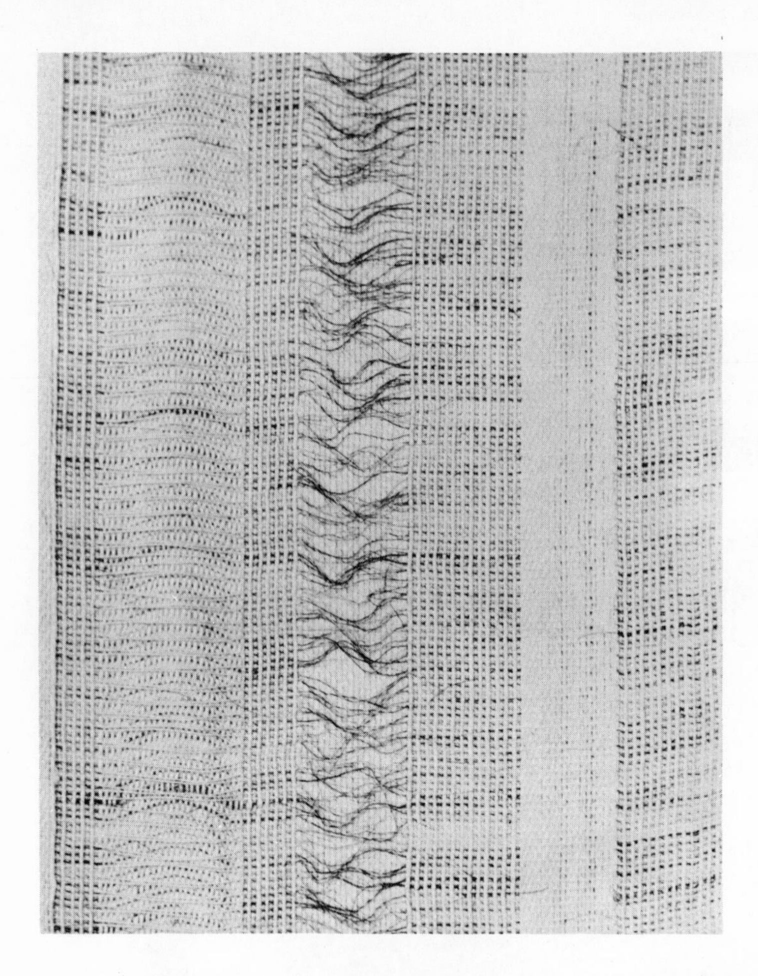

Figure 12–5. Textile woven of linen, goat hair, and Egyptian cotton. Designed by Jack Lenor Larsen and Win Anderson. Courtesy of Jack Lenor Larsen, Inc.

either in combination with synthetics or blended in unusual combinations of their own. An interesting mixture is found in the fabric shown in Figure 12–5 in which linen is combined with goathair and Egyptian cotton.

There are several ways in which fibers can be combined to create a fabric. With *plain weave,* one warp thread is interlaced with one weft thread, as in linen, burlap, and percale. When two or more threads of each kind are interlaced, the result is *basket weave,* as in monk's cloth. When a thick warp thread is used with a medium or thin weft the result is a *rib weave* as in poplin.

Floating yarn is a popular variation in which either the warp or weft yarns float over or under several opposing yarns as shown in Figure 12–6. Long floats can emphasize the texture as in pique or twills, or they can minimize it by creating greater smoothness, as in satin.

Leno weaves wrap the weft yarns around the warp, forming open effects, as found in nets of all kinds.

Pile weaves have a third set of yarns in addition to the warp and weft and this set stands in loops as in terry cloth and some novelty weaves. When the loops are cut the result is cut pile as found in velvet.

Figure 12–6. Two different uses of floats to form designs in weaving. (a) Floats are used to create bands of texture in a pattern composed of strips of varying weaves. Courtesy of Jack Lenor Larsen, Inc. (b) Floats form the triangular sections of the design as well as the rectangular sections between them, creating a rhythm of smooth-textured forms against the rougher texture in the background. Courtesy of Boris Kroll Fabrics, Inc.

Figure weaves come in many variations of complexity. There are different ways of creating designs on the hand loom by working contrasting yarns into the background at intervals (Figure 12–7). However, the Jacquard loom is usually used for machine figures. This category includes brocades and damasks as well as tapestries. Two contemporary Jacquard treatments are shown in Figure 12–8.

Figure 12–7. Designs are woven on the hand loom by means of spools holding yarns of different colors. Each color is worked into the design as needed, then broken and the end joined with the end of the next color of yarn. Here David Ortega designs one of the famous Chimayo blankets in his studio in Chimayo, New Mexico.

Tapestry

Dating from 1483 B.C. in Egypt, tapestry has been created principally on hand looms. The outstanding characteristic of tapestry weaving is the fact that no weft thread is carried entirely across the warp except in rare instances where the design requires it. Each section of the design is woven with a weft of a certain color inserted back and forth over the section where that color appears in the pattern. The weaver works from a cartoon, or actual-sized drawing, placed under the warp threads, and since the weaving is done wrong side up he notes his progress in a mirror placed on the underside.

Figure 12–8. The Jacquard loom lends itself to new and imaginative designs in contemporary fabrics. (a) Jacquard plaid with nylon warp and rayon filling, and (b) stylized floral design in nylon and rayon on a plaid ground. Courtesy of Boris Kroll Fabrics, Inc.

Tapestry was one of the few arts practiced in Europe during the Middle Ages and carried to a high degree of complexity. The Flemish and French examples such as the Unicorn Tapestries (Figure 12–9) are particularly well known. Many of them were commissioned for cathedrals and palaces and so were given excellent care. The tapestries created in seventeenth-century Paris by the Gobelin family were made by royal decree of Louis XIV. Persia and China also excelled in this skill. It is interesting to note that the characteristics we associate with other arts in a given country are expressed with equal emphasis in their weaving. The delicacy of the design in Figure 12–10 with its attention to natural forms could scarcely be anything but Oriental.

Figure 12–9. (*Opposite page*) French or Flemish tapestry from the series known as The Hunt of the Unicorn. "The Unicorn Tries to Escape," from the Chateau of Verteuil. Wool and silk with silver and silver-gilt threads. Courtesy of the Metropolitan Museum of Art, The Cloisters Collection, Gift of John D. Rockefeller, Jr. 1937.

Figure 12–10. Chinese tapestry from a set representing the Four Seasons. "Autumn," silk. From the Ch'ing dynasty (Ch'ien Lung period 1736–1795). Courtesy of the Metropolitan Museum of Art, Kennedy Fund, 1913.

Figure 12–11. "Triptych," a tapestry in three panels to be hung two inches apart, is woven in tones of red, green, white, gray, mauve, and brown. Designed and executed by Mildred Fischer. Photograph by Jack Foster. Courtesy of *Craft Horizons* Magazine.

Like many medieval arts, tapestry is enjoying a renewal of interest. After 350 years of silence, the Aubusson tapestry tradition in France was revitalized after World War II with such success that over 500 international exhibitions were held to show the work of twentieth-century weavers working in the early tradition but using contemporary methods of expression.

American weavers, on the other hand, show complete freedom from tradition. Intrigued by colors and patterns in nature, Mildred Fischer sifts her impressions of light on water, patterns in trees, people and festivity until she has abstracted them into an essence that she can interpret in yarns and fibers (Figure 12–11). Instead of forcing the fibers and the loom to work out a preconceived pattern, she adapts her impressions to the capabil-

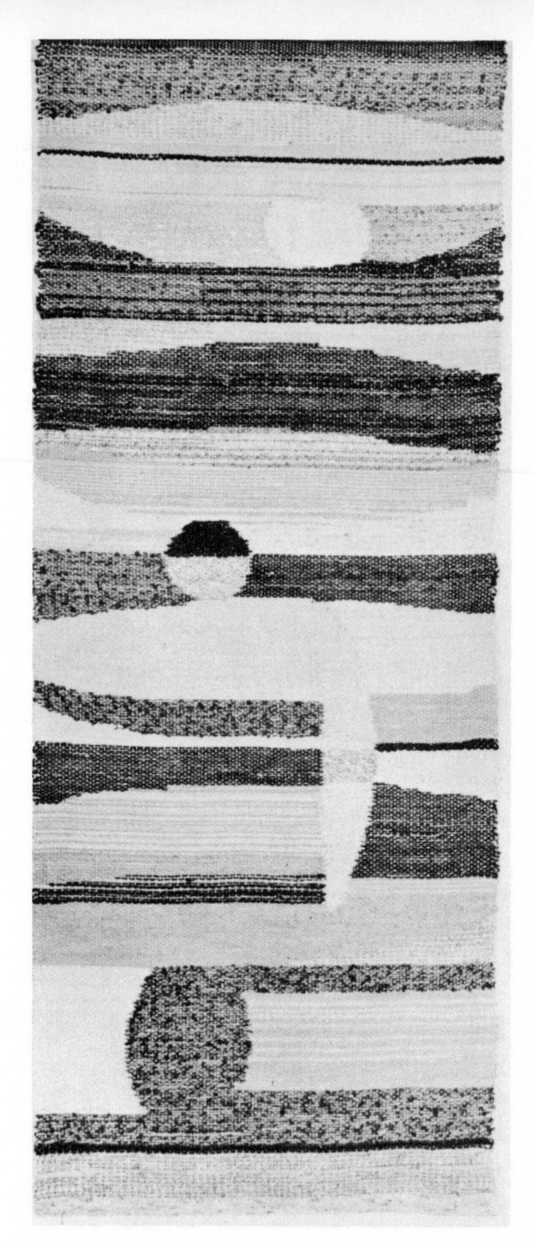

Figure 12–12. Symbolic tapestry in yellow, black, white, metallics, and orange. "Midnight Sun" by Mildred Fischer. Photograph by Jack Foster. Courtesy of *Craft Horizons.*

ities of her medium, letting the loom tell its story as well as her own in a creative partnership. Technique is not overly important, only a process of adaptation, of translating the weaver's response to her world. She may use symbols as in "Midnight Sun" (Figure 12–12), but the colors and values translate the feeling even more than the shapes depict it.

Tapestry making by means of hooking is a method used by many contemporary artists. While this is not tapestry in its true sense, the term is used because the results have a similar feeling of texture and because they are put to comparable uses. In hooking, the yarn is pulled through a stiff backing from the underside, frequently by means of a hand-held hooking machine. Loops are left on the front to form a nubby texture. No loom is involved.

Decorative Design in Fabrics

Application of design on fabrics falls into one of two general categories: embroidery or appliqué, and printing.

Embroidery is one of the most eloquent testimonies to man's need for creative expression. Since he first invented the needle from a sharp fishbone or a pointed stick he has not been able to resist the lure of bright-colored threads applied to fabrics in decorative design. From peasant costumes in cotton and wool to liturgical vestments of silk embroidered on heavy satin, intricate and colorful designs have been worked out by the painstaking process of hand embroidery. Meadow flowers and woodland birds have appeared on costumes in all parts of the world, interpreted according to the dictates of their culture. Similarly, historical events have been recorded in detail on elaborately embroidered royal mantles. Here, as in tapestry, the design characteristics of a people find insistent expression. French medieval embroidery had sweetness and grace, early Spanish embroideries reflect the Moorish influence, while the embroidery of Germany and the Scandinavian countries is largely domestic in character. The Persian embroidery in Figure 12–13 is typical of the propensity for bird forms and arabesques that arose from the Mohammedan disapproval of using the human figure in design of any kind.

In the early years in America each well-versed little girl had to finish a sampler of various embroidery stitches as a part of her education. Household linens were embroidered as a matter of course and, although quilt-making reached a high level of achievement, embroidery as such was considered a household practice rather than an artistic effort. As a result it is only recently that embroidery has come under the scrutiny of the creative artist.

The contemporary approach is marked by a bold use of color and honest regard for the stitches themselves. Heavy textures and yarns make embroidery important as expression rather than as mere enrichment of a surface. In many cases the decorative sewing is combined with appliqué, in which pieces of fabric are sewn onto the surface of the material and the embroidery worked around and over them in much the way that clay is inlaid and glazed in pottery. The total effect is imaginative, with colored fabrics and interesting yarns working together for the creation of a lively design. The fanciful wall hangings of Gisella Loeffler (Figure 12–14) co-ordinate an Old World design quality with a modern use of stitches to create an expression distinctly her own.

Figure 12–13. Persian embroidery in wool, nineteenth century. Courtesy of the Metropolitan Museum of Art, Rogers Fund, 1910.

Figure 12–14. This contemporary wall hanging by Gisella Loeffler shows a delightful imaginative approach to appliqué and embroidery. Courtesy of the artist.

Printing

Printing of design on fabric is traced to China in 1000 B.C. In the intervening ages there have been many variations in the process of application but most methods can be classified in one of four ways: direct printing, dyed method, discharge method, or resist printing.

The *direct method* includes *block printing,* the *intaglio* method, and stenciling. All are used in advertising design as well as in textiles and wallpapers. The use of linoleum and wood blocks on fabric is a particularly interesting technique, for the results can be a happy combination of fabric texture, individual design, and all-over pattern.

While block printing is done by inking the block and pressing it onto cloth or paper, the intaglio method involves engraved copper cylinders on a rotary press. Where a separate block must be used for each color many colors can be printed at one time by use of the press, even though each cylinder carries only one color. The operation of the press is faster, easier, and more flexible than the use of the block, and consequently is more widely used.

Principal among stenciling methods is the *silk screen technique* in which the design is supported by a sheet of silk stretched across a wooden

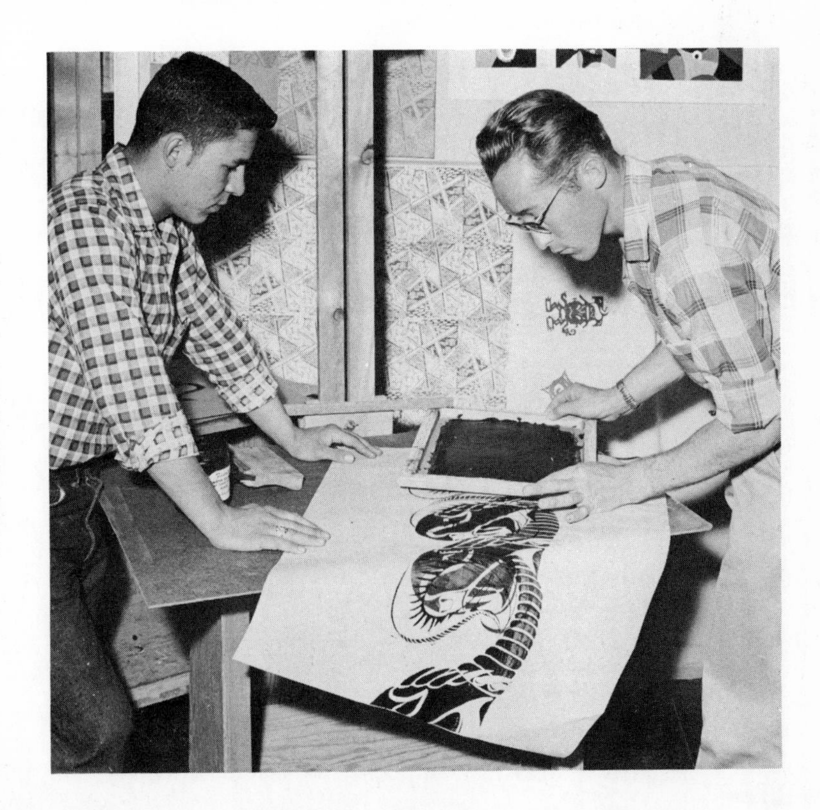

Figure 12–15. The silk screen on its frame is settled into place for the printing of the next section. Portions of the silk are blocked out with an opaque film; next, the paint will be forced through the open areas of the silk with the squeegee lying on the table between the hands of the student at left.

frame (Figure 12–15). The parts of the design to be printed are left untouched while the remainder of the silk is blocked off with a plastic coating. Ink is then pressed through the silk with a squeegee, or wide rubber-tipped wedge, imprinting the form of the design on the fabric or paper underneath. Such a process was used in the handprinting of the fabric in Figure 12–16.

The *dyed method* depends upon the preparation of the cloth by application of a mordant, a substance which combines with dye to form an insoluble compound or lake. The fabric is printed on the mordant, followed by aging, fixing, and finally by dyeing. The mordant causes the dye to produce a fast color.

The *discharge method* utilizes the action of acids, alkalis, and oxidizing and reducing agents for the destruction of dyed color. The dye is applied and then removed in patterns to produce the desired design.

Resist printing prevents dyeing from taking effect by blocking out sections of the fabric. One of the oldest forms of resist is *batik*. In the Pacific islands tapa cloth, made from steeping and beating the bark of trees, is dyed by the batik method which consists of applying wax to the areas that will not be dyed, of dipping the fabric into dye and then of peeling off the wax. A variation is the "tied and dyed" method by which fabric is tied in

Figure 12–16. Contemporary hand silk-screen print on a linen and dacron ground. Courtesy of Boris Kroll Fabrics, Inc.

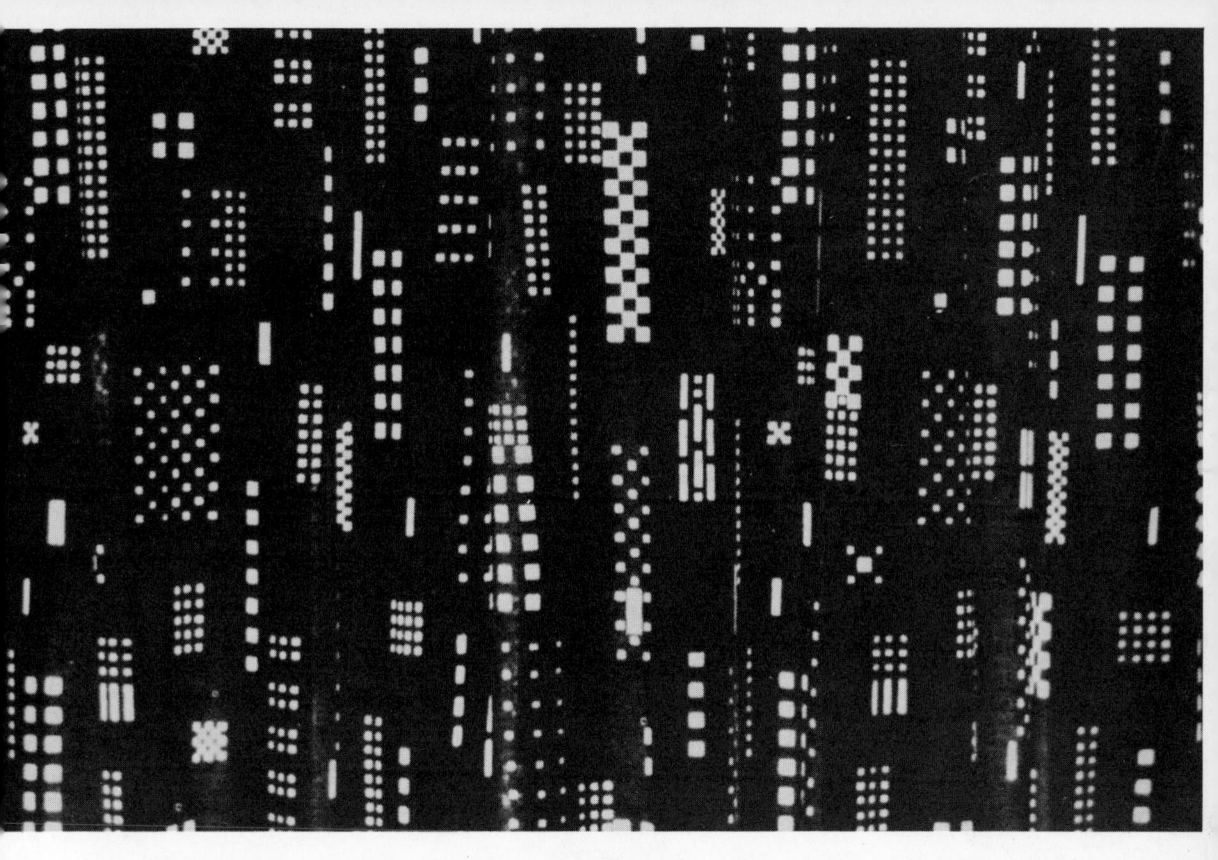

Figure 12–17. Machine-printed fabrics show tremendous variety in the use of design motifs when designed by artists for quantity production. "Manhattan" designed by Alexander H. Girard. Courtesy of Herman Miller Furniture Company.

knots and then submerged in the dye vat. The results are somewhat accidental but can be interesting.

In nature we see repetition in a subtle relationship of shapes and sizes, not in mechanical spacing. We have seen how in a field of daisies, a tide pool of foam, or in the sky full of stars repetition gives a rhythmic design in which the intervals or negative spaces are never so uniform as to create monotony. Similarly, in any all-over design unity should be retained without sameness. This is done by attention to balancing of forms and space, by arrangement of motifs in groups, or by a delicate adjustment of horizontal, vertical, and diagonal patterns. The movement created by repetition will give the fabric a rhythm that is only increased when it is hung in folds. The shapes and rhythms of the intervening or negative spaces will become important as a part of the all-over design, flowing in and out among the printed surfaces, as seen in Figures 12–17 and 12–18. It takes experience to visualize such a design from the original motif for the block or screen is a mere beginning for the flowing fabric that springs from it.

Some artists experiment with "found textures," using such materials as corrugated cardboard or wire screening for inking and printing on fabrics. Sponges, spools, wood, and erasers are other objects that can be used for

Figure 12–18. "Primavera," printed velvet inspired by Japanese prints. Courtesy of Jack Lenor Larsen, Inc.

this purpose. Textile paint, printing ink, and oil paint can be applied and "printed" on fabric, either as design or as accent for block prints. Texture, line, and shape are all important in planning any all-over design. It is neither necessary nor desirable to have three-dimensional form, as the primary interest is in surface design, not depth.

Fabrics in all their variations are a vital part of the architecture of today. Just as medieval tapestries provided warmth for cold walls and muffled the echoes of stone hallways contemporary textiles lend warmth and softness to the vast expanses of glass, steel, marble, and concrete that compose so many of our present-day buildings. Their strong tactile quality appeals to the senses lending interest to smooth surfaces, and the uncluttered lines of modern furniture provide an ideal background for upholstery of printed or woven fabrics. Movable screens covered with textiles make effective room dividers and panels of fabric are frequently used in high-fidelity equipment. Textiles are easily moved and not difficult to install. There is no breakage and cleaning is relatively simple. From every aspect, the collaboration of the architect with the textile designer offers intriguing possibilities for the future.

FOR FURTHER EXPLORATION

Block Printing on Textiles by Janet Erickson (New York: Watson-Guptill Publications, 1961). An inspiring and complete treatment of the subject written by an expert.

Know Your Fabrics by Lucy D. Taylor (New York: John Wiley & Sons, Inc., 1951). Home furnishing is considered in the light of historic and contemporary textiles.

The Joy of Hand Weaving: The Complete Step-by-Step Book of Weaving by Osma Couch Gallinger (Princeton, N.J.: D. Van Nostrand Co., Inc., 1952). A clearly written text, with projects to carry the student from simple steps to more advanced techniques.

STUDIO PROJECTS

1. To realize the possibilities of weaving, make a collection of yarns of various weights and thickness. Experiment with possible combinations by wrapping them around a small card, trying different positions, color harmonies, and varieties of texture.

2. On a simple loom weave a fabric sample of two or more different yarns. Keep in mind the principles of design: let one yarn predominate with the others forming accents. Weave a design showing rhythm, either by simple beat or by emphasis. Show balance in your distribution of color and texture.

3. Appliqué bright-colored cloth on a firm background such as hopsacking or homespun, turning the edges under and letting the shape come into being as you work. Enhance the appliqué with a variety of stitches in colored yarns or heavy embroidery thread, giving the design a modern treatment.

4. Using a piece of monk's cloth, burlap, or hopsacking run heavy threads or yarns in an interesting design. Show variety in size and color of stitches. Create as many new textures as possible.

5. Design and cut a linoleum block, first making two sketches, one of a single unit and the second showing an all-over application. Print three one-yard pieces of fabric, using different placements on each piece. Compare the final effects and decide which is most successful and why.

CHAPTER 13

Figure 13–1. Franco-Flemish woodcarving of the early sixteenth century. "Presentation of Christ in the Temple." Carved in oak approximately 35½ inches high and 10½ inches wide. Courtesy of the Metropolitan Museum of Art, The Cloisters Collection, Purchase 1950.

Design in Wood and Metal

Although wood and metal are opposite in nature, they have enough similarity in use to be considered together from the standpoint of design. Both are materials from which man has created some of his most cherished possessions and both can be used with equal effectiveness for bowls, trays, decorative panels, doors, and room dividers.

Of course, the techniques and results vary widely because of their differences. Where wood is warm with a mellow glow, metal is hard, often cold, and the glow is a sheen, frequently with clear-cut reflection. Where wood absorbs most of the light, metal when polished reflects the greater part of it outward. Although wood will burn, most metals are heat-resistant until they reach a temperature high enough to melt them. When metal is melted it is not destroyed but, cooling, solidifies to a compact mass of crystals.

Wood

Trees present infinite variety in their outer appearance and in the wood of their trunks. In many, the grain is marked by the growth of annual rings formed by the cambium, or outer layer—the only part of the tree to show active growth from year to year. In the temperate zones, the tree produces two rings of growth during the spring and summer and, since the early wood each year is lighter in color, the rings alternate between light and dark, thus forming a definite grain pattern. Grains can be varied by methods of sawing, by etching which emphasizes the grain in a three-dimensional way, and by striating which creates parallel ridges of different widths. When wood is cut parallel to the axis of the trunk the lumber is *straight-grained* unless the fibers happen to be helical, or twist around the trunk, in which case the lumber is *cross-grained*. Cross-grained lumber also results when the wood is not cut parallel to the trunk.

Woods are classified as hard or soft depending upon the type of tree from which they come. Woods from broad-leaved deciduous trees are called hardwoods while woods from coniferous trees are known as softwoods. These terms have to do with the structure rather than with the actual hardness of the wood. Hardwoods have long fiber ducts through the trunks while soft woods have no such ducts but transport the fluids from cell to cell.

Some trees shelter man against the sun and storm while others provide decorative accents to his landscape; similarly, the woods provide for his needs in many and varied ways. Fuel and construction have been major uses through the centuries, but the woods used for decorative objects disclose abundant evidence of man's adventures in adapting wood to his need for expression. The wide variations in different species and in pieces within the same tree are as fascinating as the wealth of contours and foliage within a forest. Chestnut, rosewood, satinwood, tulip, amaranth, lemon, birch, holly, harewood—what a wealth of characteristics the names imply! Rich colors, intriguing grains, facility of working, and durability are all traits that vary with the individual woods, opening a vast field of exploration for the designer. A little stain and several coats of wax can bring out beauty never suspected from almost any piece of raw wood. Ebony takes a perfect polish and teak often is merely oiled for use in contemporary furniture. Many times the grain suggests a design that far exceeds the imagination of the designer, as though the form had been held fast within the block awaiting the chisel of the artist to set it free.

Some Widely Used Varieties

Among the kinds of wood proven to be particularly useful in design, *walnut* is one of the most versatile. Known as the ideal American cabinet wood, it is outstanding for its richness of color, its durability, and beauty of grain. It can be turned for bowls or other small pieces and has long been a favorite for carving because of its ease of working and its decorative quality when polished. Much paneling in historic cathedrals and palaces was done in walnut.

Mahogany comes in many varieties from the jungles of Central America, the West Indies, and Africa. Philippine mahogany is used in large quantities for paneling and for hollow-core doors, being comparatively inexpensive yet having an attractive grain that takes a fine finish. Brazilian mahogany is particularly effective when used in decorative pieces where the grain can be exploited and a high polish applied.

Oak has been a favorite wood for floors and furniture through the years, and its resistance to wear made it one of the favorite woods for school and office furniture early in the century when the "golden oak" finish was in great demand. Although teak is being used for this purpose today, "limed oak" and "bleached oak," both light finishes, have found popularity in contemporary surroundings.

Although not adapted to carving, *maple* is widely used because of its toughness and warm color. It is one of the two woods most used for early American interiors. Its companion is *pine,* a wood that can attain a prized "antique" finish when stained and waxed. Both white and yellow pine are used in building construction, and clear white pine is used for woodcuts because of its ease of cutting and lack of flaws.

Another category that takes a beautiful finish and has a wide range of warm tones is fruit wood. Fruit woods—favored for French provincial furniture—include cherry, apple, and pear as well as some rarer varieties. They are frequently used in combination with leather and brass to give a richness and warmth of tone suggestive of fine homes and opulent furnishings.

Historic Design in Wood

The possibilities of wood reached a period of high expression during the Gothic era when cathedrals became treasure houses of carving. Panels such as the one shown in Figure 13–1 were an integral part of the medieval cathedral in Germany and France. In castles, too, woodcarving was considered an essential art, for elaborate designs graced panels on chests, coffers, and buffets. By the time of Louis XIII in France there was scarcely a square inch of wood without some sort of "turnery" from the carver's chisel. Shells, swags, flowers, fruits, and cupids were carved on any wood available until the structure of the furniture was fairly smothered in ornamentation.

The period of the great cabinetmakers of England is known for its *inlay,* its restrained carving, and the *parquetry* in which small pieces of different colored woods are laid together and sunk into the wood to form a design. Sheraton, particularly, was famous for his satin inlay and for a subtlety of carving, usually centered in the legs of chairs which had delicate reeding. In fifteenth-century Italy *intarsia* was employed. This was another means of inlay in which scrolls, arabesques, fruit, flowers, and architectural scenes or human figures were created in tiny pieces of wood inlaid against a contrasting background.

Spanish furniture also gave vital expression to the beauty of wood. Heavy paneling and strong forms have long been associated with the in-

teriors of Spanish castles where the simplicity of Moorish architecture forms an effective background for the beauty of wood and tile. The importance of wood in historic periods is a study that has filled volumes.

Contemporary Design in Wood

In contrast to the highly developed skill of ornamentation in previous periods, the designer of today expresses himself by a return to essentials, to an appreciation of the material for what it is, and to bringing out its inherent qualities.

In the wooden bowls in Figure 13–2 grain determines shape and is exploited to the fullest, emphasizing the curve of each. Because of the beauty of the grain, one feels that the bowls could not have been made from any other materials or, for that matter, from any other pieces of wood. This is an individual expression of one distinctive material which the designer guided to fulfillment.

Body-fitting forms and interesting shapes are possible through *laminated wood,* consisting of several layers of parallel grain glued together. Almost unlimited uses can be found for *flexwood* which consists of a paper-thin sheet glued to a flexible backing, making possible its use in much the same fashion as wallpaper, hung on a wall. *Plywood* has become a standby for construction and for furniture in which lightness and strength are desirable. Like laminated wood, it consists of layers, usually three or five, glued together, with the difference that they are of alternating grain for greater strength. Charles Eames' chair in Figure 13–3 demonstrates how walnut plywood can be shaped into body-fitting contours.

Although much of the process of furniture-making can now be done by machine with a man simply standing by to guide and direct the motions, the cut pieces must be joined and glued by hand, and the craftsman finds

Figure 13–2. (*Opposite.*) Although the shapes of these pieces would be possible in other materials, the individuality and beauty of these particular bowls is the result of the wood and its grain which the designer has adapted to his needs. Larger bowl of Mexican mahogany 6 inches high. Shallow bowl or platter of Macassar ebony, 7⅛ inches in diameter. Designed by James Prestini. Collection, the Museum of Modern Art, New York. Edgar Kaufmann, Jr. Fund and Gift of Dorothy Liebes.

Figure 13–3. Shaped chair of walnut plywood uses interesting grain as the sole decorative element. Shapes conform to body contours and firm support is provided by chromium legs. Charles Eames, designer. Photograph courtesy of Herman Miller, Inc., of Zeeland, Michigan.

here the same necessity for precision work that was known in the days of hand turning. He follows, too, the same principles of design. In Figure 13–4 shape and material predominate in the creation of six small tables that can be stacked for storage or placed together to form one large table. Each unit is a striking design by itself, yet each becomes a related part of the whole when all six are fitted together.

Figure 13–4. Nested tables of teak designed for use separately, as one large round table or in any number of variations. The simplicity of form and contrast of the straight brass legs serve to dramatize the wood grains. Designed by Danish architects Hridt and Mølgaard. Courtesy of John Stuart, Inc.

The endearing qualities of fine grain and warm tone are emphasized in much contemporary furniture. New methods of molding and bending make possible fluid forms suited to the relaxed postures of modern living yet retaining the qualities that have made wood loved in the past. The lounge chair by designer Charles Eames in Figure 13–5 embodies comfort and beauty in a fresh and original form. The grain of the molded wood seems almost to wrap around the chair and foot rest, as though to cradle the person within. The leather upholstery and black polished-aluminum base emphasize the interest of the wood; yet the pervading feeling is one of comfort to which the attractiveness of the material merely contributes. Recent innovations in the use of wood make such designs possible.

Figure 13–5. Lounge chair and foot rest provide relaxing support while taking full advantage of the decorative quality of the wood grain. Buffed-wax rosewood shell on base of black polished aluminum. Charles Eames, designer. Courtesy of Herman Miller, Inc., of Zeeland, Michigan.

Figure 13–6. Exposed beams and paneling of charter pecan make this interior warm and inviting. Courtesy of United States Plywood Corporation.

Wood paneling is one of the best features of many homes today. Structural members which are left exposed endow wood with a role of increased importance visually. Attractive color and interesting grain are important in paneling, much of which is rubbed with paint or stain and prefinished before it is sold (Figure 13–6). Such paneling has the practical advantage of requiring no upkeep.

The possibilities of wood reach into every corner of men's lives. From musical instruments and furniture to his home itself, from his ceremonial totems to the fire by which he dreams, wood has served man faithfully through the centuries. He has used it to whittle and carve since first he held a knife and he has learned to create from the beauty of its grain. Its hand-hewn texture has embellished his literature since ancient times, both as printed letters and as illustrations (Figure 13–7). Being organic, each piece is an entity with its own idiosyncrasies of growth and cut. Pieces sliced inches apart from the same trunk have entirely separate characteristics, although both retain the qualities of the species. What the artist achieves with wood depends upon his understanding of his individual piece and his willingness to work *with* it, releasing its hidden beauty as it suggests, adapting his methods to the material, instead of trying to bend it to his wishes. When wood is approached in this way it yields effects that no artist could anticipate and repays his efforts with a warmth and beauty not to be achieved in any other material.

Figure 13–7. The rich textural quality of a woodcut is not to be found in any other medium. *Head of L. Schames* by Ernest Ludwig Kirchner. Collection, The Museum of Modern Art, New York. Gift of Curt Valentin.

Metal

While wood devotes itself to forming an attractive background for man's activities, metal shouts its uses to the world. It peals forth from towers and belfries where bronze bells strike the hour or toll the crises in men's lives. It glows in company with the finest jewels, adorning royalty and beauty the world over, and it graces the banquet tables of every country, lending a lavish touch by virtue of its own beauty.

Metal flashes down the highways in the everchanging designs of automobiles, it streaks across the skies in planes and satellites, it rides the rails in trains, crosses the seas in ships and it is already well established in the exploration of outer space.

In comparison to wood, we think of metal as hard, cold, impersonal and unyielding, yet these characteristics are not necessarily typical. Gold, silver, and tin are so soft that they must be fortified for general use. Silver and copper warm to the touch immediately by virtue of being excellent conductors. As for being impersonal, metal has lured more men to their death than any other material, calling them into the dark recesses of the earth's surface to discover and extract the precious ore for their own use and for the money they could get for marketing it. While metal offers rigid support for our highest skyscrapers it yields willingly into delicate forms through the sensitive hands of the artist.

The most important difference between wood and metal from the artist's standpoint is the variation in the methods of manipulation. Where wood is handled primarily by the *subtractive* process, starting with a large piece and cutting, chipping, or chiseling until the desired result is attained, metal is generally handled in an *additive* manner, building up forms by welding, riveting, or pouring while in a molten condition. The form can be changed by chipping, pounding, or forging but on the whole these processes are employed for shaping rather than as methods of construction. A bowl of wood is carved from a solid block with considerable material cut away; a bowl made from metal is formed from a flat sheet and very little metal is discarded.

Characteristics of Metal

If metal is unique in some ways, the reason is to be found in three outstanding characteristics: *tensile strength, malleability* and *ductability.* Great tensile strength made possible the building of the Golden Gate Bridge (Figure 13–8). Steel cables support the entire weight of the concrete roadbed and the traffic upon it, yet the cables are so small in diameter that they actually look delicate from a distance. The concrete-enclosed towers relate the construction to the water below, but the grace of the design gives one the feeling that man has simply thrown a crossing over the deep channel rather than having erected a massive structure in opposition to natural surroundings, much as a spider spins a silken thread to transport himself over chasms that he cannot otherwise negotiate.

The second characteristic, *malleability,* takes its name from the mallets that are used to shape a sheet of metal into various forms. No other material can be so thoroughly hammered and raised without cracking and breaking.

Ductability is the capacity for being drawn out or hammered thin without breaking, and makes possible the manufacture of fine wires and sheet metal from which three-dimensional forms are made. Platinum has been reduced to wire 1/20,000 of a millimeter in diameter and gold can be

Figure 13–8. The Golden Gate Bridge spanning the entrance to San Francisco harbor gives a feeling of delicacy and strength combined. Only the tremendous tensile strength of steel cables makes possible such a graceful solution to the demands of a long span. Photograph by Harold Finke.

beaten into a sheet 1/3800 of a millimeter thick. The ductability of gold made possible its use in such works of art as the Rospigliosi Cup in Figure 13–9. This Renaissance masterpiece, attributed to Benvenuto Cellini, shows the intricate forms to which gold can be applied in the form of gold leaf. It also gives an idea of the luxurious quality which results.

Methods of Working Metal

The most usual method of creating objects from a sheet of metal is *raising* by striking blows with a hammer to elevate the outer part of a sheet of metal to form the sides. The punch bowl and ladle of Figure 13–10 were raised from a sheet of silver by designer Hans Christensen. *Beating down* is the reverse of raising, for in this process the sheet of metal is placed over a bowl-like recess the shape of the desired object and the metal is hammered down into the recess with a mallet. *Spinning* is a machine process in which cylindrical forms such as pitchers, goblets, vases, and tumblers can be formed on a lathe from flat sheets of metal. One method which cannot be simulated in wood is *casting* which depends upon the ability of metal to be melted and reformed into specific shapes. Molten metal is poured into a mold to form either solid or hollow pieces. In the latter case, when a shell of the desired thickness has formed, the remaining metal is poured off, leaving just the outer walls.

Figure 13–9. The Rospigliosi Cup from sixteenth-century Italy. Gold, enamel, and pearls, attributed to Benvenuto Cellini of Florence (1500–1571). 9 inches long. Courtesy of the Metropolitan Museum of Art. Bequest of Benjamin Altman, 1913.

Figure 13–11. (*Opposite page.*) Lynn R. Wolfe at work on the doors for the Danforth Chapel. The design is executed in copper repoussé with the raised portions textured in varying degrees to suggest modeling and to contrast with the smooth background.

Figure 13–10. Silver bowl and ladle. The punch bowl is raised from a single piece of silver shaped to give strength; the legs are added on. The ladle is raised completely from one piece of silver. Designed and executed by Hans Christensen.

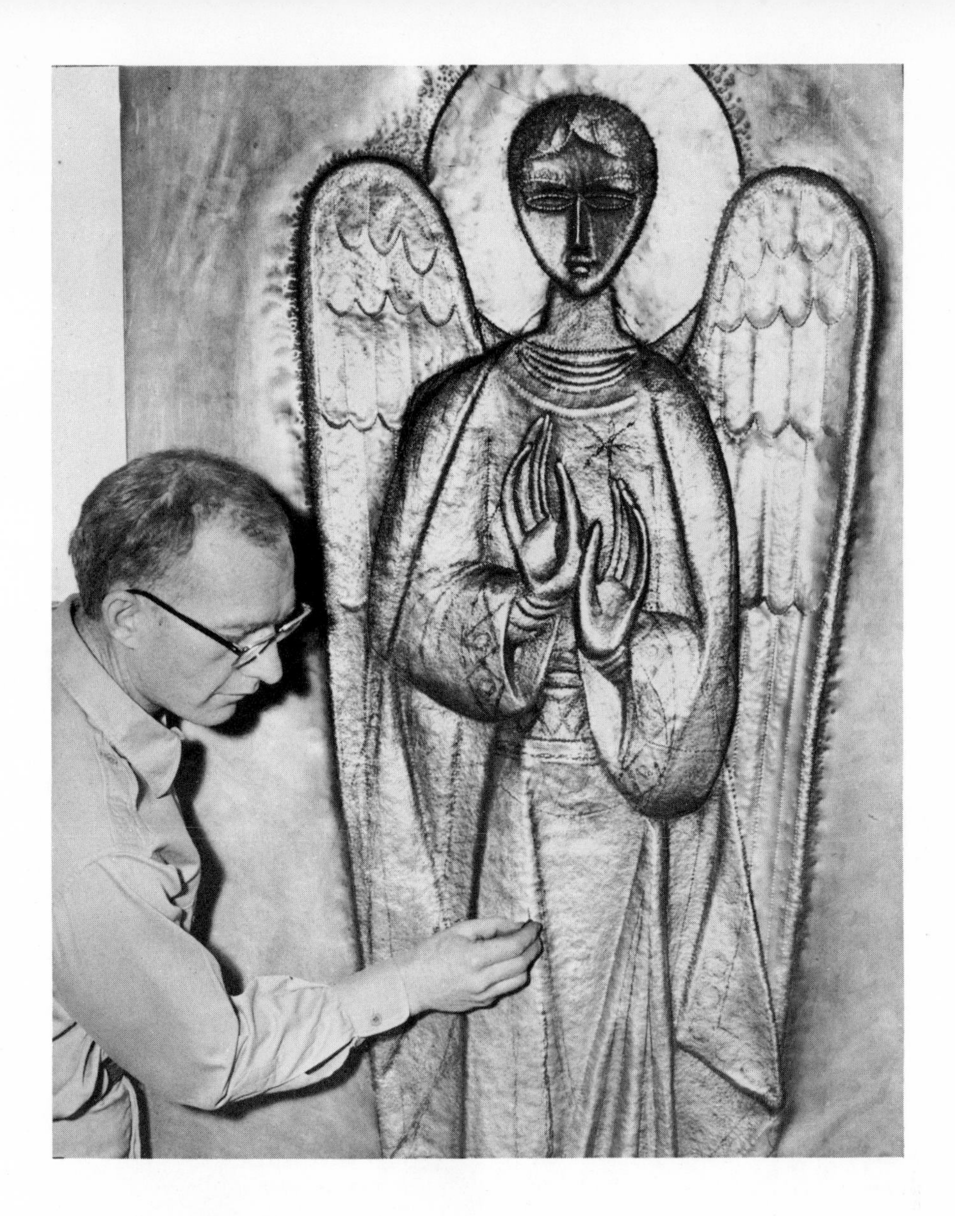

Design in Metal

The individual characteristics of various metals determine in large degree the design purposes for which they will be used. *Silver* and *copper,* both cherished for their beauty, are useful to the designer because of their easy workability. Both lend themselves willingly to *chasing* and *repoussé,* as well as to various other treatments. Chasing is accomplished with tools of hardened steel on which the tips are smooth and somewhat rounded. Their function is to sink portions of the metal to form a design in which tool marks are not noticeable. *Repoussé,* on the other hand, is created by outlining the design with a tracing tool and then raising the surface of the metal from the reverse side to form subtle modeling, as in Lynn R. Wolfe's copper doors for the Danforth Chapel (Figure 13–11). Texture and design can be added with a variety of tools, and interesting effects can be achieved by use of heat and certain chemicals. The doors of the Danforth Chapel are particularly effective because of the contrast of color and texture. The glowing tones of the copper form a rich accent to the natural fieldstone walls and the structural supports of wood (Figure 13–12).

Figure 13–12. Two views of the Danforth Chapel on the campus of Colorado State University in Fort Collins. The copper doors by Lynn R. Wolfe form a striking accent against the native stone and wood and serve to set the mood for the atmosphere of the interior. Architect: James M. Hunter. Photograph by Warren Reynolds, Infinity, Inc.

Another happy combination of copper and wood is seen in the copper doors by Irv Burkee in Figure 13–13. Here the copper is perforated and accented with heavy beaten wire riveted to the panels. Oxidation applied around the designs emphasizes the detail, while the background is rubbed with pumice to give a satiny glow.

Figure 13–13. Large copper panels with reversible designs are recessed in heavy wooden frames to form sliding doors. Designed and executed by Irv Burkee. Photograph by Bonnie Burkee.

Figure 13–14. Silver pitcher exhibiting creative use of space both within and without. Delicate balance between the interior space and the location and shape of the spout makes it possible to empty the pitcher without turning it upside down. Designed and executed by Hans Christensen.

Silver, of course, has lent itself to many intricate works in the past. Elaborate designs have graced the handles of silver tableware and ornamented large serving pieces and candlesticks. Today the tendency is for greater simplicity. This trend is exemplified by Hans Christensen's pitcher in Figure 13–14 which is strikingly simple. It is designed in such a way that it can be emptied without turning upside down. The handle is an integral part of the total design, not only in its shape and placement but in its use of contrasting material for accent.

The capacity of silver to be shaped into small decorative pieces has made it one of the favorite metals for jewelry (Figure 13–15). This is a field in which designers have shown a great deal of interest and originality.

Figure 13–15. The easy workability of silver lends itself to such fluid designs as this pin and bracelet by Helen Scheier Adelman. Photograph by Bob Pettit. Courtesy of Studio Two.

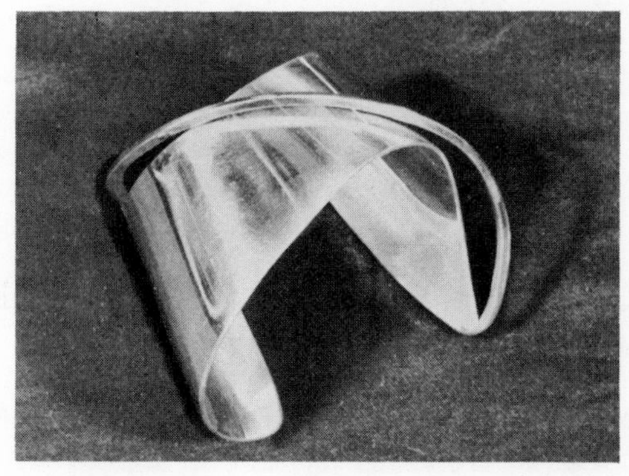

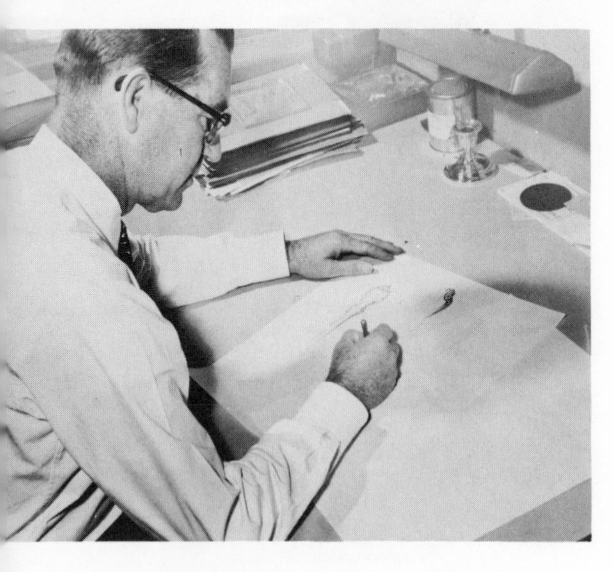

1. The designer makes the preliminary sketch.

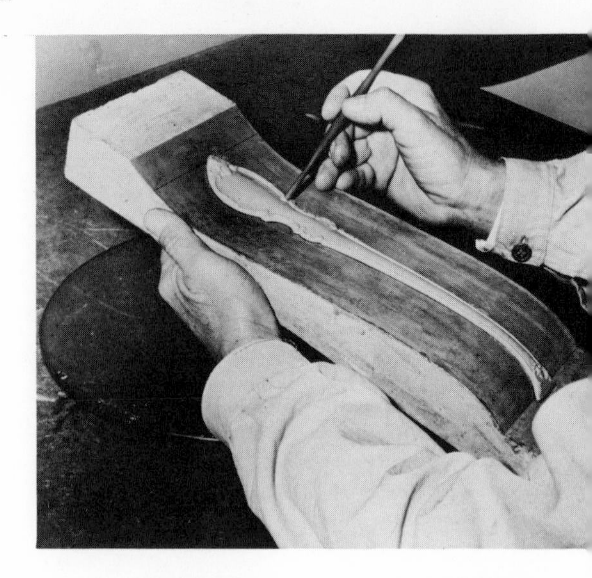

2. A large model is formed in red wax so that every detail can be perfected.

The creation of a piece of silver flatware is an involved collaboration between artist and machine, in which new shapes and forms are explored with frequently just a touch of accent (Figure 13–16).

Figure 13–16. Steps in the process of making silver flatware. Courtesy of International Silver Company.

3. A blank is made in the required size and shape.

4. The blank is punched out in its final shape and outline.

5. The blank is passed between heavy rollers to distribute the metal in correct proportion.

6. Bowl or tine is stamped in a contour die.

7. The design is now stamped on front and back of handle.

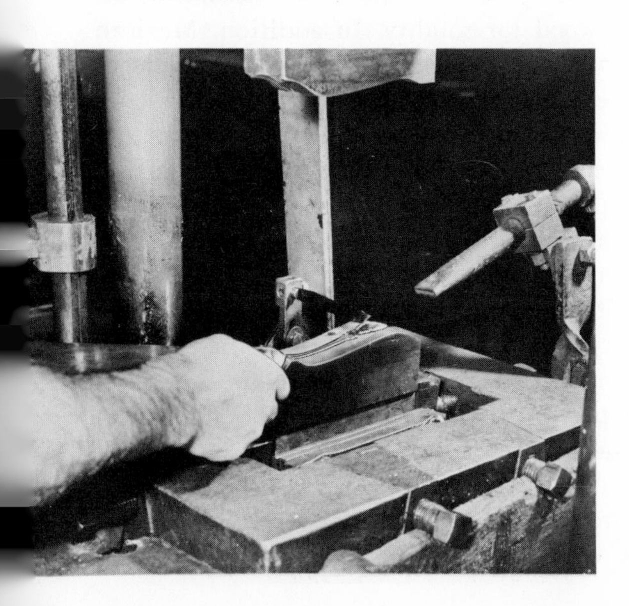

8. Hand chasing is done by a skilled craftsman.

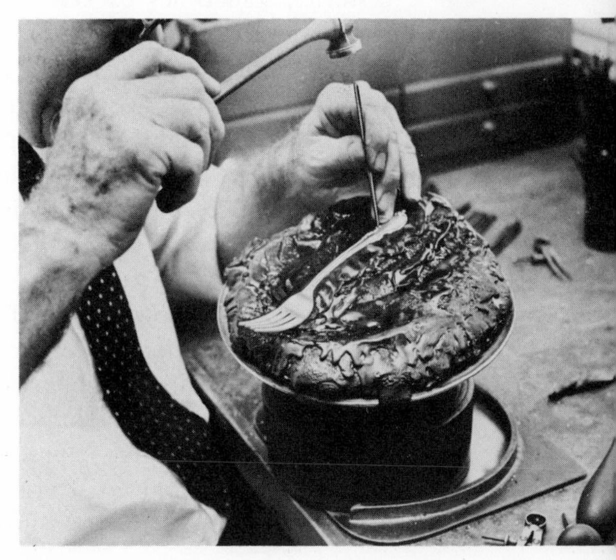

Aluminum, one of the lightest and most plentiful of metals, can be used for *repoussé* and chasing, etching and hammering. Being soft, it can be cast into many forms as well as being rolled into thin sheets for raising. *Pewter,* one of the oldest alloys known, has a long history of antique design. It is a combination in which tin is re-enforced with lead, antimony, and sometimes small amounts of copper and bismuth; it has the color of silver but with a soft glow instead of a high luster. It is frequently washed over copper to form attractive ware known as Egyptian or Chinese copper. Early American pewter is a collector's item and modern Dutch pewter is worthy of note for its contemporary designs.

Brass and *bronze* are two important alloys for decorative use. Brass, which is about 60 percent copper and 40 percent zinc, has many practical uses because it does not rust. When greater hardness is desired tin is added, and the resulting metal is employed in mechanical parts which are subjected to concentrated wear. Its decorative uses have been a chief industry of China and Persia for centuries, not only in sculpture but in vases, bowls, and trays which are inlaid or engraved with elaborate designs. Musical instruments form a large area of use and we see much brass in decorative hardware such as hinges, doorknobs, and locks. Bronze, an alloy of copper and tin with various other metals added, is darker, harder, and longer lasting than brass. It is a standby for use in bells and medals and is one of the most important materials for sculpture. The contemporary designer uses it in jewelry, desk accessories, panels, and doors.

Surprisingly, *tin* is one of the most expensive metals, yet it has many practical uses in addition to the so-called "tin" can which actually is largely zinc. It has taken the people of Mexico to give it its most imaginative uses with their lighting fixtures, trays, waste baskets, and other decorative accessories, sometimes backed with wood for solidity. In addition, Mexican tin takes on a whole gamut of fanciful forms from whimsical roosters to gaily decorated tin Christmas trees.

Iron and *steel* are so highly regarded for structural purposes that we sometimes lose sight of their potential for decorative objects. One of the principal uses of iron is wrought-iron hardware and such accessories as lighting fixtures, fireplace tools, and architectural details. Elaborately designed wrought-iron railings adorn the balconies of many countries, including the southern parts of the United States. Steel has been used widely for tableware and it shows many other possibilities depending upon the elements added to change its appearance and its degree of luster. New ovenproof serving dishes offer a line of departure for the designer who finds steel adaptable to interesting shapes and forms. Its impermeability to stains and hardness of surface give it practical advantages over silver and pewter.

Both miner and artist are lured by the attraction of metal. The many colors and sheens, the qualities that make it workable, and the opportunities for experimentation all fit it for a prominent place in the world of design. The action of various chemicals in producing oxidation as well as the results to be achieved with different tools make unusual effects possible, and the resultant work has the advantages of durability, strength, and lasting beauty.

FOR FURTHER EXPLORATION

New Furniture edited by Hatje Berd (New York: George Wittenborn, Inc., 1953). A pictorial survey of contemporary furniture in America and Europe.

Metalwork Technology and Practice by Oswald A. Ludwig (Bloomington, Ill.: McKnight and McKnight Publishing Co., 1947). Practical manual on methods of working various types of metal. Clear and concise, with illustrations.

Metalsmithing for the Artist-Craftsman by Richard Thomas (Philadelphia: Chilton Company, n.d.). Directions for making small objects in metal by the head of the department at Cranbrook Academy.

STUDIO PROJECTS

1. To acquaint yourself with the beauties of various woods, collect small pieces of several varieties. Stain each piece with walnut stain and, when dry, rub with several coats of wax. Compare the beauty of grain and tone and visualize designs that could be created from each wood.
2. Using the scale $1/2$ inch = 1 inch, draw a design for a metal room divider suitable for dividing a dining area from a living room without shutting out the view completely. Decide in advance what metal should be used and keep its qualities in mind in formulating the design.

CHAPTER 14

Design in Fashion

One of the most capricious and imaginative fields for the designer is the adornment of man himself. Seeking always to achieve new status, he utilizes his clothing as a means of expressing some of his most urgent needs.

We assume that the first coverings were donned for protection, but the anthropologists assure us that this is not the case and that even man's earliest wardrobe of skins, headdresses, and jewelry was motivated by the desire to add attractiveness to his appearance. Realizing that the Greek athletes, whose bodies were the glory of Athens and Sparta, took part in athletic events without clothing, one suspects that adornment even in ancient times may have been promoted by those of less than heroic proportions in an effort to counteract the inequities of nature's endowments. Certainly the traditional function of clothing has been to establish the status of the individual.

When status was a matter of community standing, as in the case of judges, professors, and clergymen, the garb achieved a classic quality that remained unchanged as dignity and prestige accrued to it increasingly through continued use. Academic attire dates back to the twelfth century with only minor modifications made to distinguish among different degrees and colleges. Ecclesiastical vestments have an even longer history. Both provide effective means of preserving the continuity and sense of history so important to man's feeling of his own place in time.

Figure 14–1. In nature, traditionally, the male is more lavishly clothed than the female. At left, the male redstart flashes red wing and tail patches while the female is generally duller with yellow instead of red and white undersides. At right, the male bobolink is arrayed in brown and white with black underside and a vivid patch of yellow at the back of his head; the female is mainly buff and brown. Courtesy of the American Museum of Natural History.

Where the purpose of attire has been the attraction of the opposite sex or the establishment of a reputation in society, design has been subject to as many whims as society itself. Fashion moves in cycles of from seven to ten years' duration, frequently swinging from one extreme to the other. The urgency of keeping abreast of these changes has built the fashion business into a four-billion-dollar industry employing 1,170,000 people, and the designer is at the very heart of it.

From the standpoint of the individual, the psychologists tell us that clothing has a deep-seated effect on behavior. It affects the carriage, the emotions, and the total personality to such an extent that complete character changes have been known to result from a different mode of dressing. One judge ordered a group of juvenile delinquents to give up their sideburns and leather jackets, stating that without these symbols of the cult they would be less inclined to carry on their ravages against society. Neatness in grooming carries over into other activities and the social advantages of attractive dress are far-reaching.

We tend to associate fashion primarily with women yet this is a comparatively recent development. Nature has always been more lavish in her adornment of the male, and, traditionally, it has been the male who seeks by his appearance and behavior to attract attention. This is apparent in the plumage of the birds in Figure 14–1. The gay feathers of the male are fundamental to the ritual of mating, while the reticence of female adornment becomes a matter of life and death when hiding her brood under her protective coloring. Until the nineteenth century the human male took his cue from nature. The Georgian man spent at least five times more than he allowed his wife for clothes, and it is said that his predecessors spent far more on clothes than they did on their mistresses.[1] Fine laces, furs, satins, brocades, velvets and ribbons were all within the realm of masculine embellishment from the sixteenth century on, reaching a peak of elegance during the reign of Louis XIV in France. Today, as the proportion of women to men increases, the situation has become reversed. Women in society spend ten times as much on clothes as men, and man has gained a reputation as a conservative individual.

Basic Principals of Fashion Design

A successful fashion design employs the same elements and principles as any other design with the over-all consideration that it must be adapted to the needs of the human body. It is necessary, however, to define the needs of the body in terms of personality and of the period and conditions under

[1] H. Dennis Bradley, *The Eternal Masquerade,* New York: Liveright Pubishing Corp., 1923, 265 pp.

which a garment will be worn. A woman who will stand elegantly in a receiving line does not require the freedom necessary for waltzing or walking a distance. The hoop and panniers of past periods lent themselves magnificently to life at court but can be approximated only for brief periods of formal wear in the life of the active woman of today. From the medieval coat of armor to the space suit with its built-in air conditioner, clothing must fulfill the needs of its wearer.

The same honesty that permeates the designer's work in architecture and the crafts has found its way into the design of contemporary clothing. The overemphasis on tiny waistlines and little feet has given way before the influence of modern medicine leaving the woman of today nearer to the expression of graceful, healthy womanhood than she has ever been. On the whole, her clothes display her form instead of hiding it, they offer her freedom of movement and are hygienically sound. As a result she enjoys an independence that allows her to move easily in all areas of her busy life.

In clothing as in music, *rhythm* is a predominant principle. The adaptation of a garment to the lines of the body results in a rhythmic flow of line and form that changes with every movement. A successful garment must be attractive under all conditions of standing, walking, sitting, and reaching, and it must be comfortable as well. Folds and gathers falling from strategic structural points contribute to the flow of rhythm while *repetition* of accents and trimming provides a rhythmic beat. *Emphasis* must always be, first of all, on the face, toward which all adornment directs attention. Whatever the temptation of beautiful materials and colorful design, the designer must remember that the purpose of clothing is never to dominate a person but to enhance him. The costume acts as a subtle conspirator, emphasizing all that is noteworthy but never taking the center of the stage.

Variety is essential in dress in varying degrees, depending upon the desired effect. Sometimes the most striking costume can be simple in line and solid in color, but with a single piece of jewelry to lend variety by accent. Variety can be carried to greater lengths in formal wear, where contrasting fabrics and materials are frequently set into a skirt or draped over it in panels or overskirts. In less-than-formal masculine dinner clothes a colored cummerbund and matching tie lend variety.

In fashion design *balance* can be either symmetrical or informal. We know that the human figure is never perfectly symmetrical, so clothing it in symmetrical lines may counteract its inequalities. On the other hand, informal balance may make a more interesting costume. A band of contrasting material running down one side, a clip or pin on shoulder or lapel, pleats or stitching accentuating one side all give informal balance when counteracted elsewhere by form or mass or eye-catching detail.

Form is implicit in the well-designed costume, not only in the form it clothes but in the form of the design itself. A garment that looks nondescript while hanging may take on an entity of distinction when it is filled out by a human form within. Like sculpture, it must be designed to be seen from all sides and, to show its full potential, it must be given substance. Its pleats and folds, its drapery and its hang will only be effective when they have a structure to motivate them; and then they bring out the best features of the human form itself.

As in all design, *unity* is the guiding principle in a successful costume. In this sense, unity means appropriateness of materials used together, harmony of color, and the rhythm of line in which every part is a pleasing and logical development of every other part. Unity must dictate not only the garments themselves but their relationship with the wearer and with all accompanying accessories. It can even extend to the environment and background against which they are worn.

Elements of Fashion Design

Line has been mentioned in connection with rhythm in dress; however, the lines of a garment must be considered in relation to the wearer as well as to the garment itself. The lines of apparel are determined by two factors: the fashion of the costume and the proportions of the figure. Where a design is created for an unseen market, each garment is fashioned according to standard measurements for each of a full range of sizes. Obviously, any given design will look better on some sizes than on others. However, when a designer is commissioned to *custom design* a garment for an individual he has the advantage of being able to adapt the lines specifically to achieve the desired effect.

The fact that vertical lines, on the whole, are more flattering to the average figure is attested to by the elongated proportions of fashion drawings created to sell dress designs. Where the realistic drawing of the human figure is generally seven-and-a-half heads high, the fashion figure extends to a height of close to ten heads. Such drawings emphasize a slimmed and heightened silhouette which has become accepted in the world of fashion as the ultimate in sophistication and smartness (Figure 14–2). The fact that relatively few women are able to translate this fashionable vision into their own appearance seems little deterrent to their hopes. The human longing is for a miracle of design that will transform an ordinary person into a new and exciting personality, and in the endless search for such magic the customer places vast faith in the designer.

Figure 14–2. The tall, slim fashion drawing has come to personify the height of sophistication and charm in the eyes of the American public. Courtesy of The Denver Dry Goods Company.

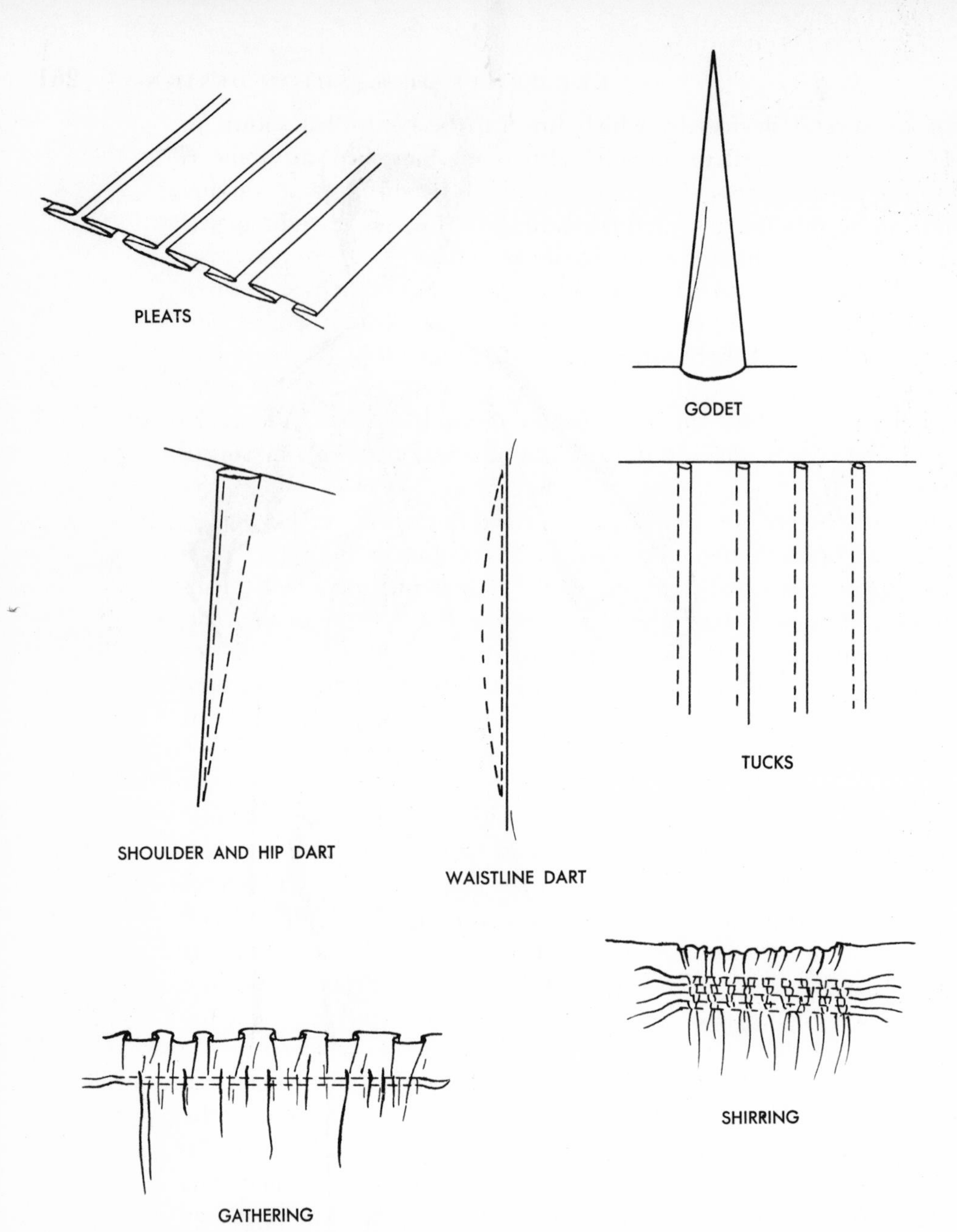

Figure 14–3. The dress designer has various devices by which he can shape his design, whether for fullness or snugness of fit.

Just as vertical lines contribute height and slimness, horizontal lines can shorten a long waist, minimize a long neck, and widen too narrow shoulders. Since the female figure is basically a diamond shape and the male a triangle, horizontal lines across the hips are not recommended for most women, yet diagonal lines in a yoke or stitching can soften the effect of too much figure by seeming to slim the fullness downward.

There are several devices by which line can be controlled shown in Figure 14–3. *Darts* are used to provide fullness for bust, hip, or elbow as well as to nip in the waist. *Tucks* can be used for fullness of varying degrees and can be very narrow, graduated, in groups placed at right angles, or in various other combinations for decorative effects. *Gathering* consists of drawing fabric up on a thread for fullness; *shirring* is composed of three or more rows of gathers. There are several kinds of *pleats* used to gain fullness at the bottom of tight-fitting skirts or at the back of coats and jackets. *Godets* are insets of fullness where the garment needs to be eased or where a contrasting material is set in for decorative effect. These are the tools of the designer, making possible the manipulation of line, form, and rhythm.

Texture is achieved by fabric or by trim, including tucks, ruffles, stitching, lace or braid. When the fabric is interesting in itself the treatment of the garment is usually simple, while plainer materials lend themselves to more elaborate design. The clean lines of the *A* shape in the coat, Figure 14–4, complement the boldly patterned wool which could never have been used effectively in a coat with intricate styling. The use of furs, the combination of silk blouses with wool suits or of men's shirts with tweed and suiting are all basically a matter of variety in texture.

Color moves with the cycles of fashion, providing one of the most exciting aspects of fashion design. More than one unlikely color combination has blossomed under the designer's brush to be echoed on Main Streets all over the country. The effects of color on eyes, hair, skin tone, and figures makes it a vital concern of fashion-minded women everywhere. While black and navy continue to be basic, the increased interest in color in all aspects of modern life has had its effect on contemporary wardrobes. Like the houses of America, the coats of American women have emerged from the conservatism of neutrals to vibrant tones that touch the entire spectrum.

Size is another element which must not be allowed to overwhelm the wearer. This does not refer to the actual size of the clothes but to the proportions of the design. Bulky collars and sweeping cloaks must be limited to figures with the height to carry them, and choice of materials must be made on the basis of size. Small people become lost in heavy woolens while oversized individuals can look ridiculous in flimsy fabrics designed to look dainty. The choice of the appropriate material at the beginning has a great deal to do with the final design having a feeling of unity and coherence.

The *shape* of a garment can be surprisingly varied, considering the fact that it is designed to cover a more-or-less standard human figure. We speak of the cut of a man's lounge suit as being quite different from that of a business suit or tuxedo. The variation comes not just in shoulder width and fit at the waist but in the draping of material from the shoulders, the

Figure 14–4. Boldly patterned wool is used in a coat style in the simple *A* silhouette. Courtesy of B. Altman & Co.

hang of the coat, and the folds in which the trousers fall from the waistline. Women's dress is even more obvious, varying as it does from sheath to full skirt with all the modifications in between. There are two primary considerations which determine the shape of a garment: first, the pattern pieces themselves which establish the shape of the various parts and of the total garment and, second, the method of construction which governs the amount and position of fullness and the way the garment hangs.

The Influence of Paris

Ever since the seventeenth century when all of Europe was dazzled by the brilliance of the French court, Paris has been the center of *haute couture,* high fashion. Many of the world's leading designers have served apprenticeships in the Paris salons, and Paris showings continue to be the focal point of the fashion world. In the meantime, centers of fashion have developed in Rome, in Madrid, and in various cities in the United States, bringing a fresh approach and the touch of custom design to a wide variety of clothing outside the realm of *haute couture.* There is a basic difference between the French and American fashion industries which modifies any feeling of competition. Parisian designers consider their creations as works of art and they insist that they are constructed with the finest workmanship. Furthermore, European women spend much of their time in the company of men and they make a habit of dressing for them. Since men are somewhat conservative in taste they approve the elegance of gradual change rather than startling innovations. These two factors indicate the tendency to spend a great deal of money on each costume rather than concentrating on amassing a vast wardrobe. In America, on the other hand, women react more favorably to the unusual, the novel, and the fad which will show them to be abreast of the latest developments. They dress more for other women and in doing so consider frequent change of great importance. Machine-made clothes fill the need by rapid and inexpensive production which makes possible continual turnover in the average woman's wardrobe.

In spite of these differences, Paris continues to be an influence on American taste. Copies of Paris originals are marketed in this country in a wide range of prices, bringing them within the budget of most American women. The names of French designers are familiar to every fashion-minded American woman, who is well aware through press releases of what has transpired at the latest Paris showings. Cristobal Balenciaga and the late

Figure 14–5. Five of the hundreds of variations that have been designed on the basis of the Chanel jacket. Courtesy of B. Altman & Co.

Christian Dior have marked a generation of fashions, and Hubert de Givenchy is known internationally for the elegant simplicity of his designs. But, perhaps no one has had more influence both here and abroad than Madame Gabrielle "Coco" Chanel, who revolutionized fashion in the nineteen-twenties. Half a century of designing has not dimmed her prestige in the world of fashion, nor lessened enthusiasm for her new collections. Slacks for women are attributed to her along with such less controversial classics as

skirts worn with sweaters, the collarless jacket, short light-colored gloves, the pillbox hat, and the entire concept of separates. Her experiments introduced the use of many materials not widely used before: cotton pique, jersey, corduroy, lamé and geometric and abstract prints. Chanel jewelry, Chanel perfume, and Chanel suits have become cornerstones of many a fashionable wardrobe. Figure 14–5 displays just a few of the classic fashions based on the chic and simple Chanel neckline and short straight jacket.

Figure 14–6. Designing accessories can be a full-time career in itself. Courtesy of The Denver Dry Goods Company.

Fashion in America

While elegance is the keynote of Parisian fashion, American designers have come into their own as creators of clothes particularly suited to the active informality of American life. Fashion centers have sprung up in Los Angeles, San Francisco, Phoenix, Chicago, Minneapolis, Dallas, and St. Louis for the purpose of creating and selling clothes for the casual life indigenous to these regions. Norman Norell, Claire McCardell, Jo Copeland, Molly Parnis and Pauline Trigère are just a few of the designers who have established themselves in the front lines of American fashion not by imitating Paris but by originating clothes for the special requirements of the active American woman.

Fashion designers in America have three main outlets for their talents. They create models for manufacturers who produce them in quantity, they make patterns for pattern companies who sell to home seamstresses, and they operate their own small shops where they design and make original models for individual customers. Some designers devote their talents to designing specific items such as hats, shoes, or accessories like those in Figure 14–6. Others specialize in a type of clothes unknown in the Paris salons which cater to women of wealth, lines such as house dresses, sport clothes, lounging clothes, and children's wear. By designing for mail-order houses and large department stores or chains of low-priced specialty shops, American designers bring fashion into millions of homes on isolated farms, or in small towns. It is these designers who have built for American women the reputation of being the best-dressed women in the world.

Sources of Inspiration

This feat has been accomplished by a constant search for inspiration. Forages into history continually inspire twentieth-century dress. The Greek chiton and the Empire waistline in Figure 14–7 have both appeared on ballroom floors periodically, and the hoopskirt of the antebellum South frequently makes its graceful re-entrance on the scene.

Extensive travel is an invaluable aid in finding inspiration. Innumerable American fashions have sprung from the soil of foreign lands, leaping from a South Sea island or a remote Italian countryside into the living rooms of America with a few deft strokes of the designer's pen. The dirndl

Figure 14–7. The soft drapery of the Grecian chiton and the exaggerated Empire waistline of the Napoleonic era emerge periodically in formal fashions.

Figure 14–8. The muu-muu has led a varied and colorful life in spite of puritanical beginnings.

skirt of the nineteen-forties came directly from the full peasant skirt of western Europe and the Mandarin influence of the sixties was translated from the Orient by way of such theatrical productions as "Flower Drum Song." Fabric design has been similarly influenced by Persian and East Indian colors and designs, South American hand weaving and embroidery and South Sea Island batiks. With increased speed and ease of travel the entire world becomes a treasure house of inspiration.

Sometimes interesting changes take place in the course of translation into American fashion. The Hawaiian muu-muu (Figure 14–8) is an example. Originally designed by missionaries to the Hawaiian Islands who were alarmed at the carefree exposure of the natives, it was first used as a kind of uniform worn by Hawaiian women in the cause of modesty. Naturally, they adapted it to their own love of color and pattern, and it became a charming garment associated with formal dress wherever Hawaiians gathered. Fashion designers were delighted with it and brought it to the mainland in an effort to carry over its gay and casual connotations, but it emerged as a lounging garment, a relative of the negligee or housecoat. Consequently, the costume originally designed for modesty in Hawaii found itself in less colorful localities considered *im*modest for wear outside the home.

Importance of the Fashion Designer

The life of the fashion designer is hectic, varied, and filled with interesting experiences. While he may not engrave the permanent impression on his environment that the architect achieves, he influences the lives of thousands of people who unknowingly are more comfortable or more festive because of his designs. In this fact we find the most important trait of any fashion designer, his interest in people. No one can design apparel successfully without a sense of the importance of all the varied feelings and relationships that arise from the wearing of clothing that is becoming, attractive, and skillfully designed.

FOR FURTHER EXPLORATION

Careers in the World of Fashion by Frieda Steinmann Curtis (New York: William Morrow & Co., Inc., 1953). Useful discussion of various types of work in fashion with many practical suggestions.

Fashions Through the Centuries, Renaissance, Baroque and Rococo by Olga Sronkova (New York: Tudor Publishing Co., 1962). A history, with many excellent illustrations, of costume in Central Europe.

STUDIO PROJECTS

1. Using a fashion figure ten heads high, design a garment making conscious use of the elements of design. Render in pen and watercolor, and be prepared to show how the elements of design contribute to its effectiveness.

2. Using the same type of figure and rendering, design a garment using the principles of design. Explain how the principles are used and how they contribute to the effectiveness of the garment.

3. Select a character from a play or other work of literature and design a costume which you feel interprets the mood and character which should be established in a dramatic portrayal of this character. Make use of both the elements and principles of design in your interpretation.

CHAPTER 15

Design in Books

A FINE BOOK HOLDS A UNIQUE PLACE among the treasures of the world. Not only does its very nature establish it as a record of great thoughts, but the use of beautiful papers, ink, type, illustrations, and binding makes the physical entity of a book an effective agent for esthetic expression in which content and wrapping create a unified work of art.

Development of Literature

From the earliest symbols scratched on stone to the mass-produced books of the twentieth century, the thoughts of man have been preserved with respect and devotion. The ancient Egyptians threaded their hieroglyphics through their painting and sculpture like a running commentary (Figure 15–1) not only on stone but on scrolls made from the thick stems of the papyrus plant. This pictorial record evolved into Greek writing (Figure 15–2) by which many of the most important works of literature were preserved on parchment made from the skin of young sheep. During the Middle Ages devoted monks and nuns kept alive the teachings of the Christian Church through parchment manuscripts elaborately illuminated with pictures and designs (Figure 15–3). This custom of illuminating, or hand painting, manuscripts extended pretty much throughout the world. Many extraordinarily beautiful books still exist in India, for example, in which illustrations consist of small painted scenes whose colors include vibrant oranges, yellows, blues, and delicately applied pure gold.

Figure 15–1. Egyptian sculpture of the Nineteenth Dynasty from Temple of Rameses I. Bas-relief in limestone showing King Rameses offering food and flowers to Osiris Symbol and the goddess Isis. Notice how the hieroglyphics form an integral part of the design. Courtesy of the Metropolitan Museum of Art, Gift of J. Pierpont Morgan, 1911.

Figure 15–2. The evolution of one segment of written language is clearly discernible in the Rosetta Stone, which shows Egyptian hieroglyphics at the top, demotic or commonly used Egyptian characters in the center, and Greek characters at the bottom. Courtesy of the Trustees of the British Museum.

Figure 15–3. Elaborate illuminations are characteristic of the manuscripts of the Middle Ages, by which devoted monks and nuns painstakingly kept alive the knowledge which was available only to a small group of scholars and clergy. Courtesy of the Trustees of the British Museum.

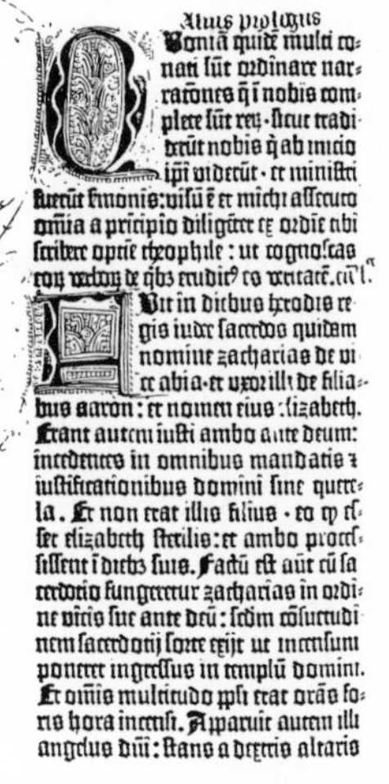

Figure 15–4. A page from the Gutenberg Bible showing the similarity between the type used and the calligraphy of the medieval manuscripts. There are forty-seven copies known to be in existence today.

Effects of Printing

The invention of the printing press in the fifteenth century had more effect on the use of paper than on the design of print. Parchment was too stiff and too expensive for the new dissemination of knowledge so paper came into wide use. However, since the inventors of the press felt it wise to remain anonymous for political reasons, the type used was copied from the calligraphy of hand-lettered manuscripts (15–4). Thus the earliest printed books had much of the aspect of medieval documents. Beyond this, the advent of movable type had widespread repercussions. The subsequent multiplication of books lowered their price to one-fifth of what it had been and brought them within the reach of multitudes who had never before owned a piece of literature. Such availability inspired interest in old manuscripts and in preserving literature in libraries. This, in turn, led to the development of bookbinding for the safekeeping of documents and literary works. Handwritten manuscripts had been bound chiefly by monks who used thick oak boards covered with tanned deerskin sometimes embellished by goldsmiths and jewelers with tooling, encrustations of gems, metal clasps, and mountings. Increased publication led to use of cheaper materials, not only paper but leather and cloth. Quarter- and half-leather bindings appeared. This paved the way for case bindings made of cloth over paper boards. A century later the culmination of the trend has come in the flexible cardboard or heavy-paper cover of the "paper back," designed for wide and inexpensive dispersal rather than for centuries of use.

Twentieth-Century Book Design

The age-old veneration for knowledge and the desire to clothe it in worthy forms call upon many facets of the contemporary designer's art. Just as principles of design govern composition of the literature within the covers, so they direct every aspect of the physical entity that becomes the tangible body of the book. Book design today falls into two categories: the book produced in quantity for the large popular market and the hand-bound book created by a small number of artist-craftsmen who continue the tradition of binding for the preservation of knowledge in our museums and libraries, both public and private.

The Popular Market

Cover Design

For the book produced in quantity, the cover design assumes the function of packaging, of making the contents of the book seem more interesting and attractive. In this highly competitive field, book covers are planned with the consciousness that in a crowded bookstore an attractive jacket may have a strong influence on sales, particularly among books whose reputation has not yet been established. A feeling for the contents is the primary consideration of the cover designer for an interpretation of the book is all-important. This can be done in several ways. Striking use of color and form is effective, with a suggestion of the contents treated in a creative way as in the jackets, Figure 15–5. Another handling is an unusual use of lettering. Figure 15–6 shows a case in which lettering gives the feeling of the title as well as spelling it out, thus becoming a visual symbol in addition to communicating the contents. Again, interpretive drawings

Figure 15–5(a-d). Color, texture, line, and shape play important roles in these interpretative book jackets designed to suggest the fascination of the contents. (a) *The Artist in His Studio* by Alexander Liberman. Courtesy of The Viking Press, Inc., Publishers.

ALEXANDER LIBERMAN

THE ARTIST IN HIS STUDIO

Figure 15–5, continued. (b) *A Treasury of Asian Literature* edited with an Introduction and Commentaries by John F. Yohannan. Designer: I. Rosenhouse. The John Day Company, Inc., Publishers. (c) *Cities and Society: the Revised Reader in Urban Sociology* edited by Paul K. Hatt and Albert J. Reiss, Jr. Designer: Paul Bacon. Free Press of Glencoe, Publisher. (d) *Textiles and Ornaments of India* edited by Monroe Wheeler with text by John Irwin and Mme. Pupui Jayaker. Designer: Norman Ives. The Museum of Modern Art, Publisher.

Figure 15–6. Lettering forms the basis of the design in this jacket, yet it communicates a feeling of the contents of the book. Donald H. Ecroyd, *Speech in the Classroom,* © 1960. Reprinted by permission of Prentice-Hall, Inc., Publisher. Designed by Irene E. Springer.

Figure 15–7. The drawing on this book jacket could be interpreted in many ways. Its effectiveness lies in its ability to stimulate the imagination and the curiosity leading the prospective reader into active interest. *Goodbye, Columbus* by Philip Roth. Houghton Mifflin Company, Publisher.

may be used, not illustrating incidents so much as giving a sense of the book and awakening the browser's curiosity. Figure 15–7 could well lead anyone to buy the book just to see how the cover design relates to the story.

Dust jackets can wear out and the case bindings underneath must be able to hold their own when left exposed. Design here is usually more conservative in all its aspects of texture and size, color and emphasis, balance and unity. Durability, of course, is the first consideration, for the life of the book depends largely upon the fortitude of its binding. Special editions frequently have end papers designed in character with the book and consistent with the binding.

Paper, Type, and Layout

The choice of paper on which a book is printed has as much to do with its general aspect as any other single feature. Upon the affinity of paper, print, binding, content, and illustrations is based the concept of organic book design.

While the basic processes for making paper have not changed in over 1800 years, there are innumerable possible variations based principally upon the raw materials from which paper is made, with modifications resulting from the textural treatment of the final surface. The cheapest grade of newsprint is made from wood pulp, and the finest paper is created from the fibers of cotton or linen rags, with the medium grades a mixture of the two, combined with various fibrous materials such as straw, leaves, and bark. Sometimes a synthetic substance is added for strength. Melamine, a plastic recently added to the paper used in dollar bills, is said to have increased the life expectancy of the bill from twelve to seventeen months.

The paper used for a leather-bound collector's volume will be quite different from that used for a popularly priced novel. Expensive books may use a heavy linen paper or an extremely thin but strong onion skin, as in religious works. Final choice depends upon the thickness of the volume and the appropriateness of the paper to the total design.

Text
Text ABCDEFGH
abcdefghijkl

FORMAL ROMAN
ABCDEFG

Bold Roman Italics
ABCDEFGHIJKLMN
OPQRSTTUVWXYZ

Gothic ABCDEFGH
Gothic abcdefgh

Figure 15–8. All the varying kinds of lettering can be classified generally in one of the four basic categories: Black Text, Roman, Italics or Gothic. Courtesy of the C. Howard Hunt Pen Company.

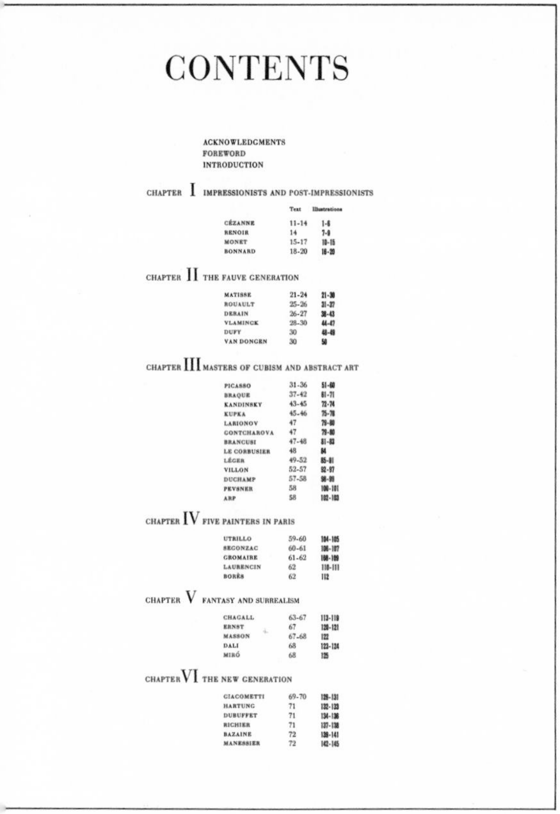

CONTENTS

ACKNOWLEDGMENTS
FOREWORD
INTRODUCTION

CHAPTER I IMPRESSIONISTS AND POST-IMPRESSIONISTS

	Text	Illustrations
CÉZANNE	11-14	1-6
RENOIR	14	7-9
MONET	15-17	10-15
BONNARD	18-20	16-20

CHAPTER II THE FAUVE GENERATION

MATISSE	21-24	21-30
ROUAULT	25-26	31-37
DERAIN	26-27	38-43
VLAMINCK	28-30	44-47
DUFY	30	48-49
VAN DONGEN	30	50

CHAPTER III MASTERS OF CUBISM AND ABSTRACT ART

PICASSO	31-36	51-60
BRAQUE	37-42	61-71
KANDINSKY	43-45	72-74
KUPKA	45-46	75-78
LARIONOV	47	79-80
GONTCHAROVA	47	79-80
BRANCUSI	47-48	81-83
LE CORBUSIER	48	84
LÉGER	49-52	85-91
VILLON	52-57	92-97
DUCHAMP	57-58	98-99
PEVSNER	58	100-101
ARP	58	102-103

CHAPTER IV FIVE PAINTERS IN PARIS

UTRILLO	59-60	104-105
SEGONZAC	60-61	106-107
GROMAIRE	61-62	108-109
LAURENCIN	62	110-111
BORÈS	62	112

CHAPTER V FANTASY AND SURREALISM

CHAGALL	63-67	113-119
ERNST	67	120-121
MASSON	67-68	122
DALI	68	123-124
MIRÓ	68	125

CHAPTER VI THE NEW GENERATION

GIACOMETTI	69-70	126-131
HARTUNG	71	132-133
DUBUFFET	71	134-136
RICHIER	71	137-138
BAZAINE	72	139-141
MANESSIER	72	142-145

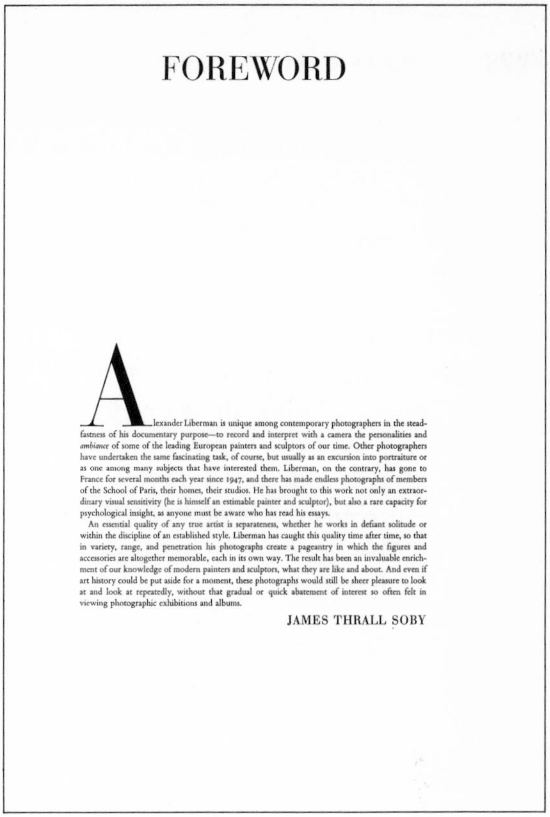

FOREWORD

Alexander Liberman is unique among contemporary photographers in the steadfastness of his documentary purpose—to record and interpret with a camera the personalities and *ambiance* of some of the leading European painters and sculptors of our time. Other photographers have undertaken the same fascinating task, of course, but usually as an excursion into portraiture or as one among many subjects that have interested them. Liberman, on the contrary, has gone to France for several months each year since 1947, and there has made endless photographs of members of the School of Paris, their homes, their studios. He has brought to this work not only an extraordinary visual sensitivity (he is himself an estimable painter and sculptor), but also a rare capacity for psychological insight, as anyone must be aware who has read his essays.

An essential quality of any true artist is separateness, whether he works in defiant solitude or within the discipline of an established style. Liberman has caught this quality time after time, so that in variety, range, and penetration his photographs create a pageantry in which the figures and accessories are altogether memorable, each in its own way. The result has been an invaluable enrichment of our knowledge of modern painters and sculptors, what they are like and about. And even if art history could be put aside for a moment, these photographs would still be sheer pleasure to look at and look at repeatedly, without that gradual or quick abatement of interest so often felt in viewing photographic exhibitions and albums.

JAMES THRALL SOBY

Figure 15–9. Two examples of page design showing attention to balance, emphasis, unity, and value. From *The Artist in His Studio* by Alexander Liberman. Courtesy of The Viking Press.

Type design has undergone many changes since the early "block books," which were printed from type cut in blocks of wood. Movable type is made from an alloy of lead—antimony, tin, and copper—a combination known as "type metal." Although designers have contributed numerous variations through the centuries, type today generally can be classified in one of four categories (Figure 15–8). The so-called modern type used for most current books is a variation of Roman type designed as far back as 1470.

The layout of every page must be designed, whether it is simply a well-placed body of print or a title page showing originality and careful attention to values. Some lines are wide apart, making for lighter value while close placement obviously gives a darker all-over tone. The size and shape of individual letters makes a difference as well. Like any other design, the layout of a beautiful page of print is a matter of proportion and value, of unity and balance. In both pages in Figure 15–9 careful attention has been given to these considerations, resulting in distinctive layouts.

Illustration

Many books today are without illustrations, but the most effective means of graphic communication is a happy balance between text and pictures. Like the Egyptians, the Japanese have long used calligraphy as an accent to their paintings, making words an integral part of design (Figure 15–10). In organic book design, we strive to make the illustrations just as unified a part of the printed text.

Although many techniques are used in book illustration, the actual processes of reproduction are done by machine. There are various technical procedures, all falling into one of three categories. The *relief* methods involve any process by which portions to be printed stand out while the background is recessed. These include line cuts, halftones, three-color and four-color processes. The *intaglio* method takes its name from the Italian meaning "to incise" and applies to any process in which the parts to be printed are cut out—as in rotogravure and photogravure. The third, *planography,* comprises all of the methods handled by plain surfaces from which prints are taken, such as photolithography and collotype.

These processes are used to reproduce in quantity any material used as illustrations. While photographs form the bulk of pictorial matter in textbooks, travel books, and special editions of many kinds, a great deal of pen-and-ink drawing is used in illustrating children's books. Books for very young children also make use of brightly colored pictures, usually done in watercolor. Occasionally, a gift edition is produced using woodcuts or wood engravings to illustrate a well-known work of literature. Both of these techniques stem from the earliest illustrations for hand-printed books, but they have a charm that cannot be replaced by more recent techniques.

The Hand-Bound Book

The culmination of all that a fine book can be is most nearly reached at the hands of a few dedicated craftsmen who restore, design, and bind books by hand. Free from the contingencies of the competitive market, these artists can devote their efforts to the creation and preservation of volumes for discriminating collectors represented by the genuine bibliophile and by libraries that are truly aware of the functions and attributes of a binding. Such people appreciate the best in materials, design, and workmanship and provide inspiration for a concept of book design that embodies the finest in art and craftsmanship. They are sympathetic to the philosophy that books, like any other work of art, are not meant to be owned by any one person but are merely to be preserved by individuals in the best manner possible until they shall be passed on to others. This does not mean that

Figure 15–10. Japanese painting in ink on silk. "River Gorge with Waterfall." From the Tokugawa Period (1603–1868). The calligraphy is echoed in the buildings, creating balance. Courtesy of the Metropolitan Museum of Art, the Howard Mansfield Collection. Purchase 1936, Rogers Fund.

Figure 15–11. Pierre Martin interprets Max Jacob's *Chronique des Temps héroiques* in two different ways, both of which are influenced by Picasso's illustrations. (*Above.*) A combination of mosaic and inlay using black and white on black, and (*opposite page*) a cubistic design in black-and-white calf mosaic.

hand binders are limited to traditional designs. Many of the hand binders of today have proven this to be one of the most exciting and imaginative of fields.

Materials are expensive and the labor involved painstaking, yet there is room for tremendous ingenuity in both. Some volumes cost thousands of dollars, and it is estimated that a minimum of twenty hours of labor is required per book. The cost is not a matter of the binding but of the decorative design.

The bookbinder of today has a long and honorable tradition behind him, starting in Ireland and spreading to England and the Italian monasteries. One of the leading influences in this country has been Hazel Dreis, who maintained her studio in California for many years, training a group of hand-picked students in the methods she learned from Lawrence Decoverly in London. In the manner of the European workshops,

Mrs. Dreis insisted that her students acquire a rich background of paper-making, music, drama, painting, sculpture and archaeology. This diverse groundwork formed the basis for intelligent and sensitive design for all types of books.

The basic purpose of a binding is that of preserving the text. Architectural solidity comes first with decorative design a function of the structure. Leather is the only practical binding for permanence and many different leathers have been used, with Nigerian goatskin as a favorite because of its durability and smooth grain. Usually these skins are not bleached, a process that threatens the lasting qualities even though it insures a smoother color. Calfskin makes possible beautifully textured bindings although, being the skin of an immature animal, it does not have the permanence of goatskin. Pigskin is most durable for very large volumes but it is a thick leather and apt to be rather stiff.

The designing of a binding is a personal alliance between the binder, the subject matter, the printer, and the paper. The use to which the volume will be put must also be considered, since elaborate decoration through gold tooling, inlay, or overlay will not hold up on active reference volumes or workbooks. The binder appraises the print, the paper, the illustrations,

and the spirit of the text and then creates his own conception of how the book shall express itself through its outer design.

Two outstanding examples of the creative bookbinder of today are Pierre Martin and Edward McLean. Working five thousand miles apart, these men have a basic similarity of approach, a consuming interest in interpretation, and the highest standards of craftsmanship.

Pierre Martin, working in Paris, has his own atelier where he creates original designs primarily for French works of literature which he considers to be of contemporary importance. A master binder after many years of apprenticeship and practice, he now experiments with unusual effects, notably a series of mosaics in leather which are extremely difficult to execute and are striking in appearance. Figure 15–11 shows two such designs in calfskin, both of which show a preoccupation with depth that is almost cubistic. He refers to some of his bindings as *trompe l'oeil* because they are so involved with a three-dimensional quality. An exploration of the possibilities of geometrical representation is a fascinating earmark of Martin's work, Figure 15–12. Feeling geometry to be a fitting symbol of our age, he uses it to interpret a variety of books, squeezing it or stretching it to produce a new dimension he labels "twisted geometry." The narrow strips of leather representing these forms are chosen with great care and meticulously integrated into a unified design.

Working in his studio in Denver, Edward McLean, trained under Hazel Dreis, binds a wide variety of books, from Latin treatises to the United States Constitution, and he did a great deal of restoration work on volumes for the Folger Shakespearean Library in Washington, D.C. under its late director, Dr. Joseph Quincy Adams. Two of his bindings for old manuscripts are shown in Figure 15–13, each with a rich but distinctive feeling stating eloquently that the manuscript within is worthy of the finest care.

Mr. McLean's belief that an interesting book design is no harder to create than a dull one is borne out in his designs for a variety of subjects, Figure 15–14. Each binding tells its own story, weather it is of the Old West or of the English theatre. In his western bindings he frequently makes use of bandana fabrics combined with the hide of unborn calves to give an unusual and authentic effect. On works which he has published himself

Figure 15–12. Two uses of Pierre Martin's "twisted geometry" expressing two books illustrated by two different artists. (*Opposite.*) Jean Giono's *Recherche de la Pureté* shows the airy effect of the illustrations by Bernard Buffet in a design of black-and-white calf inlaid with black-and-white lacquered paper, while the second (*bottom of page*) has a distinct affinity for the work of Georges Braque who provided the illustrations. Saint-Pol-Roux' *Août* is bound in light tan morocco with mosaic forms in dark plum-colored calf.

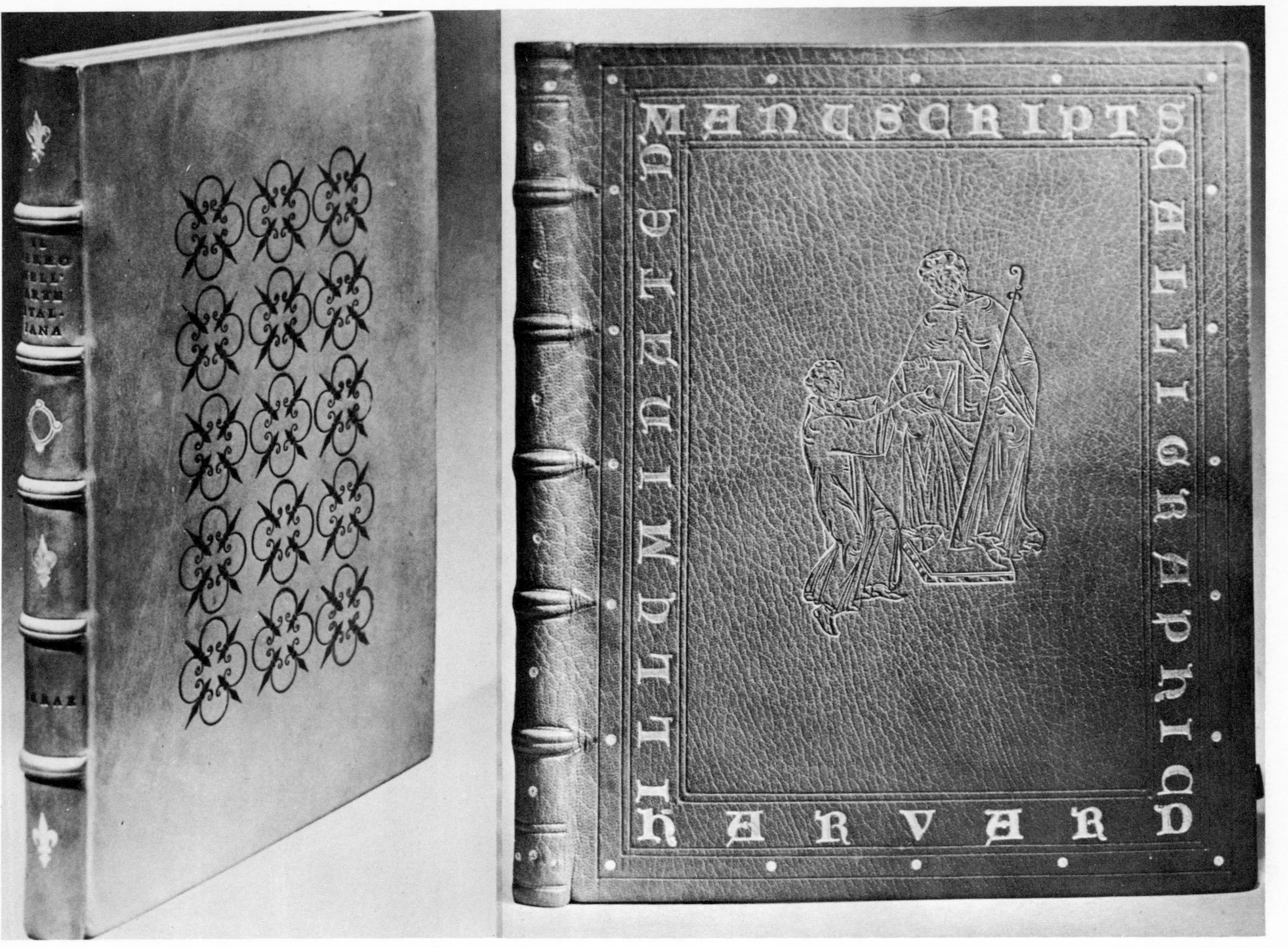

Figure 15–13. Two bindings for old manuscripts by Edward McLean. (a) Henna calf, tooled in blind and gold, and (b) a tooled

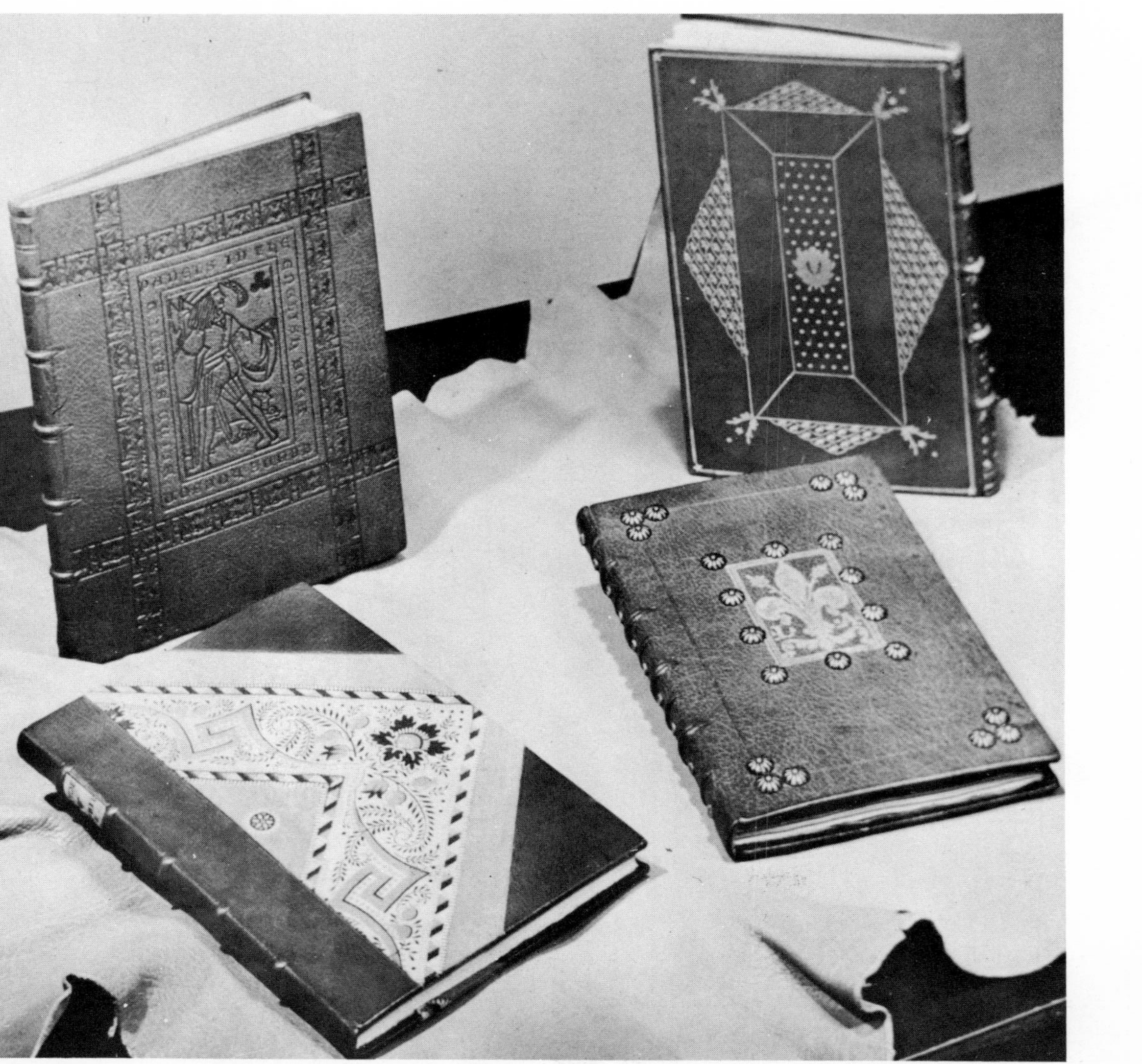

Figure 15–14. A variety of bindings by Edward McLean. Left rear, *Blind Stamped Panels in the English Book Trade* bound in dark-brown Nigerian goatskin, blind stamped and tooled in the manner of London binders *c.* 1550. Right rear, *Check List of English Plays 1641–1700* by Woodward and McManaway, tooled in gold in the manner of the Charles II period on henna calfskin. Left front, *Guide to Life and Literature in the Southwest* by Dobie, bound in mustang-colored Nigerian goatskin with bandana sides. Right front, *Fifty Printer's Marks* by Willoughby, in red Nigerian goatskin executed in the manner of early sixteenth century Venice. The stamp is a copy of the famous Italian sixteenth-century printer Giunta. Courtesy of the artist.

JOHN ROWZÉE PEYTON

3

LETTERS

FROM

ST. LOUIS

1958

EDWARD McLEAN

FOR

LIBROS ESCOGIDOS

DENVER

vicente silva

& his

40

bandits

MANUEL C.
DE BACA

TRANSLATION
LANE KAUFFMANN

ILLUSTRATIONS
FANITA LANIER

EDWARD MC LEAN · *LIBROS ESCOGIDOS* · WASHINGTON · 1947

15

NEW MEXICO

SANTOS

JAMES
MacMILLAN

COLOR PLATES
LOUIE EWING

LIBROS ESCOGIDOS

SANTA FE · NEW MEXICO · 1941

Figure 15–15. Three title pages designed by Edward McLean. Each has a flavor in keeping with the book for which it was intended. Courtesy of the artist.

he has designed the formats and especially the title pages, as well as the case bindings to go with them (Figure 15–15). His belief in expressive treatment shows as clearly in his choice of print and design here as it does in his leather bindings, for each page has a spirit in keeping with the subject it announces.

Both of these artist-craftsmen exemplify the highest standards to be found in the design and creation of books today, representing as they do a small group of artists who supplement that larger group who work with major publishing houses in producing books for wide distribution. With our tremendous market of inexpensive books available, we sometimes lose sight of the fact that knowledge is possible only because centuries of devoted craftsmen have taken the trouble to preserve it in usable form. If it had not been for bookbinding through the centuries, each new generation would have to repeat a great deal of the basic research and exploration that has gone before it. Viewed in this light, the design of books becomes not only a fascinating field for the designer but a serious responsibility to succeeding generations.

FOR FURTHER EXPLORATION

Graphic Forms: The Arts as Related to the Book by Gyorgy Kepes and others. (Cambridge, Mass.: Harvard University Press, 1949). A symposium on the book and its related arts with contributions by 15 participants in the field.

The Hand-produced Book by David Diringer (New York: Philosophical Library, Inc., 1953). An extensive treatment of the book as produced before the invention of printing.

A Book of Type and Design by Oldrich Hlavsa (New York: Tudor Publishing Co., 1962). A survey of type and modern typography with emphasis on rules of good composition.

STUDIO PROJECTS

1. Clip from magazines five examples of type showing variations in overall value. Mount in order of value, progressing from light to dark.
2. Design a book jacket for a textbook on pottery, a medical book, or a book on gardening.
3. Design and execute a woodcut illustrating a poem, a play, or some other work of literature.

CHAPTER 16

We picked 9,000 fragrant red rose petals to make one half-ounce of Yardley Red Roses Perfume for you!

Design for Selling

ADVERTISING DESIGN IS CHARACTERISTIC OF ITS TIME. Not only does it depict modern life in all its ramifications but its very nature shows clearly that it is communication designed to be viewed by people in a hurry, people with many things on their minds, people who must be caught and held a moment in spite of themselves.

Although advertising art has existed since 3000 B.C. when the ancient Babylonians used pictures to advertise their wares, and rather elaborate pictorial signs have been known since the Middle Ages in western Europe, there has never been a period when the viewer was so pressed for time and advertising so crowded with competition as in the twentieth century. Where the red-and-white-striped barber pole and the three balls of the pawnbroker's shop were sufficient at one time to announce the existence of a service, today's shopkeeper feels the need to prove that his shop is not only there, but is better than other shops available. To do this he depends upon brighter colors, bigger lettering, and flashier signs. Fortunately, he has also come to depend upon the services of the artist.

Whether or not the means of reaching the public eye can be classified as art, it employs people who must have sound art training. There are great possibilities for good design in advertising and definite strides upward have been made by many firms. Where taste is lacking it is frequently because the advertiser makes up his mind in advance as to what he wants and simply hires an artist capable of executing it, even though the artist may not agree with the approach. To bridge the gap between advertiser and artist, firms have evolved for the sole purpose of creating advertising for producers of goods and services. These firms are headed by men who know the psychology of selling and have on their staffs art directors who not only

Figure 16–1. The essence of feminine beauty and charm is intimated in this ad for perfume. Courtesy of Yardley of London. Design by Doyle, Dane & Bernbach, Inc.

know what will sell but who have art backgrounds. When an art director has reached an understanding with the advertiser he calls upon his staff of commercial artists and copy writers to carry out the proposed design with its accompanying *copy*. The procedure is often reversed, of course, and the copywriter decides what needs to be said, thinking up a catchy headline, and then calls upon the artist to put it into eye-stopping form. The larger firms employ artists who have made a name for themselves either in the field of design or as free-lance artists selling their work to various firms. As a result the advertising designs they produce are of high quality. Advertising has become an industry; advertising firms publicize their services in trade journals, newspapers, magazines; books and even motion pictures have been written about it.

The Artist and Advertising

While the philosophical question as to what constitutes a work of art has filled many volumes, there is still no unassailable dividing line between what is art and what is not. However, there are three basic principles upon which advertising design can fulfill the requisites of a work of art. First, *if the advertisement expresses the product that it advertises* it is communicating in its way just as a painting communicates an emotion or a literary work expresses a person or a philosophy. The advertisement in Figure 16–1 accomplishes this. We are attracted at once by the photograph of a beautiful rose, with petals lying casually as though it might have been laid down a moment before by a charming woman. The association of the rose with beauty and femininity is almost instinctive for anyone who has read poetry or romantic prose. Then the caption intimates that these petals are similar to 9000 "fragrant red rose petals" that have been crushed to make a half-

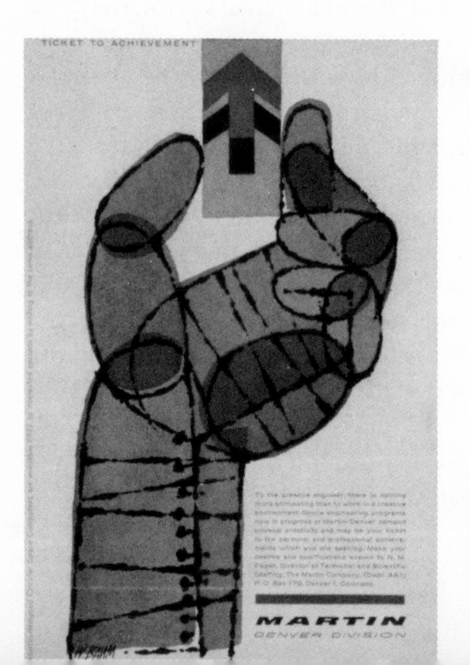

Figure 16–2. Design and layout with a feeling of a new era, in keeping with the forward-looking projects of the space age. Designed by Willi K. Baum for the Martin Company. Courtesy of the E. M. Halvorson Company, Inc.

Figure 16–3. This ad from *The Chicago Tribune* catches the eye, displays the merchandise, and arouses the curiosity, all with strikingly simple means. Designer: Robert Fabian.

ounce of red rose perfume "for you." The vision of crushed rose petals immediately brings a scent to our imagination and the idea of the perfume itself is integrated with our conception of a beautiful woman. As a result, the perfume in question has all of the connotations that the manufacturer intended for it to have, and a woman seeking allure or a man wishing to make a fitting tribute to a woman he admires could very well be persuaded that this is the solution.

Second, *if the advertisement effectively uses the elements and principles of design, it can be considered an artistic expression.* In Figure 16–2, shape, line, value, form, and texture combine to lead the eye in a rhythmic curve upward to the arrow which points the way to unknown goals with the caption "Ticket to Achievement." The technique used has a similarity to some of the techniques used in modern painting, and for this reason the eye is attracted. Then, because it is not entirely clear just what the advertisement represents, the viewer seeks out the type which relates the creative forms of the design to creativity in engineering. The total effect is one of a new approach to a new and exciting field. This is advertising, not to sell a product but to sell an institution by associating it in the public mind with the newest in scientific and engineering development.

Third, *if the advertisement achieves its goal through the first two principles and makes the viewer conscious of the product involved,* it may be said to have satisfied one of the basic principles of design, that of fulfilling its function.

These two advertisements are different in a number of ways yet they have three important characteristics in common. One advertises a product, the other an institution. One appeals to beauty and femininity, the other to science and progress. Yet both *catch the attention, hold the interest,* and *leave a definite impression.* These three steps are requisites of any effective advertisement.

Kinds of Advertising

We have spoken of advertising a *product* as opposed to advertising an institution. There are two kinds of advertising that the public is exposed to daily. Magazines, newspapers, and television screens are filled with designs and pictures publicizing specific products made by specific firms. They also carry a second kind, advertisements of the telephone, telegraph, insurance companies, railroads and airlines, all institutions that offer not a product but a *service*. Newspapers frequently carry a combination of the two. Department stores and grocery stores run full-page ads designed to convince the customer that one particular store is the best place to shop and stress the brand names that they carry in everything from girdles to canned peaches.

There is another way to consider advertising, however. This is in terms of the result anticipated. In *direct advertising* immediate results are expected in the form of an order or a request for information. Department stores carry this sort of advertising, giving the telephone number so the customer can call in and order whatever is seen in the newspaper, frequently including a coupon in the ad which the customer at a distance can fill out and mail. Grocery or department-store ads tell of special sales—another form of direct advertising—with a sense of urgency because prices will soon be higher. *Indirect advertising,* on the other hand, concentrates on building a reputation and on establishing the desirability of a product in the back of the customer's mind, for future use. Much magazine advertising is of this type, where no coupon is included or any particular store mentioned for the object advertised. The customer becomes attracted to the merchandise and when shopping next remembers the name and asks for it. Much institutional advertising is indirect. The average person does not take a trip by air frequently, and when he does he may have no choice of line because of his schedule and destination; yet his consciousness of the advertising done by the line he does take makes him feel more confidence, and it may influence him to fly at a later time instead of driving or going by train. A person may just as easily be impressed by copy that he reads for an insurance company and let it influence him in taking out his next policy.

The approach will necessarily be different in these two types of advertising. The direct ad will be gauged more to the moment, with a sense of high fashion, special price, urgent need, or some other qualification that will make the customer feel the importance of acquiring the merchandise

Figure 16–4. This ad has a strong appeal for parents, the group for which this particular insurance is intended. Art Director: Marce Mayhew. Courtesy of The Prudential Insurance Company.

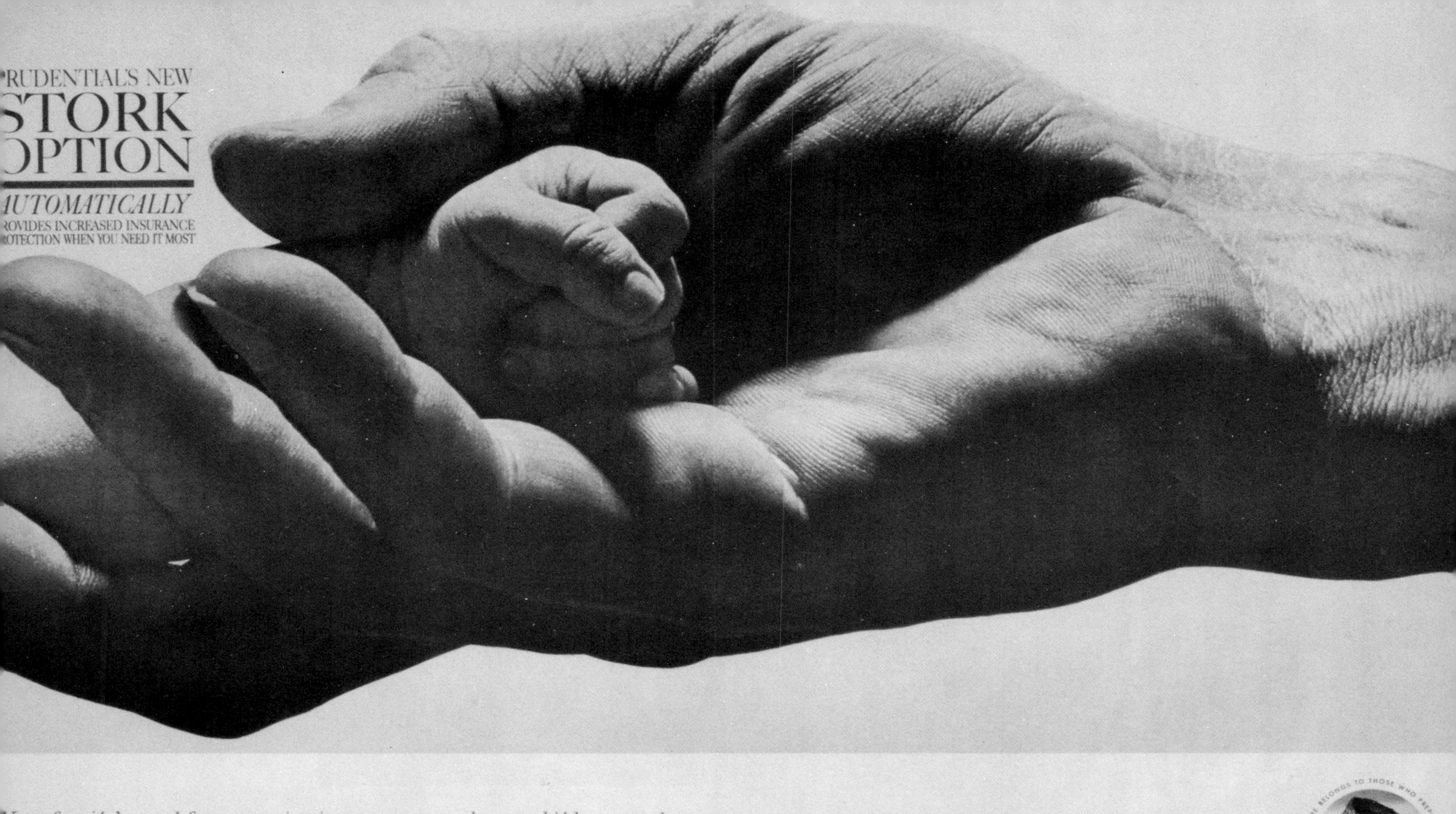
RUDENTIAL'S NEW
STORK
PTION
UTOMATICALLY
OVIDES INCREASED INSURANCE
OTECTION WHEN YOU NEED IT MOST

immediately. An ad for a cake mix may suggest the cake for dinner tonight. Overshoes advertised in the midst of a storm may be a sellout. Holiday advertising makes the most of the direct approach, of course, showing every kind of commodity as an adjunct to some festivity or as a potential gift. Direct advertising with a note of suspense can be effective, as in Figure 16–3. The design is forceful enough to lead the eye to the small print which awakens further interest with a question and an asterisk. The reader does not go on until he has read the footnoted suggestion, "See next Sunday!" When a strong follow-up appears in the Sunday paper, interest is already established and the name of the firm will stick.

Indirect advertising, on the other hand, needs a deeper current to maintain a lasting impression. Sometimes a note of poignancy is used, as in the photograph in Figure 16–4. For anyone who has loved a baby this picture will not be passed over lightly. Again, the photograph and caption in Figure 16–5 arrest the attention with a graphic story. The more one studies the faces of the children and the expression of the young mother dramatically framed by the empty chair, the more emphatic the message becomes.

Figure 16–5. No amount of written copy could hope to present as emphatic an argument for the need of insurance as this simple photograph. Courtesy of New York Life Insurance Company.

Figure 16–6. The very simplicity of this ad attracts attention. Courtesy of Gulf Oil Corporation.

Figure 16–7. Familiar comic-strip characters put the potential customer in a receptive mood immediately in addition to arousing his curiosity as to how they are going to relate to the product advertised. Courtesy of the Ford Motor Company. Peanut Characters © 1950 United Features Syndicate, Inc.

Figure 16–8. The predicament of this appealing hippopotamus enlists the interest of the passerby immediately. Courtesy of The Pacific Telephone and Telegraph Company.

Other cases use whimsy or humor, as in Figure 16–6. The ridiculous simplicity of this design attracts the eye immediately. There are wide expanses of negative space, therefore the reader seeks out the caption much as one would hunt for the kernel in a nut. With all of the space, there is still balance between the caption and the name of the corporation, and the focus of attention is directed to the bee with no difficulty. The negative approach of the caption injects an element of surprise in a business where not only positive statements but superlatives are the rule.

Humor can also be used effectively through familiar comic strips as in Figure 16–7. The reader is prepared for a humorous statement through association, so he easily responds with a chuckle when the message is brought home. Figure 16–8, on the other hand, gains its humor by a ridiculous combination of "commodities." The idea of the winsome hippopotamus sitting in a garden chair arouses the reader's curiosity immediately and he looks more closely to see what the animal can possibly be doing in such a situation. This opens the way for the punch line conveying the wide scope of use for the yellow pages, and leaves an impression of good-natured spoofing while getting the message across.

Sometimes a catch phrase is used for a series of advertisements as in Figure 16–9. Each ad has its own individual subject matter and an original approach, yet a single theme runs through the series giving unity and emphasis through repetition.

A combination of direct and indirect advertising is often used. In this case directions may be given for making something with the product advertised. Perhaps a page of recipes will be offered or a coupon will bring a free recipe book, all suggesting that the recipes involved require a specific brand of shortening, or sugar, or nuts. Pictures of rooms paneled with a certain kind of wood paneling or carpeted with a special kind of carpet may be accompanied by coupons which will bring catalogs showing samples of the various kinds and colors available through a certain company. The photographs set in motion ideas of attractiveness which are focused on a specific product once the catalog has arrived.

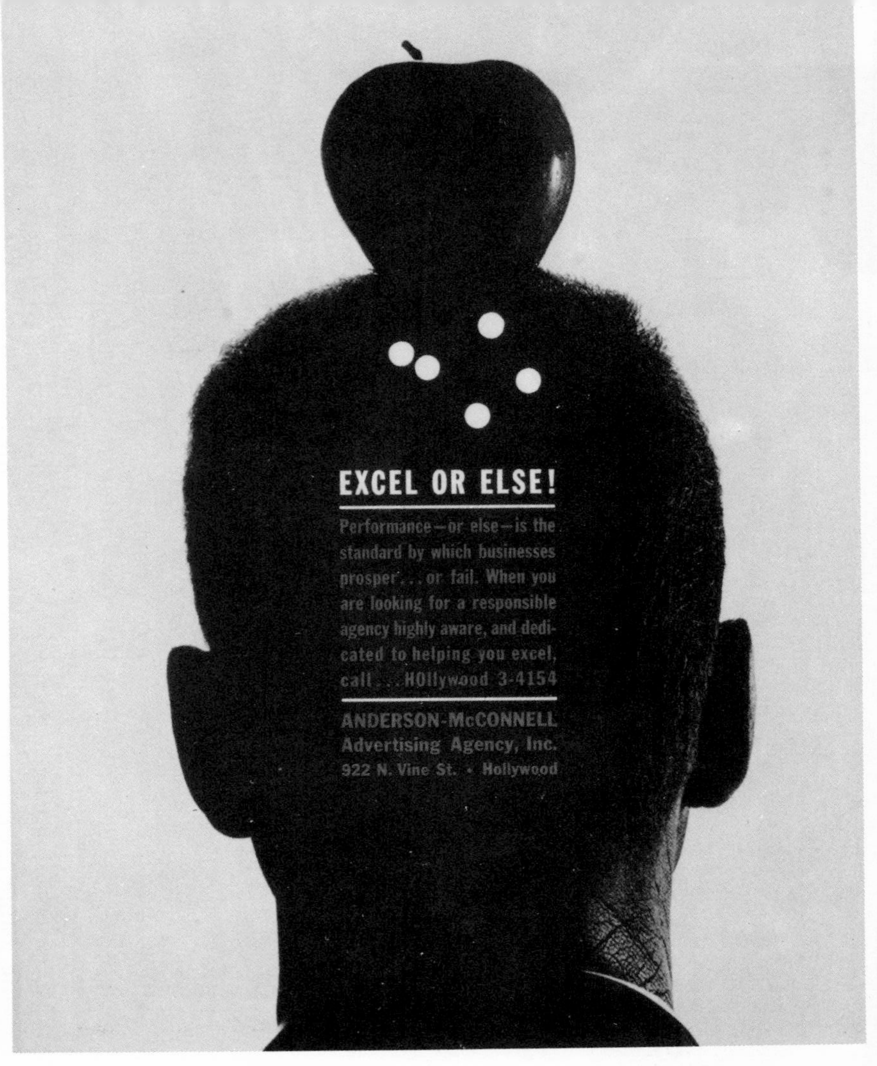

Figure 16–9. Added emphasis can be given to advertising by the use of a theme continued through a series of different but related subjects. Here a touch of grim humor adds appeal. Courtesy of Anderson-McConnell Advertising Agency, Inc.

Advertising Media

Advertising has come a long way since the days when a journeyman painter visited the farmers whose barns had the proper exposure and painted "Carter's Little Liver Pills" on the roof or the wall in letters high enough to be seen by people driving nearby in their Model T's. The barn evolved into the *billboard,* a medium so popular for advertising that highways approaching cities became veritable corridors, so little of the scenery was visible. As man's clutter and wreckage extend farther and farther beyond the cities, however, a new respect for natural countryside has arisen until it becomes apparent that the billboard is virtually doomed. Always banned from national highways and many local turnpikes, it now has been voted out of existence in more than half of the states, with more taking up the banner each year. The billboard with its quick message reaching customers on wheels will doubtless relinquish its position to the car *radio.* Meanwhile the same sort of advertising will continue in *posters* which have the advantage of being adaptable to frequent change. The eye-catching slogan and the design expressing the essence of a product are particularly suited to the poster.

Nowhere is the poster more effective than in advertising travel. So alluring is the travel poster that it has long been a fixture in foreign-language classrooms, in playrooms, and in the private collections of inveterate daydreamers. The examples in Figure 16–10 are especially articulate. The contrast between (a) and (b), for instance, is as marked as the differences between Paris and London themselves. The poster for Paris is a stylized interpretation of the things that Paris means to most people. The age-old Cathedral of Notre Dame on its tree-encircled island in the Seine is given a modern treatment that carries into the almost abstract forms of the trees in the right foreground. Geometric patches of color give a feeling of the world of art which is so closely allied to Montmartre and to the color and excitement of the city itself. The interest of the Cathedral balances the heavier forms of the foreground, and the values are carried throughout the poster in pleasing unity. The poster for London, in contrast, has the charm of an old etching, the sort of thing one might expect to find in an English bookstore or on the walls of a thousand private libraries throughout the city.

The type used for the name "London" is associated in most people's minds with "Old English" and it echoes the ancient charm and staid respectability that we look for in things English. In (c) we find an interesting mixture of the primitive and the modern, the human and the animal. The fanciful kangaroo with occupied pocket eyes a modern airliner as she hops nonchalantly across a backdrop of native textile design. The pattern of dark and light creates a subtle balance with a counterpoint of texture from the bands of pattern on the kangaroo and the more subtle tones of the textile. We have the feeling of vast resources, both in the primitive culture and in the advancements of a forward-looking country. Lastly, in (d) we have the unadulterated sense of space and speed that is the essence of the modern airliner. Triangles in blues and greens give the shape of the wingspread and the colors of air, sea, and sky, with the shape of the plane itself effectively silhouetted. Notice how simple the lettering is in each case. These are posters, meant to give the idea quickly with just the essential words to catch the eye.

Magazine advertising is advantageous in reaching a national audience and is effective for nationally distributed products or services. It also handles a limited number of large stores who welcome mail-order business or seek to reach people who visit the metropolitan centers frequently. The drawback of having to prepare copy months in advance limits magazine ads to products of moderate stability. The need for a quick, catchy message is not so urgent here, as it is assumed that anyone with time to look through a magazine will stop occasionally to read an interesting advertisement. The principal need is for a provocative headline or a design that will arouse curiosity or interest.

The *newspaper* remains the principal means of advertising for retail stores, services, and institutions such as banks and insurance, and for local tradesmen of many kinds. Because the newspaper carries the daily news of what is going on, it is read more avidly than other advertising media and

Figure 16–10. Four travel posters, each with its own distinctive message expressed in an effective way. Courtesy of the Boeing Company.

so can expect a receptive audience. Advertising design for newspapers varies from involved layouts to single figures showing fashion designs. Department stores spend 70 to 90 percent of their total media appropriations for advertising on newspapers, and smaller shops follow according to their own needs.

Hand bills and *package enclosures* are less widely used but still require the efforts of a layout designer and occasionally an advertising artist. Package enclosures, particularly, are apt to have drawings or designs accompanying statements of congratulation on having made such a noteworthy purchase.

Television, of course, is a chief contender for first place in advertising effort. Operating on the principle of making use of a captive audience, it regales thousands of people daily with every kind of jingle, animated cartoon, diagrammatical discourse, and glamorous model. It is abetted by thousands of very young addicts who recite the commercials verbatim and insist that their mothers buy the product represented by their favorite character. The use of design in television commercials is a promising field, but one that needs considerable exploration. The addition of a commentator and moving parts complicates the usual design problems, but could increase effectiveness in the hands of a skilled designer.

Type and Layout

The twentieth century has seen almost unlimited development of type design because of the growth of advertising. Figure 16–11 shows a few of the many letter styles used to express various moods and products. There is no doubt that appropriate lettering does much to attract attention and convey the message.

Because advertising design is closely tied up with copywriting, the appearance of the written matter is given equal importance with the drawing or design. In creating any advertisement, the artist consults with the copywriter before he can plan the layout, giving first preference to the catch line, slogan, or headline that must attract the attention of the reader. If the picture or design is used to attract interest, the copy is used to balance it or to underline it in some way. Whatever the final result arrived at, the copy, or printed matter, and the visual forms of the design must be in balance. The principle is the same as in book layout, yet it is complicated by the use of color and form, shape and texture in the drawing, photograph, or painted design.

The use of art in advertising has attained admirable heights in the Portfolio of Great Ideas sponsored by Container Corporation of America. Painters, sculptors and designers have been commissioned to interpret great thoughts from various cultures in such fashion that the visual arts are allied with literary and philosophic achievement. Four examples of this

How Various Letter Styles Influence Advertising

Selecting letters to harmonize with the message is just as essential as "Perfect Draftsmanship"

1 Fancy ROMAN & Italics
Is For Grace, Elegance and Feminine Appeal

2 CLASSIC ROMAN
Radiates Conservative Dignity, Permanence & Beauty

3 Texts. Church Gothic. UNCIAL
Radiate Antiquity, Quality, Craftsmanship & Reverence

4 GOTHIC AND BLOCK
Present a Sturdy atmosphere of Strength & Power

5 "Personality Script"
Commands quick Action = Speaks for itself!"

6 The "JAZZY STYLES"
Frivolous freedom effected by broken line

7 RADIO CATERPILLAR CHINA SILKS ICE
Novelty lettering individually designed to harmonize with and express the Character of the subjects

Figure 16–11. Expressive type has a great deal to do with the effectiveness of any advertisement. As shown here, type can be adapted to express practically anything. Courtesy of the C. Howard Hunt Pen Company.

happy alliance are shown in Figure 16–12. Each design expresses the basic flavor of the accompanying quotation in a way worthy of serious study.

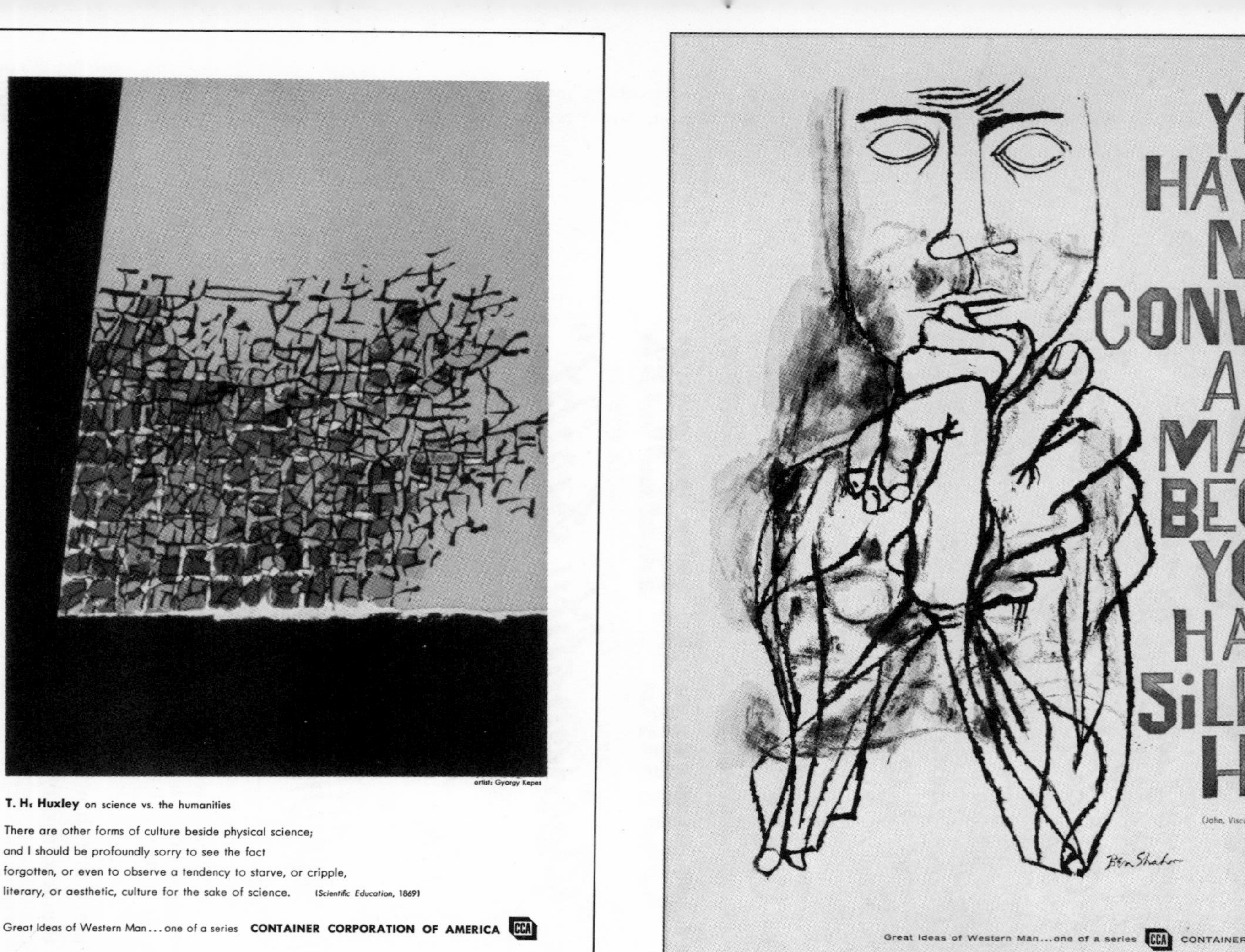

Figure 16–12. Outstanding American artists were commissioned to interpret "Great Ideas of Western Man" in the portfolio sponsored by Container Corporation of America for institutional advertising. (a) Thomas Huxley is interpreted by artist Gyorgy Kepes, (b) Ben Shahn expresses Viscount Morley.

A teacher affects eternity;

he can never tell where his influence stops

HENRY BROOKS ADAMS ON TEACHING *from The Education of Henry Adams, 1907* Artist: William Baziotes

Great Ideas of Western Man... *One of a Series* CONTAINER CORPORATION OF AMERICA CCA

Great Ideas of Western Man . . . one of a series

artist: Jacob Lawrence

Marcus Aurelius on brotherhood

Men exist for the sake of one another. Teach them then or bear with them.

(*Meditations*, VIII:59)

CONTAINER CORPORATION OF AMERICA CCA

Figure 16–12 Continued. (c) William Baziotes paints an interpretation of Henry Adams' words and (d) Jacob Lawrence symbolizes the words of Marcus Aurelius. Courtesy of Container Corporation of America.

Figure 16–13. Use of metal, glass, and plastic in a sophisticated design gives toiletries a luxurious air. The containers photographed are (from left to right) through the courtesy of Angelique International, Inc., the Renard Co., and Cara Nome Shari Toiletries of the Rexall Drug and Chemical Company.

Packaging

Once a product is advertised, it may still gain or lose a sale by its packaging. In these days of self-service stores it is quite possible for a customer to go shopping for one product and substitute another because it looks more appealing. Attractive packaging (1) helps to sell the merchandise by identifying it and distinguishing it from competing articles, and (2) facilitates a better display, thus making it easier for the merchant to put the article before the public eye. (3) It frequently improves the appearance of the merchandise itself, and (4) helps to keep it clean and attractive by protecting it. Thus (5), it helps to reduce selling time, effort, and cost. In addition to all of this, effective packaging serves practical, as well as esthetic, purposes.[1] Glamor wrappings on cosmetics not only make them look as though they belong in a luxurious boudoir, but, often, keep them from breakage and spilling, as in the case of plastic spray bottles. Tissue holders make possible the orderly use of tissues, and plastic bags protect fancy slippers, blouses, and shirts.

The role of the artist in package design can have a marked effect on sales and involves not only the principles of design but active imagination.

[1] Charles M. Edwards, Jr. and William H. Howard, *Retail Advertising and Sales Promotion* (Englewood Cliffs, N.J.: Prentice-Hall, Inc., 1943).

Cosmetics and women's toiletries show ingenuity by combining simple forms with sophisticated colors to provide a luxurious touch that women find hard to resist (Figure 16–13). Men's toiletries, on the other hand, are frequently associated with sports equipment in their wrappings or are packaged in materials resembling leather or brass. Even razors can be made to look attractive when encased in plastic and displayed in a colorful case.

A different approach is used for foodstuffs and for household necessities. In the series of cans for waxes shown in Figure 16–14, the emphasis is on clarity and simplicity of packaging with the name of the product and a few words about its virtues holding the center of interest.

Chapter 15 mentioned that book jackets are in effect a matter of packaging. The same thing can be said for record albums. Wide variety is seen in music stores, with designs ranging from dramatic photographs to imaginative linear interpretations (Figure 16–15). The record racks are among our most colorful examples of package design.

We frequently hear protests about lack of integrity in advertising in

Figure 16–14. In utilitarian products clarity of label is as important as simplicity of design in the container. Notice how each of these cans carries a line or "blurb" telling of the virtues of the product. Courtesy of S. C. Johnson & Son, Inc.

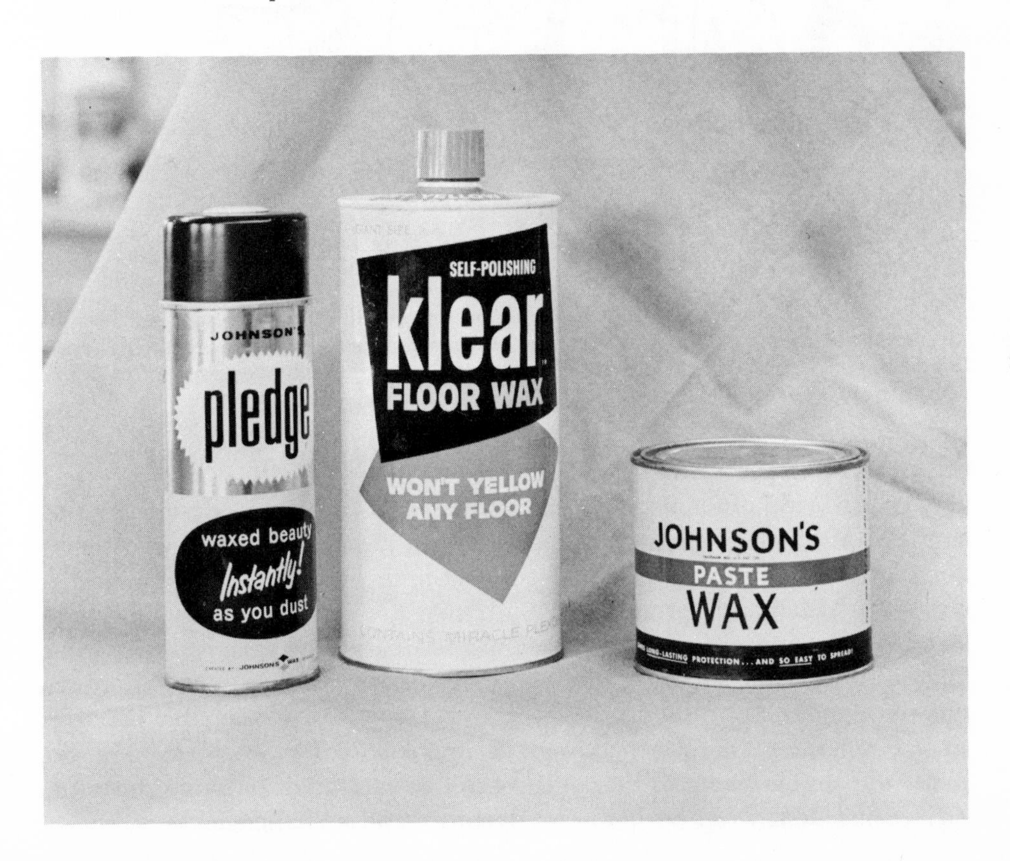

Figure 16–15. A record album is an important area of package design. In addition to interpreting the music on the record the designer uses imaginative treatment to appeal to the sophistication of the buyer. Reproduction used through the courtesy of Radio Corporation of America.

which the public is manipulated and led to buy products in spite of itself. There is a wide difference between *attracting* a buyer and deceiving him, and ethical advertisers have this fact firmly in mind. A designer who strives for an attractive package or an effective ad finds that the public appreciates his work without his promising results that are impossible. On the other hand, advertising in itself is a justifiable occupation necessary to the bringing together of the producer and consumer. It has been an economic necessity throughout the world for many centuries, and the questionable practices of a few have never overshadowed its importance for the many. For the artist who enjoys being in the midst of a high-pressured, pulsating business, advertising design can be both an adventure and a challenge.

FOR FURTHER EXPLORATION

Commercial Art Techniques by S. Maurello (New York: Tudor Publishing Corp., 1962). A manual of drawings, photographs, and instructions for producing layouts, lettering, and photography for advertising and allied fields.

Advertising Agency and Studio Skills by Tom Cardamore (New York: Watson-Guptill Publications, Inc., 1962). A comprehensive treatment of the materials and techniques involved in agency or studio work.

Type and Lettering by William Longyear (New York: Watson-Guptill Publications, Inc., 1962). Valuable reference showing hundreds of alphabets and covering the mechanics of typography and printing.

STUDIO PROJECTS

1. Design type suitable for use in a poster, expressing five different words such as fast, sweet, heavy, tragic, and funny.
2. Design a travel poster that catches the *essence* of some spot in a very simple and stylized way, using as few words as possible and adapting them to the design.
3. Design a package for a particular product, working for usability and attractiveness with the idea of selling the product by virtue of the package design.

CHAPTER 17

Figure 17–1. "The Virgin with St. Ines and St. Tecla" by El Greco. Courtesy of the National Gallery of Art, Washington, D.C. Widener Collection.

Painting as Design

In the long history of painting, the relationship of painting to design has known many subtle changes. Generations of painters would agree with Washington Allston's remark to a student: "A painter may be blessed with every gift of nature, but unless he has acquired the art of design he can never express himself."[1] Yet the emergence of the contemporary painter has brought a cry to the lips of many viewers that modern paintings are not really paintings at all but simply studies in design. Inasmuch as the earliest forms of art were designs upon primitive tools and weapons, there are those who suggest that in this relationship of painting to design a cycle has been completed. On the contrary, however, an analysis of painting as it exists today reveals not a closed door but many open ones leading into areas of unexplored adventure and experimentation.

Two Kinds of Painting

There are two basic varieties of painting: *mural painting,* which is designed to become a permanent part of a building, and *easel painting,* consisting of framed or matted works which are hung upon the walls and are easily moved from place to place.

Mural Painting

The materials for mural painting have a clear relationship to the building upon whose walls the painting is created. *Secco* (Italian for "dry") is usually dry pigment mixed with lime water and held together by *casein,* the curd found in cottage cheese, and painted directly on dry plaster walls.

1 Alexander Eliot, *Three Hundred Years of American Painting* (New York: Time Incorporated, 1957), p. 42.

Fresco (Italian for "fresh") is dry pigment mixed with lime water and painted into fresh plaster before the plaster is allowed to dry. This is a challenging and difficult process used by many of the Renaissance masters on the walls of churches, monasteries, and palaces. *Oil paint* is frequently used for murals with the painting executed on large stretches of canvas either glued or bolted to the wall.

The design of a mural is an elaborate process, starting with a small-scale drawing and progressing to full-size cartoons, or drawings, from which the finished design is painted. The total design must be appropriate to the building, not only in scale and form but in color and value, which will change radically according to the available lighting.

Easel Painting

There are many materials used today in easel painting, from the tempera of the Old Masters to experimental materials based in plastic. Most paints originate in pigments from natural sources or from chemically formulated substances, but the difference lies in the binder which holds the pigment together.

Tempera generally has egg as a binder, although animal and vegetable glues may be used. It is usually applied to a *gesso* ground built up on wood panels with white paint and glue. *Casein,* with its binder of milk curd, is used in similar fashion.

Oil paint came into general use in the fifteenth century and remains the most widely used medium today. The pigment is ground into a binder of linseed oil. This is slow drying but allows for careful manipulation. It necessitates waiting between successive coats of paint to avoid cracking because of underlayers which are not thoroughly dry. The opacity of oil paint makes possible a feeling of solidity and form and also permits painting over parts that need changing. Oil paint may be applied *alla prima,* at first, in one direct operation, or it may be built up in successive thin layers or *glazes.* The latter method accounts for much of the soft modeling of the Old Masters. It may also be applied with smooth brush strokes or *impasto,* a thick texture usually put on with a palette knife in which the painter expresses the exciting quality of paint as a plastic medium. Oil paint is used on canvas, masonite, or on wood which has been treated to give a roughness or "tooth" necessary to make the paint adhere.

Watercolor is bound by gum arabic while *gouache,* opaque watercolor, is held together with a paste of zinc oxide. Both are soluble in water and lend themselves to spontaneous and rapid painting. Used on specially prepared paper, transparent watercolor has a clarity and sparkle that sets it apart as a medium of freshness and spontaneity.

While there is evidence that *encaustic* is the oldest painting medium, having been used by the Greeks, it has enjoyed a recent rebirth of interest on the part of contemporary artists looking for new adventures in expression. Basically a mixture of hot beeswax and pigment, it is applied to wood by means of a brush or a metal instrument known as a *cauterium*. As the wax cools the cauterium is heated and successive layers are applied, achieving plasticity and making intricate modeling possible.

Among recent innovations in painting media, pigments bound with acrylic-polymer emulsion have gained considerable popularity. Water soluble yet forming a tough film, these are paints to which are attributed the combined assets of water color and oil, with a quick-drying quality which makes possible the building of layers into luminous effects. In addition, contemporary painters use enamels and ordinary house paints, exploring surface texture with plaster, sand, and gravel—sometimes using gold leaf for accent. Experimentation leads into new uses for established materials as wall as exciting and unusual combinations of the old and the new.

Attributes of Painting

In order to understand where design leaves off and painting begins and how a design becomes a painting, it is helpful to consider the three attributes that we traditionally associate with a painting. These are *subject, form,* and *content.*

Design and Subject

The painting by El Greco in Figure 17–1 has obvious subject matter, and it is easy to see that it has form. The content might be described as the deeply emotional quality we feel as a result of the elongated figures, billowing clouds, and colors—rich blues, reds, and brassy yellows—so often found in El Greco's work. There is a strong feeling of reverence combined with a supernatural quality that makes us experience El Greco's conception of heaven. We do not for a minute feel that this is an ordinary human situation because form and content interact to assure us that it is not. The content, then, is the feeling that the artist puts into the forms of his work, and it is this feeling or experience that we endeavor to share when we engage in art appreciation.

In addition to these qualities, the painting in question has a strong sense of design. We can see how the composition or structure holds together from the diagram, Figure 17–2a. The structure is based on triangular forms which reach upward and downward from the central figure of the Virgin, focusing attention on her without difficulty, since her figure forms the one strong vertical in the entire composition. The heads of the angels and of St. Ines and St. Tecla provide horizontal lines which hold the painting firmly within the canvas instead of letting it plunge downward with the predominant forms of the triangles. The composition, then, is the basic structure on which the painting is erected without particular emphasis on color or texture. In analyzing other paintings we find triangular compositions, vertical and horizontal compositions, and radial compositions. The *design* includes the composition since both are the plan or order from which the painting evolves, but it goes further, in this case including the distribution of textures around the Virgin's head and feet, the rhythm of the flowing lines, the balance of the values, colors, and shapes. Notice how the hands on the various figures form a counterpoint, not only in shape but in the diagonal lines with which they echo the larger diagonals of the basic composition. The heads, the hands, the colors and values all supplement the lines of the composition to achieve unity.

Now, if we trace the forms of the painting into an abstract design, the result looks something like the drawing in Figure 17–2. With content unnoticeable and even without color, the painting makes an interesting design. If this experiment is tried with other well-known and respected paintings, you will come to a general conclusion: a successful painting is basically a good design.

Perhaps the greatest achievement of all time in designing painting was the planning and execution by Michelangelo of the ceiling of the Sistine Chapel at the Vatican. The design problem here staggers the imagination: ten thousand square feet were to be covered with figures from the Bible, compensating for the arch of the ceiling so that they could be viewed from the floor without distortion, yet all of them had to be anatomically convincing, in innumerable states of action. The architecture of the building added the complication of lunettes, or crescent-shaped areas above the arched windows, and spandrels, or triangular spaces leading from above the windows into the vault of the ceiling. All of these areas were filled with powerful figures, three hundred and forty-three in all. The narrative was organized around three center portions depicting the origins of the world, of man, and of sin, with episodes in Noah's life characterizing man living in his sin and waiting for salvation. Around these central compositions figures are grouped, twenty youths with garlands, a chorus of seers, prophets, and sibyls, all depicting the futility of mankind while unsaved. Various Biblical episodes are shown in the triangular spaces while the prediction of the coming of the Redeemer is carried out in spandrels and lunettes showing the ancestors of Christ.

The problems of design preceded the technical difficulties of doing the work in *fresco,* color applied directly to a wet wash of lime. If the plaster was allowed to remain more than a day without painting, a film of lime was formed which caused the painting to look patchy. All of the work had to be done on a high scaffolding from which it was impossible to view

Figure 17–2. (a) A diagram of "The Virgin with St. Ines and St. Tecla" illustrates its compositional structure based on a series of triangles all leading the eye to the child. (b) A free stylization of El Greco's painting produces an abstract design of variety and interest. Notice the balance of light and dark areas and the use of texture to unify the whole composition.

the effect accurately as seen from below; consequently a meticulous design worked out in detail on full-sized cartoons was imperative. A complete appreciation of the design involved in this masterpiece can come only from

Figure 17–3. "The Creation of Man" by Michelangelo. Fresco from the ceiling of the Sistine Chapel in the Vatican at Rome. Alinari Photo.

seeing it in its entirety, yet even a fragment such as "The Creation of Man" shown in Figure 17–3 gives a sense of the rhythm, balance, and unity permeating the entire work. The forms and values balance one against the other and the directions of the bodies contribute strong rhythmic patterns. The white of the frescoed background forms an interplay of negative space which accentuates the positive sections of the painting.

Design and Form

Paul Cézanne devoted a lifetime to the study of form and its relationship to color. He did not always paint from the model, yet subject matter was important to him, especially in his landscapes which he did paint from the actual scenery of his beloved Provence. Still, even in these he was primarily absorbed in trying to expand shapes into solid three-dimensional forms with weight and volume, accomplishing this through the use of color and texture. He died believing that he had failed to express the truth he felt, but he left a legacy of canvases which became the foundation for much that later artists tried to accomplish. In "Chestnut Trees at Jas de Bouffan" (Figure 17–4) we feel the solidity of the wall and buildings and know that they are anchored firmly in the ground. The hills are firm and heavy and the trees have a strong feeling of weight as well as of pattern. The design is lyrical and rhythmic with an architectonic feeling, a term by which we

Figure 17–4. Solidity of form combines with strong design in Paul Cézanne's "Chestnut Trees at Jas de Bouffan." From the collection of The Minneapolis Institute of Arts.

Figure 17–5. Paul Gauguin's "The Day of the God" (Mahana No Atua) is lyrical, full of rhythmic shapes and rich colors. Oil on canvas, 1894. Courtesy of the Art Institute of Chicago, Helen Birch Bartlett Memorial Collection.

describe a sense of structure as though the painting were actually built of solid forms. The rhythm flows through the branches of the trees and is echoed in the smaller trees in the background, with a strong counterpoint provided by the horizontal forms of the wall. The repetition of the solidity of the buildings on the hill in the background and the rhythms of the trees provide two themes woven together into a unity.

Working at the same time, Paul Gauguin interpreted form as musical harmonies bound together in rich colors. His painting in Figure 17–5 is strong in design even without the color. After giving up a promising career in business, Gauguin lived in the South Pacific painting the natives, seeing in their lives the rhythms and designs which he transmitted to canvas. He, too, left a strong influence still felt by artists today, a lyrical approach to his work which has been carried forward by many of our leading painters. Cézanne's sense of structure and Gauguin's warmth and poetry, in fact, represent two streams of expression which have appeared repeatedly in contemporary painting.

When subject matter is as pronounced as it is in the works of El Greco, Michelangelo, Cézanne, and Gauguin, we react to the composition with a feeling of pleasure, but we have to stop to analyze if we are to appreciate fully the qualities of intellectual design that have gone into the work. However, when form and shape overshadow subject matter the design emerges readily. In a painting by Georges Braque, for instance, the design is more easily seen than the subject matter (Figure 17–6). The objects on the table appear as varied shapes represented in contrasting values while the table itself becomes a part of the series of planes supporting them. The distribution of lights and darks gives a strong sense of balance, with the dark carrying around the edges of the shapes to create unity. The composition is predominantly horizontal, varied by a few strong verticals and less obvious diagonals. Rhythm is achieved by emphasis on the center forms of the fruit and by repetition of values, textures, and shapes. Notice how the small circles of the grapes are repeated in the dark circles on the cards and again in the dots forming the texture on the table. This painting shows the inclination which later made Braque one of the originators of Cubism, one of the major trends stemming from Cézanne's interest in form. In later cubistic paintings such as Pablo Picasso's "Ma Jolie" (Figure 17–7) both subject matter and color become almost totally submerged in a design of overlapping geometric forms.

A conscious subordination of subject to design is obvious in Marc Chagall's "I and My Village" (Figure 17–8). Drawing upon his childhood memories of a small village in the Ukraine, Chagall has worked out a dreamlike design in which the images are recognizable but combined in unrealistic poses, as in *surrealism*. A circle dominates the canvas, drawing together the heads of a man and a cow which regard each other amicably, the cow evidently thinking of being milked, from the small images superimposed on her head, and the man holding a spray of leaves for her to eat. In the background the village street balances the triangle of the man's hand and the leaves, while a peasant and his wife repeat the motif of the small figures of the cow and milkmaid. The wife is turned upside down, a clear concession to design, since in this position her arms continue the diagonal of the peasant's scythe. The colors of this painting are soft and dreamlike and the values carry through in a rhythmic pattern. The overlapping planes are suggestive of cubism without losing the subject matter.

Figure 17–6. "Still Life with Grapes" by Georges Braque is a highly developed design. Courtesy of The Phillips Collection, Washington, D.C.

Figure 17–7. Pablo Picasso's "Ma Jolie" (Woman with a Zither or Guitar) loses the subject in the design of cubistic forms. Oil on canvas. Collection of The Museum of Modern Art, New York. Lillie P. Bliss Bequest.

Design and Content

All of these paintings have content, a quality that has very little to do with subject. Content cannot actually be put into words any more than the tones and harmonies of music can be written out as sentences, yet we are just as conscious of its presence as we are of the sounds of music. In a painting with subject the content is not difficult to grasp. It becomes the peacefulness of the landscape, the heroic quality of a battle scene, or the serenity of an old woman. It is the weatherbeaten aspect of an old barn which tells of howling winds and glaring sun, or the gnarled resistance of a tree that stands alone in spite of mountain gales. We do not *see* the content; we see the form, and the content is transmitted to us because of the way the form is handled. In a painting without subject this statement also holds true. In this case, however, although the content is part of the design it is sometimes more elusive, and we find that we must train ourselves to sense it as we learn

Figure 17–8. "I and My Village" by Marc Chagall is a tapestry of impressions combining a highly imaginative quality with structural design. Oil on canvas. Collection Museum of Modern Art. Mrs. Simon Guggenheim Fund.

to appreciate nonobjective form. This requires appreciation on another level than the intellectual one on which we are accustomed to approaching a work of art, for our receptivity will be more akin to an emotional or intuitive response. Just as we are learning to accept the presence of a microscopic world that we have never seen in its entirety and of the world of space whose limits we cannot fathom, in the appreciation of design we must be willing to pass through the doors opening on the world of the spirit, not only as represented in modern painting and sculpture but in music, poetry, and the theatre as well. As far back as the seventeenth century, French philosopher Blaise Pascal stated: "Human knowledge is like a sphere continually increasing, so that the larger the volume of it, the greater the number of points of contact with the unknown." Three centuries later this applies not only to the expanding fields of science but to the new intuitive expressions of art. It has been said that Einstein's Theory of Relativity seems strange only when we refuse to rearrange our patterns of thinking. The same thing could be said for modern painting.

Directions in Modern Painting

Abstraction

Development of modern painting has followed several trends, many of which have achieved an international quality, relating the work of painters in various countries by their common preoccupation with space, form, and content. A large body of this work can be categorized as some form of abstraction, or painting which in varying degrees is independent of subject matter. Tentatively appearing in the years preceding World War I, abstract painting has since developed into a dynamic characterization of the twentieth century, depicting all of its chaos, experimentation, and restless spirit with amazing vitality. Its expressions are as varied as the artists who paint, ranging from "pure" geometric forms to lyrical splashes of color.

Abstract Expressionism: Action. One of the most controversial eruptions has become known as abstract expressionism, a movement originally associated with the German artists who brought it to this country in the wake of Hitler's rise to power. It can be described as an expression of nonobjective forms created by active physical participation by the artist. This physical activity is so important a factor in one group of expressionists that they are characterized specifically as "action painters." Such action is described by the word *kinesthesia,* a term we hear applied increasingly to painting and sculpture, which relates to a feeling of muscular movement within the human body. The action painters believe that their works should

Figure 17–9. (*Opposite.*) "Mahoning" by Franz Kline. Oil on canvas. Collection of Whitney Museum of American Art, New York.

Figure 17–10. (*Right.*) Kline's painting has been compared to the broad bold strokes of Chinese characters such as these depicting 'face' (top) and 'new wine' (bottom). Calligraphy by Helen Chiang.

Figure 17–11. (*Below.*) "Number I" by Jackson Pollack is one of the dynamic action paintings for which he is best known. Oil on canvas. Collection, The Museum of Modern Art, New York.

evoke a feeling of activity in the onlooker, just as we "feel" the physical exertions of ice skating or ballet while we watch the configurations of the performance. Such an approach to painting results in vital, active and, in many cases, huge canvases.

The canvas by Frank Kline in Figure 17–9, for instance, is nearly seven by nine feet in size. A painter standing before a canvas this large can hardly hope to cover it without using his entire body. Kline paints in broad energetic brush strokes, usually black on white canvas, expressing the conflict of opposing forces. His giant forms seem to collide in mid-air like falling girders and to be held in suspension by the impact. The great black shapes have been called calligraphic designs and are frequently compared to forms of Oriental handwriting (Figure 17–10). Kline has stated that he feels the opposition of basic forces to be found everywhere in life, in the

stresses and strains of construction, in the conflict of good and evil, and in all variations of personal relationships. Thus his physical expression is not merely a working off of excess energy but a coming to terms with one of the basic precepts of life, a drastic declaration of energy and force. Sometimes his figures have a similarity to recognizable forms, such as bridges or shapes of buildings, but this is not his primary intent. Kline's interest in form is not to depict but to express the power of opposition, and thus his concern becomes involved with content.

Jackson Pollack is another expressionist in the physical sense. Trained by Thomas Hart Benton to paint with meticulous realism, Pollack eventually felt the need of a more personal expression. His great canvases were often spread out on the floor while he jabbed color at them or strode violently back and forth dribbling paint in intricate all-over designs. Layer upon layer build up until one can see planes of color and activity vibrating back and forth as one studies the canvas. As in all paintings, Pollack's work requires and deserves continued observation if it is to give forth its entire message. In Figure 17–11 our first impression is of a mess of scribbles, but as we peer into it forms and space begin to materialize. It is a little like looking at a tangle of brush and gradually seeing individual leaves and twigs and a bird hopping about. This does not mean that we are expected to find recognizable forms. On the contrary, we are invited to open our sensitivity to a different level, to sensations and reactions that come from viewing color, form, and space without reference to literal interpretation.

We notice in the work of Kline and Pollack that the traditional attributes of design are not readily discovered. In appreciating new forms of expression we must adopt new standards, not only of the importance of subject but of composition and design. It would be possible, for instance, to single out one spot on a Kline canvas and say that it is the center of interest, but it would be extremely difficult to do so with a work by Pollack. Actually, in such works a center of interest is not of particular importance. We find texture in Pollack, and repetition. We feel rhythm and balance, and there is a distinct feeling of unity. We may sense a structural sort of rhythm, but the color and value are reduced to simple terms and the texture is a matter of brush strokes in certain areas of the canvas. When we look at the design in works such as these we must react intuitively rather than intellectually. We cannot dissect these paintings and come up with clear statements that prove they have design quality, but as we develop our sensitivity we can feel that they are satisfying as designs. (Look once more at Janet Erickson's textile design entitled "After Pollack" in Figure 4–6b). They are not *merely* designs, however. The presence of content makes them paintings as well.

Abstract Expressionism: Oriental Flavor. One of the most important innovations among twentieth-century painters is the new interpretation of *space*. When perspective was formulated into an exact science at the beginning of the Renaissance, painters became fascinated by the effects that they could achieve in making two-dimensional canvas extend back into three dimensions. The painting by Giorgione in Figure 17–12 carries us not only into the cave but outside and beyond, past rocks, across meadows, over hills, and finally to the mountains. The eye travels and the spirit wanders through the skill of the painter. The work of Mark Rothko, on the other hand, might be said to be a painting of space itself. His canvases are covered with large areas of paint, usually in soft colors, sometimes with a band of dark color for emphasis. Figure 17–13 is in yellow with beige at the

Figure 17–12. (*Opposite page.*) Space reaches far into the distance in Giorgione's "The Adoration of the Shepherds." National Gallery of Art, Washington, D.C. Samuel H. Kress Collection.

Figure 17–13. (*Right.*) Mark Rothko's "Number 10" has a tranquil quality that guides the observer into reflection and meditation. Oil on canvas. Collection, The Museum of Modern Art, New York. Gift of Philip C. Johnson.

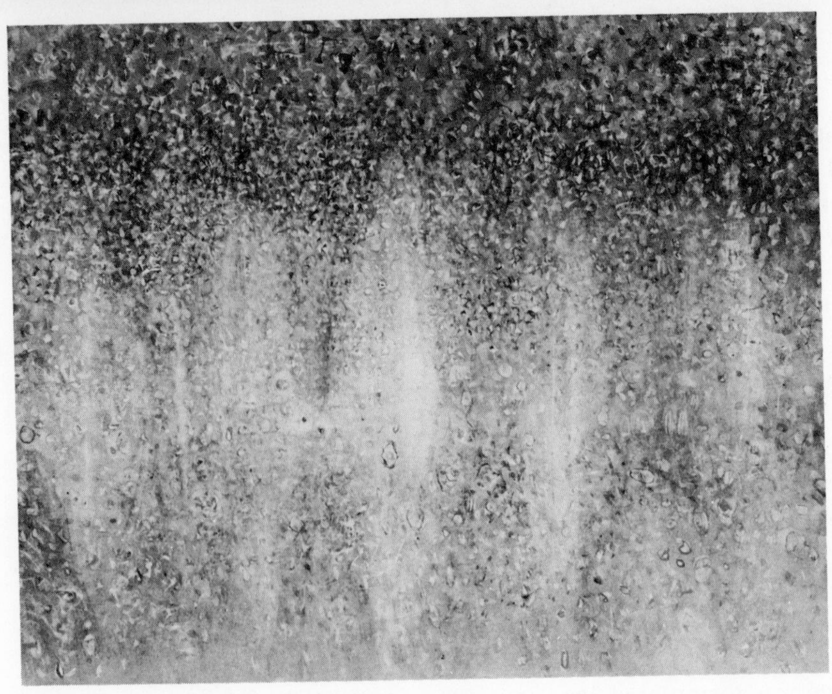

bottom and a band of blue shading into violet and white at the top. Although classed as an abstract expressionist, Rothko turns the force of Kline and the violence of Pollack into an almost Oriental serenity. His space is two-dimensional, yet as we study it we find ourselves penetrating beyond the simple surface of the canvas into new realms of thought and meditation. We look at such a canvas as the Zen Buddhists look at a single blossom in a bare room, to free the mind of detail and allow it to attain depths not possible when it is visually distracted. We are like the master Japanese gardener who, when he learned that the emperor was coming to view his beautiful chrysanthemums, cut all but one perfect blossom so his Imperial Highness could savor its full beauty alone, and thus appreciate the essence of the flower. In meditation, staring into space is not enough. A focal point is required, and Rothko's work provides it.

Mark Tobey is another painter with a spiritual tie to the Orient. After living the first part of his life in the Midwest and Greenwich Village, he took a teaching job in Seattle in 1923, and eleven years later made the trip to China which changed his outlook. His efforts to unite East and West in his work led him into the "white writing" of Figure 17–14, in which he seems to reduce the arts of both to a kind of basic calligraphy. Like Pollack's work, Tobey's paintings give rise to images within the individual mind. The "Fountains of Europe" can be seen but more is felt than just sprays of water. The white lines and the spaces which they encompass lift the receptive mind to higher states of consciousness much as music does. Again, as with Pollack, the design is a matter of texture, space, color, and rhythm combined to produce an all-over feeling of order.

Abstraction with Subject. The work of Morris Graves, another Seattle painter, shows as definite an Oriental influence as Tobey's, but it is expressed in different terms. His "Joyous Young Pine" in Figure 17–15 has a stylized

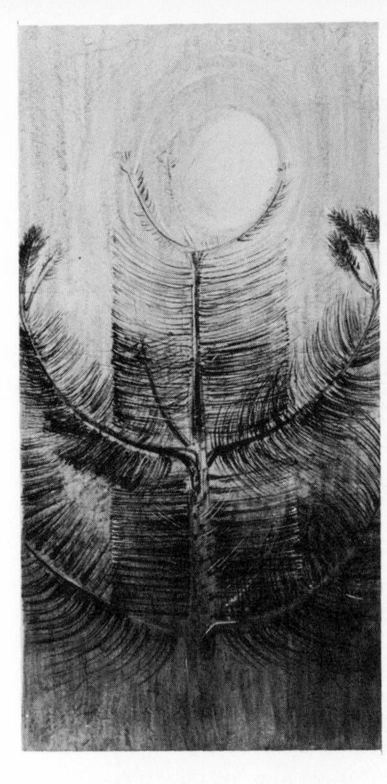

Figure 17–14. (*Opposite page.*) "Fountains of Europe," oil by Mark Tobey. Courtesy, Museum of Fine Arts, Boston.

Figure 17–15. (*Left.*) "Joyous Young Pine" by Morris Graves has a distinct Oriental feeling in its stylization and poetic design. Watercolor and gouache. Collection, The Museum of Modern Art, New York.

Figure 17–16. (*Below.*) William Thon's watercolor, "Midnight Quarry," offers solid blocks of stone and scraggly trees and allows the viewer to form his own conclusions about them. Collection of the Whitney Museum of American Art, New York. Wildenstein Benefit Purchase Fund.

quality that makes it akin to pure design with something of the feeling of a Japanese woodcut. He has been called a poet with a mystical quality in his interpretation of the Pacific Northwest and its somber seas, giant trees, fish, and birds. His work has recognizable subjects yet, as with Gauguin, the content and the design are more important.

On the opposite coast, William Thon approaches painting with a similar amount of abstraction. The rocks and trees of the Maine coast constitute the subject matter of his paintings but, as in his watercolor in Figure 17–16, he is concerned with translating them into forms and design

Figure 17–17. Another example of subject matter becoming almost totally subordinated to design is this abstraction by Karl Knaths. "Autumn Leaves," oil. The Brooklyn Museum Collection.

patterns with a feeling of light and clarity that transcends their realistic appearance.

In "Autumn Leaves" (Figure 17–17), Karl Knaths carries Braque's treatment of still life even farther toward pure design. The subject matter comes close to disappearing altogether in the shapes, forms, and textures of the composition. This sort of painting is reminiscent of the procedure followed in Chapter 6 when we abstracted a familiar object to create a design. We feel in the case of all three painters that the subject is merely a point of departure, a means of discovering designs not apparent in the casual observance of externals. The subject becomes a reason for creating a painting with a fine design quality, yet there is a sense of content deriving from the artist's feeling for his subject that lifts the work from the realm of pure design.

Geometric Abstraction. When abstraction eliminates subject matter yet does not involve the color and emotion of expressionism, it becomes geometric abstraction such as Piet Mondrian's painting in Figure 3–14. Many critics have called Mondrian's work the "purest" kind of abstraction, yet when Mondrian was feted at a dinner as the leading abstractionist of our time, he rose from the table to deny it. His argument was that where other painters depicted objects, they were actually *abstracting;* since they ended

Figure 17–18. "Illuminated Street" by Bernard Arnest illustrates the figurative approach to painting in which recognizable forms are used as symbols which summon moods or states of being. Oil on canvas. Collection of John and Dorothy Rood, Minneapolis. Courtesy of the artist.

up with only paint and canvas, which were necessarily an abstraction of an apple or a face. He, on the other hand, made no attempt to create anything but paint and canvas divided into interesting arrangements, and therefore he was abstracting nothing. This self-evaluation by Mondrian illustrates the futility of trying to pigeonhole contemporary artists into hidebound categories, for the basic spirit of painting today is one of individual exploration and of soaring above and beyond established boundaries. Even the realistic painters work in their own way, finding new approaches and new subjects.

Painting Today

Whatever the direction taken by contemporary artists, we notice one outstanding characteristic. Each has made his own contribution with a sincerity of purpose that leads him into a new and individual expression. Across the country in regional exhibitions we see copies of Pollack's dribbles and Kline's broad strokes, of Rothko's serene washes of color, and Thon's cubistically-inclined landscapes. It is possible that some of them have been done with feeling, but it is probable that many have assumed the superficial qualities of the work of these men without the attendant convictions. This is the difference between significant painting and mediocrity. We are fortunate to be living in a time when exploration and discovery are welcomed rather than condemned and when a painter with a goal in any direction can expect to be given a chance at acceptance.

Indications are that future trends in painting will be toward a wider use of the "figurative" approach which establishes contact between the painter and his public through some discernible form or symbol which can be interpreted readily by the viewer. Such a painting as Bernard Arnest's "Illuminated Street" (Figure 17–18) tends in this direction. Of this painting, the artist states: "I try to make the composition present the subject. In this work the subject is sensations of the city street with its signs, lights, wind, smoke and people. The images are adapted to the expression."

In this statement we find the artist's evaluation of the components of a painting. First comes expression and with it the composition which utilizes subject for its own ends. The composition is the structure of the design with all its color and texture, its shapes, and forms.

Whatever turn the painting of the future may take, we can be fairly certain that these things will remain important. A painting may be nonobjective or abstract. It may seem to be nothing but line or color. It may be subtle or vibrant, filled with powerful form or a feeling of mood. Its distinction will depend upon how it is put together, and from that and beyond it, upon its feeling of design.

FOR FURTHER EXPLORATION

Treasury of World Painting by A. Colombo and G. Diehl (New York: Tudor Publishing Co., 1962). Lavishly illustrated volume showing the most significant paintings of thirty-five countries, covering 3500 years of artistic expression.

Cézanne's Composition by Erle Loran (Berkeley: University of California Press, 1943). An excellent study of design in painting with photographs of the scenes painted and an analysis of the way in which the paintings were constructed.

Masters of Modern Art by Alfred H. Barr, Jr. (New York: The Museum of Modern Art, 1954). A treatise on the collection of the Museum of Modern Art with profuse illustrations and excellent text.

Pictures, Painters and You by Ray Bethers. (New York: Pitman Publishing Corp., 1948). An excellent analysis of the relationship of design to painting.

Composition in Pictures by Ray Bethers. (New York: Pitman Publishing Corp., 1949). An informative, well-illustrated discussion of the way in which paintings are put together.

Metropolitan Seminars in Art Number 1 through 12 by John Canaday. (New York: The Metropolitan Museum of Art, 1958). A discussion of the various aspects and schools of painting, with illustrations and diagrams. Good foundation for understanding painting in general.

STUDIO PROJECTS

1. To make a study of design in painting, lay tracing paper over six different paintings and trace the basic shapes. Shade in the values and indicate textures but do not draw objects. Remove the tracing and study the results as independent designs.
2. Using a large piece of masonite coated with flat-white paint and a variety of small cans of house paint, apply the paint to the board in an active physical way, concentrating on the activity rather than on the results. If necessary, think of a specific emotion as you work. When you have finished, stand at a distance and evaluate what you have done from the standpoint of design and composition. If you have worked with a feeling of harmony and purpose, the resulting painting should show unity and design.
3. Try Number 2 to music or while thinking of some specific physical activity such as ice skating. Try to get the feeling of kinesthesia into your work.

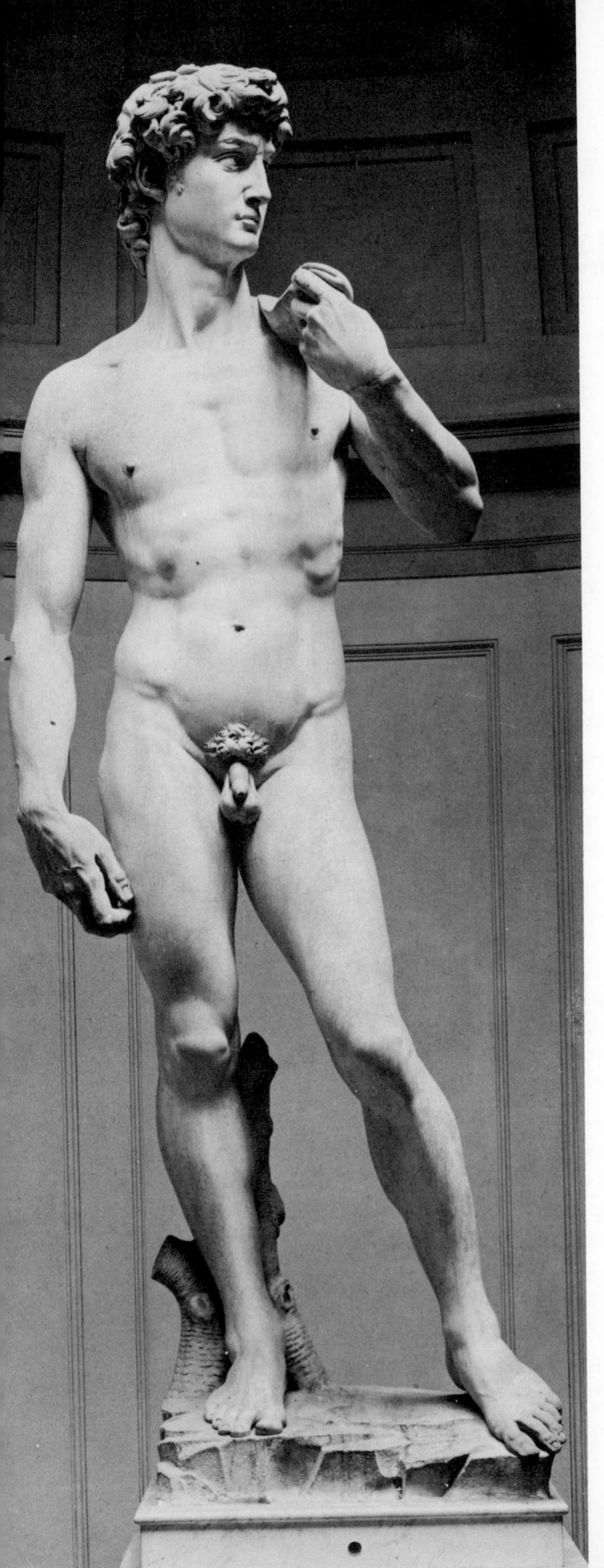

CHAPTER 18

Figure 18–1. Michelangelo's "David," one of the most beautiful sculptures of all time. Alinari Photo.

Sculpture as Design

Alexander Archipenko, asked to talk about his sculpture in 1956, stated: "Creativeness is not a human endeavor. Nature does the creating but endows certain human beings with spiritual power and facility for expressing nature's creativeness. When the spiritual power reaches a peak the result is a masterpiece."

The sculptor is perhaps better qualified than any other person to appreciate fully the fascinating discoveries to be made from natural design. The sculpture created by man is an extension of these natural forms, compounded into the forms of the human body or into some other expression of his creative instinct. Where nature's sculptural designs range from smooth pebbles that invite fondling to giant mountains that ask to be climbed, man's work encompasses a broad span from tiny amulets to monolithic buildings, poured and molded into forms that have all the attributes of sculpture. This is a field that combines the adventures of plastic expression with the satisfactions of structural design, bringing forth miracles from a block of stone, a chunk of wood, or a mass of metal.

Two Kinds of Sculpture

There are two kinds of sculpture: *free-standing,* or sculpture in the round, and *relief,* which is attached to a background. Relief can be of many gradations. Sometimes it is merely incised and becomes in actuality a drawing in stone rather than a carving. The Egyptian sculpture in Figure 15–1 goes beyond this stage to become *bas-relief* (French *bas* meaning low) in which the figures are raised above the background just enough to cast shadows. When the figures project from the background to the extent of half their thickness or more the sculpture acquires the name *haut-relief* (French *haut* for high).

Each type of sculpture has its own problems from the standpoint of design. One of the most famous examples of a free-standing figure is Michelangelo's "David" as seen in Figure 18–1. This is the work of a man who could feel a deep affection for a block of marble, who knew every crystal and vein within the stone with which he worked, and who never selected a piece of marble for his sculpture without first seeing it in the rays of early dawn when the luminous light would expose the true purity of its texture. Standing eighteen feet tall, the "David" is a masterpiece of design from every angle, the embodiment of youthful beauty and strength that seems almost to burst from the confines of its own composition. Michelangelo is frequently quoted as having said that a piece of sculpture should be so compactly designed that it could roll downhill without any part of it breaking away, and his own work exemplifies this theory. There is a solidity and a tenseness not only in the body itself but in the challenging glance and the proud carriage of the head. When the sculptor is bound by the size and shape of the block, as Michelangelo was in this piece of Carrara marble, the design problems are much greater than merely carving a convincing figure. In this case the forms of the body are contained within the shape, yet they have a feeling of intense vitality and of youthful movement that carry them beyond it.

In contrast, the Greek figures from the west frieze of the Parthenon (Figure 18–2) demonstrate the problems of vitality and movement handled in relief. Here a procession of youths leads its horses in the Panathenaic procession, the climax of the celebration to the goddess Athena in which all the citizens of Athens carry to her statue a robe woven and embroidered during the preceding four years by the maidens of Athens. The youths and horses form a part of the procession which stretches all around the Parthenon in a band 520 feet long and only three feet four inches high. Here the problem is not one of figures bursting forth from a block of stone so much as of keeping within the prescribed space and yet achieving variety, movement, and interesting design. There arose a further problem of the light being cut off from above by the ceiling of the porch and of having to adjust the various planes of the sculpture in order to avoid distortion from the view below. The sculptor Phidias solved this problem by sloping the planes of relief outward so the heavier lower parts of the body would not cast unduly deep shadows. The upper parts of the figures sometimes project as much as two-and-a-quarter inches while the lower sections do not exceed one-and-a-quarter inches. When a man was placed behind a horse, Phidias let the planes overlap like shingles in order to create more feeling of depth than would ordinarily be possible with this degree of relief.[1] Thus he not only created an interesting sculptural design, full of movement, but he actually designed the shadows to accent it and bring out its fullest beauty.

[1] Everard M. Upjohn, Paul S. Wingert, and Jane Gaston Mahler, *History of World Art* (New York: Oxford University Press, 1958), p. 90.

Figure 18–2. A feeling of great action and vitality is conveyed by these figures carved in relief on the Panathenaic frieze of the Parthenon. Photograph by Alison Frantz.

Another well-known relief design is the pair of bronze east doors created by Lorenzo Ghiberti for the baptistry of the Cathedral of Florence (Figure 18–3). This was a difficult design problem from the standpoint of both subject matter and area. These particular doors had been preceded by both the south and north doors, designed and executed, earlier in the century, by Andrea Pisano and Ghiberti respectively, and it was desirable that the basic design of the individual panels be similar enough to insure unity. However, where the earlier doors had twenty-eight panels in the shape of a Gothic quatrefoil, Ghiberti enlarged his panels in the east doors, making only ten rectangular shapes. The demands of the Old Testament subject matter made it necessary to include more than one incident in some panels and the problem of separating one from the other required considerable planning and technical skill. Ghiberti adapted his background accordingly, not keeping it on a single vertical plane but sloping it so the foreground figures are partly in the round while the background figures, which may form another scene, are in extremely low relief. Considering that some of the panels contain more than a hundred figures in addition to buildings, ships, and details of landscape, one can appreciate the dexterity involved. Critics have complained that Ghiberti treated each panel as an easel painting rather than as a piece of sculpture and this, of course, is possible in relief. At any rate, the design quality cannot be denied when one views the two doors, and their borders of larger figures interspersed with the forms of Renaissance naturalism, which create a unity that extends to the building itself. Early acceptance from the sculptural point of view was assured in part, at least, by Michelangelo's admiring statement that these doors were, in truth, beautiful enough to be the gates of Paradise.

Two Sculptural Methods

Not only do Michelangelo's "David" and Ghiberti's bronze doors represent the two *types* of sculpture but they exemplify as well the two sculptural *methods,* the *subtractive* and the *additive.* As noted in our study of design in wood and metal, these two methods are directly related to the materials used. When working with wood or stone, the sculptor uses the subtractive method, starting with a large mass and, visualizing the form within it, gradually taking off the excess until he releases the form into a structural design consistent with gravity, volume, weight, and spatial composition. This means that, as in the "David," the figure must not only stand solidly without tipping, but it must look as though it is balanced solidly in space so the viewer has a feeling of physical security as well as esthetic satisfaction when looking at it. It must be so executed that even when it is seen in three dimensions, from any side and from below, it still has the appearance of correct proportion. It must have depth of carving to give it sculptural power, yet it must retain the strength of the original mass with no sense of weakening through delving too deep. It should, furthermore, have a feeling of movement through forms and surfaces rather than through a superficial sense of texture. Sometimes a sculptor works out his design in a small model of wood or clay after making preliminary sketches on paper, for one false move in the full-scale work can be catastrophic. Usually in this first conception he thinks only in terms of large abstract masses, leaving the details to be developed as each individual mass emerges. In this way he is able to establish the rhythms among masses as well as the proportion and line. After the basic relationships have emerged he can devote himself to textures and details.

The additive method is much more flexible. Clay, wax, and metal are the usual additive materials and in all three it is possible to build up, tear down, change, and modify without danger of ruining the finished work. Frequently a metal armature is used with clay, a sort of skeleton of heavy wire which forms the basic lines and shapes and holds the clay together so that it will not crack of its own weight.

Wax is used principally as a basis for the *casting* of metal. This is a complicated process, which when understood causes us to look with renewed respect at the bronze statues in parks and city squares. The original version of the sculpture is modeled in wax, allowing for minute detail and careful manipulation of forms. Figure 18–4 (a) shows sculptor Harry Jackson work-

Figure 18–3. The bronze east doors of the baptistry of the Cathedral of Florence, designed and executed by Lorenzo Ghiberti in 1425. Alinari Photo.

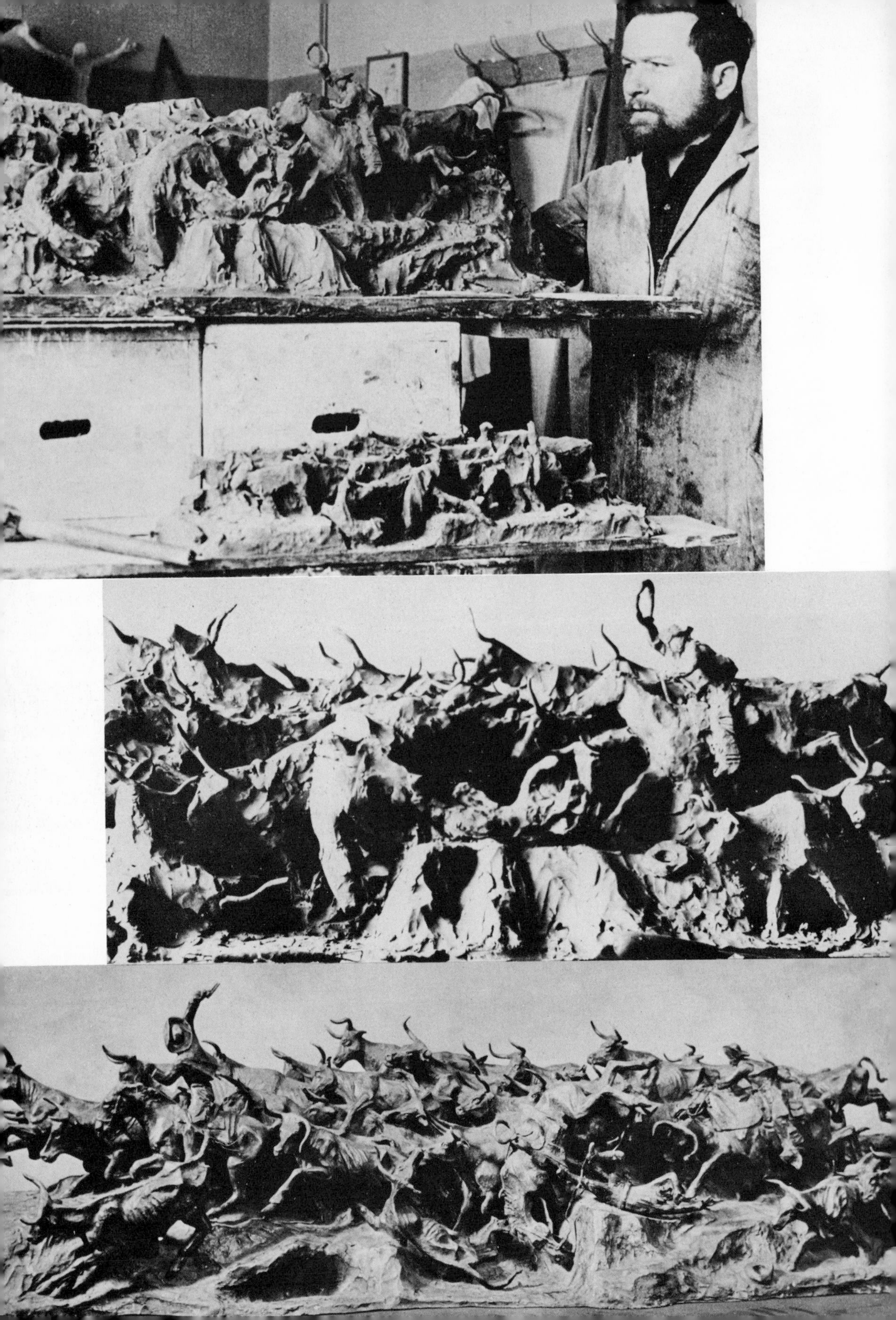

Figure 18–4. Opposite page, Top: (a) Sculptor Harry Jackson develops his full-scale model of "Stampede" in wax from a preliminary sketch in wax shown on table in foreground. *Center:* (b) Close-up of wax model. *Bottom:* (c) The finished composition after coming from the foundry. *Above:* (d), *right* (e), and (f) details of the final bronze sculpture. Photograph of (c) by Lee Bolton. All other photographs by Dr. Adrian Zorgniotti. Courtesy of the artist.

ing on the wax model of his sculpture entitled "Stampede," with a smaller sketch of the basic forms in wax on the table in the foreground. In (b) we see the full-scale model as the details emerge, and we begin to get the feeling of opposing masses and rhythms as well as the developing forms of men and cattle. When the wax model has been fully worked and is complete in every detail, the sculptor sends it to a foundry to be cast. Here a mold is built around it, usually of ceramic material. The mold is smooth on the outside but conforms to the wax model in every detail on the inside. When it is dry it is placed in a kiln and fired to a hard and solid state. During this process the wax of the model melts and runs out, leaving the empty mold. It is from this step that the process derives its name of *cire perdue* (lost wax). The mold is next filled with molten bronze or other metal which, in turn, is allowed to cool. When the metal has solidified the mold or cast is opened and the finished sculpture is revealed. Figure 18–4 (c) shows the finished bronze of "Stampede" after it came from the foundry in Italy while (d), (e), and (f) show details which help us to appreciate the meticulous modeling that can be reproduced by this method. The *cire perdue* process has a distinct advantage over the subtractive method in that several sculptures can be produced from the same mold, just as several prints can be pulled from a single woodcut. Furthermore, there is not the necessity for the compact form expressed by Michelangelo, for the additive process lends itself to extensions into space like the horns of cattle which are not in keeping with the nature of stone or the methods of working in it.

A variation of the casting process is sand casting, in which the original model in wax is packed in damp sand, in a mold that can be taken apart in halves. When the sand is tamped in place so that it will hold the shape of the model, the model is removed, the two halves of the mold are placed together, and the molten metal is poured into the mold.

Figure 18–5. Integration of sculpture with architecture and landscape design. Planted beds repeat the shapes of the sculpture. "The Texas Sculpture" designed and executed by Isamu Noguchi for the entry of the First National Bank of Fort Worth.

Other additive processes involve arc and acetylene welding, riveting, and bolting metal together into compositions of varying complexity. Some artists create "sculptures" from parts retrieved from junk yards complete with rust, broken edges, and bits of springs. These pieces are used as new forms without reference to their original purpose.

Considerations in Sculptural Design

Because from its beginning sculpture has been associated with buildings, it has certain characteristics that are more closely related to architecture than to any of the other arts. The earliest large sculptures were designed as enhancements of tombs or temples, with the purpose of preserving the souls of the dead or of paying homage to the gods. Portable sculpture, on the whole, fell into the category of charms or idols which were treasured for their beneficent effect on the hand of Fate, either as amulets to insure fertility or in other ways to oversee the well-being of the possessor. The important pieces clung closely to the building arts, so closely that much of the Egyptian sculpture in the round was firmly attached to the wall at its back, and even the Greek statues which we consider superbly finished were frequently left rough at the rear when they were located so close to the wall that no one could possibly get around behind them.

This association with architecture has affected sculptural design in several ways. One, it has put the emphasis on large forms which can be viewed from afar with no loss of detail, and which are in keeping with the larger structural forms of the building of which they are a part. Two, it has necessitated certain refinements to accommodate the lower eye level of the viewer, as we noted in Phidias' work on the frieze of the Parthenon. Three, it has required a calculated consideration of the effects of light and shade with a subsequent adjustment of materials. Unlike the painter, the sculptor whose work is commissioned to fill a certain spot need not merely hope that conditions will be right for bringing out its best points, for he is not limited to specific materials, but can make a thorough study of conditions of light throughout the day and year and attempt to choose the material that will utilize these conditions to the best advantage.

While we still have sculpture that is closely allied to architecture and are, in fact, working toward a greater integration between architecture and all the other arts, sculpture has, since the Renaissance, been freed of the restrictions imposed by attachment to buildings. The design of sculpture-in-the-round as free-standing monuments has long been a part of city planning; however, even this function traditionally placed it on a monumental scale which does not allow for the full expression of its unique esthetic qualities. An example of the contemporary handling of integration can be seen in Figure 18–5 showing two views of Isamu Noguchi's "Texas Sculpture" designed for the entrance plaza of the First National Bank Building in Fort Worth. These sculptures combine smooth and rough surfaces to suggest both the cities and the wild sweeping areas of the state of Texas, a combination of roughness and sophistication that echoes the forms of the building. Native plantings emphasize the natural textures of the stone and repeat the shapes of the sculpture.

Three Attributes of Sculpture

While sculpture is involved with the elements and principles of design in many of the same ways as the other arts, the importance of certain aspects of design is restricted to sculpture alone. On this basis, we can group its attributes under three principal headings. First of all, there must be *form.* Here we mean form in its purest sense, a three-dimensional mass of structural material. Second, there will be *organization.* This refers to the structural meaning of the form, and to the use of line, texture, light and shadow, and even color in some cases; in other words, organization of structural components into an integrated design. Third, the structure must have *content* or significance for the observer. It may be representational or symbolic or, like nonobjective painting, it may speak a language of its own through form which needs no translation into words or pictures.

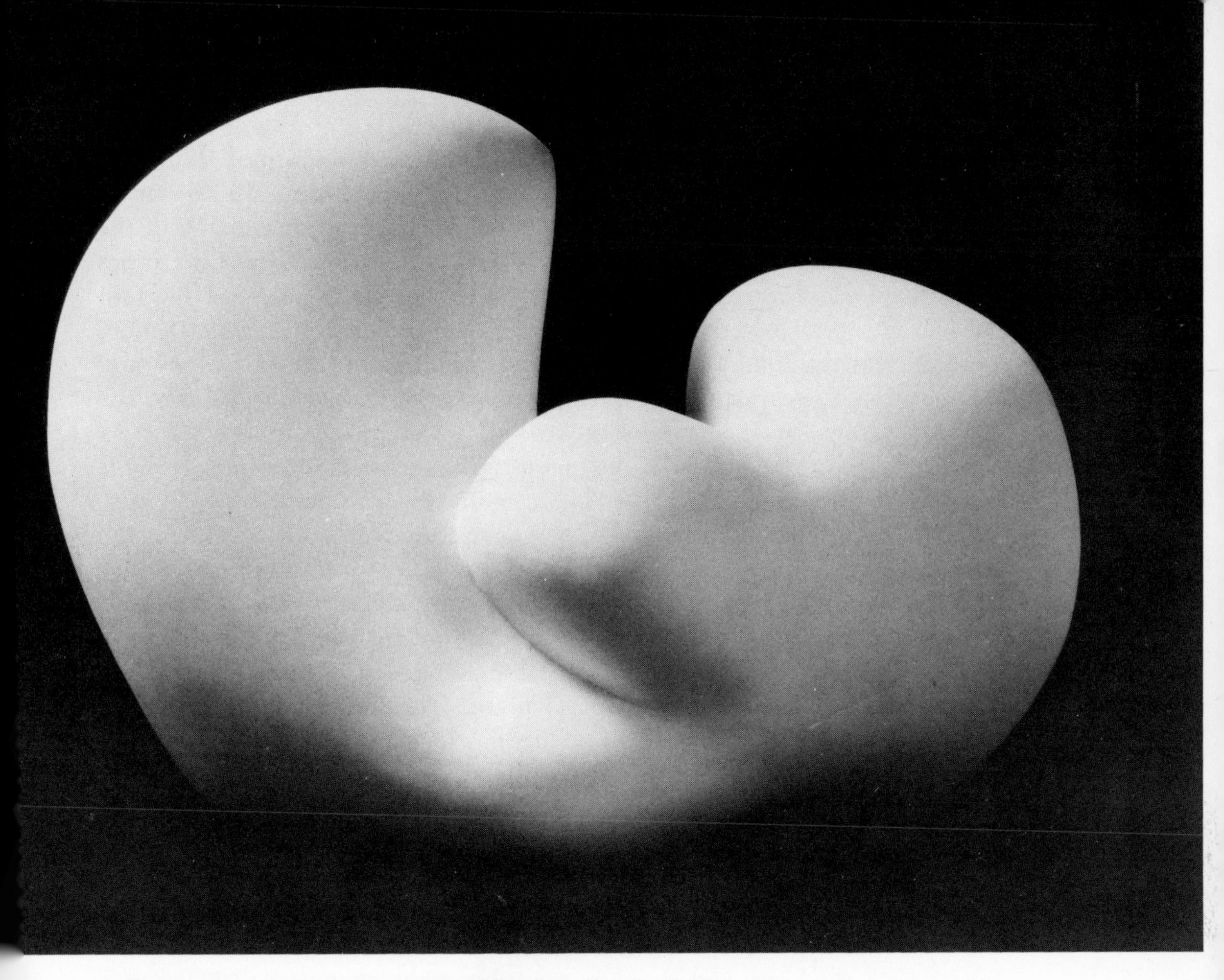

Figure 18–6. A sense of smooth solidity that impels the hands to touch it is one of the essential qualities of a piece of sculpture. "Human Concretion" by Jean Arp. Cast stone. Collection, The Museum of Modern Art, New York. Gift of the Advisory Committee. Photograph by Soichi Sunami.

Form

We have mentioned form as being of dominant importance. This is true of any of the arts, of course, but in sculpture form becomes a more physical thing than it does elsewhere. Sculptural form is not just something that the eye can see, any more than it is a tactile appeal to the hands alone. It is instead form that needs to be felt with the fingers, the arms, and the whole being. When fully appreciated, it satisfies a need to become a part of something outside our own bodies, to associate ourselves with something that can be absorbed into ourselves, just as we are absorbed by it. The sculptor Rodin spoke of his instructor, a sculptor named Constant, telling him: "When you carve, never see the form in length, but always in thickness. Never consider a surface except as the extremity of a volume, as the point, more or less large, which it directs toward you." [2] This feeling of

[2] Herbert Read, *The Art of Sculpture* (New York: Pantheon Books, Inc., 1956), p. 73.

Figure 18–7. The design of negative space is a vital part of much contemporary sculpture. "Woman Combing Her Hair" by Alexander Archipenko, bronze. Collection, The Museum of Modern Art, New York. Lillie P. Bliss Bequest. Photograph by Soichi Sunami.

Figure 18–8. The human figure is abstracted to a high degree of design in this modern cast-lead sculpture. "Reclining Figure" by Henry Moore. Collection, The Museum of Modern Art. Photograph by Soichi Sunami.

bulk and volume, of something tangible that can be embraced, is an intrinsic quality of a piece of sculpture It leads to an entirely different conception of form than the artist has in painting where the third dimension, no matter how effective visually, remains an illusion on a two-dimensional surface. Looking at a piece of sculpture should give the same feeling of satisfaction as comes from repeated fingering of a smooth pebble or of stroking the stock of a rifle to give it a hand-rubbed finish. Some people have a stronger sense of the tactile esthetic quality than others and sculptors undoubtedly are the artists who have this sense developed to the highest degree. The viewer should be conscious of a similar sense in himself when he "experiences" a piece of sculpture.

Having much in common, painting and sculpture have undergone much of the same metamorphosis so far as manner of expression is concerned. While early sculpture was concerned with subject which centered

Figure 18–9. Two versions of the human figure by Lynn R. Wolfe: (a) A solidly structural form in clay and plastic, and (b) a bronze cast in sand to produce an unusual texture that is not a surface quality but an integral part of the form itself. Courtesy of the artist.

for centuries around the human figure, we find the same emergence of form as a thing apart that we find in contemporary painting. No longer does appreciation of sculpture hinge on the sort of feeling that Pygmalion felt for his statue of Galatea when he fell in love with it and asked Aphrodite to convert it into a living woman whom he could love. A deep appreciation of sculptural form is not necessarily tied up with representation but, on a purely esthetic level, should be worthy of appreciation for itself alone. The sculpture by Jean Arp in Figure 18–6 is in this category. There is an abstract beauty of form here that needs no translation. The viewer senses the smoothness as though he were running his hands over it; in fact, he feels a need to do that very thing, to stroke it until he has absorbed all of the beauty not only of its smoothness but of the fullness of the form itself.

Organization

The second attribute of sculpture has to do with the way the forms are put together. Frequently this is a matter of materials. We find that sculptors who have done the same subject in stone and in bronze treat the two pieces quite differently, although the design is basically the same. A head in stone may be smoothly rounded while the same head in bronze will be broken into planes to distribute the reflected light in a more in-

teresting manner and to eliminate glare. As we have noted, organization may be modified to emphasize or minimize shadow patterns, depending upon the position in which the work will be placed. Textures must be organized for balance and interest, and where color is used it must undergo the same considerations. Organization of forms into positive and negative areas has been an important factor ever since Alexander Archipenko made the relationships of positive and negative volume a characteristic of his work, in the early part of the century. In his "Woman Combing Her Hair" in Figure 18–7 he surprises us with a negative form or space where ordinarily we would have expected a positive form to be, and thus establishes his work as something more than a mere replica of the human figure. While it is recognizable as having human origins, we find immediately that we are more interested in the forms and spaces than we are in the anatomical aspects of the piece. The same thing is true of Henry Moore's "Reclining Figure" in Figure 18–8. This is even more free of anatomical concerns than Archipenko's woman, yet we find ourselves carried along through a structural design of positive and negative forms that is satisfying esthetically without reference to a model. Still other interpretations of the human form are to be seen in Lynn Wolfe's two sculptures in Figure 18–9. In (a) we see the sturdy figure of a young girl in clay and plastic showing massive solidity of form with a certain youthful buoyancy, while (b) is a sand-cast

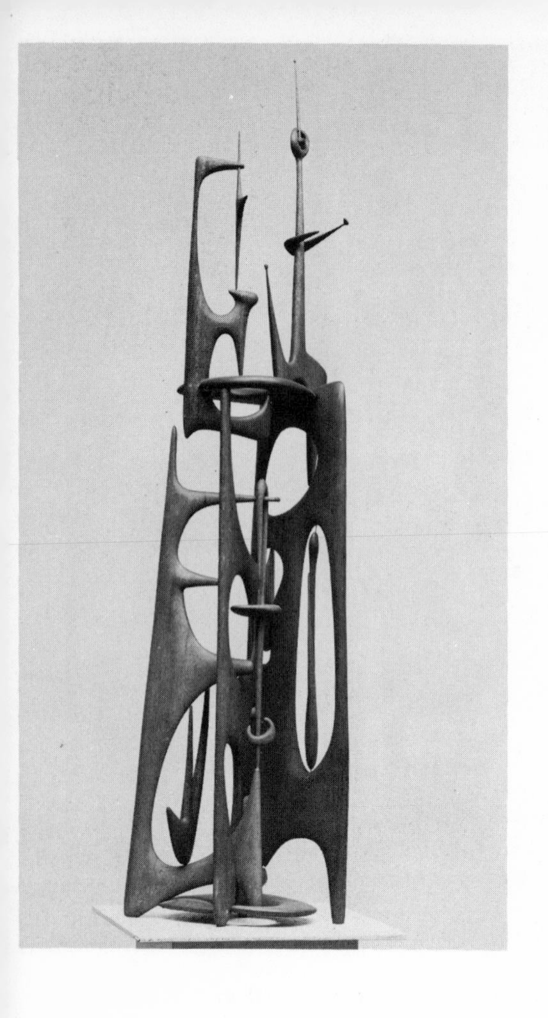

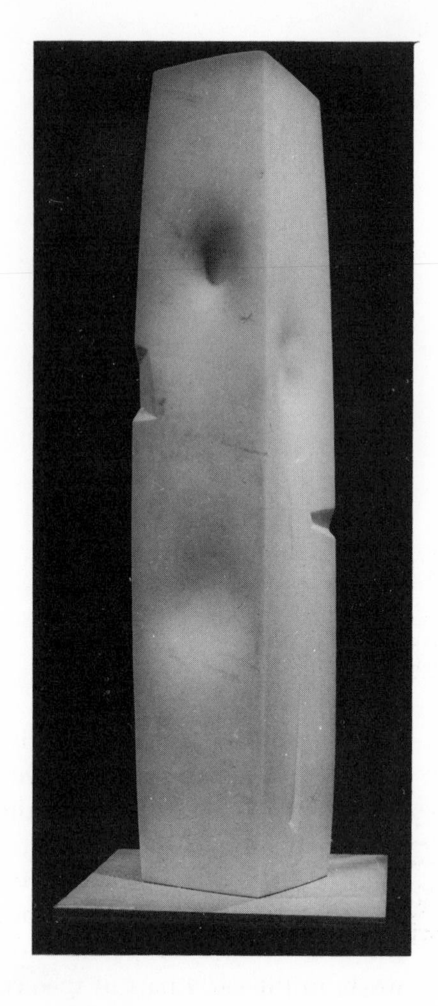

bronze with a strong linear quality and great interest in texture, not as a surface treatment but as an inherent quality of the form itself.

Content

Content in sculpture may take many forms. The positive and negative forms of Leo Amino's "Jungle" in Figure 18–10 have content because of the intricacy of the polished mahogany design. Even without the title one finds himself letting his eye wander in and out in fascination, not at the wood alone but at the interplay of wood and space. Isamu Noguchi's marble in Figure 18–11, on the other hand, is so simple that one might pass by without noticing it, yet it is the kind of form that grows more meaningful

Figure 18–10. Leo Amino's sculpture in mahogany entitled "Jungle" shows sensitive attention to negative as well as positive spaces. Collection of Whitney Museum of American Art, New York.

Figure 18–11. "Integral," a sculpture in Greek marble by Isamu Noguchi, is a subtle structure reminiscent of the refinements of a Greek temple. Gift of the Friends of the Whitney Museum of American Art. Collection of Whitney Museum of American Art, New York.

Figure 18–12. All of the soaring, gliding freedom of a bird is caught in this single piece of bronze. "Bird in Space" by Constantin Brancusi. Collection, The Museum of Modern Art in New York. Photograph by Soichi Sunami.

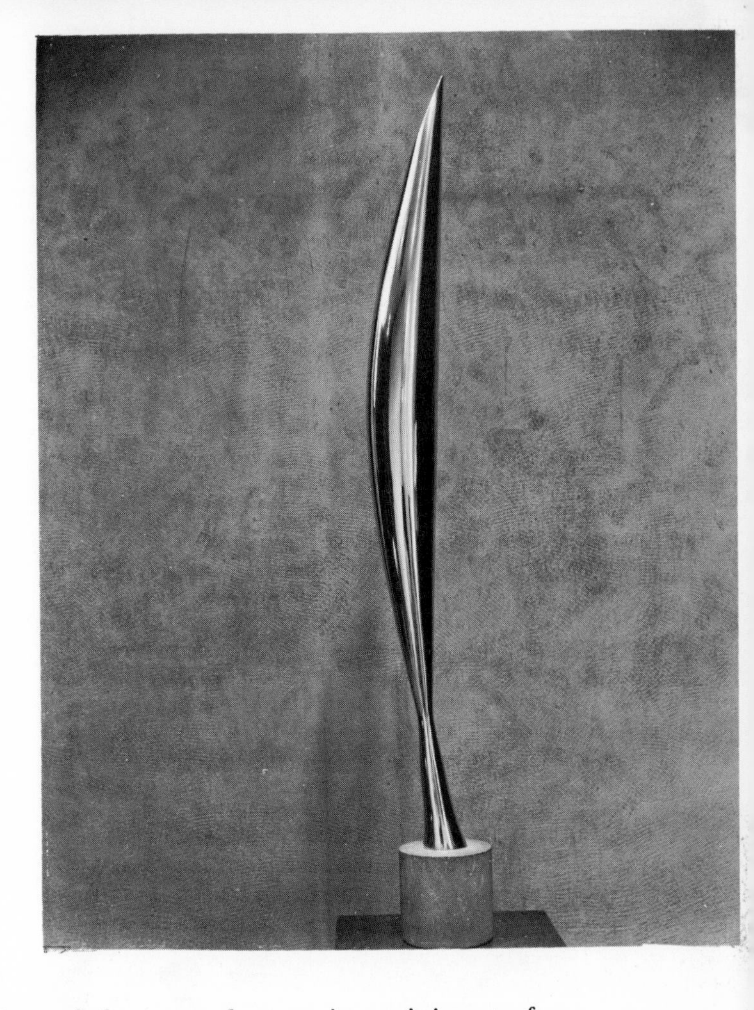

the longer one gazes. The subtlety of the upward curve is reminiscent of the modifications of Greek temples, while the indentations suggest grave steles or totem poles. One feels a sense of magic in the suggestive quality of the form itself. This sort of sculpture is the spiritual descendant of the work of Constantin Brancusi, whose "Bird in Space" (Figure 18–12) was one of the trail blazers in twentieth-century sculpture. With a complete absence of detail Brancusi transmits the feeling of freedom and rhythm, the smooth sweep of wings, and the endless soaring quality of space, all in one simple form, beautifully executed in bronze.

Content may be associated with motion. Movable sculpture is not new, yet the mobiles of Alexander Calder represent a relatively recent movement known as *constructivism* which made a concerted effort in the nineteen twenties to relate movement to sculpture in new ways. Some of the constructivist sculptures were in the nature of springs or other devices, but Calder has used sheet metal cut in various shapes which he balances delicately one against the other to produce a constant movement without any segment being set in motion by man or his inventions. The work becomes akin to fluttering leaves, swirling snowflakes, or the rippling of action across a field of grain. The fascination of this constant motion is a new

Figure 18–13. Shape, space, and movement combine with a linear design to make this construction a fascinating problem in balance. "Lobster Trap and Fish Tail," mobile by Alexander Calder. Collection, The Museum of Modern Art in New York. Gift of the Advisory Committee. Photograph by Soichi Sunami.

concept of sculpture which is referred to as the *kinetic* element. In Calder's work (Figure 18–13) is also found a linear sculpture in the wires and tubes holding the metal forms, delineating space without displacing it. Expressive of contemporary exploration is the combination of this linear sculpture with planes of clear plastic to give a third dimension through transparency. The artist today has a treasure house of new materials, and he relates them to sculpture in ways that expand the meaning of sculpture far beyond the traditional concepts.

It would seem that we have come to the opposite pole from Michelangelo's theory of compact tension, for the new forms not only reach out and define space but give the impression of limitless expansion. This, of course, is the most characteristic quality that twentieth-century sculpture can possess. Just as early sculpture evoked the gods and enhanced temples, and civic statues glorified the heroes of past eras, sculpture today reaches upward and outward in accord with the expanding outlook of its own civilization.

FOR FURTHER EXPLORATION

The Art of Sculpture by Herbert Read (New York: Pantheon Books, Inc., 1956). An excellent treatise for an introductory understanding of sculpture.

Tradition and Experiment in Modern Sculpture by Charles Seymour, Jr. (Washington, D.C.: American University Press, 1949). A comparative analysis of modern sculpture with sculpture of other periods.

Sculpture of the Twentieth Century by Andrew Carnduff Ritchie (New York: The Museum of Modern Art, 1954). A well-illustrated treatment of major modern trends accompanied by statements by some of our leading sculptors.

STUDIO PROJECTS

1. Make a collection of natural materials such as pebbles, driftwood, and anything else you feel has a sculptural quality in a tactile sense; in other words, materials you enjoy feeling with your hands.
2. Using heavy white drawing paper or Bristol board, make a three-dimensional construction you feel has sculptural quality, giving particular attention to negative and positive space.
3. Construct a mobile from wires and pieces of sheet metal, showing interest in movement as well as in shapes, forms, and divisions of space.

CHAPTER 19

Design in Photography

THE CAMERA enters the field of art with a heavy responsibility. In many quarters it is credited with having triggered modern painting by virtue of having taken the field of realistic representation out of the painter's hands. Why should the painter spend years developing skill to reproduce nature, the argument goes, when the camera can do the same thing in a fiftieth of a second?

What the camera does in a fiftieth of a second is not always art and there are thousands of snapshots lying around to prove it. What is more, the camera cannot always be depended upon for realistic representation. We say "the camera never lies," but we have all seen photographs of people caught in expressions that would never be acceptable as portraits. The term *realistic representation* brings us to a matter of semantics in which present-day critics and art philosophers make a distinction between *naturalism* and *realism*. For the sake of clarification, it is well that we understand the distinction as it is generally accepted today.

Naturalism has to do with nature and the "natural" appearance of things while realism delves further, beneath the surface, into the actual "reality" of things and people. This can become a highly philosophical distinction, but it is more understandable if we use a simple example in terms of people. When a new student comes into class we are apt to look at him with considerable interest, noting his features, his manner of dressing and his changing expressions. We make an instant evaluation of him based on his external or *natural* appearance. However, as time goes on we are thrown with him on various projects and see him under diverse conditions. We discover his ridiculous sense of humor, his dependability, his firm beliefs about certain subjects. Months later, if we recall our first impres-

Figure 19–1. Great portraiture in any medium expresses more than just one individual. This man could be all old men everywhere. Photograph by Bruce Roberts.

sion, we are amazed at how different he looks to use now. This is because we have come to know the real person, to see the *reality* of his personality and character through the outer vestiture of his appearance. This is the difference between a naturalistic view and a realistic one. A painted portrait may be a beautifully meticulous rendering of the appearance of a person, so "real" that it almost seems to speak, yet it is not realistic unless it shows us the personality and character of the person depicted. Similarly with a landscape, an old building may be painted to look like an eyesore or it may be given an inherent dignity that tells of a long useful life filled with warmth and humanity. Here we are dealing with content. What the artist puts into his work determines the difference between naturalism and realism.

A truly great work will go even further and reveal not just one person or scene but the eternal values. The portrait of a child may show one small individual dressed up and posing for a picture, or it may show the enduring restlessness of childhood restrained for a moment but bursting with eagerness to get about the business of play. Similarly the portrait of an old woman may show one tired and wrinkled individual, or it may depict the immortal sacrifice of a person who has spent a lifetime working hard for others, who has suffered most human emotions and has emerged physically exhausted but spiritually a light of strength to those around her. These are the differences to be found in representation and they are just as clear-cut in the work of the photographer as they are in painting. In Figure 19–1 Bruce Roberts achieves all the characteristics of great portraiture in his study of an old man reading his Bible. This old man has definite traits of character and personality, yet he is not just one old man. He is all old men everywhere, workworn and weary, taking comfort for a few minutes at the end of the day, seeking assurance that his struggle is not futile. Such results are not the reward for merely choosing an interesting subject. They involve the development of confidence and interest, a rapport between photographer and subject which allows the camera to bring out to the fullest the characteristics that the photographer wishes to emphasize. They hinge

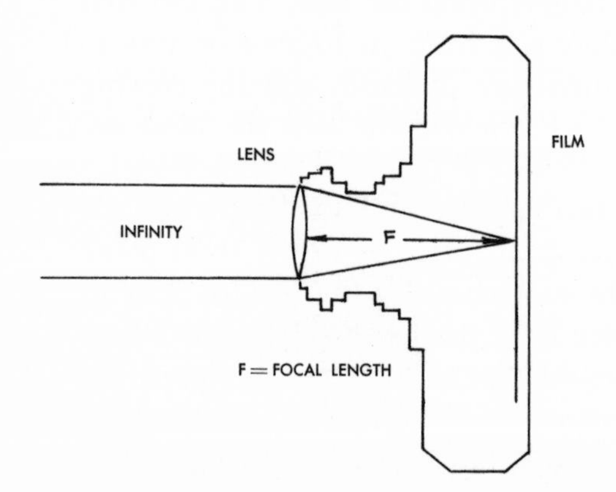

Figure 19–2. The focal length is the distance from the image to the lens.

further on technical skill, on lighting for accentuation, and focus which catches a clear image of the face while diffusing the lamp and the Bible.

The camera is the medium of the photographer just as brushes and paints are the tools of the painter, but the creative effort lies with the photographer himself, who first sees the possibilities of the subject, second has the ability to bring out the content in those possibilities, and third possesses the technical knowledge to get the effect he is after.

Technical Aspects of Photography

Since the first two qualities are useless to the photographer without the third, it would be well to look into the technical side of photography before considering its artistic aspects. Appropriately, the idea behind the camera was discovered by Leonardo da Vinci when he wrote: "Light entering a minute hole in the wall of a darkened room forms on the opposite wall an inverted image of whatever lies outside." In 1568, Danielo Barbara substituted a lens for the pinhole to achieve a clearer image and, in 1727, a German physicist strode toward the invention of film when he discovered that sunlight affects salts of silver, and made experiments with nitric acid, silver, and chalk to preserve images made through sunlight. Through many intricate steps in the intervening years the modern camera has emerged, a marvel of precision. Yet the basic principle is still the same as the one Leonardo jotted down in his notes. The darkened room (Latin, *camera*) is the first requisite, fulfilled by the interior of the camera itself. The film is the surface upon which the image is recorded, and the process of recording is effected by the admission of light through a lens.

The Lens

Just as there is no color without light, so is there no picture. The quality of the light admitted depends largely upon the lens. The fact that light rays are bent or *refracted* when they pass from air to glass or glass to air is the principle governing the manufacture of lenses and the curving of the lens to control this refraction is what makes the lens the most important and costly part of the camera.

Differences in lenses are based on two factors: the focal length and the *f*-rating. *Focal length* means the distance from the lens to the focal plane where parallel rays of light are brought to a point by the lens, as seen in Figure 19–2, in other words, the distance from the lens to the plane where the film is located. The *f-rating* expresses the "speed" of a lens by comparing its diameter to its focal length; for instance an f/8 lens has a diameter of one-eighth of its focal length. An f/3.5 lens is 1/3.5 of its focal length. The important point is that the smaller the f-rating is, the greater the speed of the lens. This is easier to understand if we remember that the smaller the bottom number of a fraction is, the larger the amount expressed. Just as ½ is larger than ⅛, so an f/2 lens is faster than one whose f-rating is f/8.

The Diaphragm

The better cameras have a diaphragm built in on the same principle as the iris of the eye. This consists of overlapping metal leaves by means of which the opening of the lens can be controlled. In other words, if the diaphragm is the iris of the eye, the lens is the pupil, and it varies in size by virtue of the adjustment of the diaphragm. Consequently, cameras are marked with *f* numbers by which the relationship of diameter to focal length can be controlled by lens settings which in reality are settings controlling the size of the diaphragm opening. These settings run something like 5.6, 8, 11, 16, 32. They are arbitrary ratios chosen because they give an accurate relationship between lens and focal length.

These relationships can become highly technical. There is a great deal of literature available to explain the physics of light refraction and the effects upon various lenses. The main reasons for changing the *f*-rating of a lens are that a wider diameter permits faster pictures while a smaller one increases the *depth of field.* An increased depth of field gives sharper focus to objects in the background or at a distance from the object upon which the lens is focused.

There are various types of lenses, all depending upon the focal length. The longer focal-length lenses shorten distances and dimensions and are known as telephoto lenses, useful in photographing wild animals and birds that cannot be approached at close range. The shorter focal-length lenses exaggerate distances at the sides of the field of vision and make it possible to squeeze more into a picture when it is taken in cramped quarters or when a wide landscape is to be included. These are wide-angle lenses.

The Shutter

Although the lens and the diaphragm control the relationship of light to film, the shutter has the final word. While the shutter is closed the film remains in darkness, but when the shutter is opened for a split second, the picture is "snapped." The diaphragm is regulated according to size, but the shutter is controlled as to length of time. Box cameras usually have a shutter speed of 1/30 of a second, while more complicated cameras can be set for from one second to 1/1250 of a second. We have all posed breathlessly for indoor time exposures in which the shutter was held open for a minute or

Figure 19–3. Comparison of exposure. (a) is overexposed, (b) is normal, and (c) is underexposed. Exposure can be controlled through the lens opening or the shutter speed. Courtesy of the Eastman Kodak Company.

more. This was necessary because of the scarcity of light. There is a definite relationship between the amount of light, or diaphragm opening, and the shutter speed. If you are photographing a race horse as 1/1000 of a second you will use a larger diaghragm opening than if you are taking a landscape at 1/25 under the same lighting conditions. The effects of various light and time relationships can be seen in Figure 19–3. Overexposure could have been caused by either too large an opening in the diaphragm or too long a time of exposure.

The Film

Today there are many types of film on the market: color and black-and-white, indoor and outdoor, still and motion picture. They are designed not only for different purposes but for varying conditions of light and color sensitivity. However, any film consists of two basic parts: the support and the emulsion.

The Support

The purpose of the support is to provide a base for the light-sensitive emulsion. The support itself is insensitive to light, transparent, flexible, chemically stable and highly volatile. It is a gelatin-like substance except in the case of some cameras which use a sheet of glass as the support of their plates which are used instead of film.

Figure 19–4. A study in the use of filters. (a) shows use of an *A* or red filter which produces exaggerated sky effects. Note the lack of detail in the model's swimsuit. (b) used a *G* or orange filter which penetrates haze and produces contrast in marine scenes. (c) was taken with a *K*–2 or yellow filter which is useful for smooth skin texture, while (d) was taken with no filter at all. All pictures were taken with Pan X film. Courtesy of Eastman Kodak Company.

The Emulsion

The emulsion starts as bar silver which is dissolved in nitric acid to form silver nitrate. This, with potassium bromide, is added to a chemically superior variety of gelatin warmed to a syrupy consistency. Since the silver and the bromide combine to form light-sensitive crystals the work is done in darkness, and the potassium and nitrate which have combined are removed from the gelatin by washing. The remaining silver bromide caught in the gelatin becomes the emulsion, with which the support is coated.

Films have four characteristics which cause the variations distinguishing them from one another: color sensitivity, speed, graininess and contrast. Some film is sensitive to blue and ultra-violet while other films have more red sensitivity or are sensitive to green. The speed of film is simply a matter of general sensitivity depending upon the manufacturing process. The longer the emulsion is "cooked," the larger the grains of silver bromide will be and the greater the sensitivity, thus requiring less light in exposure. Graininess again depends upon the size of the grains in the emulsion and it usually does not become a factor except in enlarging. Contrast is a matter of values and involves the ability of the film to distinguish between closely related tones in the brightness scale.[1]

[1] Thomas H. Miller and Wyatt Brummitt, *This is Photography* (Garden City, New York: Garden City Books, 1955), pp. 53–56.

Filters

Although films can be purchased to fit various situations, it is sometimes more effective to use filters that fit over the lens. A filter is a piece of dyed gelatin or glass which either absorbs or transmits rays of light, depending upon their color relationship to the filter. The object is to use a filter which will absorb the colors that you want to darken and will transmit the colors you want heightened. There are over a hundred available light filters, which will do everything from providing contrast in portraits to dramatizing cloud effects. Examples are shown in Figure 19–4, in which three different filters were used, causing variations in both sky and model.

Developing the Film

Developing is a process by which chemicals turn the silver particles on a film to black in exactly the same proportion as their exposure to light. Three trays of solution are used for the process which is carried out in a dark room lighted only by a special darkroom light. The paper backing is peeled off the film and a clip attached to each end of the remaining strip. Holding one clip in each hand, the photographer dips the film into water to make it pliable and then, with a gentle back-and-forth motion, he submerges the film in the first tray, containing developer. Very shortly images begin to appear and in four minutes or less, depending upon the particular developer used, the image is complete. The film is then washed back and forth in the second tray which contains cool water. Finally it is immersed in the third tray which holds fixative to neutralize the developer. Lastly, the film is washed under running water for fifteen minutes. The result is a strip of negatives which are cut apart and used for making prints, or in the case of color transparencies are mounted for projection on a screen.

Making the Prints

The printing process comes back to the effects of light. The negative is placed against a piece of glass in a printing frame with the emulsion side against a piece of special printing paper. Both are held in place by clips. There are many types of printing paper, all coated with special emulsions of one kind or another. As in the use of film, the photographer must experiment at considerable length to find the type that suits his needs with best results. With the emulsion on the paper in contact with the emulsion on the negative, the frame is held near a white light bulb for a matter of seconds. Here again, the length of exposure will affect the end result. The paper is removed and put through a second series of three trays. The developer brings out the image in a short time; the darkness desired can be controlled through this step as well as through the exposure to light. When the print is dark enough, it is plunged into the fixative in the second tray for a few seconds, and finally into the stop solution which terminates all chemical action. After this step the print can be exposed to light and left to dry.

The usual print is known as a *contact print.* Enlargements are made with a special machine which is, in effect, a camera in reverse. Suspended above the photographic paper, it projects the image from the negative onto the paper from a distance, making it larger. The projected image becomes the enlargement.

Photography as Art

From all of this, it is easy to see that wide experience is necessary to be able to judge the best lens, filters, film, printing papers, lights, and other variables for any specific purpose. These aspects of the photographer's work fall into the realm of mechanical or scientific knowledge. The fine line between good technical photography and outstanding achievement is crossed only by the photographer with creative ability, with the eye and soul of the artist, and the understanding that light, that essential of any photograph, can be his most valuable ally in design. It has been said, in fact, that in photography light *is* the great designer.

Take, for instance, the photograph in Figure 19–5. Here is the sort

Figure 19–5. A feeling of serenity, a remembrance of places almost forgotten, is induced by this study—an excellent design. Photograph by Bruce Roberts.

SAND
ELIZAB

of subject that would be ignored by anyone without a strong imagination. Yet the proper lighting and an interesting angle have created a composition of great charm and artistic merit. The eye focuses on the leaf, bathed in sunlight on the surface of the dark water. The diagonal lines of the pump and of the wood in the background lead to it. The light-touched rim of the bucket encircles it like a frame but continues around the pump, delineating the highlights of its form. The texture of the wood becomes a dramatic feature of the design accentuating the smoothness of water and metal. Here are line, form, shape, texture, rhythm, and balance. Unity is achieved by the scattered leaves which echo the center of interest and by the pervading lines of the wood. Beyond the elements and principles of design, however, there is an emotional quality, a nostalgia that brings back quiet places apart from speed and noise, close to trees and cool water, and simple fulfillment of simple needs. Shown to any number of people, this photograph would bring forth a comment beginning: "That reminds me of a place I knew as a child. . . ." This is the content, the *realism* that makes this composition far more than just a picture.

The photograph in Figure 19–6 could hardly provide greater contrast in subject matter, yet the same elements and principles of design are present. The rumble of the El as it sways along its tracks is anything but quiet and the piles of stone mounting upward are the epitome of noisy progress. Yet here, again, light has bestowed a creative touch. The opposing faces of the buildings, seized at just the moment of greatest contrast, form a pattern of light and dark broken into texture by the smaller lights and darks of windows. The dark shape of the low building in the left foreground balances the darker portions of the skyscrapers going upward, and the spot has been chosen with painstaking care to balance the light bulk of the center building with the light-washed wall at the right. These panels of light bring the eye downward to the train itself, still drenched in sunshine at the bottom of a canyon, expressing man's little activities in the contrast of his own mammoth structures. Here is all of the wonder and weight, the soaring and plunging, and above all the limitless contrast that is the essence of the city.

Light as Designer

The study of lighting effects can be a lifelong experiment to the professional photographer. Using floodlights and reflectors, he can manipulate his lighting to achieve a wide variety of effects on any given subject, and

Figure 19–6. The massiveness of the city becomes a fascinating design under the influence of light and shadow. Photograph by Todd Webb.

Figure 19–7. Light transforms these simple grasses into something full of vibrant interest. Photograph by Bruce Roberts.

it is only with such experimentation that he can choose the most effective results. He has an advantage over the painter who would like to try different colors and arrangements but can only approximate the effects through sketches before launching into his final work. The photographer can experiment endlessly and select the most successful print.

Light emphasizes a dramatic subject, but it can lend a touch of magic to a simple one as well. Ordinary grasses are transformed by back lighting and enlargement in Figure 19–7, giving the heads a glow that is accentuated by the dark outlines of leaves and stems. The composition could be compared to a study in stained glass with its black delineations and areas of light.

Light is responsible for the composition in Figure 19–8 as well, not only imbuing a simple subject with a large sense of drama but composing the areas of dark and light into an effective design. The shadow cast upon the wall falls in exactly the right place to frame the steeple in shadow, giving it a brilliance that would not otherwise be felt. The rough texture of the wall contrasts with the dark smoothness of the sky and with the impression

Figure 19–8. An imaginative eye for light and shadow made this subject into a photograph of high drama. Photograph by Bruce Roberts.

of smooth brightness formed by the steeple itself. Furthermore, the brilliance of its soaring spire achieves a spiritual quality against the brooding feeling of the foreground in which the lighting intimates other contrasts as well. This is a photograph in which the setting had to be studied and the picture snapped at precisely the right moment for the maximum effect.

Contrast the study of the steeple in Figure 19–9 which has an entirely different content. This steeple is also bathed in light but there is no ominous foreground, just the delicately blossoming tree beside it which balances the dark shape at its other side. Everything is light and beauty, as on an April morning. It is a picture that makes one think of jonquils and Easter bonnets and the clean fresh feeling of spring.

We have noted that the photographer with an artist's eye can make a dramatic subject more dramatic as well as create an aura of interest in everyday scenes. For the photographer of today, however, even this is not enough. Not only interesting angles and fascinating lighting are being explored but natural abstractions are being used in new and creative ways. Nature and art are perhaps more closely allied in photography than in any other medium, for the photographer cannot photograph what is not there. On the other hand, through the modern equipment at his disposal he can discover beauty and interest in materials never noticed by the ordinary eye. Abstract designs in driftwood, in iron fences, in animal tracks or rock crystals can, with proper lighting and enlargement, become as creative as any abstract painting. The possibilities for expression in photography from this viewpoint are virtually endless.

For simple expressiveness it would be difficult to find a more effective study than the one in Figure 19–10, showing Alfred Stieglitz' composition of the hands of Georgia O'Keeffe, his wife and a famous American painter. In this photograph Stieglitz managed to embody everything that people have ever felt about hands: their grace and power, their artistry and expressiveness, their effectiveness as instruments of creation. The hands posed against a solid dark backdrop provide the light with the best possible foil. It models the forms of the fingers and lends power to the entire composition. This is photography at its best. It is not merely a picture of something, it is the essence of life itself.

Motion Pictures

So engrossed do we become with the drama that unfolds before us on the movie screen that we seldom appreciate the knowledge and artistry that go into the actual taking of the pictures. The gigantic color films today are

Figure 19–9. The essence of spring is revealed in this simple portrait of a church steeple and blossoms. Photograph by Carl R. Hartup.

Figure 19–10. Georgia O'Keeffe's hands in the photograph by Alfred Stieglitz. George Eastman House collection.

frequently masterpieces of photography, as are many of the shorter travelogues. Selecting the angle for greatest effect, choosing details that will set the mood, the movie cameraman brings into one great unity all the artistry of set designers, costume designers, actors, and directors. There is a staff of photographers for every picture, specialists in technical equipment who know just what effects they can achieve and set about creating them in the most dramatic manner. The same is true of television. Next time you watch a singing star, or a serious drama, notice how many different camera angles are involved in a single act and analyze how much this variety adds to your enjoyment of the performance.

Moving pictures, of course, consist of small frames of still pictures, each slightly different, projected at a speed which makes the actors seem to move. There are usually twenty-four frames per second. The film, processed by professionals, is developed to the negative state which projects onto the screen as a series of positive prints.

Motion pictures have become a leading industry in the world today, converting the talents of many people and innumerable allied arts into fortune-making entertainment. When the motion pictures of today are compared with those of a generation ago we find contrast, not only in costumes and sets but in the quality of films and photography. Like any technological process, film-making is constantly changing and improving from the technical standpoint. New cameras are invented, new types of film and filters are manufactured, new methods of photographing are used in an attempt to surround the audience and make it feel that it is actually living in the picture. These changes will continue and improvements will be made. However, in motion pictures as in still photography, the unchanging attribute that is essential remains and will continue to be the creative ability of the photographer, with his imaginative eye and his sensitivity that turns a mechanical operation into art.

FOR FURTHER EXPLORATION

The History of Photography From 1839 to the Present Day by Beaumont Newhall. (New York: The Museum of Modern Art, 1949). An excellent study of photography, its roots, and development.

The Family of Man edited by Edward Steichen. (New York: The Museum of Modern Art, 1955). An outstanding collection of photographs centering around the various aspects of man's existence.

Making a Photograph by Ansel Adams (New York: Studio Book, Viking Press, Inc., 1948). A handbook full of valuable information by one of the most noted photographers today.

Feininger on Photography by Andreas Feininger (New York: Ziff-Davis Publishing Co., 1949). An inspiring treatise with complete technical information by another leader in the field of photography.

STUDIO PROJECTS

The *photogram* is a technique revived and developed by Lázló Moholy-Nagy as a medium of art expression. For exploration into this form, try the following experiments:

1. Working in a darkroom, lay various flat objects on a sheet of photographic printing paper and turn a white light on them for a second or two. Run the paper through a photographic-developer solution, then immerse in a fixing bath of "hypo," and finally wash with clear water. Study the effects and analyze possibilities for design.

2. Carry out the same experiment as in Project 1, but use both opaque and translucent objects.

3. Place two panes of glass on the photographic paper with drops of water and oil between them. Set objects nearby and hold the light so they cast shadows on the glass. Develop as before.

CHAPTER 20

The Essence of Design

To the person who has experienced art in any form, his existence and its events are never again isolated. He has entered the fellowship of creative minds, and his life touches the depths of living through the centuries. As his esthetic experience widens, he gradually becomes conscious of the interrelationship of art and life. He discovers that art has its basis in nature, that it is, in essence, an expression of the affinity with nature which the artist feels more sensitively than other men.

He finds, too, that the principles which he has learned to recognize in great art can be applied to many aspects of life not usually associated with artistic endeavor. It has been said that the solution to the evils of mankind is for everyone to be an artist in a broad sense of the word. As we realize the all-pervading influence of design, we find that the artistic approach can be applied to many of the problems of today and that a wide variety of people are, in actuality, called upon to become designers.

The Designer Today

We have studied the work of designers in many of the fields of art; now let us look at some of the other areas to which design principles can be applied. The expression "the problems of today" has undoubtedly been used since the beginning of the spoken word and in most periods of history the problems have been monumental. Yet today with the space age, a rapidly increasing population and an explosive international situation, we have challenges never before encountered. It is quite possible that within

Figure 20–1. The need for quiet spots for physical and spiritual refreshment increases as our cities grow larger and life in them more nerve racking. Grand Teton Range bordering Jackson Lake in Grand Teton National Park, Wyoming. Courtesy of United Air Lines.

our lifetime we may learn of life on other planets which may present complications seemingly fantastic to our present viewpoint. Our solutions to all of these problems will take new understanding and, in many cases, an approach differing drastically from anything we have known. Such solutions will certainly require creative imagination.

A Plan for Order

We learned in Chapter 1 that *a design is, first of all, a plan for order.* Today we find ourselves confronted by many emerging fields in which a plan for order has not yet been formulated.

Transportation. In the past fifty years our modes of travel have changed drastically. Just as an ordered system of railroads had become established the airplane evolved into a forceful contender for first choice as public transportation. Although we have a system of airports and radar control, the recurrence of air collisions shows us that we have far to go in this direction, particularly as more and more planes take to the air. Now we can see the day when rockets will become commonplace and new designs for air travel will have to be created, not only in the ships themselves but in their movements through the ever-more-crowded atmosphere. Certainly rhythm and balance will play a part in the solution.

Even on the ground only a portion of the answers have been found. In the first half of the century highway travel developed so rapidly that roads sprouted in all directions, forming a hodgepodge of thoroughfares leading everywhere. Only since World War II has a systematic effort been made to create a unified federal highway system making it possible to cross the country rapidly and easily without having to fight through the traffic of each town and city en route. Once again rhythm and balance are involved, as well as an over-riding unity. Overpasses and interchanges frequently show imaginative treatment in the handling of crossings, and improvements in base and surface treatment have resulted in superhighways. Yet as cars increase and become higher powered the fatalities on highways become appalling. This is a problem crying for solution in every part of the country.

Related to transportation is the disposal of wrecked or wornout cars. The junkyard is one of the glaring eyesores of our time, and one of the most unnecessary. Usable parts from old machines of all kinds can be catalogued in storehouses and resold with the remainder of the junk hauled to factories for melting and reuse. In small towns across the country the removal of the junkyard at the outskirts would help to restore the order of the landscape.

Population. Nowhere is a plan for order more urgent than in the design of our cities. Most of our metropolitan areas are congested because they have grown too rapidly without any all-over design. Instead of springing from human needs they have forced life into rigid molds, almost impossible situations of traffic, lack of privacy, and crushing crowds. The untangling of these problems is one of the truly monumental puzzles of our time and the city planner has become a highly trained specialist, experimenting with all possible solutions. In some cities thoroughfares are being closed for conversion into garden malls for pedestrians with traffic routed elsewhere. In other cases shoppers are encouraged to park their cars on the outskirts and take buses provided by the downtown stores. We are all familiar with the many-storied buildings devoted to parking areas and with the flourishing trend toward suburban shopping centers, yet neither of these is considered a conclusive solution. Opposing those who sponsor *decentralization,* we find a group who feels strongly that "suburban sprawl" is not the answer, pointing out that people who get away from the city at night actually barter much of their leisure time for hours spent in crowded travel. *Centralization,* on the other hand, poses immense problems of water supply, waste disposal, and the movement of traffic—among others.

Le Corbusier, the eminent architect, worked out a city plan combining the use of skyscrapers with areas of landscaping which would keep the population centralized without crowding. This sort of housing is being tried in some cities, notably in former slum areas along the East River in New York. Unfortunately, where our cities are already established the problems are multiplied by existing conditions which, for many reasons, can be removed only gradually. So many elements are involved that the solution can be neither clear-cut nor simple.

The design of a city involves a great deal beside housing conditions. Pedestrian safety, adequate lighting, safety from crime, waste disposal, changes in level, space definition, provision for focal points, and landscaping —all of these must be considered in addition to the intangible qualities that make a community an attractive place in which to live. Emphasis, balance, rhythm, form, and unity all have their place in the design of any city and each will have to be applied creatively in the improvement of our present environment. Certainly, a fresh outlook and imaginative thinking are urgently needed.

Wilderness. This is the first century in which the necessity of planning for unpopulated areas has been recognized. As a young country we have taken wilderness for granted, but with a rapidly expanding population this is no longer possible. Men conquered the wilderness by laying waste, by felling trees which in turn caused erosion leading to floods and famine. This has been the story throughout history. Today we know that our natural resources will not go on forever and we cannot afford to ignore them, much less waste them. The wilderness has a farther edge bounded by cities, and "civilization" is creeping deeper and deeper into the woods and mountains and valleys that we cherish. These things have happened by accident because man's small purposes have been given more importance than any large design.

One notable step to alleviate the situation was made in 1916 with the establishment of the National Park Service setting aside twenty-two million acres of land for ownership by the Federal Government. Through this action such scenes as the one in Figure 20–1 became permanently available for recreation and renewal.

Man's earliest gods were closely associated with nature. We find sun gods, river gods, gods of fertility and harvest over and over in the ancient religions and in the primitive expressions of religion today. So long as man lived in harmony with these natural gods his problems were elemental and simply resolved. It was only when he set forth to conquer nature, to set himself in opposition and declare himself omniscient, that complications arose, not only within his surroundings but in his own mental and physical health.

Because this country rose from the wilderness, we tend to think of taking to the woods and mountains as a regression, a "back to nature" movement. Individually, it is more of a going forward into renewed harmony with nature, appreciation of basic values, spiritual and physical rebirth, and the nurturing of peace of mind that leads to creativity. Man in a crowd becomes a victim of human values through which he gauges his life to the critical approval of his fellowmen. Man in nature has an opportunity to relate himself to a larger perspective in which he finds himself as an individual and gains the courage to pursue a goal or an ideal in spite of human pressure and the leveling influence of the crowd. Making certain that man can always get close to nature is one of the responsibilities of the planners of today, for wilderness once destroyed can never be salvaged in its entirety within a lifetime.

Reclamation. We have lost land through carelessness and greed. Figure 20–2, for instance, shows an area which was once native rangeland, then used for crop production, and then abandoned. Eventually, native range will be re-established but it is an extremely slow process. In cases such as this, man can help by reseeding with native grasses adapted to the local conditions, but he will have a long struggle before he overcomes the results of his own carelessness.

Other areas need to be reclaimed through reforestation, windbreaks, or irrigation. Ocean water is being considered as an aid in this problem, for vast sections of wasteland could become productive and attractive if only they could be reached by water. Dams and other reclamation projects are designed and constructed every year, yet local interests frequently interfere with the fruition of large-scale designs which would be of benefit to the country as a whole. As in most designs for public welfare, an interested, imaginative, and concerned public is of first importance.

Figure 20–2. A "blow-out" on sandy land in the West shows the results of man's carelessness. Colorado State University photograph.

Design in the Intangibles. There are, of course, innumerable other areas in which dedicated men and women are working to solve the problems of our day, problems which cannot always be dealt with as tangibly as land and buildings and highways. Tremendous progress in medicine has contributed to a population increase and has created a new problem of a large group of older citizens. Mental health has become a more urgent problem as a result of the crowds and pressures of modern living. The complexities of international relations are challenging the best minds the world over and remaining complicated in spite of many sincere efforts. Here, as much as in any painting or sculpture, the need is for balance, proper emphasis, and, above all, unity.

The Role of the Artist

In the involved puzzle that is the contemporary world, the role of the artist becomes increasingly important. In a primitive society the tribal artist decorates weapons and carves totems; in a complex civilization he functions as a prophet, a philosopher, and an interpreter of the changing scene. In addition, he performs the eternal service of the artist, that of endowing his environment with beauty. Today, it is natural to place great emphasis on science when scientific pursuits are opening vast horizons all around us, yet the spirit of man must also be nourished and his emotional nature must be expressed.

The Golden Mean. The Greeks based an entire civilization on Aristotle's Golden Mean. In architecture and pottery, it created a beauty of proportion that has been admired and studied for centuries. In philosophy, it sought to achieve an equally pleasing proportion in living. The Golden Mean is the ideal between two extremes. Between fear and foolhardiness, the mean is courage, between haughtiness and humility, it is an honest pride. We learn from the Golden Mean that every excess has its price to pay, not only in morality or physical well-being but in matters such as sensitivity and self-expression.

Today, the Golden Mean represents the balance that we need to achieve between art and science, but it also has personal implications for the artist. Because he is more sensitive than other men, the artist is able to create. He feels trends before the average person and as a result his work shows these trends before the layman can understand them. In this way, increased vision is balanced temporarily by scorn and rejection. Again, the increased sensitivity of the artist registers pain and sorrow as sharply as it does the interest and beauty of life, so that for every peak of exaltation he can expect to experience the plunge of despair. In order to work he must somehow strike a mean between the extremes of his experience, translating them without being completely devastated by them. The true artist does not work for the end result because the objective he seeks is never quite attained. His taste and aspirations always leap ahead of his skill, which is as it should be, for the art is in the *act* of creating, not the creation itself. Each new work thus becomes a mean between the artist's noblest hopes and his own self-doubt and is important as an experience which helps him to attain a new level of achievement.

Design as Expression

In discussing design in Chapter 1, we discovered several characteristics fundamental to creative design. In the light of our explorations into various fields of contemporary design, it might prove interesting to look at these qualities once again and see to what extent they are being expressed in the creative work of today. We have already discussed the fact that design is, first of all, a plan for order, and found that this quality applies to innumerable fields of present-day activity.

Expression of Life and Living. The second characteristic we mentioned was that *design should be an outgrowth of the material of which it is a part; it should spring from life and living, not be an external attempt at decoration.*

We have seen such expression in weaving, in which the designer used natural fibers combined with seed pods or grasses, or natural fibers hand combed and hand woven, forming a tapestry telling an entire story of life

Figure 20–3. Individuality in both structural and decorative design gives this punch set a distinctly contemporary flavor. Designed and executed by James and Nan McKinnell. Photograph by Marvin Richmond.

and living. We saw similar design in pottery in which the colors and textures of clay were the predominant feature, expressing the essence of the earth's surface in forthright shapes and forms, as in the punch set in Figure 20–3. We have seen contemporary bowls which tell the life story of the tree from which their wood was cut, and vases that portray, in one simple fluid form, the story of how glass comes to life.

Recently a one-man show of paintings was praised for the fantastic designs the painter had created, but when reporters interviewed the artist, they learned that she was making a career in thermodynamics and her paintings stemmed directly from the exquisite configurations she encountered in her work. This was design based firmly on life and living and the public, who assumed it to be imaginative, found it exciting and inspired. However, this is not always the case. Sometimes the artist is condemned because the public cannot see in his work the content he has experienced, and so says his art does not communicate. In the face of this complaint, it is important to realize that art is more than a means of communication. It is an expression of the hopes, ideals, and the highest aspirations of mankind, and in many cases much of its deeper meaning is not immediately obvious.

Greek tragedies in their original language may not communicate to an audience who knows no Greek, but they are no less authentic for this fact. The story is there awaiting the scholar who cares enough to master the

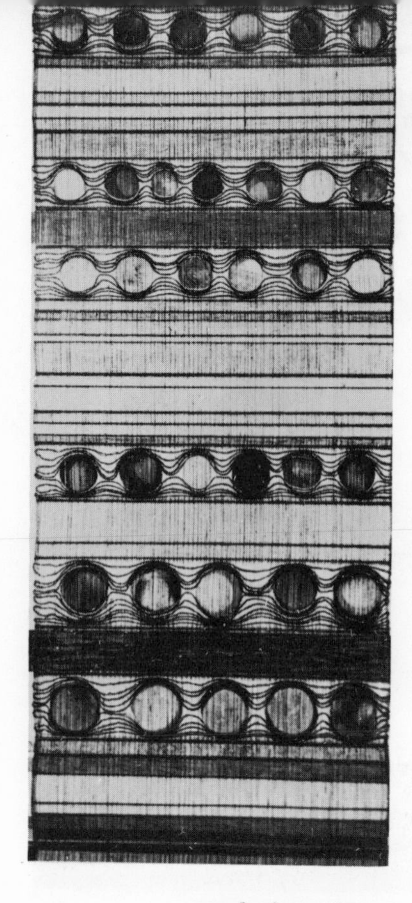

Figure 20–4. Strictly a product of the twentieth century is this acrylic room divider by Ted Hallman. Acrylic woven into a textile is a new and exciting combination. Courtesy of *Craft Horizons.*

translation. So, understanding much of contemporary art may require an extraordinary effort and repeated exposure on the part of the interested viewer. However, the value of the work does not hinge on the reaction of any particular audience. For a work to be justified, it is enough for an artist to have touched, or charmed, or transported someone, even if it is only himself, for art is primarily an *expression,* and it can express life and living in the experience of one sensitive individual with just as much justification as it can transmit the emotions of humanity.

Expression of Material. Another characteristic of design that we discovered was: *a true design has validity because it fulfills the possibilities of its material and its purpose, and its esthetic appeal stems from this validity.*

In exploring many of the fields open to creative designers today, we have constantly encountered an interest in new and exciting materials, as well as imaginative uses for old ones which result in wide fresh fields of design. We have also seen that contemporary artists are primarily interested in purpose, even though the purpose of an object may be purely decorative. When concern with purpose is combined with devotion to materials, the results are certain to have authenticity. The ceramics, glass, wood, metal, and fabrics of today have a clear feeling of sincerity. In the room divider shown in Figure 20–4 there is a straightforward quality; yet what a refreshing composition it is, with its rhythmic beat of acrylic actually woven into the textile! This design would not have been possible a generation ago. Not

Figure 20–5. "Circus," vitreous enamel-on-steel panel designed and executed by Edward Winter. The black background gives "breathing space" to the carefully designed areas of bright color: red, yellow, gray, black, white, turquoise, and gold. Photograph by The Cleveland Museum of Art.

only was the plastic not available but the very usefulness of a room divider marks it as being of our time, for the homes of the past with their closed plans lacked the flexibility which makes room dividers functional. Here both use and material are adapted to contemporary treatment to serve a current need.

Expression of Growth and Order. A fourth characteristic we attributed to design is that *good design is related to the basic natural laws of growth and order.* We have seen that architecture is most effective when it follows natural laws, that it is only possible, in fact, when it adheres strictly to the laws of physics and engineering which have their basis in nature. We have seen that the construction of a piece of pottery can succeed only when the potter follows the dictates of the material and of the laws of order which the clay itself prescribes. A piece of wood has its own laws of growth and order which no designer can ignore, for the growth rings of the wood and the resulting grain will determine the direction that the artist's efforts must take if they are to have successful results. Even in an enamel panel such as the one in Figure 20–5 the quality of the design is dependent upon certain laws of space division and interrelation of forms according to specific planning. The circus has been used in many designs, but the care with which this composition was planned and executed sets it apart. The tents are used as structural elements, yet their lilting diagonals contribute to the carnival air. The spots on the horse, repeated in the balloons and even in the moon, add further gaiety and a contrast in texture which is repeated in the horse's mane. The distinction of the panel is dependent upon its structural quality which makes it not just a circus picture but an arresting design.

Expression of Individuality. In our analysis of design and life in Chapter 1, we concluded that *for the creative artist individuality is the most important design quality of all.* This one characteristic more than any other expresses the essence of twentieth-century design. Today there are no formulae, no rules and no restrictions so far as technique is concerned. Exploration and experimentation are not only allowed but are welcomed warmly both by critics and by other artists in the field. A public looking for expressions of its own individuality can be made to appreciate unusual materials and techniques, and gradually it will accept the discoveries of the artist as it has in every period of the past.

Even such a small item as the pendant in Figure 20–6 shows the mark of today's freedom. Pendants have been designed for centuries in many ways, yet there are several hints that this one is a product of the twentieth century. The basic shape is free-form, both of the metal setting and of the stone, and yet the two shapes do not coincide. The stone is off-center and the setting has an important negative form against which the tip of the stone is silhouetted. The entire piece has a refreshing informality, yet there is balance and unity, variety and form. There is, above all, an individuality that sets this apart as an original piece of jewelry.

Figure 20–6. There is a contemporary feeling about this silver pendant arising from its form and its asymmetrical balance. Designed by Helen Scheier Adelman. Photograph by Bob Pettit. Courtesy of Studio Two.

Figure 20–7. Like a plant reaching toward the sun, the city climbs ever farther into space. New York as seen from the East River. Courtesy of United Air Lines.

The Essence of Design

The essence of design, then, is determined by many factors. It lies in an understanding of growth and order as they appear in every facet of the universe. It has been said that as our buildings climb higher and higher we grow farther and farther away from nature, and this is easy to believe as we view our great cities where from many angles no tree or patch of grass is visible (Figure 20–7). Yet space is also nature with limits far beyond our comprehension, and the farther we reach upward the farther we extend into space. We find that the basic laws of growth and order are just as much a part of space as they are of the smallest earthbound plant or animal. Furthermore, it is quite possible that in reaching upward physically we may also be stretching spiritually into new realms of intuitive understanding from which traditional concepts of representation may become as outdated as our earliest airplanes.

Design lies also in a knowledge of materials, of their possibilities and limitations and of the skill required to achieve their fullest expression. It exists in the body and mind of the artist, who receives inspirations through his senses and through the crucible of his creative power transforms them into new entities of his own making. Most of all, the essence of design is to be found in the spirit of the designer who sees the ugliness and confusion around him but who, even when most repelled by the evils of the world, carries always an overwhelming belief in the dignity and beauty of human life and an irrepressible need to express them.

Index

(Italic numbers refer to pages on which illustrations appear.)